40 Years at Farnborough

SBAC's INTERNATIONAL AVIATION SHOWCASE

John Blake and Mike Hooks

Foulis

Haynes

A FOULIS AVIATION BOOK

First published 1990

Published by:
Haynes Publishing Group
Sparkford, Nr. Yeovil, Somerset
BA22 7JJ, England.

British Library Cataloguing in Publication Data
Blake, John
    40 years at Farnborough – SBAC's international aviation
    showcase.
    1. Hampshire. Farnborough. Air displays. Farnborough Air
    Display, history
    I. Title   II. Hooks, M.J. (Mike J.)
    629.13074422725
    ISBN 0-85429-741-3

Library of Congress catalog card number 90-81743

Editor: Peter Nicholson
Page Layout: Chris Hull and Peter Kay
Printed in England by: J.H. Haynes & Co. Ltd
Typset in 11/12pt Rockwell light condensed

CONTENTS

INTRODUCTION

Introductions give authors splendid opportunities for explaining themselves. In this case, it is probably only necessary to say that what we have set out to do is to provide a general story about the content, development and context of the SBAC Shows from 1932 to 1988. Farnborough displays account for the great majority of these, but the tale would not have been complete without the inclusion of the pre-war events at Hendon and Hatfield and the immediate post-war ones at Radlett.

For reasons of space, we could not contemplate detailed coverage of every aircraft present at 36 events nor of the development of the industry. Inevitably, there were many estimable aircraft that we could not include in the narrative, but the annual lists of aircraft also included, of which more in a moment, are, we believe, the most detailed yet presented in one volume. For the rest, we have tried to give a broad coverage of the displays, with enough background history and foreground detail to make an entertaining story.

It is mostly a story about the flying display and to our many friends in the aero-engine and equipment sectors, and to the designers and organisers of the whole static side of the Shows, we can only plead lack of space for having done them less than justice.

A word of explanation on the aircraft listings. We have included registrations/serial numbers for the post-war shows from personal records and by cross-checking with lists published in enthusiast magazines. It was not possible to include the same information for the sometimes massive Service participation, particularly since many of the aircraft changed from day to day.

A cross (+) before an aircraft type in the lists indicates that it took part in the flying display, although not necessarily on every day. The letters/numbers in brackets after the registration/serial give the manufacturer's construction number where known.

Information on the actual aircraft shown at the pre-war displays is as complete as studies of contemporary magazines such as *Flight* and *the Aeroplane* allowed – the SBAC prohibited photography at its first Show in 1932 and the result is now apparent!

Many others have been involved in one way or another. We are particularly grateful to Duncan Simpson for contributing a Foreword. In the photographic sections, our thanks go to the many company PR departments which supplied material, and to the unknown photographers whose work appears here. Particularly we would thank Brian Wexham of Vickers, who gave us access to that company's photographic collection and Jack Titley of Rolls-Royce – whose photographic lenses are still going strong.

In the general narrative, much use was made of contemporary descriptions in aviation magazines and the massive series of Putnam histories was, as always, a major source of reference. Many individuals have helped with problems.

It must be said, finally, that although we have received much help from colleagues in the Exhibitions Department of SBAC, who frequently must have had better things to do than find dusty files and ancient facts for us, the views expressed in the book are entirely our own and do not necessarily reflect those of the SBAC. Errors and omissions, alas, must also, if found, be laid at our door.

John Blake
Mike Hooks

FOREWORD

One thing is certain – this book will delight the Aviation Enthusiast. It had to be written, at some stage, and who better to do so than John Blake – the commentator/raconteur, and Michael Hooks – mine of information and aviation statistician. Both have played their own part in many SBAC Shows. Their account of successive Flying Displays contain anecdotes and information that others cannot reach.

Ever since the SBAC Flying Displays began in 1932 they have provided the opportunity for customers and public to see the latest on the ground and in the air. Year by year the Show has developed, interrupted only by the war years.

After the war Radlett was used on two occasions until Farnborough was selected for subsequent years. In so many ways it was the ideal site, with rising ground to the south of the runway providing the amphitheatre for viewing the Flying Display.

In forty years at Farnborough the Show has developed from British-only into a fully International event of significant standing. The exhibition halls have been extended, the number of chalets increased and facilities improved. The flying programme has also seen change, from a wealth of prototypes in the nineteen fifties to a succession of significant new aircraft in more recent years, very often on their first public showing.

Fortunately, much remains at Farnborough as it was in 1948. The control tower, pilots tent, airfield, and surrounds at capacity, the skill of the pilots and the spectacle of the Flying Display are undiminished.

No wonder, therefore, that I have read this delightful book, cover to cover. The text and illustrations have brought happy memories, and will do so for many others in years to come.

Duncan Simpson

Duncan Simpson OBE
Deputy Director (Operations) SBAC

Spectator's eye view as the Airbus A310 F-WZLI makes a steep take off with its fly-by-wire system.

In the first two decades of the twentieth century the London *Daily Mail*, in a most enlightened manner, put up a whole series of aviation prizes, the first of the series being for model aeroplanes at an exhibition at the Agricultural Hall in Islington in 1907. Selected models were later flown at the Alexandra Palace. Alliott Verdon Roe , winner of the first prize, used the £75 that he won to help finance his first full-scale aircraft, and his subsequent career as one of the most influential founding fathers of the British aircraft industry is well-known.

The first full-scale aeronautical exhibition in Britain was at the Olympia Aero and Motor Boat Show in March 1909. It stemmed from the success of the Commercial Motor Show and was organised by the Society of Motor Manufacturers and Traders (SMMT) under the auspices of the Aero Club of the United Kingdom. This latter body had been founded on 29 October 1901 to look after the interests of private, as opposed to military, flying and which at that time (two years before the first sustained powered flight in an aeroplane) meant ballooning by the gentry. The Aero Club's official balloon constructors were the three Short brothers, also destined to do great things in the aircraft industry.

Until 1901 all matters connected with the science of flight and its practice were in the hands of the Royal Aeronautical Society, founded on 12 January 1866 and they continued to control scientific aspects of aviation. There was a third body, the Aerial League of the British Empire, founded on 5 April 1909, which was pledged to campaign for adequate air defences. From a statement issued by them (under their later title of the Air League of the British Empire) in March 1950, expressing "deep anxiety regarding the air defences of the United Kingdom and the Commonwealth", they would appear to have had little influence with successive British governments over the years.

If it seems curious that six years had passed since the Wright brothers' first flight before an aeronautical exhibition took place, it must be remembered that until the Wrights came to France in 1908, creating a huge stimulus to European thought, comparatively little progress had been achieved in Europe. Such news of what the fairly secretive brothers were up to as had been brought across by their indefatigable chronicler Octave Chanute had made comparatively little impact.

As France was, in those days, the centre of European aviation activity most of the exhibitions took place there. The first major one had been a flying meeting on 23 May 1909 at the *Port Aviation* at Juvisy, outside Paris. And then. on 25 July, Louis Blériot flew across the Channel in a monoplane of his own design. England "was no longer an island" and things were never quite the same again. In celebration of all this, a hugely successful *Grande Semaine d'Aviation de la Champagne* took place at Reims between 22 and 29 August. It was followed by an international aero exhibition in the *Grand Palais* on the *Champs Elysées* from 3 to 17 October, with flying at Juvisy.

The first British flying displays took place on 15 October 1909 at Doncaster and Blackpool. The former being unofficial and clashing with the Aero Club's official Blackpool event, that body then bared its infant teeth and took away the Aviator's Certificates of Doncaster participants – to their considerable astonishment.

Although these exhibitions were taking place in England, there was as yet little evidence of practical native progress in aircraft design. Foremost among British designers were the Short brothers, who had begun building aircraft in 1907, formed a company in 1908 and in February 1909 negotiated a contract to build six Wright Flyers and thus became the first aircraft construction company with a production line in the world. The engines selected for the six aircraft were imported from France and as the first one blew up on test and had to be hastily replaced, Shorts were probably also the first to discover the delights of international collaboration.

The hazards of exhibiting at the first British aero show at Olympia were mitigated by the fact that floor space was free and the SMMT guaranteed any losses up to £5,000. As it took place only five months after the first successful sustained flight in Britain, made by Samuel Cody at Farnborough on 16 October 1908, it is not surprising that only one of the eleven aircraft on view, J.T.C. Moore-Brabazon's Voisin *Bird of Passage* had actually flown. Having learned to fly in France he brought the aircraft back to England and became officially the first Englishman to fly. (Cody was still an American citizen). *Bird of Passage*, incidentally, was actually being built for Henry Farman, when "Brab" spotted it on a visit to the Voisins' factory. He had a persuasive tongue and the Voisins' business ethics, like others in the perilous business of aircraft building, were nothing if not flexible in the face of hard cash.

There were no less than 36 engines on display at Olympia and 15 manufacturers exhibited accessories of various kinds. The show ran for nine days and ushered in five years of quiet development in aviation, up to the outbreak of the First World War, when things became a touch phrenetic.

Many names familiar in subsequent SBAC shows appeared at Olympia, though of them all, only Short Brothers were still trading under their own name in 1990. Elliott Brothers who, like Shorts, were to become established at Rochester, showed their "complete aeroplane board", containing three instruments. Two designers showed all-steel aircraft; Howard Wright of Britain displayed a biplane with a light and delicate structure and Louis Breguet of France one of massive construction, some structural members of which were nearly three inches (7.62 cm) in diameter. The Wright featured reduction gearing to its contra-rotating airscrews while the Breguet could fold its wings and tail, leaving it looking remarkably like a hospital trolley.

Frederick Handley Page exhibited his first aircraft, to the designs of a gifted Hungarian, José Weiss. A twin-propeller, swept-wing, tail-less monoplane, it had a graceful, curving wing whose deep centre section and heavily washed-out tips bore some resemblance to Gustav Lachmann's aerodynamic compound sweep wing of 1947, which was still keeping the company's Victor airborne in 1990, as a tanker in Royal Air Force service. The model Lester-Best airships featured airscrews running in swivelling, slotted boxes and providing an early example of vectored thrust, as resurrected by Airship Industries in the 1980s. Swivelling propellers had first been introduced by E.T. Willows of Cardiff on airships of his own design, the blades being made by Handley Page.

A 1988 aerial view looking across a part of the static park with the exhibition halls behind.

The origins of the Society of British Aircraft Constructors lay in the announcement of the names of seven individuals, all prominent men in the young aircraft industry, who signed a Memorandum of Association to form the Society. Their names, listed alphabetically with their descriptions as subscribers to the Memorandum were:

V.Caillard, Wolseley Motor Car Company Ltd
R.O.Cary, Sopwith Aviation Company Ltd
A.T.Dawson, Beardmore and Company Ltd
H.White Smith, The British and Colonial Aeroplane Company Ltd
G.Holt Thomas
H.F.Wood, Vickers Ltd
Howard T.Wright, J.S.White and Company Ltd

All were described as aircraft constructors. The document was dated 28 March 1916 and it should be noted that all seven joined as individuals, company membership as Ordinary Members following on 6 April 1916. The new body held its first meeting on 13 April.

Howard Wright had been one of the first British designer-constructors, settled in one of the arches beneath the railway near Battersea in 1907 after working with Sir Hiram Maxim on the latter's steam aeroplane. (Maxim had bought the family engineering business). He built a biplane for T.O.M. Sopwith in 1910 in which the latter won the Baron de Forest prize. In 1912 he joined Samuel White at Cowes – a firm of boatbuilders who had turned to aviation.

George Holt Thomas began a career of management in aviation as early as 1906. He organised Louis Paulhan's successful London-Manchester flight, took up a licence to build Farman aeroplanes and founded the Aircraft Manufacturing Company, engaging Captain Geoffrey de Havilland as a designer in 1913. The company in later years became the de Havilland Aircraft Company. Holt Thomas was also involved in the design and building of the first blimp airships.

Reginald O.Cary was one of the band of dedicated men gathered round Tom Sopwith and was another management man. A member of the Royal Aero Club, in 1916 he had been a director of the company since it was formed in 1914 and was also general manager, adding to his more normal duties that of leading the works band, for which he also provided violin solos. He had been appointed general manager in 1913, having gained experience as manager to Gustav Hamel and with the Universal Aviation Company under L.D.Gibbs and Co. After the war he managed the company's Paris office.

Captain, later Major, Herbert F.Wood served with the 12th Lancers before learning to fly at the Bristol School at Brooklands (where Vickers later established a school). He joined the aviation department of Vickers, Sons and Maxim at Erith, becoming manager on 28 March 1911 and was largely responsible for taking on construction of the French R.E.P. monoplanes. Virtually the founder of the Vickers aviation department, and an active test pilot, he was manager at Weybridge, where the department had just settled in 1916. He died, sadly for the company, in the post-war influenza epidemic.

Henry (later Sir Henry) White Smith was a nephew of Sir George White, founder of the British and Colonial Aeroplane Company on 19 February 1910 and was its first secretary. The company later became the Bristol Aeroplane Company (which had been registered as a dormant company in 1910). He became the centre of a celebrated dispute between Captain Murray Sueter of the Admiralty (to whom Smith had just sold twelve Scouts) and Colonel Sefton Brancker of the War Office, who told him he should have asked the War Office first and tried to snaffle the contract. He became a director on 23 January 1917, remaining company secretary. In the latter capacity he organized licence production of monoplanes by Caproni in 1921.

V.Caillard and A.T.Dawson represented manufacturers who had become involved in aircraft engines as well as airframes. Beardmore built the Austro-Daimler under licence, which mostly powered the FE2B and, like the Wolseley Motor Car Company, built the dismal BE2c for the War Office. Wolseley also built Hispano-Suiza vee-eights under licence, naturalising it as the Viper, as well as batches of the S.E.5a into which it was put.

No distinction was made initially between aircraft and engine constructors; member number 50, Brazil, Straker (Cosmos Engineering) being the first "engine" member. They joined on 2 May 1916, so initial response was pretty swift. As they were all sponsored by the Secretary (Henry White Smith), the Society, one suspects, was doing some active promotion. The matter of what sort of aviation company you were was the subject of a question on the application form; the only member too grand even to answer that one was Hooper of St James. So we don't know what they did.

For some curious reason, in 1917-1918, seven companies became "honorary members, aero engine section". Of these, only Rolls-Royce have survived, but now pay a subscription like everyone else.

In April 1916, the Society of British Aircraft Constructors, while making it clear that they would not attempt to interfere in Service matters (there was a war going on at the time), and would not operate in the interests of individual members, announced that arrangements would be made for the exchange of members' views on technical and other matters within the industry. Out of that commitment has eventually arisen the network of committees, sub-committees, groups and working parties, both national and international, that constitute the backbone of SBAC contribution to the industry today.

While many members were wartime growths or pre-war companies that failed to survive the trauma of returning to peace-time levels of work, most of the familiar names were included: Avro (A.V.Roe and Company), Blackburn, Boulton-Paul, Bristol, Handley Page, Short Brothers, Sopwith (which re-emerged after the war as Hawker), Vickers and Westland.

The same year that saw the birth of the SBAC witnessed the appearance of another organisation, the Association of British Motor and Aircraft Manufacturers, but little seems to have come of it before it faded away. The SBAC, however, flourished and by 1920, when some of the dust had settled, was happily co-operating once more with the SMMT over another Olympia Show. It ran for twelve days with twenty-eight aircraft on show, only twelve of which were military.

All but five were British, although 13 of the 24 engines displayed were foreign, reflecting the large wartime reliance placed on foreign engine production for British aircraft during the war and the 1919 disaster of the ABC engine programme.

Royalty attended, in the persons of the Princess Marie Louise and the Duke of York, (later to become King George VI) and Royalty opened the final Olympia Show in 1929. On that occasion it was the Prince of Wales who, as King Edward VIII, was the first monarch to take a notable interest in civil and Service aviation. (His father had disliked aeroplanes.) History, absorbed in other aspects of his public and private life, has largely ignored the very considerable contribution to British aviation made by his keen interest in both industry and the Royal Air Force.

In 1920 the Air Ministry staged the first of a succession of highly popular annual flying displays at Hendon to present their Royal Air Force to the public. They ran annually on the last Saturday in June until 1937, after which it was decided that Hendon had become too small for modern military aircraft, and one of their features was a small enclosure of prototypes which became known as the New Types Park. There, behind a neat enclosure of chestnut palings, the latest – or almost the latest – products of industry were displayed to tempt possible Service or foreign buyers

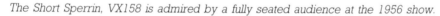

The Short Sperrin, VX158 is admired by a fully seated audience at the 1956 show.

1932

THE FIRST SHOW
27 JUNE

In 1932 the SBAC sought permission from the Air Ministry, which was readily given, for the New Types Park to be left in place, together with the attendant display facilities (and the chestnut palings) until the Monday following the RAF Pageant. The Society could then, having tidied the place up on Sunday, insert a few more of their own New Types into the Park and invite foreign guests to inspect the latest products of its members. This, with a view to purchase and to see a selection of them put through their paces by company or Service test pilots. Not all the 15 aircraft in the New Types Park were present at, or flew at, the SBAC Show and an additional 19 civil and military types were wheeled out on Monday. Starting a tradition that was to carry forward into current Farnborough Shows, several carried on with passenger demonstrations in the evening.

The public were not admitted and nor were cameras. Those guests and members of the Press so rash as to arrive carrying photographic apparatus had it removed politely by a lady member of the SBAC staff! The logic of this general ban appears to have been that it would have been impolite to let the British Press take pictures while guests could not. One of the exhibited aircraft, the Bristol Type 120, complete with new and exciting gun turret, was whisked away during Monday morning and not seen again. Security was evidently taken quite seriously, but the camera ban aroused Press protest and was not repeated.

In the morning the distinguished guests, who included General Italo Balbo, the charismatic Italian Air Minister, were let loose among the exhibits. Luncheon was served in an adjacent hangar at 13.00, presided over by the SBAC Chairman, Sir John Siddeley, chairman and managing director of Armstrong Siddeley Motors. He was plain John Davenport Siddeley CBE until created a Knight Bachelor in the Birthday Honours and his knighthood was conferred, to quote the citation, "for public services in connection with mechanical developments in the Defence Services". Patently, the language of the College of Arms had not yet caught up with that of the Industrial Revolution.

The flying programme, organised by the Royal Air Force display team, commenced sharp at 14.30 as instructed. Unfortunately, the lunch was less precisely controlled and, as Leonard Bridgman put it, writing the affair up for *The Aeroplane*, "L'heure militaire failed to coincide with the tail end

of the *déjeuner civil*".

As a result, the Chairman's speech of welcome was drowned by the opening roar of two Rolls-Royce Kestrels in the Handley Page Night Bomber, which was promptly followed by the same company's Gugnunc. None of the guests therefore saw the aircraft, which were allowed to fly again at the end of the Show (Mr Frederick Handley Page had a forceful and persuasive personality) and the incident undoubtedly gave birth to the strict SBAC rule that the flying programme takes precedence over chalet hospitality.

Undoubtedly the Night Bomber, called Heyford in its production form, was the most important aircraft at the Show. The last biplane bomber in the Royal Air Force, serving in eleven squadrons and carrying on in odd jobs until 1941, it had a top speed of 140 mph (225 km/h), replacing earlier H.P. designs, the Hinaidi and Hyderabad of 109 mph (175 km/h) and the ageing Vickers Virginia, capable of a brisk 93.5 mph (150 km/h) "in the dusk with a light behind her".

Designed to the same Specification, B.19/27, the Fairey Night Bomber also flew in the afternoon. A more advanced design, it was a monoplane of striking appearance and although of better performance than the Heyford, the latter was preferred by the conservative Service test pilots. (The Heyford was described by H.A.Taylor as "quaint-looking, practical, but slow"). It was the practical bit that did the trick; the Hendon, as the Fairey aircraft was later named, suffered several development problems and required a change of engine (from the Bristol Jupiter to the Rolls-Royce Kestrel) with considerable redesign of the wing, to eradicate undesirable flying characteristics. Ironically, the Hendon was ordered into production in October 1934, to replace the Heyford. Fourteen were built and delivered to No. 38 Squadron, RAF at Mildenhall. Sadly for its future, the new monoplane bombers of the next generation were coming through by then and the Hendon died an early death. It was the only twin-engined Fairey design to see production; the others, the F.2 fighter of 1917 and the advanced but unlucky Rotodyne of 1957, which was killed largely by commercial and political indecision, remained prototypes and the Double Mamba of the Gannet was generally considered to be a single entity.

The quality of flying at this first show set standards that have been maintained ever since and was enlivened when Philip Lucas, who was demonstrating the Jupiter-engined Hawker Hart, scooped up from the grass on take-off a considerable length of heavy steel balloon cable, and flew his entire display trailing it from his tail skid. The pilot was the only person

The Armstrong Whitworth Atlanta G-ABPI made its first public appearance at the 1932 SBAC Display.

The Handley Page Heyford prototype J9130, seen prior to its SBAC Display debut.

Gloster's only four-engined aircraft, the TC-33 J9832. Note the new Types Park No.6.

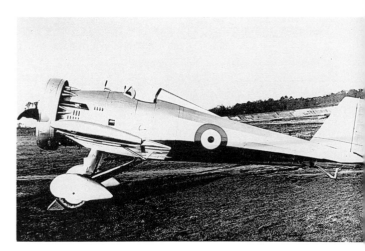

The Vickers Jockey prior to application of its RAF serial J9122.

Originally built as the Westland Wapiti V, registered G-AAWA, this later became the Wapiti VII G-ACBR and eventually the prototype Wallace K3488. It appeared at the 1932 Display with Class B marks P6.

G-ABEG was the seventh Westland Wessex; it was a company demonstrator.

on the aerodrome neither aware of, nor alarmed by, this fact.

All but four of the eleven Service prototypes displayed in 1932 entered service with the Royal Air Force. The story of one of them, the Westland PV6 (Private Venture) shows what an adventurous life a prototype might lead in those days. Starting life as the Armstrong Siddeley Panther-engined Wapiti Mk V with lengthened fuselage, by the time it got to Hendon it was the Wapiti Mk VII with a Bristol Pegasus. It reappeared later in this form as a new type, the Wallace Mk I, spending the interval in between these incarnations as the prototype and then more-or-less standard production Wallace. With the civil registration G-ACBR, it became the back-up aircraft to the Westland P.V.3 in the 1934 Everest expedition. In those hard times, there was obviously, in Westland's eyes, no point in wasting a perfectly good airframe.

The Westland Wessex, displayed in 1932, was of interest as being the last civil fixed-wing aircraft produced by the company.

There was an exhibition of ground equipment, housed in two marquees at the back of the SBAC enclosure alongside the New Types Park (rudely referred to by some spectators as the Amusement Park). Here 16 companies displayed their products, including such survivors as Smiths Instruments (later Smiths Industries), Cellon, subsequently part of the Titanine group and Vickers. In front of the tents stood eight aircraft engines and out in the open, a solitary forerunner of the Equipment Terrace, stood a fire engine.

1932

+	Armstrong Whitworth Atalanta	G-ABPI (AW.740)	
+	Armstrong Whitworth Atlas II	G-ABIV (AW.696)	
+	Armstrong Whitworth A.W.16	A-2 (AW.722)	
+	Avro Cadet	–	
+	Avro Tutor	–	
+	Avro 626	–	
+	Avro 627 Mailplane	G-ABJM (502)	
+	Blackburn Segrave	G-ABFR (3169/2)	
+	Blackburn B-2	G-ABUW (3580/1)	
	Blackburn C.A. 15C Biplane	G-ABKW (2781/1)	
+	Bristol Bulldog IIIA	R-5 (7560)	
+	Bristol Bulldog TM	K2188 (7643)	
+	de Havilland D.H.80A Puss Moth	–	
+	de Havilland D.H.82 Tiger Moth	–	
+	de Havilland D.H.83 Fox Moth	G-ABUO (4000)	

+	Fairey Firefly III	S1592 (F.1137)	
	Fairey Gordon	–	
	Fairey Night Bomber (Hendon)	K1695 (F.1271)	
	Fairey IIIF	–	
+	Gloster TC.33	J9832	
+	Handley Page Gugnunc	K1908 (1)	
+	Handley Page H.P.38	J9130	
	Handley Page H.P.42W	G-AAXF (42/8)	
+	Hawker Fury	–	
+	Hawker Hart		
+	Hawker Hart	G-ABTN (H.H.3) Bristol Jupiter engine	
+	Hawker Horsley	J8620 A.S. Leopard engine	
+	Saro Cloud	K2681 (A.19/3)	
+	Spartan Cruiser I	G-ABTY (24M)	
+	Spartan Three-seater	G-ABTR (101)	
+	Vickers Jockey	J9122	
+	Vickers Vildebeeste	–	
+	Westland Wessex	? G-ABEG (WA.1901)	
+	Westland P.V.6	P-6	

1933

THE SECOND SHOW
26 JUNE

The SBAC Show unlike the RAF Pageant on the preceding Saturday, which had been visited by low clouds, driving rain and general meteorological beastliness for the first time in its history, was blessed with fine weather. This time the flying display took place in the morning, followed by the official luncheon. They were not going to go through all that business with Handley Page again. By an odd coincidence, the same two aeroplanes opened this second display (the flying order each year was chosen by lot). The welcoming Chairman this time was Mr Herbert H. Thomas of the Bristol Aero-

A general view of the aircraft park. In the foreground, the Napier Javelin engined Percival Gull.

plane Company.

After lunch, guests were free to inspect the exhibits, in a flurry of photography, sketching and note-taking, while passenger flying took place in those aircraft suitable for this pursuit. Thirty-nine companies appeared in the static show, with nine engines on view. Foreshadowing the combined displays that were to become a Show feature, de Havilland sent on their Dragon and Tiger Moth as a pair after a formation take-off and during the day the new Leopard Moth flew unconcernedly over the assembled guests. No-one was unduly worried, although such a casual insertion into the flying programme would hardly do for today's Flying Control Committee.

Hawker's company demonstrator Hart, G-ABMR, was among the military aircraft to appear, sporting a most ele-

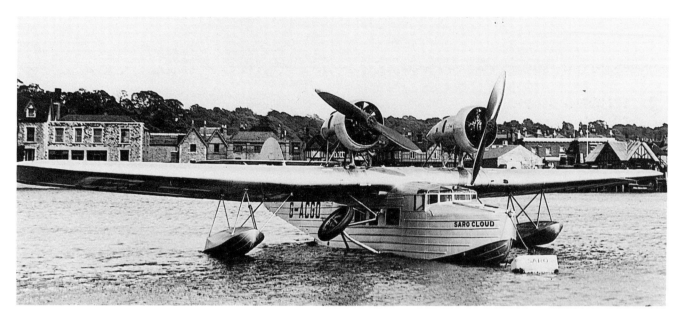

Saro Cloud G-ACGO shown moored at Cowes was a 1933 exhibit.

gant pair of spats. Later, 'BMR followed up a lengthy test-bed and test flying career as a post-war company hack and was raced in the National Air Races, painted in the rather lugubrious company colours. She reappeared later in resplendent silver (and the markings of No. 57 Squadron) and graced the display scene for many more years, incidentally giving Duncan Simpson the opportunity of becoming the only post-war Display pilot and SBAC official in current practice on a pre-war Display aircraft. She then retired to a well-earned rest in the Sydney Camm Memorial Hall in the RAF Museum at Hendon.

There was now virtually complete separation from the founding New Types Park. Very few of the exhibits were common to both events and the number of civil aircraft in the Monday display had increased considerably, the Blackburn Civil Monoplane having been the only non-military aircraft in the Royal Air Force New Types Park on Saturday.

In the flying display itself, perhaps the most startling exhibition came from the Supermarine chief test pilot, J. "Mutt" Summers, who looped the company's Seagull V, a staid, pusher biplane amphibian later to win fame as the Walrus. This manoeuvre took both his directors and the designer – and very probably the Seagull V – completely by surprise. The designer was that same Reginald Mitchell who also designed the Spitfire. As the Seagull was only on its third outing, having flown for the first time on 21 June, the general astonishment was understandable.

Even shorter on airborne time before the event was the General Aircraft Monospar ST-6. It had flown for the first time *that* day, the Air Ministry airworthiness team spending the whole of Sunday completing the paperwork.

Among other exhibiting aircraft the Avro Mailplane was in

its final metamorphosis into a very rapid single-seat test-bed for the 700 hp Armstrong Siddeley Tiger IV and was therefore being exhibited by Armstrong Whitworth, parent company of the engine builders, rather than the aircraft's makers. This was the first occasion on which this subsequently quite common practice was to be seen. The elegant Fairey Firefly, the last production aircraft of this type from Avions Fairey at Gosselies, Belgium, later became the prototype Mk IV with a Hispano Suiza engine and was bought back by the English company.

The Vickers M.1/30 S1641 broke up in the air in November 1933.

1933

Westland Wapiti J9102 was shown as a test-bed for the Bristol Phoenix compression-ignition diesel engine.

The Fairey Long Range Monoplane on show, K1991, was the second of two built and the one on which S/Ldr O.R.Gayford and Flight Lieutenant G.E.Nicholetts had just regained the long-distance record for Great Britain on 6-8 February, flying the 8,597 km (5,341 miles) from Cranwell to Walvis Bay in South West Africa in 57 hours 25 minutes. This achievement gave Great Britain, briefly, all three of the world aviation records – speed, altitude and distance.

All official records homologated by the *Fédération Aéronautique Internationale*, the governing body for such things, are established in metric measurements. The subsequent translation into native English units gives rise to such unlikely results as height records measured, apparently, to the nearest inch, which is absurd.

The speed record was held until 10 April by Flt Lt G.H.Stainforth on the Supermarine S.6B at 655 k/h (407 mph), when it was taken by Italy. The altitude record was held by Cyril Uwins, at 13,404 metres (43,976 ft), and was achieved in a Bristol Pegasus-engined Vickers Vespa. It was next taken by France on 28 September 1933. Uwins was the chief test pilot at Bristol and was to hold the post for 30 years, from 1918 to 1947 (a record in itself).

Among the static exhibits was a Westland Wapiti test-bed for the compression ignition Bristol Phoenix; research into the inherently safer heavy oil aircraft engine being popular at this time. Shortest-lived of all the 1933 display crop was the Vickers M.1/30, which disintegrated comprehensively in the air on 23 November next, dropping its (dummy) torpedo in a churchyard while the crew parachuted to safety.

Another view of the aircraft park from the Heyford.

1933

	Armstrong Whitworth Atalanta	G-ABTM (AW.786)
+	Armstrong Whitworth A.W.16	G-ACCD (AW.828)
	Avro Cadet Three-seater	–
	Avro Club Cadet	–
+	Avro Tutor	G-ABGG (476)
	Avro 626	–
+	Avro 627 Mailplane	G-ABJM (502)
+	Blackburn Ripon	K3589 (5568/1) became prototype Baffin
+	Blackburn B-2	G-ACBK (4700/6)
	Blackburn B-2	G-ACEM (5093/1)
	Blackburn C.A.15C Monoplane	G-ABKV (2780/1)
	Blackburn M.1/30A	K3591 (3900/1)
+	Bristol Bulldog IIIA	R-7 (7745)
	Bristol Bulldog TM	K2188 (7643)
	Bristol 120	K3587 (7562)
+	de Havilland D.H.82A Tiger Moth	G-ACFA (3187)
	de Havilland D.H.83 Fox Moth	G-ABKS (4015)
+	de Havilland D.H.84 Dragon 1	G-ACCE (6010)
+	de Havilland D.H.85 Leopard Moth	E-1 (7000) flew over
+	Fairey Firefly IIM	– (AF.5050)
	Fairey Fox III	G-ABYY (F.1842)
	Fairey Long Range Monoplane	K1991 (F.1671)
	Fairey Seal	–
	General Aircraft Monospar ST-4	G-ACGM (17)
+	General Aircraft Monospar ST-6	G-ACGI (14)
+	Gloster SS.19B (Gauntlet)	J9125
+	Handley Page Gugnunc	K1908 (1)
+	Handley Page Heyford	K3489
+	Hawker Hart	G-ABMR (H.H.1)
	Hawker Horsley II	J8003 R-R Condor engine
	Hawker Nimrod	K2823
+	Hawker High Speed Fury	K3586
+	Percival Gull	G-ACHA (D.30) Napier Javelin engine
+	Saro Cloud	G-ACGO (A.19/5) A.S. Serval engines
	Saro Cutty Sark	C-ACDP or 'R (A.17/10 or /11)
+	Spartan Clipper	G-ACEG (201)
+	Spartan Cruiser II	G-ACDX (4)
+	Supermarine Seagull V	N-1
	Vickers Vespa VI	K3588
+	Vickers Victoria V	K2808 Bristol Pegasus engines
+	Vickers Vildebeeste	0-7
	Vickers M.1/30	S1641
+	Westland Wallace	K3562
	Westland Wapiti	J9102 Bristol Phoenix engine
+	Westland Wessex	G-ACHI (WA.2151)

1934

THE THIRD SHOW
2 JULY

The third SBAC Show took place in brilliant sunshine, the timetable was unaltered and general arrangements were much as before. Before taking a look at the Show it is worth quoting the Chairman of the SBAC, who was still Herbert J. Thomas. In his speech on this occasion he said:

"In spite of propaganda to the contrary, I personally feel most strongly that a strong, competent air force is the finest guarantee for the security of peace of any country in the present conditions of political development."

In view of the attitude of the politicians of the day, this was a bold and positive statement; 55 years of political and other developments have done nothing to modify its truth.

Many interesting and trend-setting aircraft appeared at Hendon that year. One was the Hawker High Speed Fury, which was evolved from the Intermediate Fury and led directly, through tests with the Rolls-Royce evaporative cooling Goshawk engine, to Hawker's later P.V.3 entry for Spec. F.7/30.

The neat but unconventional Westland P.V.4 was designed to the same Spec. and had the "steam-cooled" Goshawk mounted below and behind the pilot. This gave him a superb view but initially had the severe disadvantage of setting fire to the rear fuselage. When he first flew it Harald Penrose complained that the slipstream over the gull wing just behind him almost pulled his head off and it was subsequently deemed to be a good defence to instal a cockpit canopy. F.7/30 was an interesting Spec. and drew a large number of responses, the eventual winner being the Gladiator; but the limitations of vision suffered by the compilers of the Specification resulted in biplanes with little advance over aircraft already

Recognisable in the line up are the Westland P.V.7, Fairey G.4/31, Fairey Seal, Avro 626 and Vickers Vellox.

in service. Recognition of this impediment by the private sector did, however, lead to the independent development of the Spitfire and Hurricane.

For the first time an engine manufacturer (as opposed to an airframe manufacturer who also owned an engine company) entered an aircraft in the flying display, D. Napier & Son presenting the Dagger-Hart and Rapier-powered Airspeed Courier. Air Vice-Marshal A.E. Borton, a director of the company, flew the latter a fortnight later in the King's Cup Air Race. There was also, for the first time, an autogyro.

Shortly after luncheon, Flt Lt A.G.Pickering arrived in the Supermarine Scapa flying-boat, S1648, (whose two Kestrels gave the big boat a speed of 143 mph (230 km/h) and put up an unscheduled but very convincing demonstration, causing *The Aeroplane*'s correspondent to comment, a little waspishly:

"To come out of a lunch marquee feeling good and to see a big flying-boat standing on its head apparently 500 ft (152 m) above the grass at Hendon is disconcerting."

No less than 48 companies took part in the static display. Such items as covered cockpits and split flaps now appeared as a matter of course, while new engines included the neat and business-like Napier Dagger, designed by the great Major Halford and the Bristol Perseus with Roy Fedden's adaptation of the Burt-McCollum sleeve-valves, (whose patents were about to expire). It was the first successful aero-

Hawker's Fury demonstrator G-ABSE.

engine of this type.

Installed in a tight-wrapped cowling in the nose of a Hawker Hart, the Dagger produced 705 hp at 12,000 ft (3,659 m) at a high-stepping 4,000 rpm.

Blackburn had entered four B.2 trainers to replace cancelled entries of their Torpedo Spotter Reconnaissance prototype, which was still in Ministry hands, and their

The Supermarine Scapa S1648 took part in the flying programme.

day-and-night fighter. As, even in those days, time was at a premium, with four minutes allowed per aircraft to a maximum of eight minutes per company, they flew them as a team.

The big Vickers Vellox, a most advanced design, with electric instruments, pneumatic brakes and wing and tail de-icing, was fitted out as a passenger transport with stressed seats, full soundproofing, galley and toilet. Sadly, toilet and all, it found no takers and eked out its days, *sans* everything, as a freighter, while another exhibit, the Wolseley A.R.9-engined Envoy, wound up its career, as did several others of the type, as a participant in the Spanish Civil War.

Contemporary comment on the novelties shown at the Display was not always favourable: C.G.Grey, the formidable and opinionated Editor of *The Aeroplane*, pointed out that flight refuelling, though a pretty parlour trick, was of no conceivable military value. Another writer took an interesting view of the state of British aeronautical progress: "....the character of the machines in this enclosure does disclose the lines along which new equipment for the Royal Air Force is being developed. Their aerodynamic and structural design discloses the technical progress of the Air Ministry if not of the Aircraft Industry.

This twofold aspect of the New Types Park should be properly appreciated, for obviously criticism of design and layout cannot be justified if it is of features imposed in the Specifications laid down by the Air Ministry," which in view of things like F.7/30, was percipient of him.

1934

	Airspeed Courier	G-ACLF (12)	de Havilland D.H.85 Leopard Moth	–
+	Airspeed Courier	G-ACNZ (20) Napier Rapier engine	+ de Havilland D.H.86	G-ACPL (2300)
+	Airspeed Envoy 1	G-ACMT (17)	+ Fairey Hendon	K1695 (F.1271)
	Armstrong Whitworth A.W.19	A-3 (AW.923)	Fairey Seal	K3577 (F.1910)
+	Armstrong Whitworth A.W.35 Scimitar	G-ACCD (AW.828)	Fairey G.4/31	F-1 (F.1926)
+	Avro Cadet	–	+ General Aircraft Monospar ST-6	G-ACIC (20)
	Avro Commodore	G-ACNT (691)	+ General Aircraft Monospar ST-10	G-ACTS (32)
	Avro 626 Trainer	G-ABJG (496)	+ Gloster SS.19B (Gauntlet)	J9125
	Avro 642/2M	G-ACFV (642)	+ Handley Page Heyford II	K3503
+	Blackburn B-2	G-ACAH (4700/2) Blackburn Cirrus Hermes IVA engine	+ Hawker Fury	G-ABSE (H.F.4)
+	Blackburn B-2	G-ACLC (5290/1) D.H. Gipsy III engine	+ Hawker Hart	K2434 Napier Dagger engine
+	Blackburn B-2	G-ACPZ (5290/3) D.H. Gipsy Major engine	+ Hawker Hart	G-AMBR (H.H.1)
+	Blackburn B-2	G-ACRA (5290/4) Blackburn Cirrus Hermes IV engine	+ Hawker Hart	K3020 Bristol Pegasus engine
			+ Percival Gull Six	G-ACUP (D.46)
	Blackburn B-6 (Shark)	K4295 (5060/1)	+ Saro Cloud	G-ABCJ (A.19/1A) Napier Rapier engines
+	Bristol Bulldog IVA	R-8 (7808) Bristol Perseus engine	Saro Cloud	K2681 (A.19/3) A.S. Serval engines
+	Cierva C-30P	G-ACIN (659)	+ Short Scion	G-ACUV (S.774)
	de Havilland D.H.82A Tiger Moth	–	+ Spartan Cruiser II	–
			+ Supermarine Scapa	S1648 flying only
+	de Havilland D.H.84 Dragon 2	G-ACOR (6073)	+ Vickers Vellox	G-ABKY (1)
			+ Vickers Vincent	S1714
			+ Westland F.7/30	K2891
			+ Westland P.V.7	P7

The sole Vickers Vellox G-ABKY was eventually sold to Imperial Airways who used it as a freighter.

Westland's F.7/30 was another one-off, powered by a Rolls-Royce Goshawk VIII engine with evaporation cooling.

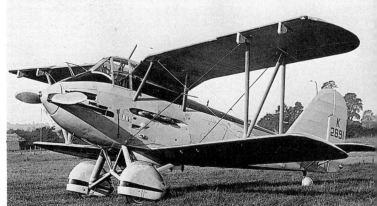

1935

THE FOURTH SHOW
1 JULY

On Monday, 1 July 1935, the SBAC staged what was to be their last appearance at Hendon. Aircraft were getting both faster and heavier and more demanding of space and the encirclement of houses that was eventually to destroy the airfield had already begun. Moreover the effort required to subdue the numerous relics of the public's presence on the preceding Saturday was proving something of a strain. The following year they would move the Show to Hatfield, after some debate among member companies over a possible transfer of the whole affair to Olympia. The advantages of this course were outweighed by the overall expense of the move and recognition that the flying display was one of the event's main attractions.

Concentration among military aircraft builders on the recently-introduced Expansion Scheme and the consequent preoccupation in industry with production meant that very few of the exhibited aircraft this year were actually prototypes.

Sixty-five exhibitors spread their wares in the big Royal Air Force transport shed, housing what the SBAC were now officially calling the Static Display. In response to pressure, and taking advantage of a captive audience, the public were admitted to this Static Display on Saturday, during the RAF Pageant, on payment of sixpence (2½p to younger readers). Ticket holders in the ten shilling (50p) enclosure at the RAF event were admitted during the afternoon and those in the cheaper pens after the flying.

Among the distinguished visitors greeted by the Chairman of the SBAC, Sir Robert McClean, chairman also of Vickers (Aviation) Ltd, was Prime Minister Stanley Baldwin's new Secretary of State for Air, Sir Philip Cunliffe-Lister, GBE, MC. Appropriately he was also Conservative Member for Hendon. His predecessor, the highly air-minded Marquess of Londonderry, had departed with Ramsay Macdonald's defeated administration.

Among items significant of future developments Bristol's sleeve-valve Perseus reappeared, having been shown the previous year in a rather startled Hart. Two more examples of this admirable power plant, though not at the Show, were running experimentally as number two and three engines in the four-engined RMA *Syrinx* of Imperial Airways, replacing the two inner Jupiters, sheathed by neat Townend rings, driving four-bladed propellers and giving the old girl a slightly unfinished air.

The Westland-Hill Pterodactyl was grounded, both its pilots being indisposed, and "Mutt" Summers flew the new Vickers P.V. bomber (later to become the Wellesley) with the undercarriage locked firmly down, treating the big aircraft "with more respect than he usually gives to family models", as *The Aeroplane* put it.

Mr Pickering of Supermarine also flew his mount, the Seagull, with the amphibian's wheels down, looping it twice (it was obviously a compulsive manoeuvre with this aircraft) in the course of a very spirited display. The Australian government had just put in an order for the Seagull and one was serving in the Royal Navy as tender to HMS *Nelson*, tucked into a nesting place abeam the bridge on the port side – about the only place to put it in that cluttered flat iron of a ship. (The concentration of weight aft made her occasionally a brute to steer and on her trials she ran aground, appropriately on Trafalgar Bank outside Portsmouth and took several days to refloat. The wardroom's temper was not improved by a polite note from the army regiment in one of the forts offering honorary membership of their mess during their stay.) The Seagull V was, incidentally, the first flying-boat capable of full-load catapulting.

Chris Staniland rolled the Fairey Fantôme immediately after take-off and went on to give his usual brilliant aerobatic display, the powerful 860 hp Hispano-Suiza *moteur-canon* engine and exceptionally clean airframe permitting effortless upward rolls. The aircraft was an entrant in a Belgian Air Force competition for a new fighter and, having a French engine, was evidently the exception proving the SBAC rule about "British goods only allowed". (The Americans call this protectionist attitude NIH – Not Invented Here.)

Among other offerings were the Handley Page H.P.47 "most-purposes monoplane" with full-span leading-edge slats, spoilers and slotted flaps. Also, Edgar Percival's wickedly quick Mew Gull, now sporting flaps and brakes after his dramatic arrival at Cardiff/Pengam Moors in the 1934 King's Cup Air Race, when he had only just squeezed into that small riverside airfield without the benefit of either of those aids to safe arrival.

The High Speed Fury was there, streaming black smoke from an over-rich mixture, and Avro were showing both the military 652 – prototype of the Anson coastal-reconnaissance bomber – and the civil version, employed by Imperial Airways (on charter work only; they had a safety rule that said that all line aircraft must be four-engined). Originally the two civil aircraft had been christened *Avalon* and *Avatar*, but

The Fairey Fantome F6 runs up before its display in front of the Fairey Hendon.

The Hawker High Speed Fury K3586 with the evaporative-cooled Rolls-Royce Goshawk engine.

Bristol's one-off Bullpup J9051 had a Bristol Aquila sleeve-valve engine.

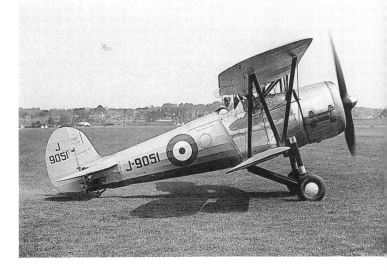

shortly before the Display the latter, with a few swift strokes of silver paint, had become *Ava*. The story ran that her arrival at a Balkan airport with the members of some commercial delegation caused a noticeably cool reception; it was subsequently explained that the word painted on her bows had unfortunate connotations in the local language and it was hastily shortened on the spot.

This was, incidentally, the year that saw the first moves to break the 12-year-old monopoly of Imperial Airways, with government backing being given to the newly-formed British Airways. This move followed the recommendations of an Inter-Departmental Committee set up, under the chairmanship of Sir Warren Fisher, to consider the implications of a "chosen instrument" policy.

1935

From de Havilland came the cabin Hornet Moth, acknowledgement that the private owner needed some protection from the weather, replacing the original Moth which was now being phased out of production.

Significantly, the point was raised in the aeronautical press that the Show should last at least three days in order to give guests the chance to cover all the exhibits thoroughly, even at the risk of having to move the site – which of course SBAC were already beginning to contemplate.

The Vickers G.4/31 biplane K2771 was built to meet the same specification as the company's private venture PVO-9.

1935	
+ Airspeed Courier	G-ADAX (26)
+ Airspeed Envoy II	G-ACVJ (30)
Armstrong Whitworth A.W.23	K3585 (1251)
+ Armstrong Whitworth A.W.35 Scimitar	G-ADBL (AW.460)
Avro Cadet	G-ADCX (813)
Avro 652	G-ACRM (698)
+ Avro 652A Anson	K4771
+ B.A. Eagle	G-ADGJ (121)
+ B.A. Swallow	G-ADDB (32)
+ Blackburn Shark	K4362 (5670/14)
+ Bristol Bulldog IVA	R-8 (7808)
+ Bristol Bullpup	J9051 (7178)
Bristol 130 (Bombay)	K3583 (7809)
Cierva C-30A	G-ACWO (717)
de Havilland D.H.82A Tiger Moth	G-A---
de Havilland D.H.85 Leopard Moth	G-ADCO (7093)
de Havilland D.H.87 Hornet Moth	G-ADIS (8001)
+ de Havilland D.H.88 Comet	K5084 (1996)
de Havilland D.H.89A Dragon Rapide	–
de Havilland D.H.89M	K4772 (6271)
Fairey Hendon	K1695 (F.1271)
+ Fairey Fantome	F6 (F.2118)
+ General Aircraft Monospar ST-25 Jubilee	G-ADIV (46)
+ Gloster Gladiator	K5200
+ Handley Page H.P.47	K2773
+ Hawker High Speed Fury	K3586
+ Hawker P.V.3	1-PV3
+ Hawker P.V.4	IPV4
+ Parnall Heck	G-ACTC (341)
+ Percival Gull	G-ADEP (D.49)
+ Percival Mew Gull	G-ACND (E.20)
+ Saro Cloud	G-ABCJ (A.19/1A) Napier Rapier engines
+ Short Scion 2	G-ADDN (S.785)
+ Supermarine Seagull V	A2-1
+ Vickers G.4/31	K2771
+ Vickers G.4/31	PVO-9
Westland Pterodactyl V	K2770
+ Westland Wallace	K4346 Bristol Pegasus I.M3 engine

The Saro Cloud G-ABCJ was powered by Napier Rapier engines.

A relaxed scene in the aircraft park; the Parnall Heck flies past and in the foreground the A.W. Scimitar G-ADBL.

1936

THE FIFTH SHOW
29 JUNE

The reasons for moving the Show from Hendon have already been mentioned. Undoubtedly the increasing growth and importance of the SBAC event was edging it towards a separate existence, which may have coloured the decision a little. There seems, as well, to have been a desire to move away from the restrictions inevitably imposed by employment of Service property and Service personnel and facilities. As one of the prime facilities available at Farnborough for the control of current Displays is the admirable police and security network provided by the Ministry of Defence, that reasoning, if true, now seems curious.

After a hot and humid Saturday for the Royal Air Force Hendon Display, Monday opened with rain and low cloud and the flying, scheduled for a 10.30 start, was postponed until the afternoon, the display being dramatically opened by Summers in the prototype Spitfire, as guests were assembling after lunch. The great majority of the aircraft taking part were civil; few of the new generation of military prototypes were either ready or available.

There *were* military entries; the Gloster Gladiator, displaying a new cowling, three bladed Fairey airscrew and cockpit hood was to be the last biplane fighter in Royal Air Force service. It was flown by Jerry Sayer of Hawker, a reminder of the 1934 take-over of Gloster by that company. The Westland A.39/34, modestly displayed by Harald Penrose, was firmly restricted to "straight and level" manoeuvres – possibly the antics of certain test pilots with military prototypes at previous shows had alarmed the management. The Lysander, as it became in service, was "remarkably quiet, even when flat out", to quote O.V. Holmes. In 1940, "Tich" Holmes was engaged in a remarkable clandestine operation, landing an ex-Olley Air Service Rapide (still in its pre-war markings) and with long extension exhaust pipes for silence's sake, on Paris racecourses at night to deliver and collect sundry persons after the fall of France. Telling this story to the author after the war, he was contemptuous of the hideous racket kicked up by the Lysanders used for this purpose in later days. Curious.

The Bristol 130, in the hands of A.J. "Bill" Pegg, now boasted turret defence, three bladed airscrews and a production order and the company were also showing the Type 142, referred to colloquially as the Rothermere Bomber. (Lord Rothermere

had commissioned it from the company as a very fast twin-engined private aircraft called *Britain First*). The eventual Service development, the Blenheim, was among those not yet ready for public viewing.

A significant entry, displayed by Flt Lt J.E.Moir, was the Phillips and Powis Miles Hawk Trainer. Hawk Trainers were already in use at the firm's Elementary Flying Training School and when a new version, modified to meet Specification T.40/36, was ordered, it was the first monoplane trainer to serve the Royal Air Force. It was also a significant exception to the new "metal only" rule of the Air Ministry.

Aerobatics were again the order of the day; the Fairey Battle was rolled convincingly by the celebrated Chris Staniland, though its vertical manoeuvres, which tended to be on the grand scale in this big and rather underpowered aeroplane, were much hampered by height restrictions. The Vega Gull started its demonstration with a series of loops and was thrown about both fast and slow by Edgar Percival. As he reached the top of a particularly sharp loop the bi-lingual commentator, Captain Rex Stocken, pointed out that the aircraft could be folded up by one person; "...but", said *The Aeroplane* rather smugly, "it wasn't".

Once again, many aircraft made last-minute arrivals with only an hour or two in their log books. PVO-10, the Vickers fighter, arrived late, though it was not for that reason that it never secured a production order.

There were 93 companies in the Static Show, including nine engine manufacturers and the whole thing was patently getting too big for a one-day event. Sir Robert MacLean was again chairman, and, in a speech whose commendable

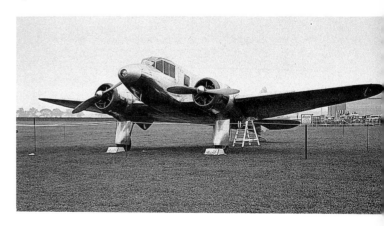

The Bristol 143 R-14 was shown alongside the company's 142 but had Aquila engines in place of the latter's Mercurys.

The third pre-production Blackburn Shark II K4882 was converted to the prototype Mk.III.

The Hawker Hurricane prototype K5083, seen at Brooklands.

Running up the Vickers Venom PVO-10 at Brooklands.

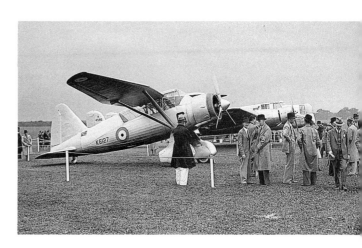

Prototypes of the Westland Lysander, K6127, and Armstrong Whitworth Whitley, K4586.

The Handley Page H.P.52 K4240, prototype of the Hampden.

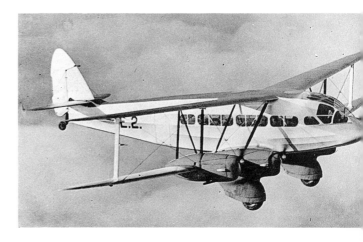

The de Havilland D.H.86A prototype in Class B markings.

brevity was duly noted, welcomed the distinguished guests, who included the *Staats Sekretar, Deutsches Luftministerium, General de Flieger* Erhard Milch, General Lindquist, the Finnish Chief of Air Staff and a delegation from the Latvian Air Force.

Among the awards in the Birthday Honours, announced that week, was an Air Force Cross for a young Flying Officer, Jeffrey Kindersley Quill.

1936

+ Airspeed Envoy II	G-ACVJ (30)
+ Armstrong Whitworth Whitley	K4586
+ Avro Anson	K6174
Avro Cadet 2	G-ADJT (849)
B.A. Eagle	–
+ B.A. Double Eagle	G-ADVV (901)
+ B.A. Swallow	G-ADDB (32)
+ Blackburn Shark II	K4882 (6020/3)
+ Bristol 130 (Bombay)	K3583 (7809)
+ Bristol 142	K7557 (7838)
+ Bristol 143	R-14 (7839)
de Havilland D.H.82A Tiger Moth	G-AEID (3498)
+ de Havilland D.H.86A	E-2 (2342)
de Havilland D.H.87B Hornet Moth	G-ADMT (8093)
de Havilland D.H.89A Dragon Rapide	YR-DRI (6330)
+ de Havilland D.H.90 Dragonfly	G-AEBU (7501)
+ Fairey Battle	K4303 (F.2121)
Fairey Swordfish	K5970 (F.2195)
+ General Aircraft Monospar ST25 Jubilee	G-AEDY (72)

+ General Aircraft Monospar ST25 Jubilee	G-AEGX (80) ambulance version
+ Gloster Gladiator	K5200
+ Handley Page H.P.52 (Hampden)	K4240
+ Hawker Hurricane	K5083
+ Heston Phoenix	G-AEHJ (1/3)
Percival Gull	–
Percival Mew Gull	–
+ Percival Vega Gull	–
+ Phillips & Powis Miles Hawk Trainer	
+ Phillips & Powis Miles Nighthawk	L6846 (285)
+ Phillips & Powis Miles Whitney Straight	G-AECT (290)
+ Short Scion 2	G-AEIL (PA.1003)
+ Short Scion Senior	G-AECU (S.834)
+ Supermarine Spitfire	K5054
+ Supermarine Walrus	–
+ Vickers Venom	PVO-10
+ Westland Lysander	K6127
Westland Wallace	–

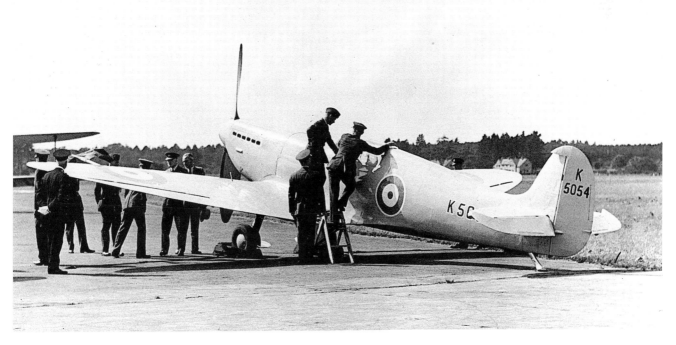

The prototype Supermarine Spitfire K5054 at Eastleigh.

1937

THE SIXTH SHOW
28-29 JUNE

For their sixth – and as it was to turn out – their last Display before the outbreak of the Second World War, the SBAC announced several changes in the arrangements. Motivated no doubt by considerations of public safety they banned foreign visitors from the show and the event was now spread over two days, in recognition of the fact that a single day was just not enough to absorb all that was to be seen and learnt.

The decision to ban foreigners, which caused unfavourable comment at the time, was the result of a mounting realisation of the deterioration of the international situation. In the previous year the first fruits of the series of re-armament programmes were becoming known, with the Air Estimates, presented on St Patrick's Day, 17 March by Sir Philip Sassoon, Under-Secretary of State for Air, announcing an end-of-year goal for Home Defence of 1,500 aircraft in the first line. The significance of this appears when the figures are laid alongside equivalent totals for overseas (270) and the still much-neglected Fleet Air Arm (around 220). Just before this, on 3 March, the re-armament White Paper had stated that home defence strength was to be increased to 1,750 aircraft. Four days later, on 7 March, Hitler re-occupied the Rhineland and announced to British Ministers in Germany at the end of the month that the Luftwaffe had achieved parity with the Royal Air Force. On the other side of the world Japanese aggression in China was about to break out into total war.

One further pointer to the future conduct of the Display, though not one influenced in any way by the political situation, was provided by the vice-chairman of SBAC (and chairman of Rolls-Royce), F.H.Sidgreaves, CBE, speaking at the Flying Display Dinner, who disclosed that the following year the public might be admitted, after a day devoted solely to "the trade". One of the guests at the dinner, incidentally, was Sir Henry White Smith, who had been elected secretary of SBAC on its foundation, 20 years previously.

On this occasion, Monday, 28 June was devoted to examination of the static display, with flying on the following day, each aircraft exhibitor being allotted a maximum twelve minute slot. The occasion was also marked by the first appearance of the most famous – or infamous, depending on your point of view – of all SBAC commentators, Major Oliver Stewart, MC. In subsequent years his *bons mots* and his clashes with successive presidents were to become legendary, even if occasionally unrepeatable.

In deference to the political situation, the more secret of the military aeroplanes on view were roped off from all but distant inspection.

The accelerating pace of re-armament and the fruits of the less unlikely Air Ministry Specifications of recent years resulted in what was undoubtedly the most exciting show to date. Most of the new military aircraft were on view, together with a new generation of engines. Rather surprisingly, although they had appeared the previous year, neither Spitfire nor Hurricane were in the flying display; nor was the Battle. On the other hand the Harrow, a foundling transport hastily converted to bomber status to swell the Air Estimate figures, *was* flown and was described by the Press as "a modern high-speed bomber". It was also the subject of a spirited drawing in *Flight* by F.Gordon Crosby, under attack for some reason by Spanish-marked He 112s. Although Harrows were all replaced by Wellingtons in squadron service before the war – the latter offering increases in speed and bomb load but initially poorer armament – the Harrow had one moment of glory, mine-laying in the winter of 1940-41; an operation code-named by some anonymous humorist at Air Ministry "Operation Mutton".

This vintage display was dominated by Philip Lucas and the beautiful de Havilland Albatross, powered by four closely-cowled Gipsy Twelve engines, which were designed specifically for it and gave the 22 seater airliner (spanning two feet more than the Lancaster), a top speed of 225 miles an hour (362 k/h). Originally intended for trans-Atlantic routes, Imperial Airways' fleet of seven – the 'F' class – served European schedules until the outbreak of war, then flying wartime runs to Lisbon and Iceland, until lack of spares forced the scrapping of the two survivors in 1943. It was largely on A.E.Hagg's experience with the Albatross that the success of the Mosquito was founded.

It could be said that at this show died the concept of the light bomber. Neither the Hawker Henley nor the Fairey P.4/34, destined to carry the banner of the Hart, saw service in that now defunct rôle, although the Henley lingered on as an unsatisfactory target tug, when it might well have been a far more successful light bomber than the Battle (which would not have been difficult) and the Fairey design gave birth to the Fleet Air Arm's Fulmar.

Specification F.5/34 gave birth to the Vickers Venom and the Gloster "Un-named Fighter", the latter as shapely as the Venom was not. Both were radial-engined (respectively the

625 hp Aquila and 840 hp Mercury) and though carrying the same armament as the successful contenders to this Specification, the Hurricane and Spitfire, they were considerably less powerful. Gerry Sayer produced a sparkling aerobatic display on the Gloster, though some of the impact was lost by his having to stay high because of the Air Ministry "part publication" rules for what would then have been described by the Press as a "hush-hush" aircraft.

Like the light bomber, the general purpose aircraft was fading from the Air Staff's mind, the Vickers Wellesley being its last example. The latter, this time cleared fully for display flying, was in sombre green and brown camouflage, as were the Whitley (which had won the B.3/34 contract to which the Harrow had been converted) and the Bristol Blenheim, now appearing for the first time in its full military form.

Glowing in their coats of training yellow, the de Havilland Don and Airspeed Oxford, represented single and twin engined approaches to Specs for pilot, radio and gunnery trainers. Although an official change of plan put paid to the Don, the Oxford went on to a long and honourable career, being memorable for having the first properly designed instrument layout in a Royal Air Force aircraft, and also for demanding the trainee pilot's full and undivided attention.

Among the experimental types, the agility of the sleeve-valve Perseus-engined Hart and the remarkably short take-off and steep climb of its Mercury-powered stablemate with the "infinitely-variable" controllable-pitch Rotol airscrew, were notable. Both were quite quiet in flight, unlike the big Blackburn Shark, unkindly described by one spectator as sounding like "a tram going round a corner". The strength and buoyancy of Blackburn aircraft for the Fleet Air Arm were well-known and A.J.Jackson describes one Shark that was returned to service after being towed twenty miles at sea, inverted and still carrying a torpedo. The type first appeared at an SBAC Show in 1934 and now sported a long cockpit canopy and three bladed airscrew.

Geoffrey Tyson looped the Anson and John Lankester Parker arrived *hors concours* in the big Short Empire boat *Calpurnia*, ushering in the greatest period of British flying boat development in a series of grass-cutting passes during the luncheon interval, with what F.D.Bradbrooke in lyrical mood called "a subdued but authoritative hissing of horsepower". Sadly, it would fall to Tyson to close that period with the Saro Princess at a later Show.

Among the civil offerings, only the Vega Gull, developed into the Proctor, survived in any numbers. A.E.Clouston, who had been trying out the little Hafner A.R.III Gyroplane during lunch, took it up again to close the flying display and the show and that was that for nine long years.

Gloster's F.5/34 fighter bore a strong family resemblance to the Gladiator.

The D.H.91 Albatross as shown at Hendon with inset vertical tail surfaces, later changed to oval endplates.

A stately flypast by the Short S-23 G-AETW Calpurnia.

1937

+	Aeronca 300	G-AEVE (AB.120)	
	Aeronca 100	–	
	Airspeed Envoy III	F-AQAA (70)	
+	Airspeed Oxford	L4534	
+	Armstrong Whitworth Whitley	–	
+	Avro Anson	–	
+	Blackburn Shark	K8495 (6790-46)	
+	Bristol Blenheim I		
+	C.W. Cygnet Minor	G-AEMA (0001)	
+	de Havilland D.H.86B	–	
	de Havilland D.H.89A Dragon Rapide	G-AEOV (6342)	
+	de Havilland D.H.91 Albatross	E-2 (6800)	
+	de Havilland D.H.93 Don	E-3 (9300)	
	de Havilland Technical School T.K.4	E-4 (2265)	
	Fairey Swordfish	–	
+	Fairey P.4/34	K7555 (p.2266)	
	Gloster Gladiator	–	
+	Gloster F.5/34	K5604	

+	Hafner Gyroplane	G-ADMV (A.R.IIi)	
+	Handley Page Hampden	K7271 flying only	
+	Handley Page Harrow	K6933 or 34	
+	Hawker Hart	K3020 Bristol Mercury engine	
+	Hawker Henley	K5115	
	Hawker Hurricane	K5083	
+	Hawker P.V.4	K6926 Bristol Perseus engine	
+	Heston Phoenix	G-ADAD (1/1)	
+	Miles P.6/36 Kestrel	– (330)	
+	Miles Magister	L5916	
+	Miles Whitney Straight	–	
	Percival Gull Six		
+	Percival Mew Gull	G-AEXF (E.22)	
+	Percival Vega Gull	G-AEYD (E.60)	
+	Short Scion Senior	G-AECU (S.834)	
+	Short S-23	G-AETW (S.839) flying only	
+	Supermarine Walrus	L----	
	Tipsy S-2	G-AEYG (106)	
+	Vickers Venom	PVO-10	
+	Vickers Wellesley	–	
+	Westland Lysander	K6127	

The de Havilland Don shortly before the Show, with New Types Park No.1 and Class B markings E-3.

A production Vickers Walrus shares a line-up including a pair of Aeroncas, the Westland Lysander prototype and a Gloster Gladiator.

1946

THE SEVENTH SHOW
12-13 SEPTEMBER

The first of the post-war SBAC Shows took place at the Handley Page aerodrome at Radlett, tucked into the corner of the triangular site between Watling Street and the railway, just over seven years since the start of the war and nine years since the previous Show. Handley Page had moved to Radlett in 1930, after the site had been accidentally discovered by their chief test pilot, Major Jim Cordes following a precautionary landing. Cricklewood, for so long the company's factory and airfield, had succumbed, like its neighbour, de Havilland's Stag Lane, to the familiar demands of North London expansion and had been sold to property developers.

It was an exciting, prestigious and portentous occasion; not all the portents being favourable, as it turned out. Most of the fruits of wartime research, development and production, as much in the equipment as in the airframe and engine sectors, was on display (or as much as was thought suitable for exposure to bulging foreign eyes and notebooks). Unfettered yet by the national reluctance to exploit British invention that seemed to dog later years, the aircraft manufacturers emerged from the war as the largest industry in the country and in broad terms, despite subsequent knocks from frequently unexpected quarters, it never lost that position.

Engine development, in particular, had been spectacular; in this field, Britain was, for the moment, firmly in the lead with the only practical jet engines in the world – opposition from the Germans, who had been building the more advanced but tricky axial flow turbines, having been dealt with by methods considerably more direct and effective than normal commercial practice might have condoned. In this area we were, for the moment, in the delightful position of passing technical expertise and experience to the Americans, rather too freely at times, it might be added, though no-one regarding the respective industrial bases of the two countries could have expected *that* situation to last for long.

British achievement over the past eight years had been brought sharply into focus the previous year when the Royal Air Force High Speed Flight, back in business 15 years after the last Schneider Trophy race, raised the World's Air Speed record to 975.875 k/h (606.38 mph). On 7 September 1946, six days before the Show, G/Capt. E.M. "Teddy" Donaldson, DSO, AFC, one of three remarkable brothers in the Service, jacked the record up another ten miles an hour (16 k/h) flying the FAI prescribed course between Bognor and Worthing at

an average speed of 991.36 k/h (616 mph). The trophy itself was on view in the entrance to the static exhibition.

The record was now within nudging distance of the first official record over 1,000 k/h, for which Louis Blériot had long ago offered a prize.

One of the exhibits at the Show was a clipped-wing Mk IV Meteor from Gloster's Experimental Flight, basically similar to Donaldson's record-breaking EE549, and which had come over to Radlett from Moreton Valence in eight minutes. That modish cropped span, which in conjunction with redesigned ailerons gave much improved performance in roll, was to become a standard feature on Service Mk IVs.

By far the most important single feature of this first (and still private) post-war display was the emergence from security-darkened obscurity of the jet engine. A little brief publicity had been given to the Meteor when it emerged as the first Allied jet in 1944 (largely because as a killer of the Fieseler Fi 103 flying bomb it was in the public eye anyway) and rather more media inches were devoted to the Messerschmitt Me 262. The latter, unlike the Meteor, featured in a number of combats with Allied bombers and fighters. A persistent and successful Me 262 bomber attacking Nijmegen bridge, upon which the author was standing at the time, gave him his first sight of this novel invention.

For the 1946 Show Thursday was devoted to the static show and ground inspection of aircraft and Friday the 13th, in defiance of superstition and in unexpectedly good weather in the afternoon, to two separate displays either side of lunch.

The static exhibition was housed in the two Handley Page engine-running hangars in the south-west corner of the airfield, their impressive bulk enlarged by a tented extension to accommodate the 194 exhibitors. The majority of the exhibited aircraft were ranged outside the adjacent main hangar. Recalling the heady optimism of the immediate post-war period, it is sad to think how few of these gleaming prototypes and production aircraft would survive the unremitting challenge from across the Atlantic.

The aircraft for the flying display were towed away to the north side, as they still were 42 years and 30 Shows later, extracted from the static park to cross the main runway to the operational side.

The flying display included, inevitably, a number of established military types, as well as novelties, the most important of these being the jet fighters and the most significant the demonstration of flight refuelling techniques by two Lancasters, and the appearance of a solitary helicopter. Jeffrey

Quill arrived with the Supermarine E.10/44, the first type to be fitted with the Rolls-Royce Nene. The machine, said *Flight*, "gave an instant impression of solidity", which was probably fair enough. It had evolved from the Spiteful/Seafang, which had been Supermarine's final attempt to improve the Spitfire. The result, even with a laminar-flow wing which the company had been pondering since 1943, was not epoch-making but the "jet-Spiteful", made fully carrier-compatible in 1947, evolved into the Attacker and the Navy's first operational jet. Unlike its contemporary, the Gloster Meteor, the E.10/44 still carried a tail wheel – it was intended for naval use and conformed to current deck-landing techniques, although Lt Cdr E.M."Winkle" Brown, had made the first-ever carrier jet trials with the nose-wheel equipped Vampire aboard HMS *Ocean* as long ago as 3 December 1945 and two Meteor IIIs had been "navalised" for the same purpose.

Despite the appearance of the new jets, piston engines continued to dominate the production scene at the display. The prototype Mosquito was there, surrounded by a heterogeneous collection of warlike stores (possibly the first occasion this now common piece of showmanship was employed at a display). With it, to keep the nostalgia going was Jean Batten's famous record-breaking Gull Six, adding lustre to Edgar Percival's post-war Proctors.

Other reciprocators included the Centaurus-powered Blackburn Firebrand IV, a 51 foot (15.5m) span, 8½ ton single seat torpedo fighter and the Hawker Sea Fury Mk X. The latter claimed a top speed of nearly 440 mph (708 km/h) (and was the vehicle for a virtuoso display of aerobatics by Bill Humble). While the Seafang was also there, with a Rolls-Royce Griffon that would push it along at 475 mph (764.4 km/h), the writing was on the wall and it was generally accepted that the limits of speed behind an airscrew had been reached.

Two research aircraft claimed attention. The advanced and elegant D.H. 108, planned scale model for the original three-engined, tail-less and swept-wing Comet airliner project, was represented by the second of three built. (A significant step towards the civil jet airliner was present in the Nene-Lancastrian test-bed). Where the first D.H. 108, TG283, had been used to explore the basic characteristics of control, the second was built with a much modified wing to take the design to supersonic speeds. Geoffrey de Havilland Junior demonstrated it at Radlett with a fine display of aerobatics. The aircraft had already flown at speeds in excess of the official World Speed Record (held by the Meteor) and was prepared after the Show for an officially observed attempt. Tragically, during a practice run at around Mach 0.9, the 108 broke up in flight, killing the pilot, on 27 September.

The second research aircraft existed only in model form, but must be mentioned in the general post-war atmosphere of British aeronautical research. This was the Miles M.52, intended to fly at 1,000 mph (1,610 km/h) on a Whittle W.2/700 giving eventually, it was planned, slightly over 4,000 lb (1,815 kg) of thrust at full speed. The design was very advanced, with a bi-convex wing, power-operated controls and all-moving tailplane and the pilot in an "escape pod" cockpit acting as a shock cone in the engine intake. (The design, incidentally, went back to 1943.) In 1946, when the M.52 was virtually completed, the whole project, with three aircraft under construction and the first flight planned for just before the SBAC Display, was cancelled.

The official statement said that it would be "uneconomic to pursue the original line of attack in research into supersonic flight embodied in the M.52 and it was therefore abandoned in favour of later developments." £100,000 of the tax-payer's money went down the drain – a situation with which that unfortunate person would become increasingly familiar as the years went by. What all this actually meant was that as German research into wing sweep-back as a means of delaying compressibility at high sub-sonic speeds became available and with rather dubious logic, (while attempting to conceal the fact that this country had not thought of it too) Government dropped all supersonic research not employing sweep-back. The result was that the United States, not Great Britain, achieved the first level supersonic flight – without swept-back wings. Under the wartime arrangement to pool knowledge, incidentally, all Miles's drawings, design data and calculations were apparently made available to the Americans. No comment on this early example of political folly need be given. It was in connection with this episode that *The Aeroplane*, writing of the post-war industry, said: "Its positive approach contrasts so markedly with the depressing exhibition of restrictionism shown by political planners." In retrospect, "restrictionism" seems quite mild.

Explaining the abandonment of the project to Parliament, the Director-General of Research at the Ministry of Supply, Sir Ben Lockspeiser, announced "We have not the heart to ask pilots to fly the high-speed models, so we shall make them radio-controlled." This rather less-than-satisfactory reply (although radio-controlled model tests were made) was taken by some to be an attempt to divert attention from a rather less than-satisfactory handling of the whole thing. Nevertheless, Geoffrey de Havilland did lose his life in a similarly advanced project.

Short's twin-engined, contra-rotating Sturgeon was billed as "the first modern twin designed for naval operation". This was perhaps not quite true, 13 Grumman F7F-4N Tigercats having been given arrester gear for that purpose a short time earlier, but certainly the only previous British twins to operate on carriers had been converted RAF types, the Sea Mosquitos of No. 811 Squadron, who received them just a month before the Radlett show.

In the civil field, Avro showed the Tudor I, which was the first pressurised British airliner and a long tradition was maintained with the appearance of a flying-boat; one of BOAC's Short Hythes, flown by Captain Stone. With the exception of the Gemini (flown by F.G.Miles, who was probably the only chairman and managing director of a member company personally to display his wares in an SBAC Flying Display), all the light aircraft present were developments of wartime aircraft and all did well in the immediate post-war period, but they were virtually the last British light aircraft so to do.

In the years to come, British manufacturers, despite good, competitive designs, never seemed to be able to master post-war conditions. Miles and Percival struggled on until both were overwhelmed by economic conditions and only Auster, marketing an essentially pre-war and fairly basic product, sold large numbers all round the world – a process that probably owed as much to the inspired pilotage and golden North British tongue of Ranald Porteous as to anything else. Auster's military Mark VI would re-emerge some years later as the Beagle-Auster Terrier after a useful second career with gliding clubs and they attempted to show the Arrow – until the SBAC realised there was an American engine under the bonnet (ugh!) and had it wheeled away smartly. 1946 also saw the first of an apparently endless succession of appearances by the de Havilland Dove.

The end of the year witnessed the end of a massive general advertising campaign in the British, Commonwealth and foreign press, started in 1944 by the SBAC on behalf of industry, emphasising the wartime achievements of British companies in aircraft, engines and the industrial base. This was intended to bridge the gap until the individual companies could gather themselves together and once more launch their own sales programmes. One of the features of the campaign was the commissioning of a series of paintings for the advertisements, principally by Terence Cuneo and Frank Wootton and featuring aircraft and industrial capacity, many of which still adorn the Society's offices. This habit of artistic support set off a decade and a half of similar behaviour among aviation companies and the covers of both *Flight* and *The Aeroplane* positively blazed with artistic talent.

Aerial view of the first post-war SBAC Display at Radlett; three-fifths of the aircraft are in military marks.

1946

+	Airspeed Consul	G-AICZ (4317)	
	Airspeed Horsa I	LG875	
+	Armstrong Whitworth Whitley V	LA951 tug for A.W.52G	
+	Armstrong Whitworth A.W.52G	RG324	
+	Auster Arrow J/2	G-AICA (1878)	
+	Auster Autocrat J/1	G-AHSM (2107)	
	Auster AOP.VI	VF482	
	Avro Anson C.XIX	VL294	
+	Avro Lancaster B.III	G-AHJT (S4/VA2505) Flight refuelling	
+	Avro Lancaster B.III	G-AHJU (S4/VA23094)	
	Avro Lancastrian III	G-AHBY (1293)	
+	Avro Lancastrian I	VH742 R-R Nenes in outer nacelles	
+	Avro Lincoln B.II	RF360	
+	Avro Tudor 1	G-AGRF (1254)	
	Avro York 1	G-AGOA (1228)	
+	Blackburn Firebrand TF.V	EK742 (3380/184)	
+	Bristol Brigand TF.1	RH748 (12636)	
+	Bristol Buckmaster T.I	RP151 (12055)	
+	Bristol Freighter 2A	G-AHJC (12735)	
+	Cierva W.9	PX203	
+	de Havilland Dove I	G-AHRJ (04004)	
	de Havilland Hornet F.III	PX313	
	de Havilland Leopard Moth	G-ACTJ (7075)	
	de Havilland Mosquito I	W4050	
+	de Havilland Mosquito PR.34	RG231	
+	de Havilland Sea Hornet F.20	TT186	
	de Havilland Sea Vampire F.20	TG328	
+	de Havilland Vampire F.1	TG285	
+	de Havilland D.H.108	TG306	

	de Havilland Technical School T.K.2	G-ADNO (1998)	
	Elliott Eon Olympia	–	
+	Fairey Firefly Trainer	F1 (F.7661)	
+	Fairey Firefly FR.IV	TW693 (F.6024)	
+	Fairey Spearfish	RA356 (F.7870)	
+	General Aircraft Hamilcar X	LA704	
+	Gloster Meteor F.IV	EE525	
+	Handley Page Halifax B.III	NA295 tug for Hamilcar	
+	Handley Page Halton	G-AHDS (1350/SH.22C)	
+	Handley Page Hastings I	TE580	
+	Hawker Fury I	LA610	
+	Hawker Sea Fury FB.X	TF895	
	Hawker Tempest VI	NX233	
	Kirby Tutor	–	
+	Miles Aerovan 3	G-AIDI (6383)	
+	Miles Gemini 1A	G-AIDO (6306)	
+	Miles Marathon 1	G-AGPD (6265)	
+	Miles Martinet TT.1	RG906	
+	Miles Messenger 3	HB-EIP (4690)	
	Percival Gull Six	G-ADPR (D.55)	
+	Percival Prentice	TV163	
	Percival Proctor 1	G-AHMV (H.547)	
+	Percival Proctor 5	G-AGTC (Ae.3)	
+	Short Hythe (Sunderland)	G-AGKY flying only	
	Short Sturgeon 1	RK787	
+	Supermarine Seafang F.32	VB895	
	Supermarine Seafire F.47	PS944	
+	Supermarine Spitfire T.VIII	N32 (6S/729058)	
+	Supermarine E.10/44 (Attacker)	TS409	
+	Vickers Viking C.IA	VL226 (127)	
+	Vickers Warwick C.III	HG248	
+	Westland Welkin II	PP370	

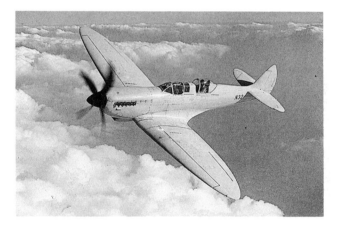

The Supermarine Spitfire T.VIII trainer, marked N32 in an all-yellow scheme. It later became G-AIDN.

The Westland Welkin high altitude fighter programme was cancelled. One Mk.1 was converted to Mk II PF370 with radar nose and other changes.

de Havilland Sea Hornet F.20 TT186 and the prototype Mosquito W4050.

The experimental Cierva W.9 to specification E.16/43 used jet thrust to compensate for torque.

1947

THE EIGHTH SHOW
9-12 SEPTEMBER

The Show remained at Radlett and was still a purely private occasion, with invited guests only. However, the Society's President, W.R.Verdon Smith, in his welcoming speech referred to the fact that government assistance was being sought to find a site for the event with facilities for the public.

The additional day was a non-flying one for technicians (who were presumably supposed not to be interested in what happened to aeroplanes after they had built them). The period of the first week of September had been chosen in 1946 after careful consideration of met. records and was to become one of the immutabilities of the occasion (with one disastrous exception), as was the venue, following this final Radlett display. In deference to the general climate of austerity imposed by government, the Society replaced the traditional first-day banquet with an austerity cafeteria lunch.

Numbers of aircraft in the Flying Display fluctuated from a maximum of 46 to 41 on the opening day, when the Press attended and the weather was uncharitable and a couple of entries failed to make it in time. The exhibition area had gone up to 63,000 square feet (5,853 sq. m). There were 188 exhibitors, fewer than in 1946, but the figure would remain roughly constant for another five years.

There was a novelty not often to be repeated, with no less than twelve gliders and sailplanes, the three big experimental tail-less beasts from General Aircraft and nine more elegant civil ones, presented by Slingsby, Short Brothers and Elliott's of Newbury (EoN). Elliott's also showed the shapely four-seat A.P.4 Eon light aircraft – the initials recording the designers, Aviation and Engineering Products, Ltd. It came to a curious end. In 1950, by which time it had acquired a more powerful Gipsy Major 10 in place of its Cirrus Minor II, it took off (or attempted to do so) at a meeting at Lympne, with a glider attached and no-one aboard either craft, finishing up in a heap in the hedge.

This was to be one of the last public appearances of the great Austrian gliding pioneer Robert Kronfeld, who was killed shortly afterwards testing one of the tail-less GAL 56s.

Many of the wartime "left overs" and some newcomers that found no favour had disappeared, including the gaggle of Spitfires (now represented only by a two-seat Mk VIII and a Seafire 47), the curious General Aircraft Hamilcar X powered glider and the massive Fairey Spearfish, 60 ft (18.3 m) span, 11 ton (9,979 kg) intended successor to the

Barracuda. The sad Tudor was represented by the solitary Mark VII, with the Merlin engines replaced by Hercules. Earlier Marks had fallen considerably short of promise, which, with endless alterations to the Specification by the British Overseas Airways Corporation blighted its future as a production airliner. Its demise was further hastened by the loss of two of the Mk IVs operated by British South American Airways. Nevertheless, the design was fundamentally sound and Tudors served with success for several years as freighters.

With increasing emphasis being placed by the civil Corporations on recovery of pre-war traffic on the main European and Empire routes, airliners presented at the immediate post-war Displays were of particular interest.

A Government White Paper published in December 1945, announced the future formation of three commercial transport Corporations, covering respectively European and internal services, Atlantic, Commonwealth and Far East routes and lastly South America. One of these, British Overseas Airways Corporation, had come into being from a merger of Imperial Airways and British Airways on 4 August 1939, taking over responsibility for such commercial routes as survived and beginning operations on 1 August 1940. On 2 March 1941, it began the famous service to and from Sweden, latterly using Mosquitos and on 23 May recommenced trans-Atlantic services with three Boeing 314 flying-boats. These were ordered "privately" by Lord Balfour, which started a terrible row with Churchill and Lord Beaverbrook, who had not been consulted. At the end of May 1945, the London-Sydney service was started in conjunction with QANTAS, using Lancastrians. In November, Lord Winster, the Minister of Civil Aviation in Attlee's Labour Government, announced that the second and third Corporations, British European Airways and British South American Airways, were to be formed, all three under public ownership and the full government monopoly came into being on 1 August 1946.

In all this, the Government were actually implementing the views expressed in the Conservative administration's White Paper of March 1945, from Lord Swinton, the first Minister of Civil Aviation. He in turn had based the Paper on the Cadman Report made to him as Secretary of State for Air in 1938. So the new Corporations had actually quite an ancient lineage.

In 1947 most routes, including those to South Africa and Australia following the withdrawal of the ageing C class boats, were being flown by "interim" types – Avro Yorks and Lancastrians and the Hythe class Sunderland conversions – but the new British airliners intended to replace them were appearing at Radlett. One, the Vickers Viking, had been introduced to service by BEA already, just before the previous SBAC Show, on 1 September 1946, taking over from their previous aircraft, the ex-Transport Command Dakotas of No. 110 Wing, Royal Air Force.

Prominent among the prototypes in the afternoon's opening "heavy" circus was the Handley Page Hermes II, flown by S/Ldr H.G."Hazel" Hazelden, the company's new chief test pilot (following the unfortunate death of Flt Lt J.R.Talbot in the crash of the Hermes I in 1945). Lacking the ten hours airborne time demanded by the Ministry before allowing an aircraft to display in public, it made them up in circuits at Radlett before the Show, flown by a very bored chief test pilot. Like its military version the Hastings, developed in parallel and also flying at Radlett, it was a tail-wheel aircraft and was a development model for the nose-wheel Hermes 4. Twenty-five of the latter had been ordered by the Ministry of Supply for BOAC at the beginning of the financial year in April.

The Marathon took off on three engines. In fact, everybody in the opening circus, which had taken off and assembled during lunch and consisted of the Hermes II, Tudor VII, Hastings C.1 prototype, Lincoln, Valetta, Marathon, Dove and Bristol Freighter, performed a pass on half power, feathering one or two airscrews as appropriate. In the case of the

Freighter, carrying a three-ton truck, this was particularly impressive.

Not to be outdone, the duty flying-boat at the Display, BOAC's recently-commissioned Short Solent 2, *Scapa*, pounded steadily past the crowd with two feathered on one side.

One of two versions of the Fairey Firefly was a Mk IV with its Rolls-Royce Griffon fitted experimentally with contra-rotating airscrews and, virtually alone among the jet-powered fighters, the piston-engined Hawker Sea Fury, in the hands of "Bill" Humble, produced an impressive aerobatic display.

The Ghost-powered Vampire, flown by John Cunningham was employed for high-speed, high-altitude tests of that engine, and there was a Lancastrian with Ghosts in the outboard positions, utilising the drawings prepared by Rolls-Royce for the Nene-Lancastrian mountings to save time. Employed for endurance and fuel consumption tests, it was displayed by Chris Beaumont of the de Havilland Engine Company.

A circus of light aircraft included the Auster Autocrat, the progenitor of a long line of similar aircraft. First production

Airliner line up, with Avro Tudor VII G-AGRX, Airspeed Ambassador G-AGUA, Handley Page Hermes II G-AGUB and, just visible, Handley Page Hastings TG502.

FORTY YEARS

of Auster Aircraft Ltd (the name was registered in 1946) and first really successful British light aircraft post-war, with over 400 built by the end of 1947, it had two distinctions to its credit by the time it appeared at the Show that year. The prototype, built up from the remains of a 1939 Taylorcraft Plus D, had conducted the first post-war charter flight on 1 January 1946 when civil flying once more became legal in Britain. (On the same day, Heathrow was transferred to the Ministry of Civil Aviation by the Air Ministry). In more spectacular fashion, ten months later, Autocrat G-AERO, owned by Temple Press and visiting HMS *Illustrious*, made the first landing of a civil aircraft on an aircraft carrier.

Others in the "light" circus were the Messenger, Gemini and Aerovan from Miles, who were also showing a Merchantman crammed with Biro pens – symbolic, no doubt, of the launch of the Miles-Martin pen company. Much was made in early advertising of the fact that the pen would write under water; in those pre-Cousteau days, one would have thought

The interesting little Portsmouth Aerocar G-AGTG was exhibited at two Shows but was scrapped in 1950.

that a rather under-utilised accomplishment. There were the inevitable stories about losing a year's supply of ink to atmosphere above 10,000 ft (3,050 m).

The Heston A.2/45 Air Observation Post, the curious twin-boom, high-wing Portsmouth Aerocar and the Cunliffe-Owen Concordia, the latter a twin-engined ten-seater for which a market did not exist, failed to survive, but the neat little Percival Merganser grew up to be the much better-known Prince.

1947

+	Airspeed Ambassador	G-AGUA (61)
+	Airspeed Consul	G-AJWR (5162) Ambulance version
	Airspeed Consul	G-AJWS (5170)
+	Avro Lancastrian	VM703 D.H. Ghosts in outer nacelles
+	Avro Lincoln B.2	RE348
+	Avro Lincoln B.2	RA716/G Bristol Thesus in outer nacelles
	Auster Avis	Z-2
+	Auster Autocrat J/1	G-AJEM (2317)
+	Auster Autocrat J/1	G-AHHD (1976)
	Auster AOP.VI	16658 Canadian Army
+	Avro Tudor VII	G-AGRX (1261)
	Blackburn Firebrand TF.V	EK743 (3380/155)
+	Blackburn S.28/43	RT651
+	Boulton Paul P.108 (Balliol)	VL892 Bristol Mercury
+	Bristol Brigand TF.I	RH797 (12671)
	Bristol Buckmaster T.I	RP151 (12055)
+	Bristol Freighter 2	G-AIFF (12766)
+	Bristol Freighter 21E	G-AIMW (12812)
+	Cierva W.9A	PX203
+	Cunliffe-Owen Concordia	G-AKBE (2)
+	de Havilland Chipmunk	G-AKDN (11)
+	de Havilland Dove 2	G-AJLW (04033)
	de Havilland Dove 2	VT-CRT (04057)
	de Havilland Leopard Moth	G-ACTJ (7075)
	de Havilland Mosquito	W4050
	de Havilland Sea Hornet F.20	VR837
+	de Havilland Tiger Moth	G-AIRR (84086) tug for Nimbus
+	de Havilland Vampire F.I	TG443
	de Havilland Vampire F.III	VF345
+	de Havilland D.H.108	VW120
+	Elliott Newbury Eon	G-AKBC (EoN 1) glider tug
	Elliott Eon Olympia	–
	Elliott Eon Baby	–
	Elliott Eon Primary	–
+	Fairey Firefly Trainer	MB750 (F.7661)
+	Fairey Firefly FR.IV	TW695 (F.6045)
	Fairey Gyrodyne	G-AIKF (F.8465)
+	General Aircraft GAL 56/U	TS510-D
	General Aircraft GAL	56/V.24 TS507
	General Aircraft GAL 56/V.36	TS513-B
+	Gloster Meteor F.IV	RA449
+	Handley Page Halifax A.IX	RT894 tug for GAL 56/U
+	Handley Page Hastings C.I	TG502
+	Handley Page Hermes II	G-AGUB (HP.74/1)
	Hawker Fury I	NX802 Centaurus engine
	Hawker Fury I	VP207 Sabre engine
+	Hawker Sea Fury FB.X	TF955
+	Heston A.2/45	VL529
	Kirby Gull IV	–
	Kirby Kite II	–
	Kirby Tutor	–
+	Miles Aerovan IV	G-AJWK (6417)
+	Miles Boxcar	G-AJJM (6696)
+	Miles Gemini IA	G-AIDO (6306)
+	Miles Marathon 1	G-AGPD (6265)
+	Miles Merchantman	U-21 (6695)
+	Miles Messenger 2A	G-AKBO (6378)
+	Percival Merganser	G-AHMH (AU.1)
+	Percival Prentice T.I	VR192
	Percival Proctor I	G-AHUX (K.244)
	Percival Proctor IV	G-AJMP (H.742)
	Percival Proctor VI	XI (Ac. 140) floatplane
+	Portsmouth Aerocar	G-AGTG (2)
+	Reid & Sigrist Desford	G-AGOS (3)
	Scottish Aviation Pioneer I	VL515 (101)
+	Short Nimbus	BGA470 (S.1312)
+	Short Solent	G-AHIS (S.1305) flying only
+	Short Sturgeon I	RK787
	Slingsby Gull	–
	Slingsby T.21B	
+	Supermarine Attacker	TS409
+	Supermarine Seafire F.47	VP248
	Supermarine Sea Otter	G-AIDM (014352)
	Supermarine Spitfire T.VIII	G-AIDN (6S/729058)
+	Vickers Valetta C.I	VL249 (158)
	Vickers Viking IB	G-AJJN (289)
+	Westland Wyvern TF.I	TS371

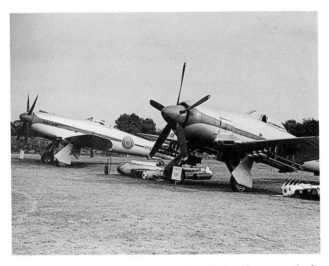

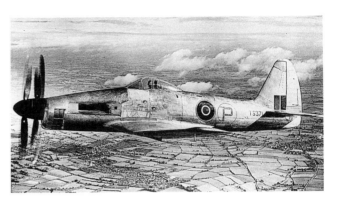

The Westland Wyvern prototype TS371 with Rolls-Royce Eagle engine.

The third de Havilland D.H.108 VW120 in a military domi-nated section of the aircraft park. Only one of the aircraft in this picture has survived – the Reid & Sigrist Desford G-AGOS.

The Hawker Fury 1s VP207 and NX802 with respectively Napier Sabre and Bristol Centaurus engines.

1948

THE NINTH SHOW
7-12 SEPTEMBER

The 1948 SBAC Show had to do with two very important changes; it was the year in which the location was moved to Farnborough and it was the first year in which the public were admitted to inspect, in the air and on the ground, the aircraft, engines and equipment for which they had, after all, very largely paid.

The Show was officially opened by the Minister of Supply, Mr G.R.Strauss, and as well as the trade days on Tuesday, Wednesday and Thursday and a technicians' day on Friday, with no flying display, there were now two public days at the week-end. A separate static display had been introduced in 1947.

One hundred and eighty-seven exhibitors were accommodated under the 60,000 square feet (5,574 sq.m) of shelter provided by two of the Royal Aircraft Establishment's hangars.

At the Show was the fastest helicopter in the world, the first jet approved for civil use, the first two and four-engined jet airliners and the first turboprop trainers, as well as the holder of the World Altitude Record. Once again there were circuses of heavy and light aircraft in order to fit everybody in within the time available. One new feature in the flying arrangements was the appearance of extra aircraft solely on public days. A novelty to be expanded in future Shows, but on this occasion it consisted solely of the third de Havilland 108, flown by John Derry, fresh from his supersonic plunge from 40,000 ft (12,192 m) on 6 September in the first successful British assault on the sound barrier. It was explained that the significance of this lay in it having been achieved with a turbine engine. Captain Charles "Chuck" Yeager had already flown the straight-winged Bell X-1 to M:1.015, equivalent to 670 mph (1078 km/h), in level flight at 42,000 ft (12,800 m) on 14 October 1947, but this aircraft was powered by an experimental rocket engine. At that time, it was not widely known that the turbine-powered North American YP-86A had reached Mach 1 plus on 25 April.

Comment has already been made about *l'affaire* M.52; in the official letter from the Ministry of Supply to Miles Aircraft it was stated that it was expected to be several years before supersonic flight would be achieved.

This year's flying-boat was again a Short S.45 Solent, flown by Captain Alcock of BOAC (who feathered two again). The marine aircraft tradition on the Empire routes died hard and in 1946 BOAC had borrowed a "civilised" Short Seaford – a type which had been intended to replace the Sunderland in Coastal Command. Twelve were ordered the same year, offering promenade, cocktail bar and dining saloon luxury for 30 passengers and taking over the run to Johannesburg on 4 May 1948. It was no doubt in celebration of this event (the boats subsequently served the route for two and a half years without accident) that Shorts presented G-AHIM, RMA. *Scarborough*, but the occasion marked also the end of a great era of British aircraft manufacture, for the twelfth and last of these Solent 2s, launched at Rochester on 8 April, was the last aircraft ever to leave that historic slipway.

Far more impact, however, was made by a flying-boat that never saw service – indeed, with the collapse of the Japanese, the original purpose of Specification E.6/44 had virtually disappeared. The thunderous and dramatic appearance of Geoffrey Tyson (himself the mildest of men) in the Saunders-Roe SR.A/1, inverted and scandalously low, across the A235, was a sight still savoured by those who saw it. The SR.A/1 was the world's only single-seat, jet-powered, fighter flying-boat, with two Metrovick (Metropolitan-Vickers) Beryl turbojets, developing, in the third and final airframe as the F.2/4A Beryl MBV 1, 3,850 lb (1,746 kg) static thrust and sending the SR.A/1 along at 512 mph (824 km/h), rather faster than the current World Speed Record for marine aircraft. Despite its representing an obsolete conception, the SR.A/1, unknown to most people watching it, had its place in the pioneering events at the Show, for it carried the first Martin-Baker ejection seat.

Armstrong Whitworth, one of the concentration of aeronautical talent at Coventry's Baginton aerodrome showed both prototypes of their remarkable A.W.52 flying wings. Nearly as big across as a Lancaster, powered by two Rolls-Royce Nenes or Derwents, the aircraft was developed from the earlier glider version and was seen as leading eventually towards a six-jet airliner. Interest in the tail-less aircraft as a practical design revived after the war, following the success, aerodynamically speaking, of the Messerschmitt Me 163 and the discovery of several advanced projects from Horten and Henschel, among other German researchers. The Horten brothers were far advanced down this road and Dr. Reimar Horten, bobbing up in Argentina after the war, like several of his countrymen, built a commercial version of the Horten VIII/I. But the outlay of time and money usually proved too great against only minimal gains. Only Northrop, in the United States, persevered with this format and emerged in 1988 as the progenitor of the stealth bomber.

Another prototype, however, George Edwards' splendid Vickers Viscount, was poised at the beginning of its remarkable success story. Few watching the display would have predicted that it would still be in demand forty years later – except perhaps its designer. The outcome of a proposal put up by Rex Pierson, then Chief Designer of Vickers, in response to the IIB specification of the Brabazon Committee, design responsibility fell upon George Edwards after the death of Pierson in 1948. The new Rolls-Royce Dart propeller turbine was chosen as power plant, with other engines in mind should the Dart fail, which of course it did not. Britain, it should be remembered, held a virtual monopoly in the propeller turbine field.

Two prototypes at the Show had cause to grumble at the success of the Viscount; the alternative Vickers aircraft, the jet-powered Nene-Viking (the first turbo-jet airliner in the world) was not seen to be as desirable as the Viscount and was dropped, and the Airspeed Ambassador, with two closely-cowled Bristol Centaurus piston engines, which only enjoyed a limited success. It did, however, give Vickers a nasty turn, for when an order was placed by the Ministry of Supply for the smaller Ambassador on behalf of British European Airways – somewhat to their astonishment and on rather non-commercial grounds – Vickers almost abandoned Viscount development in disgust. In the end, only 20 production Ambassadors were built, although it was an excellent design, which survived an incident-packed development period.

George Errington was Airspeed's chief test pilot and secured his – and the aircraft's – place in Farnborough history in 1948 by conducting the whole Ambassador display on one engine, feathering the port airscrew before starting his take-off run and not releasing it until after the landing; a feat that has, not surprisingly, never been repeated at subsequent Displays.

It is intriguing to consider that both Vickers and Airspeed had, so to speak, hedged their bets; there was a piston alternative to the Viscount, with two Centaurus and the Ambassador wing was originally designed to take four Napier Naiad or Mamba turboprops.

The Viscount had started out as the Viceroy (a name used by Airspeed, incidentally, before the war), but India became independent in 1947 and the title became redundant, so the name was changed.

Two contenders for the 100 km closed circuit speed record, the de Havilland 108 and de Havilland Vampire were taking part in the Show. The latter actually held the FAI Class C.1 record, John Cunningham having flown VF332 to 799.6 km/h (496.88 mph) at Lympne on 31 August 1947. Also flying was the much modified third production Vampire, TG278, test-bed for the Ghost engined version which became the

Venom. This particular aircraft, with 8 ft (2.4 m) added to the span and a special hood, was taken to 18,119 m (59,446 ft) by Cunningham in a successful attack on the World Altitude Record on 23 March 1948.

The third and last D.H.108, with redesigned nose and cockpit area in a fuselage little resembling that of the Vampire from which it sprang, and with a Goblin 4 engine giving rather more thrust than earlier versions, raised the closed-circuit record to 974.02 km/h (605.23 mph) on 12 April. During the private days at the Show John Derry pushed the 108 through the sound barrier, as already described, and went on to give a flawless aerobatic display on the public days, with a particularly meritorious appearance on Sunday, when the weather was bad enough to stop the rest of the flying. Indeed, the weather had not been kind during the week, being bad enough on the opening Tuesday to prevent twelve of the military jets from flying.

Among other novelties was the first real Short Take-Off and Landing (STOL) demonstration by the Scottish Aviation Pioneer. This aircraft, which had appeared the previous year in response to Spec. A.4/45, now carried a 250 hp D.H.Gipsy Queen 34 and an array of full-span slats and Fowler flaps that enabled it to land into a 15 knot (27.8 km) wind in 20 yards (18.29 m).

Just before the Show, a naval order for the Attacker was announced, and the newest naval prototype, the Hawker P.1040 to Spec. N.7/46, was being shown by Squadron Leader T.S."Wimpey" Wade, having made its first flight just over two weeks previously. This powerful, well-balanced fighter from Sydney Camm and his team presented the settled Hawker philosophy for the single seat fighting aircraft and took full advantage of the wing-root intakes and aft engine to get the pilot right up in the nose, where he could see "What In Hell Is Happening", to quote Roger Bacon. Grumman had taken the same design decision in the United States of America with the Panther. The arrival of the turbine brought fresh hope to designers of single-engined military and naval aircraft; behind those monstrous piston engines pilots had been retreating further and further from the outside world.

Once more a "heavy" (sic) circus opened the Show, led by the Hastings and including the Lincoln, Valetta, Marathon, Dove and Bristol Freighter (flown by Bill Pegg). Again this featured a feathered run. Sadly, financial problems exacerbated by a savage winter and inadequate power supplies had forced the closure of Miles Aircraft earlier in the year and Handley Page had taken over the production run of the Marathon (25 each for BEA and BOAC) and were presenting the aircraft at Farnborough.

The "light" circus that closed Tuesday's display, the weather being too much for the military, contained the Chrislea Super Ace, Portsmouth Aerocar, Auster A.2/45 and Chipmunk. The military circus contained the Sea Hornet, Spitfire Trainer, Brigand (with four 500 lb (227 kg) bombs, Sea Fury, Firefly Trainer, Sturgeon "long nose" TT 2, Meteor 4, Athena 2, Balliol 1 and Meteor 7. The Spitfire Trainer was subsequently presented to the Hampshire Aeroplane Club (which also owned a D.H.86B Express four-engined biplane) by Lord Louis Mountbatten, Club President and a Vickers director. Forty years and several owners later it was still going strong.

The Boulton Paul Balliol 1 and Avro Athena 1 were designed to Spec. T.7/45 for a turboprop trainer (the Balliol 1 was the world's first single engined turboprop to fly). Upon the cancellation of this requirement they reverted to the piston power of the Merlin under Spec. T.14/47, the Balliol achieving the major order for the Royal Air Force.

The helicopter was just beginning to make its mark in aviation, having, like the jet, received a brief baptism at the end of the war. Flying at Farnborough were the Bristol Type 171 Mk 2, with Alvis Leonides engine and the remarkable Fairey Gyrodyne. The latter, flown by Basil Arkell, had achieved a new World Class record for helicopters (and the first British helicopter record) on 28 June, reaching 200.04 km/h (124.3 mph). This very complex but ingenious helicopter combined a conventional rotor with an airscrew, the latter providing most of the thrust in forward flight, enabling a low disc loading to be attained and holding much promise for helicopter development. Fifteen years of research, design and construction by Fairey did not compensate for the fact that this did not turn out to be the main stream in the future of the rotary wing.

The Gyrodyne suffered a fatigue failure of the rotor head and crashed on 17 April 1949, during preparations for a new record attempt.

1948

+	Airspeed Ambassador	G-AKRD (62)	
	Airspeed Consul	G-AJLN (5132)	
+	Armstrong Whitworth A.W.52	TS363 R-R Nenes	
	Armstrong Whitworth A.W.52	TS368 R-R Derwents	
+	Auster Autocrat J/1	G-AJIZ (2343)	
	Auster Avis	G-AJXW (2838)	
+	Auster T.7	VF665	
+	Auster A.2/45	VL522	
+	Avro Athena 1	VM125 A.S. Mamba	
+	Avro Athena 2	VW890 R-R Merlin	
+	Avro Lancastrian	VM732 R-R Avons in outer nacelles	
+	Avro Lincoln B.2	RE292	
+	Avro Lincoln B.2	RE339 Bristol Theseus in outer nacelles	
+	Avro Tudor 8	VX195 (1249) four R-R Nenes	
	Blackburn Firebrand TF.5	EK844	
+	Blackburn S.28/43	VF172	
+	Boulton Paul Balliol 1	VL935 A.S. Mamba	
+	Boulton Paul Balliol 2	VW897 R-R Merlin	
+	Bristol Brigand B.1	RH809 (12683)	
+	Bristol Freighter 21E	G-AIFO (12775)	
	Bristol 171 Mk.2	VW905 (12869)	
+	Chrislea Super Ace	G-AKUX (106)	
	Chrislea Super Ace	G-AKUY (107)	
	Cierva Air Horse	G-ALCV (W.11/1)	
	Cierva Skeeter 1	G-AJCJ (W.14/1)	
+	de Havilland Chipmunk	G-AKDN (11)	
+	de Havilland Dove 1B	G-AKSV (04161)	
	de Havilland Mosquito TT.39	PF606	
+	de Havilland Sea Hornet F.20	VR892	
	de Havilland Vampire F.I	TG278 D.H. Ghost engine, extended wing tips	
	de Havilland Vampire F.3	VF332	
	de Havilland Vampire F.B.5	VV218	
+	de Havilland Vampire F.B.5	VV219	
+	de Havilland D.H.108	VW120	
+	Elliott Newbury Eon	G-AKBC (EoN 1) glider tug	
	Elliott Eon Olympia	–	
	Elliott Eon Intermediate	–	
	Elliott Eon Primary	–	
+	Fairey Firefly AS.5	VT487 (F.8371)	
+	Fairey Firefly T.1	DK429 (F.7685)	
+	Fairey Gyrodyne	G-AIKF (F.B.1)	
	Fairey Gyrodyne	G-AJJP (F.B.2)	
+	Fairey Primer	G-ALBL (F.8455)	
	General Aircraft GAL 61/U	TS515	
+	Gloster Meteor F.4	VT256	
+	Gloster Meteor F.4	RA490 Metrovick Beryls	
+	Gloster Meteor T.7	G-AKPK (G.5/201)	
+	Handley Page Hastings C.1	TG527	
+	Handley Page Hermes 4	G-AKFP (H.P.81/1)	
+	Handley Page (Reading) Marathon 1	G-AILH (6430)	
+	Hawker P.1040	VP401	
	Hawker N.7/46	VP413	
	Percival Prentice 1	G-23-1 Argentine colours	
+	Percival Prentice T.1	VR211 (PAC/035)	
+	Percival Prince	G-ALCM (P.50/1)	
	Percival Proctor 4	G-AKYJ (H.789)	
	Percival Proctor 5	G-AKYA (Ae.112)	
	Planet Satellite	– (1) no marks, became G-ALOI	
+	Portsmouth Aerocar	G-AGTG (2)	
+	Saunders-Roe SR.A/1	TG271 flying only	
+	Scottish Aviation Pioneer	G-31-1 (101)	
+	Short Sealand	G-AIVX (SH.1555)	
+	Short Solent 2	G-AHIM (S.1301) flying only	
+	Short Solent 2	G-AHIS (S.1305)	
+	Short Sturgeon TT.2	VR363 (SH.1560)	
+	Supermarine Seagull ASR.1	PA143	
+	Supermarine Spitfire T.8	G-AIDN (6S/729058)	
+	Vickers Valetta C.I	VW140 (310)	
+	Vickers Viking	G-AJPH (207) R-R Nenes	
+	Vickers Viscount 630	G-AHRF (1)	

The Saunders-Roe SR.A/1 TG271 usually flew inverted down the runway!

G-AIKF was one of two Fairey Gyrodynes shown.

Left: The unconventional Planet Satellite was of magnesium alloy construction with a pusher airscrew. It never flew.

Above: The second Blackburn B-48, to specification S.28/43, was VF172 and was intended to be a Firebrand replacement. Only two were built.

Two prototypes of the Supermarine Seagull amphibian were built – PA143 was the first.

The Auster A.2/45 VL522 failed to win a production order but led eventually to the Auster AOP.9.

Avro Lincoln RF530 was used as a test-bed for the Napier Naiad turboprop, mounted in the nose.

Armstrong Whitworth A.W.52 TS363 landing over Farnborough's famous Black Sheds, used as the East Exhibition Hall in 1948.

1949

THE TENTH SHOW
6-11 SEPTEMBER

The pattern and scale were very much the same as in 1948, with 185 exhibitors occupying 64,000 square feet (5,946 sq.m) of hall space.

There was no flush of record-breaking this year, but one or two very significant "firsts", of which the most exciting was the appearance of the de Havilland Comet. The first production jet airliner in the world, it was designed by a team headed by R.E.Bishop. After a wide variety of configurations had been explored, including a tail-less, swept-wing version based on the D.H.108, a fairly conventional aircraft emerged at Hatfield and was given its first flight by John Cunningham on 27 July. As was the established custom at a time when the industry was still in the grip of the Ministry of Supply, a specification was issued (22/46) to cover two prototypes designed to fill the Brabazon Committee's Type IV proposals.

The grip of this Ministry, continuing after the war, was intended to act as a strengthening influence on an industry still struggling to adapt to the free-for-all of peacetime conditions. It had been loosened already in one respect, for in January the Government announced that the British Airways Corporations would in future be able to order their aircraft directly from the manufacturers. Up to then, the Ministry had acted as agents for orders from the Corporations or the Ministry of Civil Aviation. That their decisions were not always free from outside pressures was shown by the affair of the Ambassador, but letting the Corporations loose on the manufacturer turned out to be a mixed blessing; one of their first victims had been the unhappy Tudor, subject of literally hundreds of modifications at the final design conference.

Immediately following its triumphant appearance at Farnborough, the Comet prototype set about a series of high-speed proving flights to check fuel consumption under airline conditions, beginning with a run to Castel Benito and back at 448 mph (720.98 km/h) in October.

Apart from the Comet, the first pure jet airliner in history, the only four propeller turbine airliners in existence were also on display: Hermes 5, Viscount, Apollo and Marathon 2. So it was hardly surprising that *Flight* should note the presence of numerous representatives from at least fifteen major airlines. The Armstrong Whitworth Apollo was, like the Viscount, designed to Brabazon II proposals but with four axial-flow compressor Mambas designed by near-relation Armstrong Siddeley, had a more advanced engine than the cen-

trifugal compressor Dart in the Viscount. It was the Dart, however, that flourished, the Mamba that died. And that was the end of the Apollo and other Mamba-powered designs, including the Marathon 2.

The fourth turboprop airliner, the Theseus-powered Hermes 5, virtually a direct conversion from the Hercules driven Hermes 4, suffered a similar fate to the Apollo, for the 2/47 specification to which it was designed, for a Constellation replacement (as the Hermes 4 had been a Tudor II replacement), resulted in a win for the rival Bristol Britannia. A large part of the failure was undoubtedly due to the numerous faults that plagued the Theseus. It was a brave sight in the Farnborough skies, nevertheless; with a top speed of 350 mph (563 km/h) and gross weight of 85,000 lb (38,555 kg), the heaviest and fastest turbine airliner in the world.

On a smaller scale, Bristol displayed the Air Coach version of the Freighter, with 48 seats.

Shortly after being appointed chief test pilot to the Bristol Aeroplane Company at Filton, and two days before the opening of the Farnborough Display, A.J. "Bill" Pegg lifted the Brabazon I off the specially-built runway for the first time. At an all-up weight of 129.5 tons (131,5 tonnes) and 230 ft (70 m) span it was the biggest and heaviest aeroplane ever flown in Britain. The occasion is sufficiently commemorated by Bill Pegg's comment to his co-pilot, Walter Gibb: "Well, my side's airborne; what about yours?". On the occasion of the Display, no landings or take-offs were attempted, the aircraft flying in from, and returning to, Filton.

When the specification was issued, only Bristol, among companies with big aeroplane experience, really had the capacity to tackle it and drew heavily on the work already done on a 300 mph (482 km/h), 100 ton (101.6 tonne) bomber project with engines buried in the wings. Sadly the Brabazon, and its stable mate the Brabazon 2, the latter designed to cruise at 330 mph (531 km/h) on eight coupled Bristol Proteus propeller turbines, with 100 passengers and a crew of twelve, were well ahead of the structural and economic parameters of the day. Lord Brabazon of Tara commented later that the Brabazon I specification was the only one where their traffic forecasts had gone astray, for they had reckoned a 50-passenger layout would be ample on the North Atlantic and BOAC actually preferred half that figure.

In one respect, however, the Brabazon proved to be prophetic. The Select Committee on Estimates, reporting on the project on 9 April 1948, noted that the total cost of two prototypes, runway and buildings, was now expected to amount to £11,056,500 – an increase of 40 per cent on the original estimate. By no means the last the British public would hear of that song.

Star of the show, without a doubt, was the magnificent presentation of the new English Electric Canberra by "Bea" Beamont. Designed as a Mosquito replacement capable of carrying an 8,000 lb (3,629 kg) bomb at 540 mph (869 km/h), for 1,600 miles (2,575 km) at 50,000 ft (15,240 m), the Canberra was designed by a team led by the gifted but restless W.E.W.Petter, who had left Westlands and moved to English Electric specifically to create this high altitude bomber. By great good fortune, Rolls-Royce were working on an advanced axial-flow turbine, the AJ.65, for precisely the same purpose and when Petter and his team proposed to adopt the engine for their design, Rolls-Royce went ahead on their own, without waiting for the Ministry of Supply to issue a specification. The engine, later to be named Avon, became one of the most successful British turbines ever built.

Petter had designed a most elegant wing for his bomber, giving optimum performance at all speeds and altitudes and the slender proportions of the engine enabled it to be mounted ahead of the main spar, only the jetpipe passing through the latter, while the diameter was only marginally greater than the depth of the wing. Eventually the Canberra replaced every other bomber in the Royal Air Force, equipping a total of 61 different squadrons in the course of its Service life and attracting numerous export orders.

Nothing could have better underlined its superior qualities than "Bea's" display, featuring very tight, high-G turns within the limits of the airfield.

Among the military offerings on display were no less than four Meteors, one with re-heat to its Derwents and one with Avons; both aircraft were presented by Rolls-Royce. The spectacular climbs on re-heat by the Derwent-Meteor gave the public its first sight and sound of this thrust-multiplier and they were suitably impressed. The Avon-Meteor, with a great deal more power than it well knew what to do with, was even more dramatic, gliding down from 6,000 ft (1,828 m) to run across the field with both HP cocks turned off, trailing plumes of unburnt fuel and pulling up into an upward roll. With that confidence born of working for Rolls-Royce, the pilot waited until he was on the way down again before relighting the engines. With nearly three times the thrust of the "cooking" Mk 4, RA491 (later used for trials with the French SNECMA Atar) reached 40,000 ft (12,192 m) in some four minutes.

With what Chris Wren described as the Meteorific display of the Mk 8, Farnborough *aficionados* were introduced to one of the outstanding display pilots of all time – Jan Zurakowski. Over a period of several years his carefully-timed and spectacular sequences on various Meteors became high points of successive Farnborough Shows.

The Supermarine 510, flown by Mike Lithgow, was certainly the fastest aircraft in the Show with speeds around 670 mph (1,078 km/h) – this representing M:0.88 at Lithgow's operating height of 100 ft (30.5 m). At that height, though not at that speed, he also produced some very tight radius turns.

The 510 was intended as a Meteor replacement and was based on an Attacker fuselage. The first British all-swept aircraft, it achieved M:0.93 (the Spitfire had got to M:0.92) and was only limited by considerable trim changes at that number. Together with a second aircraft, intended to "get ahead" of the Hawker P.1040 (which became the Sea Hawk), it finished up as a prototype for the Swift.

New Royal Air Force equipment figured prominently in the 1949 Display. Apart from Bomber Command's Canberra, Coastal Command would receive the massive Avro Shackleton, whose second prototype appeared at the Show. Few watching it would have thought that, like the Shows, it would celebrate forty years of life in 1988 and look like going on for another five years.

The little Cierva Skeeter, the huge Cierva Air Horse and the Bristol Type 171 had all been seen statically in 1948. The first two flew in 1949 and did so again in 1950 but the 171 had its rotor disintegrate dramatically at the start of its second flight, three days before the Show, fortunately without injuring anybody.

Powered by a Rolls-Royce Merlin 24, with three 47 ft (14.3m) rotors, the Air Horse had flown at 14,000 lb (6,350 kg) – the highest all-up weight yet achieved by a helicopter – on 7 December 1948 and was now displayed by Alan Marsh, its extraordinary shape and great lazily turning blades creating a most vivid impression. Tragically, the following year, a rotor hub failed and Marsh and his crew were killed.

Westland embraced the helicopter when their various military and civil fixed-wing projects ran out of steam and rather than commence from scratch in this new field took on a licence from Sikorsky to build their S-51. Six of these American four-seaters had been imported in 1947 and Westland were now offering a licence-built version with a 540 hp Alvis Leonides 521 replacing the 450 hp Pratt & Whitney Wasp Junior.

As far as light aircraft were concerned, the representation was poor and there did not seem to be any particular indication in all this that Britain might recover her pre-war position in this field.

Among naval offerings were the prototype Attacker F.1 in the hands of Les Colquhoun, the Supermarine Seagull and the Westland Wyvern TF.2. The Seagull was a remarkable design, for all that it was never taken up by the Navy. Conceived in 1940 as a Walrus/Sea Otter replacement, it finished up as a large, 15,000 lb (6,804 kg) amphibian with an 1,815 hp Rolls-Royce Griffon and a speed range of 260 to 35 mph

(418-56 km/h), thanks to the ingenious variable-incidence wing.

The Wyvern TF.2 was an interim type between the Python-powered production Mk 4 and the Rolls-Royce Eagle piston-engined T.F.1. Petter (of Canberra fame) had originally designed it for a fully-forward pilot with the engine behind him and a long shaft drive, rather like the Westland F.7/30 before the war. The Wyvern, which was not only the com-

pany's first naval design to see service since the Walrus of 1921 but their last fixed-wing design, finally entered service in 1953. The Mk 4, of which 94 had been built when production ceased three years later, equipped four first-line and two training squadrons and saw brief glory in the 1956 Suez campaign – if glory was to be extracted from that essentially dismal political adventure.

1949

+ Airspeed Ambassador	G-AKRD (62)	
+ Armstrong Whitworth Apollo	G-AIYN (AW.3137)	
+ Auster Autocar J/5B	G-AJYK (2908)	
+ Auster Autocrat J/1	G-AJIZ (2343)	
Auster Avis 2	G-AJYF (2907) fuselage only	
+ Auster T.7	VF665	
Avro Athena 1	VM129 R-R Dart	
Avro Athena 2	VW892 R-R Merlin	
+ Avro Lancaster B1	TW911 A.S. Pythons in outer nacelles	
+ Avro Shackleton 1	VW131	
Avro 19 Srs.2	G-AHKX (1333)	
Avro 707	VX784	
+ Boulton Paul Balliol 2	VR591	
+ Bristol Brabazon	G-AGPW (12759)	
Bristol Freighter 21	G-AIME (12795)	
+ Bristol Freighter 31	G-18-2 (12732)	
+ Chrislea Super Ace Srs.2	G-AKVB (1·10)	
Chrislea Super Ace Srs.4	(G-AKVS) (126) ambulance, no markings	
+ Cierva Air Horse	VZ724 (W.11/1)	
+ Cierva Skeeter I	G-AJCJ (W.14/1)	
Cierva Skeeter 2	G-ALUF (W.14/2)	
+ de Havilland Chipmunk T.10	WB549 (C1/0001)	
de Havilland Chipmunk T.10	WB550 (c1/0002)	
+ de Havilland Comet 1	G-ALVG (06001)	
+ de Havilland Dove 1	G-AKSV (04161)	
+ de Havilland D.H.113	G-5-2 (13001)	
de Havilland Sea Hornet PR.22	VZ658	
+ de Havilland Vampire FB.5	VV454	
de Havilland Vampire FB.5	VV217	
+ de Havilland Venom 1	VV612	
+ English Electric Canberra 1	VN799	

+ Fairey Firefly AS.5	WB310 (F.8528)	
+ Gloster Meteor F.4	RA435 reheat R-R Derwents	
+ Gloster Meteor F.4	RA491 R-R Avons	
Gloster Meteor T.7	VW482	
+ Gloster Meteor F.8	VZ438	
+ Handley Page Hermes 4	G-ALDA (H.P.81/2)	
+ Handley Page Hermes 5	G-ALEU (H.P.82/1)	
Handley Page (Reading) Marathon 1	G-ALUB (101)	
+ Handley Page (Reading) Marathon 2	G-AHXU (6544) A.S. Mambas	
Hawker Sea Fury FB.11	VX642	
Hawker Sea Fury T.20	VX287	
+ Hawker N.7/46 (Sea Hawk)	VP413	
+ Hawker P.1052	VX279	
+ Percival Prentice T.1	VR211 (PAC/035)	
Percival Prentice T.1	VS639 (PAC/273)	
+ Percival Prince 1	G-ALFZ (P.50/2)	
Percival Prince 1	G-ALJA (P.50/3)	
Percival Survey Prince	G-ALRY (P.50/8)	
Percival Proctor 5	G-AGTC (Ae.3)	
+ Short Sealand 1	VP-TBA (SH.1565)	
+ Short Solent 3	G-AHIU (S.1307) flying only	
Short Sturgeon TT.2	TS477 (SH.1578)	
+ Supermarine Attacker	TS409	
+ Supermarine Seagull ASR.1	PA147	
+ Supermarine 510	VV106	
Vickers Valetta C.2	VX571 (423)	
+ Vickers Varsity T.1	VX828 (501)	
+ Vickers Viscount 630	G-AHRF (1)	
+ Westland Wyvern TF.2	VP113	
Westland-Sikorsky S-51	G-ALEG (WA/H/2) spraying equipment	
+ Westland-Sikorsky S-51	G-ALIK (WA/H/3)	

The prototype de Havilland Comet G-ALVG made its first flight on 27 July 1949.

Roland Beamont flew the blue English Electric Canberra prototype VN799 at Farnborough. After several hops, it made its first flight on 13 May 1949.

The mighty Cierva Air Horse VZ724 was the largest British helicopter, powered by a single Rolls-Royce Merlin engine geared to the three rotor drives. Development was abandoned after the crash of this, the first of two prototypes to fly, in June 1950.

Another experimental installation, with the Handley Page (Reading) Marathon 2 G-AHXU sporting a pair of Armstrong Siddeley Mamba turboprops.

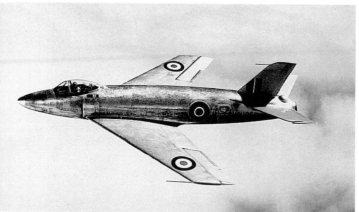

Seldom seen with its wings folded – a Royal Navy requirement – the Short Sturgeon TT.2 TS477 with its attendant
Short's crew and period van.

The Supermarine 510 VV106 with an unusual combination of
Type D roundels on the wings and Type C1 on the fuselage.

Bristol Freighter G-18-2 was the military prototype, formerly
G-AGVC.

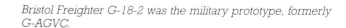

1950

THE ELEVENTH SHOW
5-10 SEPTEMBER

The background pattern for the 1950 event remained very much as before; the system was working nicely and the overall size in terms of exhibitors and exhibits had not greatly altered; exhibition space remained at 64,000 square feet (5,945.8 sq.m.). Commencing on Tuesday with Technicians' (or Preview) Day, there were then three Trade Days with the week-end devoted to the public. Admission prices were 3s (adult), 1s 6d (children), £1 (cars) and £5 (coaches). In 1990 terms, personal admission came to 15p and 7.5p respectively.

The weather chose once more to be capricious. Technicians' Day was one of brilliant sunshine but Wednesday produced gale force winds and lowering clouds. Although conditions for flying were better on Thursday, there was still a strong wind at 20 degrees to the runway and by Friday the rain had set in again fairly steadily. The low cloud base prevailing for much of the week put rather a damper on vertical manoeuvres and there were more high speed passes and tight turns evident than aerobatics.

The crowd line was now established where it remained 38 years later, parallel to the southern edge of runway 07/25 and the exhibition area was transferred to the area south east of that. The exhibition was now housed in a purpose-built marquee, which was to become the largest of its kind in the world, erected on the end of runway 29 and static display aircraft were placed on the large oval hard standing, forming the centre of Camel Way, with the equipment park in the middle. Flying display aircraft were parked on the main runway (07/25) and marshalled into the old public viewing area to the north.

For some reason, on a contemporary plan of the layout, the NW-SE runway was marked, not as 11/29 but 12/30. In 1988, when Heathrow changed its runway headings by one degree to keep pace with shifts of the magnetic pole, the RAE were asked if they were about to do the same.

"Dear me, no!" said Don Hickman, Farnborough's SATCO, "Things change much more slowly in Hampshire". Actually, being a civil servant, he is a CATCO; the familiar SATCO is apparently an acronym for something quite different in the Civil Service.

The Ambassador had suffered its share of incidents during its development; the prototype had had a dramatic undercarriage failure in 1947 and in July, 1950 the third, production prototype aircraft, G-ALFR suffered a similar embarrassment. (This was the aircraft that was to shed both engines in an otherwise uneventful heavy landing later in the year.) As a result it was the second prototype, pressurised and fully sound-proofed and furnished and sporting early Centaurus 630 engines, less powerful than those in production aircraft, that appeared at Farnborough. There it provided a noteworthy challenge to the Viscount in terms of quietness and a smooth ride. The aircraft appeared in BEA markings, anticipating slightly its first appearance on scheduled service as the Elizabethan class a year later. It was Airspeed stylists who created the "wrap-round" nose end to the livery cheat lines, establishing a clever visual effect and a firm precedent. Later they extended the scheme to the nacelles of G-AKRD during part of its long life as a test-bed for the Bristol Proteus and Rolls-Royce Tyne, minimising the bulk of the Proteus nacelles.

The Armstrong Whitworth Apollo appeared again, much of the time with two airscrews feathered – which enabled the *cognoscenti* to observe that it now had four-bladed airscrews on number two and three engines. Plagued by constant engine problems and with the company heavily occupied with other work, the Apollo never regained the ground lost to the Viscount, nor did it attract a single order. The two built reverted to the Ministry of Supply and Service serials and faded from the scene.

The civil Viscount present was the prototype "stretched" Series 700, flown by "Jock" Bryce. First flown only nine days previously, it could carry eleven more passengers and cruise almost 50 mph (80.5 k/h) faster than the Type 630 which had inaugurated world turbo-prop services between London and Paris on 29 July and which was sitting in the Static Park. That same 630, G-AHRF, later ran a similar service to the Scottish capital for the Edinburgh Festival.

Solitary champion of British light aircraft hopes was the new Auster Aiglet. Its ebullient pilot, Ranald Porteous, was to become one of the Farnborough legends and one of the very few pilots ever to have an aerobatic manoeuvre named after him. Auster history began with the construction in England in 1939 of the American Taylorcraft. (Taylor himself was British.) One was on loan to the Royal Artillery Flying Club at the outbreak of war and became a pioneering factor in the subsequent formation of the Air Observation Post squadrons in 1941 – and the survival of British Taylorcraft. The Taylorcraft licence lapsed after the war and the company, now Auster Aircraft Ltd, continued military production and began an assault on the civil market. Selling initially through car

The Vickers Viscount 700 prototype G-AMAV in a steep low-level turn with everything down.

The Short S.B.3 WF632 was an ugly conversion of the last Sturgeon airframe for the anti-submarine role. Radar would have been fitted under the nose and Armstrong Siddeley Mamba engines replaced the Sturgeon's Rolls-Royce Merlins.

dealers, by 1950 the 130-150 hp three-seat Autocrat was the standard model and the Aiglet Trainer was a short-span, semi-aerobatic version. Mind you, in Ranald's hands, the aerobatics were not all that semi.

This year the Brabazon was present on the ground as well as in the sky, though railed off from curious eyes (Heaven knows why). "...the central stateroom", said *The Aeroplane*, "...is more reminiscent of a ship than of an aeroplane." Frankly, so was most of the rest of it. Also roped off from close inspection, with rather more justification, was the prototype Comet, resplendent in BOAC colours, resting most of its weight on the huge single main wheels that later gave way to more practical and better-looking multi-wheel units.

The international situation in September 1950, was more than a little strained and was to have profound effects on the aviation industry. The Korean War had broken out with the North Korean Army's invasion across the 38th Parallel on 25 June and following the appeal of the United Nations Security Council, Sunderlands of No. 88 Squadron, Royal Air Force were out on blockade duty by mid-July, with the two squadrons of the Far East Flying Boat Wing, Nos 205 and 209, joining in later. These were the only Royal Air Force operational aircraft to see service throughout the conflict.

The Royal Air Force expansion and re-equipment that was evident at Farnborough formed part of the general strengthening of defence forces announced by the government at the end of August, and was tied in with considerable changes in trade structure and increases in pay from 1 September. In March, the Service had been 10,000 bodies short of the Defence White Paper target; somewhat ironically, earlier in the year, concern had been expressed by the Ministry of Civil Aviation that insufficient trained pilots were leaving the Services to fill the needs of civil aviation.

Following the startling appearance of the prototype B.1 Canberra at the 1949 Display, Roland Beamont flew the fourth prototype in 1950 as well as the first prototype B.2. This was the definitive bomber version, now a three-seater, with a glazed nasal position for the bomb-aimer and wingtip drop tanks. It had already been seen at Paris and Antwerp and not long after the Farnborough Show the remarkable news was released that the Americans were proposing licence production in the United States – the first time a British design had won this distinction since the D.H.4 in 1918. The Canberra, in various guises, was to be one of the Farnborough hardy annuals over the next nine years. In 1989 it was still in service with the Royal Air Force at Wyton. As a direct result of the international situation the original order for 132 Canberras was supplemented by a second one for 215. In order to accommodate this large "peace-time" order, English Electric's facilities had to be duplicated by parallel production at Short Brothers & Harland, Handley Page and A.V.Roe.

As well as the test-bed Avon and Sapphire Meteors, presented by the respective engine companies, a production Gloster Meteor F.8 was being demonstrated experimentally (and aerobatically, including an outside loop) with a pair of 1,000 lb (453.6 kg) bombs beneath the wings. This might have been prophetic of Korean service, which saw massive ground support operations, but only No. 77 Squadron, Royal Australian Air Force, took the Mk. 8 to that war. These were to replace their Mustangs, coming as a great surprise to the squadron, who were expecting to get the F-86. Indeed, the choice of the Meteor was an odd one; its performance, except in the climb, was inferior to the MiG-15 and it was not equipped with bomb racks, though it could undertake rocket attacks and later in its career did so with conspicuous success. One wonders if any of the Australian pilots who had their sturdy Meteors savaged by the superior MiG reflected that the latter owed its genesis to the sale to the Soviet Union by a British government of 55 Rolls-Royce Nene engines in 1946 and 1947.

The Meteor 8 entered service with Fighter Command at the end of June 1950 with No. 245 Squadron, subsequently equipping a further 19 squadrons of the Royal Air Force and ten of the Royal Auxiliary Air Force. WA878, however, after its Farnborough appearance, remained in the hands of the Gloster Aircraft Company Ltd and never saw squadron service.

There was still a conspicuous lack of a competent night fighter. Squadrons were currently equipped with the de Havilland Mosquito, which continued in service until 1951, the last one built, in the previous November, being an NF.38. Specification F.44/46 had therefore requested tenders for a replacement. No satisfactory bid was received and Armstrong-Whitworth, who, like Gloster, were part of the Hawker Siddeley Aviation group, and already engaged in building Meteors, were invited to develop a night fighter to F.24/48, based on the Meteor. The second prototype NF.11 was demonstrated at the 1950 Show by J.O.Lancaster and starting in the following year, the type eventually equipped 21 squadrons, mostly attached to the two-squadron day fighter bases.

De Havilland had shown the Vampire NF.10, a private venture night fighter, in 1949, intending it primarily for export; but when the first sales were blocked it bounced back into the Royal Air Force, equipping three squadrons from July 1951. Conversion from the Mosquito was made simple by the adoption of a Mosquito-style cockpit, the two fuselages being much of the same size. It was only a temporary issue until the equally private venture Venom night fighter arrived – which was itself a temporary issue until the Meteor 11 arrived. The latter met RAF safety requirements in having two engines, and what was more, actually conformed to an official specification.

Anyway, in 1950, they showed the Venom night-fighter, which was a standard day fighting single seat Venom with new, side-by-side accommodation and radar. In due course it became the Venom NF.2 and succeeded the Vampire with No. 23 Squadron, the launch unit for both types, and No. 33, the only other unit to get the Mk 2.

All these were comparatively pedestrian developments; virtually no more than up-dating of current equipment. There were, however, two swept-wing single seaters, developed from straight-winged ancestors. Both would become the subjects of accelerated development as a result of fears that the Korean War might escalate. For one this would bring great success, for the other, comparative failure.

Hawkers entered the arena of jet aircraft design with a proposal for a jet-powered Fury, based on the Rolls-Royce Nene, which masqueraded at that time under the uninspiring title of B.41. Refinement of this proposal (the P.1035) resulted in the P.1040, which surfaced in 1945, but, offering little increase in performance over the Meteor (currently holding the World Speed Record), was of no particular interest to the Air Staff. Gloster's original decision to go for two engines to get superior performance was still paying off.

Inspired, perhaps, by the similar story of the Sea Fury, the Admiralty, however, were interested; the P.1040 became the N.7/46 (and appeared at Farnborough in 1949) and saw service as the Sea Hawk. At the same time as the P.1040 was being born, Hawker proposed a swept wing variation, which appeared in 1948 as the P.1052 – virtually a swept-wing N.7/46. A whole series of forced-landings delayed its tests but led to a new prototype, this time with swept tail surfaces as well and a redesigned, single tailpipe replacing the forked layout of the earlier aircraft. This, the P.1081, was flown at the 1950 Display by "Wimpy" Wade, Hawker's chief test pilot. Still powered by the 5,000 lb (2,268 kg) static thrust Rolls-Royce Nene, the new aircraft turned in a speed of M:0.89 at 36,000 ft (10,973 m) and 604 knots (1,119 k/h) at sea level and climbed usefully to 35,000 ft (10,668 m) in just over nine minutes. With half as much power again, the new Meteor 8 achieved 460 knots (852.5 k/h) at 40,000 ft (12,192 m) but, as the Australians were to find useful in Korea, climbed to 30,000 ft (9,144 m) in 6.5 minutes. In 1948 a design for a Meteor replacement was started, based on the P.1081 and emerged as the P.1067 Hunter.

Sadly, on 3 April 1951, the P.1081 crashed, killing the chief test pilot, "Wimpy" Wade.

Vickers Supermarine, like Hawkers, were drawn into production of a new fighter designed round the Nene, and from the straight-winged Attacker, chief designer Joe Smith evolved the swept-wing Type 510. Unlike the Hawker P.1052 and P.1081 which, like their parent, the Sea Hawk, were tricy-

cles from the start, the Supermarine prototypes (two were ordered from each company) were tailwheel aircraft. Both, however, unlike the P.1052, had swept tail surfaces and were the first all-swept British aircraft.

The first Type 510 appeared at the 1949 Show and had subsequently been considerably modified at Boscombe Down. The second prototype, having progressively absorbed the modifications and become the Type 528, now appeared at Farnborough with reheat (afterburning to new readers), which was not used at the Show, nosewheel undercarriage, provision for armament and a name – Swift. It had also acquired yet another type number; 535. At a later stage in its career it appeared briefly as Prometheus for its starring rôle in the film *Sound Barrier*.

Under the Ministry of Supply's hastily conceived Super Priority programme at the time of the Korean War, intended to spool up supply of equipment to the Royal Air Force from the idling speed of peacetime provision, the Swift was thrust into production rather before it was ready and its first launch into Service use was embarrassingly fraught with problems.

Both Handley Page, with the H.P.R.2, and Percival, with the P.56, were contending for the new basic trainer order, to team up with the Vampire T.11 in replacing the Prentice/Harvard combination. The new trainer would, in fact, be the P.56 Provost, continuing the tradition of side-by-side seating but eliminating the eccentric third seat of the Prentice, intended for the pupil-next-for-duty.

Blackburn's Y.B.1 and Fairey's 17 were fighting a similar battle for a naval anti-submarine aircraft. The two prototype Y.B.1s had been Griffon-powered, but it was now, like the Fairey 17, carrying the neat Armstrong Siddeley Double Mamba. The Fairey, which won the draw and became the Gannet, took full advantage during the Show of its ability to perform in a most sprightly manner on one half of the Double Mamba and one of its contra-rotating airscrews.

Two single Mambas powered the Short S.B.3, a curious aircraft derived from the Sturgeon. The jet exhausts pointed downwards and, the single-shaft engine producing exhaust thrust varying with demand, gave a startling demonstration of assymetric vectored thrust if one engine was throttled back. The deep proboscis housed a radar operator squatting above his equipment and did not, as was suggested, reflect the common naval practice of locating the heads in the bows of the ship.

Test-beds were still much in evidence: the Avon-Meteor, the bet-hedging Tay-Viscount (in case the Dart turned sour) and a Lincoln sprouting two Bristol Theseus propeller turbines; the latter an engine that did not achieve its potential and contributed to the downfall of the Hermes 5.

1950

+ Airspeed Ambassador	G-AKRD (62)	
+ Armstrong Whitworth Apollo	G-AIYN (AW.3137)	
+ Armstrong Whitworth Meteor NF.11	WA547	
+ Auster Aiglet J/1B	G-AJYW (2663)	
Auster Autocar J/5B	G-AJYV (2927)	
Auster J/5A	G-AJYL (2889)	
+ Avro Ashton 1	WB490	
+ Avro Athena T.2	VR569 (1519)	
+ Avro Lincoln B.2	RA657 Flight Refuelling	
+ Avro Lincoln B.4	SX972 Bristol Proteus in outer nacelles	
+ Avro Shackleton GR.1	VP257	
Avro 707B	VX790	
+ Blackburn & GAL Universal Freighter 1	WF320 (1000)	
+ Blackburn Y.B.1	WB797	
+ Boulton Paul Balliol T.2	VR602	
+ Bristol Brabazon	G-AGPW (12759)	
Bristol Freighter 31	G-AGVC (12732)	
Bristol Freighter 31 (Military)	G-AINK (12826)	
de Havilland Chipmunk T.10	WB723 (C1/0175)	
+ de Havilland Comet 1	G-ALVG (06001)	
de Havilland Dove 1	G-ALBM (04170)	
+ de Havilland Heron 1	G-ALZL (10903)	
de Havilland Vampire FB.5	VZ831	
de Havilland Vampire NF.10	G-5-2 (13001)	
de Havilland Vampire Trainer	G-5-7 (15000)	
+ de Havilland Venom NF.2	G-5-3 (12000)	
+ English Electric Canberra 1	VN850	
+ English Electric Canberra B.2	VX165	
Fairey Firefly AS.6	WD850 (F.8678)	

Fairey Firefly TT.1	SE-BRL (F.6033)
+ Fairey G.R.17 (Gannet)	VR557 (F.8271)
+ Gloster Meteor F.4	RA491 R-R Avons
+ Gloster Meteor F.4	VZ389 Flight Refuelling
+ Gloster Meteor F.8	WA820 A.S. Sapphires
+ Gloster Meteor F.8	WA878
Gloster Meteor GAF	G-AMCJ (G.5/1210)
+ Handley Page Hermes 5	G-ALEV (H.P.82/2)
+ Handley Page (Reading) H.P.R.2	WE505
Handley Page (Reading) Marathon 2	G-AHXU (6544) A.S. Mambas
Hawker Sea Fury FB.11	WE686
+ Hawker Sea Hawk F.1	VP413
+ Hawker P.1081	VX279
+ Percival Survey Prince	G-ALRY (P.50/8)
Percival Sea Prince C.1	WF136 (P.57/4)
+ Percival P.56 (Provost)	WE530
+ Scottish Aviation Pioneer 2	G-AKBF (101)
+ Short Sealand	G-AKLO (SH.1564)
+ Short S.B.3	WF632 (SH.1599)
Supermarine Attacker F.1	WA471
+ Supermarine Seagull ASR.1	PA147
+ Supermarine 535	VV119
+ Vickers Valetta T.3	VX564 (485)
Vickers Varsity T.1	VX835 (202)
Vickers Viscount 630	G-AHRF (1)
+ Vickers Viscount 663	VX217 (2) R-R Tays
+ Vickers Viscount 700	G-AMAV (3)
+ Westland Wyvern TF.2	VW867
+ Westland-Sikorsky S-51	G-ALIK (WA/H/3)

The Bristol Brabazon G-AGPW makes a stately turn over the Farnborough runway. In the foreground is Vickers Valetta T.3. VX564.

The second Vickers Viscount, VX217, was used as a test-bed for the Rolls-Royce Tay turbojets (nothing to do with the present Tay engine, the second use of the name).

The Supermarine 535 VV119 led to the 541 which in turn became the Swift.

Avro Ashton WB490 runs in over the first English Electric Canberra B.2 prototype, VX165.

Westland Wyvern VW867 with an Armstrong Siddeley Python engine – a sound not to be forgotten!

1951

THE TWELFTH SHOW
11-16 SEPTEMBER

In 1951 over half of the 36 flying and 13 static aircraft in the Display were gas-turbine powered; it was ten years since the Gloster E.28/39, the first British jet aircraft, had flown in the hands of Gerry Sayer; the first propeller-turbine airliners, all British, were well in service and the orders for the revolutionary Comet were coming in.

Nineteen aircraft were making their first appearance in public at Farnborough. For the first time, the Royal Air Force were taking part as an "exhibitor", with an aerobatic team from No. 54 Squadron, the four Vampire 3s, led by Flt Lt Clay providing the finale on the Sunday. They were originally billed to appear much earlier in the programme, but one suspects that the urge to produce a memorable closing number proved irresistible. The squadron had already achieved fame by making the first jet trans-Atlantic crossing in 1948 with six Vampires, led by the Commanding Officer, S/Ldr R.W.Oxspring DFC, and shepherded by a navigating Mosquito.

Despite the presence of the next generation of fighters and bombers for the Royal Air Force, there were rumbles of discontent expressed in the technical press. Employment levels in the aviation industry were falling, there seemed to be very little co-ordination between the Ministry of Supply, the Corporations and the constructors – the continuing changes of policy and requirements that hampered the finalisation of the Bristol Britannia being a case in point – and there was considerable anxiety being expressed over the current official policy of buying military aircraft from the United States of America. All was not yet financially well with the State Corporations either, as they groped for a coherent policy of re-equipment and the most cheerful headline *The Aeroplane* could come up with as a comment was "B.O.A.C. Loses Less".

As far as buying American was concerned, the Air Staff had really had very little choice. Relations with the communist world were getting worse (as someone put it at the time, "the cold war was hotting up") and there was no telling if the Korean pot would boil over. It would be some years until the Hunter and Swift would be ready and in the meantime the formation of the first of twelve squadrons of F-86 Sabres, ten of which would eventually face the Warsaw Pact forces in Germany, began a programme to bridge the equipment gap. The swept-wing, four-jet Valiant was some way off service, the more conservative Short Sperrin was still only a proto-type and in the meanwhile a combination of government policy and Treasury parsimony had reduced the strategic force to a handful of frighteningly obsolete Lincolns. It was hardly surprising, therefore, that the Royal Air Force should be forming nine squadrons of Boeing B-29s, supplied under the American programme of military aid to Europe from spare aircraft cocooned in storage.

There was one minor declaration of confidence; the SBAC closed its last overseas office, in Buenos Aires. The Society had set up offices immediately after the end of hostilities, in the Middle East, India, Pakistan and Buenos Aires, to maintain commercial contacts in these areas until such time as individual members could re-establish their own sales networks. Evidently, this was now considered to have come to pass.

After all that, new aircraft and engines crowded the Farnborough scene, the flying, in spite of the weather, was superb and the future looked bright for the Industry, even if the present in post-war Britain in general was a bit austere.

To offset the gloom and distract the nation, we had the Festival of Britain, referred to unkindly by its critics as the "*fête worse than death*". The only sensible bit of the whole thing was Basil Spence's sombre but inspiring Exhibition of Fuel and Power in Glasgow, but there was an aeronautical section among the Emetts and the Skylon and the shuttered concrete of the South Bank; the D.H.88 Comet of 1934, the spare Supermarine S.6B of Schneider fame and a couple of gliders A parade of historic aero-engines did at least include the Derwent, Ghost, Python and Proteus. There was also the flight deck of the new Comet, which inspired the French to borrow it for the Caravelle, and a section through a double-deck airliner fuselage. Unless intended as a vague reference to the Princess this last was something of a mystery, as there *were* no British double-deckers and it could hardly have been part of a Stratocruiser. Power Jets Ltd arranged a "gas turbine week" for the occasion, with the surviving Saro SR.A/1 landing on the Thames and being towed to a mooring at the South Bank.

At Farnborough in this Festival year, totals of guests and members of the public continued to rise, with 28,000 at the preview on Tuesday (Press and Technicians' Day) and the three succeeding Trade Days, including 2,472 invited foreign guests from 79 countries. A final official count of 180,000 bodies through, round or over the turnstiles at the week-end, included, allegedly some 140-150,000 on the Sunday. The imbalance on the Public Days was probably because Saturday was a day of persistent rain and low cloud. Sunday, a day of admirable weather, saw the ticket control apparatus severely strained by the rush, and a lot of people got in free in the process of easing the jam at the gates and car parks. At one time, the tail-back of cars had reached Bagshot and people were still coming in when the flying had stopped.

The weather generally was irritating. Tuesday was inclement, Wednesday a lot better and Friday perfect. Thursday was so rotten that there was no flying at all.

One noticeable alteration in the layout this year brought the exhibitors' hospitality caravans back from the barrier and into a position on the hill pretty well where "A" row of chalets later sat. Not surprisingly in view of the attendance, every inch of space west of that, right up to the N/S runway, was car parks. The end of the exhibition marquee crept a bit further up R/W 29, with 66,000 sq ft (6,131.6 sq m) of floor space.

The flying opened with a "heavy circus", largely composed of the now familiar test-beds deploying the still multiplying new engines intended to maintain Britain's turbine lead. Bill Pegg of Bristol flew the Proteus-Lincoln and Mike Randrup another, fitted with a nose-mounted Napier Nomad driving co-axial airscrews, whose start-up procedure closely resembled a badly-managed firework display. There was also the Avro Ashton, the Mamba-Marathon (except on Tuesday), Shackleton, Hermes V and Viscount. Tuesday, regarded as a bug-exorcising exercise for the trade days, was just that, with the Wyvern T.F.Mk 4, Sapphire-Canberra (which lost the port engine dramatically on the take-off roll), Supermarine 508 (which arrived late) and Firefly non-starters as well as the Marathon. The latter, incidentally, contrived to be a complex entry, built by Handley Page (Reading) who had taken it over from Miles, operated by Armstrong-Siddeley as a Mamba test-bed and actually presented by de Havilland, who were displaying their reverse-thrust airscrews, with test pilot de Villiers turning in some startling short stops.

The Shackleton was a production M.R.Mk 1A. Replacing the Maritime Reconnaissance Lancasters of No.120 Squadron at Kinloss in April 1951, the first of fourteen squadrons in Coastal Command to receive it, the 1A established the Shackleton's reputation for longevity, serving in the M.R. role until 1972.

Another production Royal Air Force aircraft at the Show was the Meteor N.F.Mk 11, complete with wing-mounted cannon. Deliveries, to No. 29 Squadron, had commenced the previous month at Tangmere, just down the road. The twentieth production aircraft flew at Farnborough, displaying the new 100-gallon (455 litre) wingtip drop tanks. At a later stage of its career this airframe would be employed by the de Havilland Propeller Company for missile trials.

The presence of the Airspeed-converted prototype Vampire T.Mk 11 trainer tied in with the recent announcement of a production order for the Provost, its stable mate in the

new training programme. Chris Beaumont displayed the old prototype Venom, now fitted experimentally with reheat for the Ghost. Another prototype, appearing for its second Show, was the Type 535, understudying for the production Type 541 Swift. Dave Morgan had suffered a forced landing following an engine failure in the latter, which consequently could not appear at Farnborough.

In parallel with the Swift, Supermarine had a twin-engined design under way to a naval requirement, based round the Rolls-Royce AJ.65 axial-flow turbine, later named the Avon. In order to get the required performance, particularly in rate of climb, weight was to be saved by deleting the undercarriage. Take-off would be from a catapult and landing on a specially-designed "carpet". Work on the Type 505 began in 1945 and a great deal of work on the catapult-and-carpet idea was undertaken at Farnborough. When the Navy, rather predictably, one feels, lost interest in the idea two years later, Supermarine, who were not about to drop a lot of useful design work, installed a conventional nose-wheel undercarriage and came up with the 508.

The result was a large, clean, purposeful-looking beast, with unswept wings and a vee-tail – dictated by strength/weight considerations and by the engine exhaust layout. Flown at the 1951 Show by Mike Lithgow, it possessed full potential for a production fighter, but nothing, as it happened, came of that, although it reappeared in later years with swept wings and an order from the Royal Navy as the Scimitar.

Naval offerings at the Show included the Westland Wyvern, recovered from its temporary fit of sulks on the Tuesday. It was one of a batch of thirteen T.F.Mk 2, virtually to definitive production Mk 4 standard, carrying wing fences and a representative load of four cannon and a 20 inch (50.8 cm) air torpedo, but lacking the rudder mass balance. As in the preceding and succeeding shows, the Wyvern gave a sprightly performance, including climbing rolls after take-off.

Westland paid the penalty of pioneering when they set out, with the Wyvern, to tackle Spec. N.11/44. The range, speed and capacity demanded required a very powerful engine and therefore a very large aircraft. They wanted to design the new aircraft round a propeller-turbine, but the only suitable engine available for the six prototypes and the ten pre-production airframes, laid down simultaneously · to cut development time, was the experimental Rolls-Royce Eagle. This 24-cylinder reciprocating monster was laid out like the Napier Sabre and had rather more problems than even that sophisticated piece of temperament achieved.

First flight took place on 12 December 1946, but as no-one else showed the slightest inclination to employ the Eagle, all the engine development problems had to be worked out at the expense of the Wyvern. This, and a later decision to go for a turbine after all, which resulted in two further development programmes being started for the Rolls-Royce Clyde and Armstrong-Siddeley Python, lead to prodigious extra outlays of time and money. There were other problems, too. Airbrakes had to be incorporated as nobody wished to compound the already complicated problems surrounding the co-axial airscrew/engine combination by suggesting reverse thrust propellers; and no less than three test pilots were killed in unfortunate crashes.

Another naval aircraft, the Fairey Gannet, now in production form as a three-seater, was demonstrated by Peter Twiss and Gordon Slade. The Firefly A.S.Mk 7, also a three-seater, which would hold the naval anti-submarine fort until the Gannet A.S.Mk 1 entered service, was also there. Peter Twiss, who took over the Gannet on Wednesday, lifted it off on one Mamba and, having lit the other boiler with the utmost despatch, demonstrated a lively climbing roll. Rumour had it, incidentally, that when Sir Richard Fairey, having sent the Specification terms down to his design team, enquired how they were getting on, was told: "Oh, we reckon we can meet this by re-engining the Swordfish."

The fighters, as usual, stole the show; their impact emphasised by the fact that by this, the fourth year at Farnborough and the fourth year of public attendance, the names of test pilots were beginning to be familiar and linked to their displays in the popular mind. Neville Duke, one of the two stars of the Display, flew the indecently fast and exceedingly handsome P.1067. He had taken it off on its first test flight, not from Hawkers' new aerodrome at Dunsfold, but from Boscombe Down, only five weeks previously. It was the first prototype of the Hunter and the machine with which he was, two years later almost to the day, briefly to hold the world speed record.

He also flew the P.1052, now flourishing an arrester hook as a broad hint to the Royal Navy. Two prototypes of this aircraft were built and it first appeared at Farnborough in 1949. As a result of a series of modifications and an accident to the first aircraft, VX272, the strengthened rear fuselage with hook, on the aircraft at Farnborough had actually belonged to the second prototype, VX279, which had itself now been converted into the P.1081. A notable feature of his display was the half-Cuban which he was using as a turn-round manoeuvre, with remarkable economy of space.

It had been intended further to modify the P.1052 to take the Armstrong-Siddeley Snarler rocket motor to enhance climb performance, but this eventually wound up at the back of the P.1072, statically displayed only in 1951. Mention has already been made of the Supermarine 508 and 535; the latter, which was hardly new or terribly secret, was nevertheless carefully packed away in the "secret" enclosure along with the Valiant, P.1067 and 508. One must assume that the organisers, having been informed by the makers "for the purpose of the exercise, *that* is a Swift", behaved as if it were.

The Vickers Valiant was an aircraft that was probably more exciting to the Air Staff than the new fighters. Thanks to the advent of the powerful turbine, advances (largely German-inspired) in high speed aerodynamics and the concentrated fury of a single nuclear weapon, the wartime concept of strategic attacks by a mass of heavily armed, piston engined, bombers at comparatively low level, had vanished for ever. In their place was the prospect of a small, economic force of nuclear-armed, swept-wing jets, riding high above any foreseeable opposition at near sonic speeds.

In Korea, where the Americans, *faute de mieux*, were employing piston-engined bombers on daylight missions, there had arisen a further complication in the difficulty of escorting them with the much-faster and incompatible jet fighters.

Now on view for the first time was the first of these new bombers, so gracefully proportioned that it was a shock to find how big it was, when near it on the ground. It was powered by four of the ubiquitous Rolls-Royce Avons but in common with the "belt and braces" philosophy of those days, a second prototype would carry four Armstrong-Siddeley Sapphires to guard against any failure of the former engine.

In the event, there were no failures. The new bomber flew for the first time from Wisley, then still a grass airfield, on 18 May, in the hands of "Mutt" Summers and "Jock" Bryce, in plenty of time for the latter to display it at Farnborough. It was later destroyed in January 1952, catching fire in the air from a wet start relight, but was swiftly replaced by the almost-completed second aircraft which was by then fitted with the thoroughly successful Avon.

As an even more basic piece of "belt and braces", against the possibility that the whole concept was too advanced, a more sober, straight-wing alternative had been built by Short Brothers, without taking any leaps into untried theory. The design emerged as the S.A.4 Sperrin and two prototypes were ordered and completed even although it was realised that the design would be obsolete very shortly. Relations with the Soviet Union, aggravated by the recent Berlin blockade, were very bad and no chances could be taken of not having a fairly immediate Lincoln replacement.

After a first flight on 10 August, the Sperrin was flown at Farnborough by Tom Brooke-Smith ("Brookie" to everyone in the industry) and later, although it was denied service status by the success of the Valiant, it led a useful life on research projects.

A small, bright blue triangle was also flying at Farnborough that year. Intended for research into the low-speed end of the delta's flight envelope, the Avro 707B was displayed with tremendous dash by Roly Falk, a cheerful giant of a man who had at one time been involved in the Spanish Civil War –

an unusual accomplishment in a British test pilot – and was accompanied by another small delta, the Boulton Paul P.111. Designed to explore the trans-sonic characteristics of the delta wing, the latter displayed a fierce pugnacity and possessed distinctly hairy-heeled landing characteristics.

Finally, in this *annus mirabilis*, there was "Zura". Jan Zurakowski flew the Private Venture, ground attack Gloster Meteor, fully loaded with 24 90-lb (40.8 kg) rockets and 100 gallon (454.6 litre) wingtip tanks. On this unpromisingly burdened mount he proceeded to demonstrate his "cartwheel". This shattering and improbable manoeuvre he had apparently thought out while engaged in production testing de Havilland Hornets. He pointed the Meteor vertically upwards and as the speed fell off to the stall, simultaneously opened one throttle while fully retarding the other, spinning the aircraft round its vertical axis (which was parallel to the ground) and holding the rotation through several cycles in the descent.

He was unable to demonstrate it at all on Saturday because of the weather, but on Sunday, lacking adequate clearance below cloud he commenced the manoeuvre "VMC on top" and energed, tumbling wildly through the clouds into the astonished view of the public.

Two events that took place just before the Show underlined the quality of British airframes and engines at this period. On 31 August Flt Lt R.B.Prickett, the Armstrong-Siddeley test pilot flying the Sapphire-Canberra at the Display, had set up four World Class records in the Time-to-Height category. The category had only been introduced in 1950 and these were the first attempts, the results being respectively 3,000 metres (9,730 ft) in 76 seconds, 6,000 metres (19,700 ft) in 110 seconds, 9,000 metres (29,500 ft) in 145 seconds and 12,000 metres (39,400 ft) in 187 seconds. On the same day Beamont flew a Canberra across the Atlantic from Aldergrove to Gander in 4 hours 18½ minutes at an average speed of 480 mph (772.5 k/h).

1951

	Aircraft	Registration
+	Airspeed Ambassador 2	G-ALZP (5213)
+	Armstrong Whitworth Meteor NF.11	WD604
+	Auster Aiglet Trainer J/5F	G-AMKF (2709)
+	Auster B.4	G-AMKL (2983)
+	Auster S	WJ316
+	Avro Ashton 2	WB491
+	Avro Lincoln B.4	SX972 Bristol Proteus in outer nacelles
+	Avro Lincoln B.4	SX973 Napier Nomad in nose
+	Avro Shackleton MR.1A	WB822
	Avro 707A	WD280
+	Avro 707B	VX790
+	Blackburn GAL Universal Freighter 1	WF320
+	Boulton Paul P.111	VT935
	Bristol Brabazon	G-AGPW (12759)
	Bristol Freighter 31	G-AINO (12830)
	Bristol 171 Mk.3	G-ALTC (12897) inside Bristol Freighter
	Bristol 171 Mk.3	G-ALSX (12892)
	de Havilland Chipmunk 22A	G-ALWB (C1/0100)
	de Havilland Comet 1	G-ALYS (06005)
+	de Havilland Dove 2	G-ALBM (14170)
+	de Havilland Heron 1	G-ALZL (10903)
+	de Havilland Sea Venom NF.20	WK376
+	de Havilland Vampire Trainer	G-5-7 (15000)
+	de Havilland Venom	VV612 with reheat
+	English Electric Canberra B.2	WD933 A.S. Sapphires
+	English Electric Canberra PR.3	VX181
+	English Electric Canberra B.5	VX185
+	Fairey Firefly AS.7	WJ216 (F.8827)
	Fairey Gannet AS.1	WE488 (F.8749)
	Gloster Meteor F.8	WA820 A.S. Sapphires
+	Gloster Meteor GAF	G-7-1 (G.5/1210)
+	Handley Page Hermes 5	G-ALEV (H.P.82/2)
	Handley Page (Reading) Marathon 1	G-AMEO (112)
+	Handley Page (Reading) Marathon 2	VX231 (6544) A.S. Mambas
+	Hawker P.1052	VX272
	Hawker P.1067 (Hunter)	WB188
	Hawker P.1072	VP401 Snarler rocket
	Percival Prince 2	G-AMMB (P.50/13)
+	Percival Provost	WG503
+	Percival Sea Prince T.1	WF120
+	Scottish Aviation Pioneer 2	G-AKBF (101)
+	Short Sealand	G-AKLV (SH.1570)
+	Short Sperrin	VX158 (SH.1600)
	Supermarine Attacker FB.1	G-15-110 for Pakistan
+	Supermarine 508	VX133
+	Supermarine 535	VV119
+	Vickers Valiant 1	WB210
	Vickers Varsity T.1	WF330 (522)
+	Vickers Viscount 700	G-AMAV (3)
+	Westland Wyvern TF.2	VW870
+	Westland-Sikorsky S-51	G-ALIK (WA/H/3)

Services participation in the flying programmes:
de Havilland Vampire: four from 54 Squadron.

WG503 was the third prototype Percival Provost, but the first to have the Alvis Leonides engine selected for production aircraft.

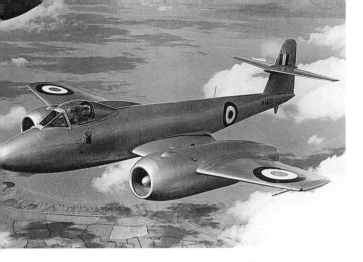

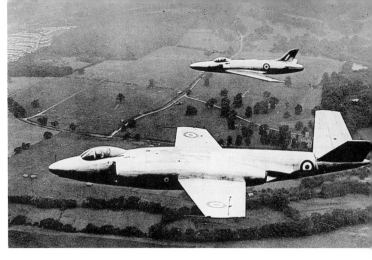

Gloster Meteor WA820 with Armstrong Siddeley Sapphire engines established four time-to-height records immediately prior to the Show, including 3 min 9.5 sec to 12,000m.

A poor photo, but it shows the V tail and general appearance of the Supermarine 508 VX133.

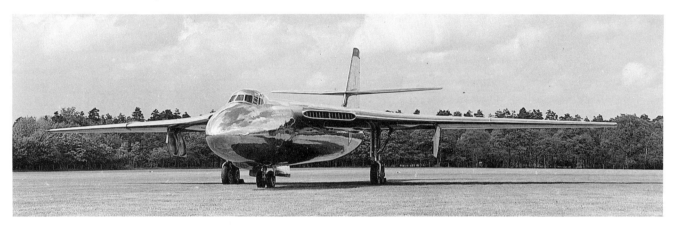

The clean lines of the prototype Vickers Valiant WB210 are evident in this view at Wisley prior to its Farnborough appearance.

The Blackburn & GAL Universal Freighter WF320 and Bristol Brabazon G-AGPW at top left and right dominate the static park. At the bottom, the Mamba Marathon in RAF colours as VX231 has its roundels well inboard.

1952

THE THIRTEENTH SHOW
1-7 SEPTEMBER

Farnborough 1952 was remarkable for a number of reasons. Total attendance came to the staggering figure of 338,000 plus; over 300,000 of these coming in on the two public days. Farnborough popularity had reached a peak, with almost half as many spectators again as in the previous year. Exhibition space was increased to 68,000 sq. ft (6,317.4 sq m), and there were 38,000 invited guests on the Trade Days, including 4,126 from overseas, representing 94 countries. There were 220 exhibitors, 34 more than in 1951.

The Show now lasted a full week, Monday 1 September to Sunday 7 September and there was a Public Premium Day on Friday, when for a slightly larger fee – to reduce attendance – the public could have more elbow room and almost console themselves for not having been able to scrounge a Trade Day ticket. Sonic bangs were permitted, if rather disappointingly achieved and the Duke of Edinburgh came to the Show on the second day. The following day the Minister for Defence, Field Marshal Viscount Alexander, who had taken over the post from Sir Winston Churchill in March, arrived by helicopter. There were now no less than 61 hospitality caravans on "Members' Row" and a Members' Luncheon Room was inaugurated. The word of the week was "Reheat", the thunderous roar that accompanied its sudden and unfamiliar application being sometimes taken for a sonic bang by the timorous or uninitiated.

On the obverse side, the weather was reportedly the worst on record, forcing Wednesday's display, which for some reason was scheduled for the morning, to retreat to a more familiar period after lunch, spoiling the Public Premium Day (which had been gleefully interpreted by exhibitors as Family Day and resulted in some very overcrowded caravans) and producing pouring rain from a wretchedly low cloud base until early afternoon on the Sunday. As a minor benefit, the vast wings and hospitably open doors of the Blackburn Freighter gave shelter at least to some of the multitude, 1,000 of whom reportedly were passing through its cavernous interior every hour.

The Boulton Paul P.120, built to extend the knowledge of deltas at high speed, had crashed as a result of tail flutter the week before the Show and could not take part; on Saturday the Scottish Aviation Prestwick Pioneer struck a sodium light on take-off and executed a breath-taking return to earth trailing one half of its elevators attached only by the control cables. Tragically, John Derry and Tony Richards were killed when the de Havilland D.H.110 prototype broke up during one of its runs on Saturday. One of the engines fell among the crowd, killing 29 people and injuring 60 more.

The occasion did not lack those who pointed out that it was the thirteenth Display.

There were 35 aircraft in the Flying Display and a further 20 on static display only. The flying programme contained a very high proportion of prototype or experimental types, but no fewer than 27 of them would in time achieve production status and civil or military service. Several were old friends, if only from the previous year; there were no less than four different Canberras flying, the Short Sperrin was back in an all-grey colour scheme (actually it was the second prototype) and the second prototype Valiant flew, showing its new intake shapes.

All six of the "super priority" types were flying and on view together for the first time: Valiant, Hunter, Swift, Javelin, Canberra and Gannet. For all the fuss about this programme, it was to be a long time before any of the magnificent six saw squadron service. One of the holes in the defence programme had been plugged earlier in the year by the arrival of the first two Lockheed Neptunes from the United States. Provided under the Mutual Defence Aid Pact to close gaps in the British defences, they slipped quietly into St Eval on 13 January.

The star of the 1952 Show, both aerodynamically and on grounds of sheer pilotage, was without doubt the Avro 698 Vulcan prototype. As yet un-named, it had first taken the air at Woodford on 30 August, only three days before its first public appearance at Farnborough (it did not fly on Monday). When Wing Commander Roly Falk brought the huge white delta round for its first thunderous pass, flanked by the bright blue and orange triangles of the 707A and B, and proceeded to give a masterly display at very low altitude, it was difficult to realise that his total flight time on the aircraft was about two hours – or that he was flying it solo. The delta shape, which dominated Farnborough '52 with the three Avros and the Gloster Javelin, was a logical extension of the swept wing to obtain low wing loading and good manoeuvrability at high altitudes and possessed other advantages as well.

The prototype 698 was powered by four Avons, as the Bristol Olympus, the chosen production engine, was not yet available and despite its dramatic appearance was of fairly conventional construction. It did, however, introduce a major novelty in its approach and landing. The delta wing gave the capability of landing at low speed and a high angle of attack and the chosen technique of descent with throttle closed and stick checked to give a constant angle of attack resulted in an eye-catching arrival without the normal flare. In later years it was to become a matter of pride with Vulcan display pilots to hold the high alpha altitude as long as possible, in some cases not lowering the nose wheel until turned off the runway and well down the perimeter track.

Three experimental Canberras took part in the Display, presented by Armstrong-Siddeley (Sapphire), Rolls-Royce (Avon with two-position afterburners) and Bristol (Olympus). It might have been expected that this barrage of excess power would have outshone the modest performance of the fourth Canberra present, a standard production T.4 trainer for the Royal Air Force, but for the fact that "Bea" was flying the latter. As it was, his incomparable skill produced what one aeronautical journal termed "the most beautifully timed and placed performance of the day".

Proceedings opened with a "heavy circus" again, which included the Shackleton – this time the new Mk 2, which flew for the first time on 17 June. The two 20 mm guns that had graced the nose of the prototypes but vanished from the lumpy nose of the Mk 1 were back in a new, streamlined front end and the retractable radar dustbin was further aft. At a top weight of 42.5 tons (46 tonnes), a span of 120 ft (36.5m) and packing nearly 10,000 horsepower, it was, and would remain for many years, an impressive display item when boldly handled.

Among the fighters, both Hunter and Swift were flying, though they were not to enter squadron service until 1954. The Hunter would equip a total of 38 squadrons, replacing the Meteor, Sabre and Venom, while the Swift, a most unlucky aircraft, went solely to No. 56 Squadron at Waterbeach, where the various airframes spent much of their early days in the hangar covered in snag sheets. However, it was to have its moment of glory later, as will appear.

The Gloster Javelin, the Royal Air Force's first true all-weather fighter, with comprehensive electronics and radar, was designed to cope with the new breed of high altitude, high subsonic speed bombers that would soon be in service. Its delta shape emerged via a swept-wing, Sapphire-engine Meteor development, which it was proposed to arm, at one stage, with a 4.5 inch (6.35 cm) recoiless cannon.

A great deal was already known about deltas, much of it from the work of Lippisch and other German designers, but combining it with a T-tail, as in the Javelin, uncovered a number of fresh problems. The Boulton Paul P.120 had been intended to resolve many of these, but crashed early in its programme, as already noted, due to tail flutter. The prototype Javelin also crashed and burned, with both elevators torn off. Bill Waterton, Gloster's chief test pilot, was awarded the

George Medal for saving the records of the flight after executing a skilful crash landing. Later, Peter Lawrence was to be killed in another Javelin, victim of the first of the deep stall accidents.

Despite these alarming problems, the Javelin, in competition with the D.H. 110, had already been selected as the next all-weather fighter for the Royal Air Force by the time it flew at Farnborough. The need for an effective aircraft in this category was underlined by a message received at Royal Observer Corps Group Headquarters, Rudloe Manor, during an exercise about this time: "Owing to the weather, the all-weather fighters will not be flying."

Among naval offerings in 1952, both the Gannet and Wyvern were present in more-or-less production form. On the civil side, proceedings were again enlivened by Ranald Porteous in the aerobatic Auster Aiglet Trainer, who inserted a flick-ish rolling movement into the top of a loop. Frequently referred to as a Porteous loop, Ranald himself called it the "avalanche", because that was what it felt like when it hit you. He also drew attention to the virtues of his mount by landing on one wheel.

The greatest civil triumph of the Display, undoubtedly, was the first appearance of the Bristol 175, christened by some anonymous genius at Filton, the Britannia. It was originally designed by Dr A.E. Russell and his team for four Centaurus piston engines, but was built with Bristol Proteus propeller turbines installed in its elegant nacelles. Three prototypes had been ordered by the Ministry of Supply as the nearest practical response to a requirement of BOAC for a "Medium Range Empire" type, while the Corporation were making up their Corporate minds a process that took a good long time, and tended to interfere with design continuity.

It must be admitted, though, that with the foreign travel allowance for British citizens recently reduced to £25, prospects for mass travel in what was left of the medium-range empire must have been difficult to assess.

When the big, handsome, laid-back Britannia cruised by on the murmur of the admirable Proteus, it was immediately christened the "Whispering Giant". Following the precedent set some years previously by the Ambassador, it appeared in full airline colours, although some years from actual service. (It was the Corporations incidentally, who pioneered the practice of painting the tops of fuselages white, to reflect heat.)

Great Britain has been noticeably slow in following up the promise of the helicopter, but the 1952 Show did produce some activity and promise, in the shape of two production aircraft and two prototypes. The little two-seater Skeeter had been designed by Cierva as far back as 1946 and when the company was taken over by Saunders-Roe in 1951, the latter continued development and were now marketing it with the 180 hp Blackburn Bombardier, as the Skeeter 3B. Seventy-seven Skeeters were built for the British and German armies and the German Navy, but there were no civilian orders although no less than seven did subsequently appear on the civil register.

The other production helicopter, the Westland Dragonfly, had been in naval service since 1949. A British version of the Sikorsky S-51, it featured a more powerful engine (Alvis Leonides) and in the version shown, an HR.3, new metal rotor blades.

Bristol had two new helicopters on display; the Type 171, later named the Sycamore and the twin-rotor, twin-engined Type 173. The latter was flown by "Sox" Hosegood, who proved convincingly that the 173 manoeuvred on the ground by using engine differentials like a fixed-wing twin and walked it about on its hind legs like a Lippizaner before lifting off; apparently a perfectly normal procedure. The 173 was a good example of an enduring British habit of producing promising prototypes from first class ideas by first class designers (in this case Raoul Hafner) and failing to follow them up. Subsequent success by Boeing-Vertol in this field points the moral.

What should have been quite clear, but equally was apparently not, was the folly of even contemplating the construction of the Saunders-Roe Princess, also making its first appearance at Farnborough. This 100 ton (101.6 tonne) ten-engined behemoth first took the air on 20 August, flown by Geoffrey Tyson. Designed for 102 passengers or 250 troops (even in those days they packed 'em in), it was a classic example of "Nostalgia rules!" and an exceedingly expensive way of seeing out the flying-boat. In reply to a question the Secretary of State for Air, Lord De L'Isle and Dudley stated that the estimated cost for the three Princesses order had risen from the 1946 figure of £2,800,00 to £10,000,000 four years later.

Nevertheless, there it was, sailing majestically down the runway and cruising about among the tents, as dignified and useful as a Victorian battleship and arousing very much the same emotions.

To close the account of 1952 on a more exciting note, it was announced that on 26 August "Bea" Beamont and Peter Hillwood, with S/Ldr Watson as navigator, had made the first double air crossing of the Atlantic in a day, flying a Canberra. This was done in VX185, the Avon R.A.7 powered prototype B.Mk 5, between Aldergrove and Gander Lake. Not the airport – the finishing line being set between two mark boats. Outward time was 4 hours, 33 minutes and 17.08 seconds and the return was flown in 3 hours, 28 minutes and 18.13 seconds to give a West-East average speed of 605.52 mph (974.5 k/h).

1952

+	Armstrong Whitworth Meteor NF.11	WM166
+	Auster Aiglet Trainer J/5L	G-AMMS (2720)
	Auster Autocar J/5G	G-AMPA (2987) spraying equipment
	Auster B.4	G-AMKL (2983)
+	Avro Shackleton MR.2	WG531
+	Avro 698 (Vulcan)	VX770
+	Avro 707A	WD280
+	Avro 707B	VX790
	Blackburn GAL Universal Freighter 1	WF320 (1000)
	Bristol Freighter 31	NZ5906 (12929) RNZAF
+	Bristol 171 Mk.3	G-ALSX (12892)
+	Bristol 173 Mk.1	G-ALBN (12871)
+	Bristol Britannia 100	G-ALBO (12873)
	de Havilland Chipmunk T.10	WP838 (C1/0721)
+	de Havilland Comet 1	G-ALVG (06001)
	de Havilland Comet 1A	CF-CUM (06013)
	de Havilland Dove 2	G-AJLW (04033)
+	de Havilland Heron 1	G-ALZL (10903)
	de Havilland Sea Venom NF.20	WK385
	de Havilland Vampire T.11	WZ429
+	de Havilland Venom 1	VV612 with reheat
	de Havilland Venom FB.1	WE281
	de Havilland Venom NF.2	WL808
+	de Havilland D.H.110	WG236 crashed 6 September
+	de Havilland D.H.110	WG240
+	English Electric Canberra B.2	WD933 A.S. Sapphires
+	English Electric Canberra B.2	WD943 R-R Avons with reheat
+	English Electric Canberra B.2	WD952 Bristol Olympus
	English Electric Canberra B.5	VX185
+	English Electric Canberra T.4	WN467
	Fairey Firefly AS.7	WJ149 (F.8759)
	Fairey Gannet AS.1	WE488 (F.8749)
	Gloster Meteor T.7	WL453
+	Gloster Javelin FAW.1	WD808
+	Handley Page (Reading) Marathon T.11	XA250 (102)
+	Hawker Hunter F.1	WB195
	Hawker Sea Hawk F.1	WF147
	Percival Prince 2 (VIP)	G-AMMB (P.50/13)
+	Percival Prince 3B	G-AMKY (P50/36)
+	Percival Provost T.1	WE522
+	Percival Sea Prince T.1	WM735 (P.57/49)
+	Saunders-Roe Princess	G-ALUN (SR.901) flying only
+	Saunders-Roe Skeeter 3B	WF112 (W.14/3)
	Saunders-Roe Skeeter 5	G-AMTZ (SR.907)
+	Scottish Aviation Pioneer 2	G-AKBF (101)
	Short Sealand	G-AIVX (SH.1555)
+	Short Sperrin	VX158 (SH.1600)
	Supermarine Attacker FB.2	WK338
+	Supermarine 508	VX136
+	Supermarine 541	WJ965
	Supermarine Swift F.1	WK194
+	Vickers Valiant 1	WB215
	Vickers Varsity T.1	WF429 (704)
+	Vickers Viscount 701	G-ALWE (4)
+	Westland Dragonfly HR.3	WG707
+	Westland Wyvern TF.4	VZ750

Ranald Porteus and his inimitable one-wheel landing with the Auster Aiglet Trainer G-AMMS.

The prototype D.H.110 WG236 was lost on 6 September in a fatal crash at the Show.

The Saunders-Roe Princess G-ALUN over the Isle of Wight flew in daily for its Show slots.

Pest Control's Auster Autocar G-AMPA with underwing spray gear and a particularly patriotic rudder!

Dove G-AJLW was shown at Farnborough in this silver and blue scheme with the US flag on the tail but no registration; in fact it was never exported.

1953

THE FOURTEENTH SHOW
5-11 SEPTEMBER

The great exhibition marquee had expanded again, up to 110,000 square feet (10,219 sq.m) and was stretched down R/W 29 halfway to the intersection with the active display runway. Exhibitors' caravans had become so popular a feature that now they reached right round the static park, in two rows, up to the crowd barrier. Further along that same fence lay the two marquees housing the President and his guests and the Press. It cost an adult 20s (£1) to get in on Friday, 5s (25p) on the other public days. Private cars on Friday, 20s (£1). If he came with five of his mates in a car at the weekend, the whole lot got in for thirty bob (£1.50). Children under 16 were half-price, motor cycles 5s (25p) or 2s 6d (12½p) and bicycles 2s 6d (12½p) or, on Saturday and Sunday, 1s (5p). (Why don't they still charge for bicycles?)

The weather was irreproachable, in contrast to one or two other Shows. Not all the aircraft turned up on Monday; Neville Duke's scarlet Hunter, the new holder of the World Speed Record, did not arrive until Tuesday; nor did the Gannet, the Princess, or the Valiant, the latter delayed by a minor problem with the fuel supply. The Viscount did not turn up until after the flying was over on Monday. For once, on this one day, take-off was from the Laffan's Plain end, giving everybody an inordinately long taxi. Well, almost everybody; "Sox" Hosegood in the Bristol 173 not only took off in far less distance than anybody else, bar his fellow helicopters, but did it backwards.

One of the most dramatic presentations in any Show closed the flying programme; the glittering cohort of the deltas, the two huge white Vulcans flanked by the blue, orange, red and silver of the four little 707 research and training aircraft. Passing in vic on Monday, in diamond on the other days, they were a sight no-one who saw it will ever forget.

The specialist press drew attention to the swing from immediate post-war experiments to production aircraft, a point made by the President of the SBAC, Mr Burroughes, at the traditional eve-of-Show dinner. The Korean War had ended on 27 July and with the urgency of achieving maximum output of existing designs that had been envisaged in 1950 now removed, the balance between rearmament and the related subjects of export and development had changed.

This was the great year of "sonic booms", with everybody in the caravans telling everybody else how they were caused, without anybody apparently really knowing, and pilots experiencing considerable difficulty, either at height or in a dive, in pointing their bangs at the airfield so the spectators could actually hear the wretched things. Bill Bedford, Mike Lithgow and Dave Morgan, respectively flying the Hunter 2, Swift 3 and Swift 4, had only limited success and added to the mystery by producing double, rather than single, booms.

This affair of the booms had another claim to historical fame, giving rise to one of the earliest examples of "Franglais". Franglais is, of course, the truly Gallic art either of translating literally a word or phrase that the *Académie* has not succeeded in finding already in the French language or leaving it in English, but spoken with a French accent. This was done originally for convenience's sake, later simply to irritate the Academicians (which it did), and eventually out of pure snobbery. At first, authority tried to have nasty English expressions like "briefing" replaced by good old Gallic words, such as *"le briefage"* but this failed to work. So did literal translation, in many cases – who could take *souscoup volante* seriously as a flying saucer? Thus, when the best that the French language could produce for a sonic boom turned out to be *grondement sonique*, it was promptly Franglaised into "le double bang".

Two research aircraft caught the eye. The Boulton Paul P.111, now equipped with airbrakes and called the P.111A, still flung itself impetuously at the runway after its display and required the additional comfort of a braking parachute – the latter in itself quite a Farnborough novelty, the only other deployment being from the Sapphire-Vulcan when it had to abandon its display. The little Boulton Paul delta gave an exciting performance; compact, extrovert and quick in reaction, it was a highly suitable mount for the company's chief test pilot, "Ben" Gunn.

Even more intriguing than the P.111A was the new Short S.B.5. This had been built to Specification ER.100 as a research vehicle into the low speed characteristics of very sharply swept wings, with specific reference to the English Electric P.1. Three different sets of P.1 wings were built for the S.B.5, giving sweep-back angles of 50, 60 and 69 degrees. The urgent necessity for information in an area far beyond contemporary knowledge justified a special research aircraft and it flew for the first time at Boscombe Down, with 50 degrees of sweep, on 2 December 1952. At Farnborough it carried the 60 degree sweep wings and still had the high-mounted, variable-incidence tailplane, which was moved down onto the fuselage at the end of the year. It was demonstrated by Tom Brooke-Smith, who probably had, through

Short's involvements in research, more exciting aeroplanes to play with than any other test pilot.

This was the first time that all three of the V-bombers were seen together at Farnborough. With the Mk.1 Valiant well on its way to production status, Vickers were showing the Mk.2, designed for the specialist low-level pathfinder role with NATO forces. The most obvious difference was the relocation of the main undercarriage into streamlined fairings, the result of the necessary "beefing-up" of the structure for the new task. Clothed in decent black, the sombre Valiant, flown by "Jock" Bryce, remained a prototype; the Canberra was found to be more suitable and moreover was readily available for the job. Curiously, after the last Valiant had disappeared, condemned to early retirement by structural fatigue, the Vulcans of the V-force found themselves adapting to a low-level task, faced with changing NATO requirements and increasingly sophisticated defences.

With the Vulcan, the public was already familiar, but the Handley Page Victor, latest of the three new bombers intended to re-equip the Royal Air Force and designed to the same high-altitude, high sub-sonic speed requirement, was new. It had made its first public appearance at the Queen's Coronation Review fly-past at Odiham on 15 July.

The official Specification, B.25/46, was written around the proposals made to the Air Staff (before that body had even drafted a requirement) early in 1946, much as the B.9/48 Spec. was drawn up round Vickers' Valiant proposal. The design, like many that issued from Cricklewood, was inspired and very advanced; Godfrey Lee, who put it forward, had had access to swept-wing work done by Arado when he was in Germany with a technical commission. Heart of the design was the advanced "crescent" wing, which solved the various problems of low-speed stability and critical Mach numbers with an aerofoil of decreasing sweep to the tips and the latest high-lift devices (in which H.P. was something of a specialist). Painted for the occasion in black and silver-grey, with a red cheat line, it made a most impressive appearance at the Display. Very few people knew at the time that "Hazel" Hazelden had performed the whole demonstration on the first day on three engines, plagued by a minor fuel flow problem.

Handley Page invariably offered civil versions of most of his big aircraft and the Victor was no exception. A model was displayed on the company stand at Farnborough, which, owing to the highly secret nature of the Victor wing had appeared only as a fuselage the year before, looking, as someone said, rather more like a proposal for a rocket. In 1953, with the real thing in plain sight (though confined to the north side, like the Vulcans, when on the ground) it appeared complete.

That wingless wonder on the company stand recalls to mind a large cut-away model of an H.P.42 which used to be on display in the Paris offices of Imperial Airways. A note on it, in French, reassured nervous passengers that the absence of wings on the port side was caused only by the requirement to get the model into the glass case.

Both the Hunter and Swift were now in production and most attention focussed on Neville Duke's record-breaker. This was the original prototype, modified to take a Rolls-Royce Avon RA.7R with reheat which gave 9,000 lb (4,082 kg) of thrust when lit. In Hunter genealogy this made it the one-and-only Mk 3. Modifications included a more pointed nose and remodelled windscreen and the airbrakes were in the intermediate flank position on the fuselage. Painted scarlet to aid camera interpretation, the aircraft gained the World's absolute speed record over a 3 km (1.8964 miles) course off the South Coast on 7 September (the second trade day), achieving an average speed of 1,171 k/h (722.6 mph). The previous record, set by a North American Sabre, had lasted only 21 days, and Duke's, as it turned out, only lasted 19, being (briefly) eclipsed by Mike Lithgow in the Swift. The latter record was set up in Tripoli, where temperatures were more favourable and raised the record to 1,184 k/h (737.7 mph). That record stood exactly nine days, when it returned to the United States in the even better climatic conditions at Salton Lake. The Swift had already made headlines, on 5 July, when Mike Lithgow flew from London to Paris in 19 minutes, four seconds.

The Wyvern had just started service with the Fleet Air Arm's No. 813 Squadron as the S.4, the aircraft displayed being one of a batch of upgraded Mk 2s. The Fleet Air Arm, incidentally, had just come back officially into existence. In the political in-fighting that went on after the First World War, the Royal Air Force gained administrative and technical control of naval aviation. The Navy retained operational control, but pilots had to be members of the Royal Air Force – causing some complications in promotion and career structures. In 1924 it became the Fleet Air Arm of the Royal Air Force, and was belatedly handed back to naval control in May 1939. It continued to be called Fleet Air Arm during hostilities, but post-war was officially once more Naval Aviation, the name Fleet Air Arm being re-instated on 20 May 1953.

This year the D.H.110 appeared in naval markings, foreshadowing its eventual career as the Sea Vixen. New on the scene was the prototype Short Seamew, a tribute to Bill Stout's axiom of "Simplicate and add more lightness" and the direct result of the campaigning for less complex and less heavy anti-submarine aircraft by Rear Admiral Slattery, who had been in charge of Projects and Development at Short's new home in Belfast since he retired as Chief of Naval Equipment. Convinced by his eloquence, the Admiralty issued Specification M.123 for such an aircraft and accepted the Seamew as the result.

Powered by a single Mamba, it was a very basic aeroplane indeed. Construction of the first prototype was rushed through following the order in April 1953 and completed in 15 months. Despite a crash on 23 August, when it sustained considerable damage, it was present at Farnborough, but the backlash of the accelerated completion of the design began to show up in major re-design requirements, especially of controls. Hopes of a NATO order to follow that from the Navy proved still-born.

There had been great hopes that the Comet 2 would be present at Farnborough, but the company could not spare the aircraft.

The Bristol Freighter/Wayfarer has been rather neglected so far in this narrative. It made its earliest appearance at Radlett and was even then attracting orders at a handsome rate. In 1953 it was represented by the Mk 32, a production aircraft for Silver City, whose Ferryfield-Le Touquet car service was the best-loved and best-known aspect of the type's service world-wide.

Conceived as a commercial vehicle based on the successful military career of the Bombay, it emerged as a twin-Hercules cargo or passenger aircraft with a disposable load of some 13,000 lb (5,897 kg) and a range of over 1,000 miles (1,609 km). Silver City took the first of fourteen Mk 32 Superfreighters, designed to their requirement, on 31 March 1953. Two hundred and fourteen of this admirable aircraft were built, seeing service with several Air Forces, as far afield as New Zealand.

The first "real" Canadian aeroplane to display (most of the Chipmunks were built in England) was the D.H.C.2 Beaver, a prototype converted from a Canadian Mk 1, on the British register and now powered by an Alvis Leonides. With greater span and bigger fin, it was effectively a Mk 2. The first of a long and continuing line of Short Take-Off and Landing (STOL) aircraft from the company, the Beaver served, and in 1989 was still serving, with the British Army. Half of the total of 1,692 built went to US Army and USAF units and it operated in over 60 countries.

The Chipmunk, in the Static Park only in 1953, had one current claim to fame: His Royal Highness the Duke of Edinburgh had started his flying training in one at White Waltham the previous November. In January 1953, he was promoted to Marshal of the Royal Air Force, which must have made life interesting for his instructor.

Two Viscounts were present, one in Air France colours, the second, G-AMAV, taking time off from preparations for the impending London-Christchurch, New Zealand air race. Although air race preparations prevented the appearance of the Mk 7 Canberra, Walter Gibb had made sure that the type remained in the headlines by taking the Class C (Aeroplane) Height Record to 19,406 m (63,668 ft) on 4 May that year.

1953		
+ Auster Aiglet Trainer J/5L	G-AMMS (2720)	
Auster B.4		
Ambulance/Freighter	XA177 (2983)	
+ Avro Shackleton MR.2	WG796	
Avro Vulcan 1	VX770 A.S. Sapphires	
+ Avro Vulcan 1	VX777 Bristol Olympus	
+ Avro 707A	WD280	
+ Avro 707A	WZ736	
+ Avro 707B	VX790	
+ Avro 707C	WZ744	
Blackburn Universal		
Freighter 2	WZ889 (1001)	
Boulton Paul Sea Balliol T.21	WL715	
+ Boulton Paul P.111A	VT935	
+ Bristol Britannia 100	G-ALBO (12873)	
Bristol Freighter 31	G-AINL (12827)	
+ Bristol Freighter 32	G-AMWF (13133)	
+ Bristol 171 Mk.4	G-AMWI (13070)	
+ Bristol 173 Mk.2	G-AMJI (12872)	
de Havilland Chipmunk T.10	WZ884 (C1/0924)	
de Havilland Comet 1A	F-BGNX (06020)	
de Havilland Dove 2	G-ALFT (04233)	
de Havilland Dove 6	G-AMZN (04437)	
de Havilland Heron 1	PK-GHB (14015)	
+ de Havilland Heron 2	G-AMTS (14007)	
+ de Havilland D.H.110	WG240	
+ de Havilland Canada Beaver		
2	G-ANAR (80)	
+ English Electric Canberra B.2	WD930 R-R Avon RA.14S	
+ English Electric Canberra B.2	WD952 Bristol Olympus	
+ English Electric Canberra B.2	WJ716	
English Electric Canberra		
PR.3	WE146	
Fairey Firefly T.7	WM873 (F.8728)	
Fairey Gannet AS.1	WN341 (F.9113)	
+ Gloster Meteor T.7	WS141	
+ Gloster Javelin FAW.1	WT827	
+ Handley Page Victor	WB771	
Hawker Hunter F.1	WT557	
+ Hawker Hunter F.2	WB202	
+ Hawker Hunter 3	WB188	
Percival Pembroke C.1	WV701 (P.66/4)	
+ Percival Provost T.1	WV471	
+ Percival Provost T.1	WV472	
+ Saunders-Roe Princess	G-ALUN (SR.901)	
+ Saunders-Roe Skeeter 5	G-AMTZ (SR.907)	
+ Scottish Aviation Pioneer 2	G-ANAZ (103)	
Short Seamew AS.1	XA209 (SH.1606)	
+ Short SB.5	WG768 (SH.1605)	
+ Supermarine Swift F.3	WK195	
+ Supermarine Swift F.4	WK198	
+ Vickers Valiant 2	WJ954	
+ Vickers Viscount 700	G-AMAV (3)	
Vickers Viscount 708	F-BGNN (14)	
+ Westland Dragonfly HR.1	VZ966	
+ Westland Wyvern S.4	VW870	
Westland S-55 (Whirlwind)		
HAR.1	XA863 (WA.2)	

This did not qualify for an Absolute World Record, which since 1931 had been in the hands of the balloonists and in 1953 stood at 22,066 m (72,394.5 ft) set up in 1935 by Captains Anderson and Stevens of the United States Army.

(Continues on page 73.)

1955 Avro Canada CF-100-4B 18321 was shown statically while its stablemate, 18322 was flown with verve by Jan Zurakowski.

1955 Handley Page Herald G-AODE in the type's original four piston engine configuration and Queensland Airlines titles – an option subsequently cancelled.

1955 Bristol Sycamore HR.14 XJ364 in camouflage and with main rotor blades folded.

1956 Gloster Javelin FAW.4 XA764 shares the static park with Venom WX931, Canberra XK951, Comet XK695 and Twin Pioneer G-AOEO.

1957 4X-AGB was the second of three Bristol Britannia 313s for El Al, Israel's national airline.

1958 The last of 15 Fairey Gannet A.S.4s delivered to the West German Naval Air Arm was UA-115, seen on a Farn-borough public day. One T.5 was also supplied.

1960 Avro Shackleton MR.3 XF708 of 201 Squadron lands after a 22 hour patrol – part of this year's Service participation.

1959 Avro Lincoln B.2 G-APRJ (ex-RF342) used by Napier for icing research with 6ft specimen wing sections on top of the fuselage wetted by a vertical spray mat.

1962 Avro Vulcan B.1 XA894 makes a low pass, clearly show-ing the Olympus engine under test for the TSR-2.

1962 Blackburn Buccaneer S.1. XK533 of No. 700Z Flight based at Lossiemouth was one of four in the Services participation this year.

1964 More Service participation in the combined assault; Whitworth Gloster Argosy XN857 prepares to move out having offloaded troops while Royal Navy Westland Wessex run in.

Top:
1966 The Beagle 206 quartet awaiting take off clearance; five aircraft were shown and shared the flying between them through the week.

Above:
1966 Breguet Atlantic No. 15 about to touch down on the "piano keys".

Left:
1966 The first Fairey F.D.2, WG774, rebuilt as the BAC 221 to test the Concorde's wing shape.

1966 Hants & Sussex Aviation converted de Havilland Chipmunk G-ATTS to turbine power with a Rover TP.90.

1972 Hindustan Gnat E1069 was one of two shown.

1974 Lockheed's C-5A Galaxy 00454 dwarfs the same company's Orion and Blackbird.

(continued from page 64)

Blackburn showed the Universal Freighter 2, the production prototype Beverley, carrying a couple of 7-ton trucks and the Princess was back, for the last time, looking, as *The Aeroplane* put it, "more like a ship dragging its anchor than an aeroplane flying at 150 knots or so."

Non-event of the season: The Minister of Transport and Civil Aviation, Mr A.T.Lennox-Boyd, withdrew the passenger-carrying ban on the Tudor.

The Avro delta formation seen at Farnborough – Vulcans VX770 and '777, and two 707As, a 707B and 707C.

Another delta – Boulton Paul's P.111A VT935 in modified form since its 1951 appearance and sporting a bright yellow scheme with black trim.

Avro Shackleton MR.2 WL796 complete with airborne lifeboat (number 804 for the enthusiasts!).

The Bristol 171 Mk.4 G-AMWI carrying an external load.

Bristol 173 Mk.2 wearing BEA trim and King Arthur Class name Sir Bors – sounds (and looks!) like a railway engine. Noteworthy is the use of civil marks G-AMJI and serial XH379. The three "spare" wheels underneath belong to a Bristol 171.

The Exhibition and associated tents, with two separate aircraft parks. The close proximity of the car parks to the large tents will never be seen these days!

1954

THE FIFTEENTH SHOW
6-12 SEPTEMBER

The fifteenth SBAC Farnborough Show was a little bigger, a little better than its predecessors; and a good time was had by all. For the second time running, Thursday was a civil day, with no military aircraft flying (though that rule seemed to stretch a little here and there).

Monday was still referred to as "preview" or "rehearsal" day, with Tuesday as opening day, although the distinction was becoming a little vague. Presumably, there were still enough hiccups for a trial day to be a good thing. The main exhibition hall had expanded to 110,000 square ft (10,219 sq.m) and this year had moved off Runway 29 (presumably because it was getting too near the active) and was sited in the general area since occupied by the exhibition halls in later years.

Not all the aircraft flew every day, apart from the restrictions on Thursday; the weather on Monday was lousy, to put it mildly, with low clouds and driving rain and both the Javelin and the D.H.110 were unable to take off and had to content themselves with taxying. The Supermarine 525 was not even there. It has to be borne in mind that at every Show there would be a number of brand new prototypes, displaying under considerable performance restrictions and probably not yet equipped with full flight instrumentation. Despite this, and with a cloud base of between 500 and 800 feet (152-244 m), virtually all the aircraft present actually flew under the positive and impeccable radio and radar control from Farnborough Tower. The RAE's Air Traffic Control personnel seldom get even a mention on these occasions, but upon their shoulders as much as the pilots' rests the responsibility for a close-knit and safe display. On this occasion their efforts were duly noted by the Press. There were no diversions necessary, even though conditions were such that aircraft were frequently invisible to the spectators.

Opening day was blessed with good weather, as was Tuesday and Sunday, but Friday in particular was another nasty.

At the pre-Show Dinner, some Members were complaining that, like the Show, it had got very crowded (and very hot). The President, the tall, genial J.J.Parkes, chairman of Alvis and an aviation enthusiast who flew his family around in the company's immaculate Puss Moth at week-ends, assured those present that the Show would continue to be an annual event and announced that the labour force in the Industry had risen to 230,000 from its 1948 level of 145,000. Guest of Honour was the Minister for Transport and Civil Aviation, Mr Duncan Sandys. In view of the effects of his "shot-gun marriages" when he came later to rationalise the aircraft companies, some members might well have looked back on that evening with a feeling of having nursed a viper in their hospitable corporate bosom.

For the first time, there was no flying boat at the Show; not even a seaplane, though *The Aeroplane* and several persons in the industry quite obviously, if a trifle irrationally, still hankered after them, even if not on quite the same grand scale as before. One other feature from previous Shows had also been quietly consigned to oblivion, when Duncan Sandys made the announcement that as neither the Services nor the civil sector could find the slightest use for them, the Brabazons, one built and one building, were to be scrapped.

It is doubtful if anyone was surprised, though in view of the fact that the cost at that stage amounted to £8 million, having risen from an original £2 million estimate, more fuss might have been made. Bristol came out of it with a lot of experience, the country's largest and most expensive assembly hall (useful for the Britannia) and a runway that enabled No. 501 Squadron, the local Auxiliary unit, to take off five-abreast in their Vampires. There is a dip in the middle of that runway, from which much of the outside world is invisible and the story runs that the pilot of a Chipmunk ground-looped at the bottom and, being urged to clear rather than wait for his compass to recover its wits, enquired plaintively if anyone could see which way he was facing.

Sonic booms were now forbidden over land, but there was a dispensation for the SBAC Show, provided pilots could keep their booms within the aerodrome boundary. In view of increasing complaints of damage, pilots were not encouraged to try this tricky operation.

The B.2/Olympus-Canberra was the aircraft used to obtain the Class C Altitude Record. Of the other Canberras in the Display, the prototype of the new night intruder B.8 had been converted from the solitary Mk 5 and was also the holder of the double Atlantic crossing record. This new Mk 8 successfully concluded the Canberra's attempt to take over virtually all the front line tasks of the Royal Air Force.

The Sapphire Vulcan represented a step in the development of this aircraft, which ended up in production form powered by the Bristol Olympus. The Sapphire powered a wide variety of airframes, largely in its capacity as an alternative to the Avon, but enjoyed an independent success beyond being a mere understudy.

1954

+	Airspeed Ambassador	G-AKRD (62) Bristol Proteus	
+	Armstrong Whitworth		
	Meteor NF.14	WS848	
+	Auster Aiglet J/8L	G-AMYI (3151)	
	Auster AOP.9	WZ664	
+	Avro Shackleton Mr.2	WR969	
+	Avro Vulcan 1	VX770 A.S. Sapphires	
	Blackburn Universal Freighter		
	2	WZ889 (1001)	
	Boulton Paul Sea Balliol T.2	G-ANSF (BP.6c)	
+	Bristol Britannia 102	G-ANBA (12902)	
	Bristol Freighter 31M	G-18-166 (13173) for Pakistan AF	
+	Bristol 171 Mk.4	G-AMWI (13070)	
+	Bristol 173 Mk.2	XH379 (12872)	
	de Havilland Chipmunk T.10	G-ALWB (C1/0100)	
+	de Havilland Comet 2	G-AMXD (06026)	
+	de Havilland Comet 3	G-ANLO (06100)	
	de Havilland Dove 6	G-AMZN (04437)	
	de Havilland Heron 2	TC-HAK (14056)	
	de Havilland Vampire T.11	XE824	
	de Havilland Venom FB.4	WR374	
	de Havilland Venom NF.3	WX791	
	de Havilland Sea Venom		
	FAW.21	WM569	
+	de Havilland D.H.110	WG240	
+	de Havilland Canada Beaver		
	2	G-ANAR (80)	
+	English Electric Canberra B.2	WD933 A-S Sapphires	
+	English Electric Canberra B.2	WD952 Bristol Olympus	
	English Electric Canberra B.6	WJ771	
+	English Electric Canberra PR.7	WJ820	
+	English Electric Canberra B (I) 8	VX185	
	Fairey Firefly U.8	WM882 (F.8937)	
+	Fairey Gannet AS.1	WN360 (F.9132)	
	Fairey Gannet AS.1	WN391 (F.9152)	
+	Fairey Gannet T.2	WN365 (F.9137)	
+	Fairey F.D.1	VX350 (F.8466)	
+	Folland Midge	G-39-1 (FL.1)	
	Gloster Javelin FAW.1	WT827	
	Gloster Javelin FAW.1	WT830	
	Gloster Javelin FAW.1	WT836	
+	Gloster Javelin FAW.1	XA544	
	Gloster Javelin FAW.1	XA546	
	Gloster Meteor T.7	G-ANSO (G.5/1525)	
+	Gloster Meteor F.8	WA982 R-R Soars at wing tips	
+	Handley Page Victor B.1	WB775	
+	Hawker Hunter F.1	WT631	
+	Hawker Hunter F.2	WN909	
+	Hawker Hunter F.6	XF833	
+	Hawker Sea Hawk FB.3	WN107	
	Hunting Percival Provost T.1	WW393	
+	Hunting Percival Provost T.1	G-AMZM (P.56/20)	
	Hunting Percival Provost T.53	UB201 (PAC/F/180) for Burmese AF	
+	Hunting Percival Jet Provost T.1	XD674 (PAC/84/001)	
	Hunting Percival Pembroke C.1	WV733 (P.66/26)	
+	Hunting Percival Pembroke C.51	OT-ZAH (P.66/28)	
+	Saunders-Roe Skeeter 5	G-AMTZ (SR.907)	
+	Saunders-Roe Skeeter 6	G-ANMH (SR.905)	
+	Scottish Aviation Pioneer 2	G-ANRG (SAL/PP/105)	
+	Short Seamew AS.1	XA209 (SH.1606)	
+	Short Seamew AS.1	XA213 (SH.1607)	
+	Short Sherpa	G-14-1 (SH.1604)	
	Short SB.5	WG768 (SH.1605)	
	Supermarine Swift F.3	WK195	
+	Supermarine Swift F.3	WK247	
+	Supermarine Swift F.4	WK273	
+	Supermarine 525	VX138	
+	Vickers Valiant B.2	WJ954	
+	Vickers Varsity T.1	VX835 (502) Napier Elands	
+	Vickers Viscount 700	G-AMAV (3)	
+	Vickers Viscount 720	VH-TVA (44)	
	Westland Whirlwind HAR.1	XA871 (WA.17)	

Of true research aircraft this year there were only the Fairey F.D.1 and the Short Sherpa. The F.D.1 was the smallest aircraft at the Show and one of the most unusual ever shown. Fairey became interested in designing a small, vertically-launched fighter, largely for shipboard work and persisted in its development undeterred by the nasty history of a similar German attempt ten years previously, the Bachem Natter. As with the Miles M.52, current caution in official policy confined Fairey initially to a series of unmanned models. Experiments continued for some time, with varied success but were alarming enough to cause them to be transferred, first to a ship and later to the Woomera range in Australia. The design of the manned aircraft was very ingenious and a model had appeared at the previous Show, but problems were endless and when eventually official interest waned the F.D.1 was completed as a normal research aircraft on a conventional undercarriage.

Powered by a Derwent engine, it possessed a very small airframe with disproportionately large controls (a relic of its VTO youth) and sported a vestigial horizontal tailplane which was to have been removed when the aircraft was proven, but never was. Structural restrictions with the tail limited the speed severely, far below the 628 mph (1,011 k/h) calculated top speed at height. In the event, however, the F.D.1 did provide the company with a good deal of information for the design of the F.D.2. Not surprisingly, it shared with the P.111 the distinction of having the fastest landing speed at the Show and like the P.111 streamed a braking parachute.

The Short S.B.4 Sherpa bore the same relation to a proposed large bomber as did the Avro 707 and Handley Page H.P.88, but the Short proposal was a very advanced tail-less design incorporating rotating wing-tips for lateral and vertical control. Geoffrey Hill, collaborating with Shorts on the project, had much practical experience in both fields from his pre-war series of Pterodactyl aircraft, built by Westland. The wing-tip controls were exceedingly sensitive to wing twist at high speed, and to eliminate this Hill and Short's chief designer, David Keith-Lucas, evolved the ingenious "aero-isoclinic" wing, a structural concept that kept the angle of attack of a swept wing constant whatever the torsional load and eliminated buffet. Ingenious as it was, it remained experimental and the Short bomber was never built.

The Viscount appeared only on the civil day: a Series 720 for 53 passengers, with Dart 506s, which was about to be delivered to Trans-Australia Airlines as the first of their order. Viscounts had been very much in the news the preceding year, when Captain Baillie of British European Airways set a London-Melbourne record of 35 hours, 46 minutes and 47.6 seconds. This occurred between 8 and 10 October, in the course of the London-Christchurch air race, organised as part of the latter city's centenary celebrations. The speed section, incidentally, was won by a Canberra flown by Flt Lts R.L.E. Burton and D.H. Gannon, in an elapsed time of 23 hours, 50 minutes and 42 seconds over a distance of 11,792 miles (17,977.6 km).

There was little new among the helicopters and light aircraft, but in the trainer category was the smart maroon and white Boulton Paul Balliol 2 demonstrator, its civil C of A only a fortnight old. The Balliol had been around since 1948 and

it was now in Royal Air Force service, replacing the Harvard at No. 7 F.T.S. Balliol production for the RAF was cut back when official policy changed again, this time in favour of a jet-powered advanced trainer, which would be the Vampire T.11.

Another trainer, making its first appearance, in the hands of Dickie Wheldon, was the Hunting Percival Jet Provost, a company private venture in anticipation of a what they correctly saw coming as an official requirement. As in previous years on the Piston Provost, the pilot included a long, multi-turn spin in his sequence.

One event, not directly concerned with Farnborough, needs recording. On 3 August, Captain R.T.Shepherd had lifted three and a half tons of Thrust Measuring Rig off a runway under the power of two Rolls-Royce Nenes with their jet pipes combined into one vertical efflux. The Flying Bedstead had arrived and so had vertical take-off and landing. For the record, the American airscrew-driven Convair XFY-1, powered by an Allison YT-40 turboprop had actually made the first successful free vertical take-off two days earlier, but that particular concept turned out to be a blind alley.

The five Gloster Javelins comprised of the third, fourth and fifth prototypes plus the first and third production aircraft.

The Short Sherpa G-14-1 was built to test the company's isoclinic wing for its proposed P.D.1 bomber. The name is an acronym for Short & Harland Experimental and Research Prototype Aircraft.

The Airspeed Ambassador G-AKRD was a test-bed to gain experience with the Bristol Proteus 705 engines for production Bristol Britannia 100s.

The Supermarine 525 VX138, basically a swept wing version of the 508 but with conventional tail surfaces, led to the Scimitar.

FORTY YEARS

Gloster Meteor WA982 was used by Rolls-Royce as a test-bed for Soar engines, mounted on the wing tips.

The Fairey F.D.1 VX350 provided much data on the longitudinal and lateral stability and rolling performance of the broad delta shape, but was quite a handful in other than calm conditions.

Boulton Paul's civil Balliol demonstrator G-ANSF was finished in an attractive maroon and cream trim.

1955

THE SIXTEENTH SHOW
5-11 SEPTEMBER

The 1955 Show saw the initial presentation of the truly super-sonic English Electric P.1, the forerunner of the Lightning, which provided the first of a whole series of stunning perfor-mances by "Bea" Beamont, chief test pilot of the company.

Another newcomer was the "droop-snoot" Fairey F.D.2 research aircraft; a supersonic delta design that was later to recapture the World Absolute Speed Record for Britain. The Short Sperrin, now launched firmly on its useful, if unspec-tacular career of research, carried the big de Havilland Gyron, claimed to be the most powerful aero engine in the world, in one nacelle. Planned to provide the power for the Hawker P.1121 project, it was sacrificed with the aircraft to the unmitigated folly of the "no more manned fighters" ministerial decision. More significant, as it turned out, was the Avro Ashton flying with the first of the new, economic, by-pass engines, the Rolls-Royce Conway. Producing 13,000 lb (5,897 kg) thrust, the design reduced specific fuel consump-tion, surface temperature and noise, the latter greatly assisted by new tailpipe designs from Rolls-Royce.

"Sound and fury are a normal accompaniment of progress", said *The Aeroplane* in its pre-Show editorial, going on to point out that the by-pass engine gave a promise of more power for less noise. "Which", as the leader concluded, "should avoid fury".

In a light-hearted mood, and to the profound surprise of the assembled heads of A.V.Roe, "Roly" Falk rolled the second prototype Vulcan. The manoeuvre put considerable strain both on a number of the rivets on board and the pilot's relations with management. The name "Roly", incidentally, though causing confusion at the time, had nothing to do with this manoeuvre. The gallant Wing Commander had been christened Roland, that was all.

He was flying XA890, the silver-grey second production aircraft and after a dashing climbing turn on take-off, returned at 1,000 ft (305 m) to pull up into a climbing roll. He had intended to do this in 1954, but his chosen vehicle had been *accidenté* and was not available. But he took the Avon-powered prototype over the vertical and got a deal of stick for it.

There were to be no supersonic bangs at this, or any future Farnborough – at least, not intentionally. That brief flirtation with showmanship was over.

The number of exhibiting companies rose to 307, topping 300 for the first time. Reflecting this, the main exhibition hall had grown to 112,000 square feet (10,407 sq. m). Prices for entry on the public days remained unchanged.

The weather was generally good. The Prime Minister, Sir Anthony Eden, visited the Show. (His predecessor, Sir Win-ston Churchill, had resigned on 5 April, towards the end of the previous Administration.)

The SBAC moved into its new offices at 29 King Street, St James's, London SW1, where, in 1990, it still resided.

Once again, the Canberra was in the news, setting up several startling new records, this time between London and New York. On 23 August Johnny Hackett and Peter Money-penny of English Electric flew the 3,457.96 mile (5,565 km) distance in 7 hours, 29 minutes, 56.7 seconds at an average speed of 461.12 mph (742 k/h). The return trip took 6 hours 16 minutes, 59.5 seconds at an average speed of 550.35 mph (885.7 k/h) and, with a swift turn-round of some thirty minutes at Floyd Bennett Field, gave an out-and-back record time of 14 hours, 21 minutes, 45.4 seconds and an average speed over the distance of 481.52 mph (774.9 k/h).

On 29 August, Walter Gibb did it again, with the old height-record Olympus-engined Mk 2, setting a new altitude of 20,083 metres (65,876 ft) in Class C (Aeroplanes). Earlier in the year, on 28 June, S/Ldr (later Air Marshal Sir Ivor) Broom flew *Aries IV* of the Empire Air Navigation School from Ottawa to London, covering 3,330 miles (5,359 km) in 6 hours, 42 minutes.

The standard trick for cramming more aircraft into a dis-play of limited duration was used again and the Show opened with two circuses. Leading the first was the production pro-totype Ambassador, loaned the year before to Napier for flight trials with the 3,000 ehp N.El.1 Eland. Though owned by the Ministry of Supply, it was equipped to full BEA standards in case they needed another aircraft. The Eland, already flying in a Convair 340 and a Vickers Varsity, fitted neatly into the existing Centaurus bulkhead, making conversion easy and the pilot for the test programme, Captain Ron Gillman (who had survived a mid-air collision in cloud in another Ambas-sador), was convinced the conversion was worth while. It came too late in the aircraft's career to arouse interest, however and the airframe was restored subsequently to con-ventional piston power.

Other aircraft in the heavy circus included the Ashton, now

1955

+	Airspeed Ambassador	G-ALFR (65120) Napier Elands	
+	Auster Aiglet Trainer J/5L	G-ANXC (3135)	
+	Auster AOP.9	WZ715	
+	Avro Ashton 2	WB491 R-R Conway under fuselage	
+	Avro Shackleton MR.3	WR970	
+	Avro Vulcan B.1	XA890	
	Avro Canada CF-100-4B	18321 RCAF	
+	Avro Canada CF-100-4B	18322 RCAF	
	Blackburn Beverley C.1	XB263	
+	Bristol Britannia 100	G-ALBO (12873)	
+	Bristol 171 Mk.4	G-AMWI (13070)	
+	Bristol Sycamore HR.14	XJ364 (13241)	
+	Bristol 173 Mk.2	XH379 (12872)	
	de Havilland Chipmunk T.10	G-ALWB (C1/0100)	
+	de Havilland Comet 3	G-ANLO (06100)	
	de Havilland Dove 6	G-AMZN (04437)	
	de Havilland Heron 2	G-AMTS (14007)	
+	de Havilland Heron 2	G-ANCJ (14082)	
	de Havilland Sea Venom FAW.21	WW219	
	de Havilland Vampire T.11	XH276	
	de Havilland Venom FB.4	WR497	
+	de Havilland D.H.110	XF828	
+	de Havilland Canada Beaver 2	G-ANAR (80)	
+	English Electric Canberra B.2	WD952 Bristol Olympus	
	English Electric Canberra T.4	WT489	
+	English Electric Canberra B(I)8	WT328	
+	English Electric Canberra PR.9	WH793	
+	English Electric P.1	WG763	
	Fairey Gannet AS.1	XA349 (F.9241)	
+	Fairey Gannet T.2	XA522 (F.9342)	
+	Fairey Jet Gyrodyne	XJ389 (F.9420)	
	Fairey Ultra-light Helicopter	XJ924 (F.9423)	
	Fairey Ultra-light Helicopter	XJ930 (F.9425)	
+	Fairey F.D.2	WG774 (F.9421)	
+	Folland Gnat 1	G-39-2 (FL.2)	
	Gloster Javelin FAW.1	XA563	
	Gloster Javelin FAW.1	XA564	
+	Handley Page Herald	G-AODE (147)	
+	Handley Page Victor B.1	WB775	
	Hawker Hunter F.4	WT780	
+	Hawker Hunter F.4	WV385	
+	Hawker Hunter F.6	WW593	
+	Hawker Hunter Two-seater	XJ615	
	Hawker Sea Hawk FGA.4	XE443 (AW.6364)	
+	Hunting Percival Jet Provost T.2	XD694 (PAC/84/011)	
+	Hunting Percival Pembroke C.1	WV750 (P.66/60)	
	Hunting Percival Pembroke C.52	83012 (P.66/61) Swedish AF	
+	Hunting Percival Provost T.53	382 (PAC/F/387) Iraqi AF	
+	Saunders-Roe Skeeter 6	XK773 (SR.904)	
+	Scottish Aviation Pioneer 2	G-AODZ (SAL/PP/115)	
+	Scottish Aviation Twin Pioneer	G-ANTP (501)	
+	Short Seamew AS.1	XA213 (SH.1607)	
+	Short Seamew AS.1	XE171 (SH.1775)	
+	Short Seamew AS.2	XA209 (SH.1606)	
+	Short Seamew AS.2	XE172 (SH.1776)	
+	Short Sperrin	VX158 (SH.1600) D.H. Gyron lower port nacelle	
+	Supermarine Swift FR.5	XD904	
	Supermarine Swift FR.5	XD905	
+	Vickers Valiant B.1	WZ365	
+	Vickers Viscount 724	CF-TGV (59)	
+	Westland Widgeon	G-ALIK (WA/H/3)	
+	Westland Whirlwind HAR.5	XJ396 (WA.60)	

Services participation in flying programme:
Hawker Hunter, four from 54 Squadron, aerobatic team.
Hawker Hunter: four formations of 16.
Vickers Valiant: twelve in six pairs

carrying the new Rolls-Royce Conway under its stomach, the Gannet T.2 trainer, displaying remarkable climbing powers and the Short Sperrin, with what one presumes to be No.2 engine position (that is, the lower berth on the port side), now occupied by the imposing bulk of the 15,000 lb thrust de Havilland Gyron and giving very nearly twice as much thrust available on one side as on the other. The Sperrin aborted its take-off on Monday and did not display that day.

In the second, less-heavy circus was Dickie Wheldon with the Provost T.53, which was the version for the Iraqi Air Force. Armed with two machine guns and underwing stores it had some claim to be one of the very first trainer-cum-light-attack types that would in later years form such a considerable part of the Farnborough Display. Also present was Ranald Porteous in the Auster AOP.9 (he substituted the civil Aiglet Trainer on public days), the Scottish Aviation Pioneer, vying with the Auster for STOL honours, a production Hunting Percival Pembroke C.1, and the de Havilland Heron 2, cruising by comfortably on the port two as though it were a Dove.

Following a lead given previously by Gloster with their five Javelins, Shorts were represented by no less than four Seamews, in an inter-Service formation that culminated in a climbing, rolling break with number four, in the box, completing a loop. The prototype and first production aircraft represented Coastal Command and the second prototype and fourth production aircraft, the Fleet Air Arm.

Another circus was composed of civil aircraft; Twin Pioneer and Handley Page Herald – both newcomers – Viscount and Britannia. The last-named was an old friend, G-ALBO, first prototype, standing in for one of the first three production aircraft, which were busy on trials. The Viscount, a Type 724, was the fourteenth of the fleet ordered by Trans-Canada Airways and a scoreboard by the aircraft in the Static Park announced the state of play on orders. On Monday it stood at 234; KLM had just ordered twelve and the first of 60 for Capital Airlines in the United States had been delivered on 17 May.

The Scottish Aviation Twin Pioneer, referred to by one of

The Folland Gnat G-39-2 made its first Farnborough appearance – Midge G-39-1 had been shown in 1954.

the lesser Press rather obviously as the Double Scotch, but to be known affectionately by the squadrons that flew it as the Twin Pin, was a logical development from the Pioneer. It first flew, in 16-seat civil guise, on 25 June 1955 and was ordered by the Royal Air Force, already familiar with the performance of the single engined aircraft, but in view of the fact that four of the five squadrons that eventually used it were to operate in Aden, Kenya and the Far East, it would undoubtedly have benefited from a more powerful engine.

Another brand-new prototype on display for the first time was the Fairey F.D.2, which was to have a fairly long and useful career. Its importance, historically, lay in being the first practical proof that the Ministry of Supply now recognized, very late in the day, that its policies had put Britain at considerable disadvantage in supersonic research. Two companies, English Electric and Fairey, responded to E.R.103, calling for a supersonic research aircraft and by coincidence, both were flying at Farnborough in 1955 as the P.1 and F.D.2. The former was twin-engined and the prototype for a new fighter; the latter purely for research and powered by a single Avon. In a later, developed version, it provided useful data in the Concorde programme. Like its tiny stable-mate the F.D.1, it landed very fast and required the services of a cluster of braking parachutes.

The new, nose-wheel Shackleton M.R.3, held improved anti-submarine equipment and had a patrol capability of 18 hours. Eight were sold to the South African Air Force. At one time it was proposed to re-engine the Shackleton with Napier Nomads and a Mk 1 was actually converted to take two in

the outer nacelles, but did not fly. The prototype Mk 3, piloted by Johnny Baker, had only flown for the first time on the Friday before the Show.

The Orpheus-powered Gnat, elegantly attired in pale blue and recovered from recent trim problems, put up one of the best solo displays of the week in the hands of Ted Tennant; among its less orthodox features were inboard ailerons doubling as flaps. The Jet Provost now carried its definitive short undercarriage and hydraulic systems and once more, all three V-bombers appeared. The Valiant was sporting the huge underwing fuel tanks fitted for the London-Christchurch air race, the Victor was painted a dashing sky blue.

The appearance of the Swift as the FR.5 marked its Service rehabilitation. Serving in the (very) low-level reconnaissance role at very high speeds, Nos 2 and 79 Squadrons in West Germany, paid for their dedication to this ultra-demanding task with 13 aircraft lost out of the 64 issued to them. The attrition problem of very fast, very low-level training was to remain an acute one for Strike Command.

Bill Bedford demonstrated the pale green two-seat Hunter, an aircraft which was to become one of the Farnborough favourites, but honour for the most sensational, skilful and polished displays yet seen at the Show, went however to Jan Zurakowski.

Like Bill Waterton of Gloster, "Zura" had gone to work for Avro Canada. Waterton had test-flown the original, Avon-powered CF-100 Canuck, a massive twin-engined fighter designed for Arctic defence and "Zura" the first Avro Orenda-powered one. Now he was flying it at Farnborough – a very different mount from the lively P.V.Meteor in which he had last appeared. The Show aircraft was one of three CF-100 4B sent over for British evaluation.

Scottish Aviation's Pioneer G-AODZ in a typical pose above the runway.

The highly polished Scottish Aviation Twin Pioneer G-ANTP complete with St Andrew's Cross on the central fin. Note the large flaps.

The elegant shape of the Airspeed Ambassador G-ALFR used as a test-bed for the neatly cowled Napier Eland turboprops.

The empty weight of this 52 ft (16 m) span beast was 35,500 lb (16,102.45 kg); he rolled it vertically, pushed it round a half-outside loop from the inverted (Waterton had done that, too, in a Javelin) and in a final supreme demonstration of skill, brought it down in a long falling leaf – a manoeuvre consisting of a series of left-and-right incipient spins and one that very few pilots would tackle confidently today, even in a Tiger Moth.

The Royal Air Force were at Farnborough this year in some strength, outnumbering display aircraft by some margin. Their proceedings opened with a display of formation aerobatics, which included formation changes during manoeuvres, from the well-known four aircraft of No.54 Squadron, who had exchanged the Vampires of their previous Farnborough display for Hunters and were led this year by Captain Irving, who was on an exchange posting from the United States Air Force.

The second item was a fly-past by 64 Hunters of all fighter Marks, in "box fours of four" from eight of the 15 squadrons then equipped with the type. After them came six "squadron pairs" of Valiants from six squadrons in a less dashing and more widely-spaced procession. This demonstration of the new striking power of the Royal Air Force was a stirring sight and the Service content of the Shows was to remain high for many years to come.

The Fairey F.D.2 WG774, a supersonic research aircraft which, six months later, established a world speed record of 1,132 mph – 310 mph above the previous record.

The Saunders-Roe Skeeter 6 XK773 undertook trials with the Central Flying School at South Cerney in late summer and appeared at Farnborough in this silver scheme with yellow training band.

The only Avro Ashton 2, WB491, as a test-bed for the underslung Rolls-Royce Conway engine intended for BOAC's Boeing 707-420s.

1956

THE SEVENTEENTH SHOW
3-9 SEPTEMBER

On 10 March, the World Absolute Speed Record returned to the United Kingdom, with Peter Twiss flying the Fairey F.D.2 – or Delta Two, as it was usually called, over a course between Ford and Chichester. The record was interesting for several reasons. It was the first set under the new rules of the *FAI* which allowed records in this category at altitude, over a 15-25 km (9.32-15.53 miles) course; it drove the record up by a convincing 498.7 km/h (310.7 mph) and it was the last time the record was ever held in British hands and it gave us the Triple Crown, holding the speed records on land, sea and in the air – a unique performance. The average speed homologated over two runs in opposite directions came out at 1,822 km/h (1,132 mph). Speed records had been falling fast in those days, but this one did not return to the custody of the United States of America until 21 months later. The attempt was not just for publicity, but formed a serious part of the collecting and collating of information on supersonic flight.

The weather frogs got it totally wrong again and the first week in September, allegedly the best time of the year on average, turned out to be about the worst, with heavy rain for most of the Show and bitterly cold. The Show went on, nevertheless, and with the best test pilots in the world and probably the best air traffic controllers, the weather had little effect, except on attendance figures, which dropped sharply on the public days. Prices remained unchanged, a wistful reminder in these inflated days of the stability of the economy in the mid-fifties.

Following in the wake of First Secretary Nikita Khrushchev's U.K. visit in April (when another Soviet visitor was Andrei Tupolev), there was a heavy Soviet presence at Farnborough, with civil and military missions headed respectively by P.V.Dementjev, Minister for the Aircraft Industry and Chief Marshal of Aviation P.F.Zhigarev, Commander-in-Chief of the Soviet Air Force. In the other direction, the British Secretary of State for Air, Neville Birch, had been flown to the Soviet Air Force Day on 24 June at Tushino, in a Comet T.1 of No.216 Squadron of Transport Command. (*The* Comet T.1, in fact; the first aircraft, and only T.1, received by the unit, it was used for crew training, all the other 14 Comets eventually taken on charge being C.1s.)

There was one major change in the layout of the Exhibition. This year, four permanent terraces were built along the face of the famous hill that has been such a blessing to Farnborough by giving everyone a good view of the flying. Their purpose was to give a decent anchorage to the 140 entertainment complexes set up this year by exhibitors, and good, all-weather access – just as well, in the circumstances. Thus were born the now-familiar chalet rows.

For the main exhibition hall, 13 miles of standard width, blue and white canvas were required to cover the 113,000 square feet (10,498 sq.m) of its floor. It was now the largest single tented structure in the world.

The Flying Display ran its own preview this year, with a solitary performance by an Armstrong Whitworth-built Hunter 5 (WN960) before the Show opened. All Mk 5s, like the Mk 2s, were built by Armstrong Whitworth Aircraft and both marks had Armstrong Siddeley Sapphire engines. They equipped five squadrons from 1955 until 1958.

The Javelin, having first flown two years previously, was now on the line, as the first delta and the first dedicated all-weather fighter to enter Royal Air Force service. It had powered ailerons and power-assisted tail controls, reached 40,000 ft (12,192 m) in half the time of the Meteor it replaced and was designed to fight at 50,000 ft (15,850 m). The 40 built equipped No. 46 Squadron (from 29 February) and, later, No. 87 in West Germany. The three Javelins flown at Farnborough marked further development of the basic type. One was the trainer T.3, flown by Geoff Worrall, with a revised canopy – the instructor sitting high on his ejection seat, to see over the pupil's head (a very early application of this layout) and having sighting periscopes on either flank for weapon instruction on the 30 mm Adens. First flight had been only eight days before the Show, by Zurakowski, who got around.

One of the others, flown by Peter Varley, was a production Mk 4, with an all-flying tail, which finished up at the Central Fighter Establishment at West Raynham. The other, recorded as a Mk 7, was in fact a Mk 2, but carried the Sapphire Sa.7s of 11,000 lb (4,990 kg) thrust (and consequently the bigger intakes and tail pipes) of the Mk 7 and the flying control system of the Mk 8. Later in its career this rather bewildered airframe turned up at Boscombe Down painted bright orange all over.

The Rolls-Royce reverse thrust test-bed Hunter was the prototype aircraft of its mark, built round the middle portion of

1956

	Auster Agricola	ZK-BMK (B.103)
+	Auster Alpine J/5R	G-ANXC (3135)
	Auster AOP.9	XK417
+	Avro Lincoln B.2	G-37-1 R-R Tyne in nose
+	Avro Vulcan B.1	XA892
+	Blackburn Beverley C.1	XB289
+	Bristol Britannia 101	G-ALBO (12873) Bristol Proteus and Orion test-bed
	Bristol Britannia 301	G-ANCA (12907)
+	Bristol 171 Mk.4	G-AMWI (13070)
+	Bristol 173 Mk.2	XH379 (12872)
	de Havilland Comet C.2	XK695 (06030)
	de Havilland Dove 6	G-AMZN (04437)
+	de Havilland Heron 2	393 (14105) Iraqi AF
	de Havilland Sea Venom FAW.21	XG671
	de Havilland Vampire T.11	XK627
	de Havilland Venom NF.3	WX931
+	de Havilland D.H.110	XF828
+	English Electric Canberra B.2	WD930 R-R Avon RA.29 test-bed
	English Electric Canberra B.2	WJ582
+	English Electric Canberra B.2	WK163 Napier Scorpion rocket in bomb bay
	English Electric Canberra B(I)8	XK951
+	English Electric Canberra PR.9	WH793
	Fairey Firefly U.9	WB257 (F.8483)
	Fairey Gannet AS.4	XA425 (F.9295)
+	Fairey Gannet AS.4	XA426 (F.9296)
+	Fairey Ultra-light Helicopter	G-AOUK (F.9426)
+	Fairey F.D.2	WG774 (F.9421)
+	Fairey F.D.2	WG777 (F.9422)
+	Folland Gnat F.1	XK724 (FL.2)
+	Gloster Javelin T.3	WT841
	Gloster Javelin FAW.4	XA764
+	Gloster Javelin FAW.7	XA778
+	Handley Page Herald	G-AODF (148)
+	Handley Page Victor B.1	XA917
+	Hawker Hunter F.4	XF310
+	Hawker Hunter F.6	XG128
+	Hawker Hunter F.6	XG129
+	Hawker Hunter F.6	XF833 R-R Avon with reverse thrust
	Hawker Hunter FGA.6	XG131
+	Hawker Hunter T.7	XJ615
+	Hawker Sea Hawk FGA.6	XE456
+	Hunting Percival Jet Provost T.2	XD694 (PAC/84/01)
	Hunting Percival Jet Provost T.2	G-23-1 (PAC/84/013)
+	Hunting Percival Pembroke C.1	XK884 (P.66/82)
+	Hunting Percival President	G-AOJG (P.66/79)
+	Saunders-Roe Skeeter 5	G-ANMI (SR.906)
+	Saunders-Roe Skeeter T.11	XK479 (S2/3012)
+	Scottish Aviation Pioneer CC.1	XL664 (SAL/PP/135)
+	Scottish Aviation Twin Pioneer	G-AOEN (502)
	Scottish Aviation Twin Pioneer	G-AOEO (503)
	Short Seamew AS.1	XE174 (SH.1778)
+	Short Sperrin	VX158 (SH.1600) D.H. Gyron in each lower nacelle
	Supermarine Swift FR.5	WK296
+	Supermarine Swift FR.7	XF113
	Supermarine N.113 (Scimitar)	WT854
+	Supermarine N.113 (Scimitar)	WT859
+	Vickers Valiant 1	WB215 D.H. Super Sprite rockets under wings
+	Vickers Viscount 802	G-AOJA (150)
+	Westland Whirlwind HAR.5	XJ396 (WA.60)
+	Westland Widgeon	G-AKTW (WA/H/001)
+	Westland Widgeon	G-ALIK (WA/H/3)

Service participation in flying programme:

Hawker Hunter: four from 43 Squadron, aerobatic team.
English Electric Canberra: four from 231 OCU, formation team.

the abandoned supersonic P.1083; installation of the reverse thrust equipment was done by Miles Aircraft. The two-seat T.7 was on one occasion flown by Lieutenant General Alexei Blagoveschensky, chief test pilot to the Soviet Air Force.

Canberras there were, in profusion; five altogether. (The 500th built, an export B(I)8, had been completed in August.) Two were test-beds; one modified to carry the Napier Double Scorpion rocket motor in the bomb bay. The second was an elderly B.2, carrying an Avon RA 29 in the port nacelle, a reminder of the days in 1951 when only the Canberra could undertake really high altitude work and when a large number of production aircraft seemed to be poached by Ministries and various research establishments.

The high altitude performance of the Canberra facilitated testing of rocket engines, which operated most happily at high altitude and the rocket boosted the aircraft's ceiling considerably. It was a Scorpion-powered Canberra that later took part in the upper-air sampling after the British atomic tests on 11 October. Talking of such things as test-beds, this year saw

the final appearance of the venerable Lincoln in the flying display, carrying the 4,500 hp Rolls-Royce Tyne intended for the Vickers Vanguard. Bearing the maker's B class registration G-37-1, it was in fact RF533 of the RAE, beefed-up for the nose-mounted Tyne. Upon the solitary power of this formidable proboscis it went howling past with the four Merlins feathered. It was not the final appearance of the Lincoln at the Show, however, for RF402 turned up in the Static Park three years later bearing the Napier de-icing rig and civil marks.

The Swift was a production Mk 5, carrying the big ventral fuel tank which had been tested on the prototype and with the wing fences and cranked, saw-tooth leading edge that dramatically improved its flying characteristics. The Valiant, WB215, was the second prototype, now fitted with de Havilland Super Sprite high-test peroxide motors intended considerably to improve take-off performance. Nothing came of the scheme, which was never officially adopted, but the Valiant force had a busy year, with a No.49 Squadron aircraft

A view from the aircraft park plus Short's Sperrin with D.H. Gyron engines in each lower nacelle. In the foreground D.H. Vampire T.11 XK627, Short Seamew XE174 and Hunting Percival Jet Provost G-23-1.

dropping the first British atom bomb (on Australia) and becoming the first and (until the Falklands and Operation Black Buck) only V-bomber to drop bombs in anger, during the Suez campaign. Four squadrons, one from Wittering (No.138) and three from Marham (Nos 148, 207 and 214), being involved in this last effort.

Supermarine also provided the only really new military aeroplane at the Show. This was the N.113, later to be named Scimitar, with the Supermarine Type number 544. Both first and second prototypes were there, the former with anhedral tailplane as on production aircraft, the latter with dihedral. It was the largest, heaviest, most powerful (and noisiest) fighter the Royal Navy had yet acquired and the first that could carry out a nuclear strike. It was also, sadly, the last aircraft to carry the Supermarine name, which had dated from 1913 but was about to vanish in the Vickers empire of which it was a part.

The prototype Britannia, good old G-ALBO, was back, this time wearing Proteus 705s in the inner nacelles, a Proteus 755 at number one and an Orion at number four, which must have made servicing a bit of a nightmare. The prototype long-fuselage Britannia 301 represented future production, which had been set back by a recurrence of icing problems encountered during tests in the inter-tropical front.

The Sperrin first prototype, which had displayed with one de Havilland Gyron in 1955, now turned up (for the last time) carrying two, one in each of the lower berths of the over-and-under nacelles. The Gyron programme winding up in 1957, the Sperrin languished at its Hatfield base until finally scrapped.

Bristol Britannia G-ALBO with its inboard Bristol Proteus 705s stopped. The working engines are a Proteus 755 and Bristol Orion.

The Skeeter 5 was now carrying a kind of bowler hat on its head full of liquid rocket fuel for tip mounted propulsion nozzles. Bristol's Type 173 was the second prototype, the Mk 2, now fitted with a tailplane with endplate fins. This was the aircraft which had appeared at previous Farnboroughs, briefly with stub wings, then with upswept tailplane to meet a naval interest that later expired, and it was currently on loan to British European Airways Helicopter Unit for operational trials. It carried BEA markings and was named *Sir Bors*, but retained Royal Air Force markings as XH379. Very confusing.

Conspicuous by its absence was the English Electric P.1., the aircraft being fully committed to a demanding test programme since its Farnborough appearance the previous year.

Two Royal Air Force formation display teams assisted at the Display, one with four Canberra T.4s from the OCU and the official Hunter aerobatic team from No. 43 Squadron, led by F/Lt P.E.Bairsto.

Avro Lincoln G-37-1, test-bed for the nose-mounted Rolls-Royce Tyne, flies past on Tyne power only.

Troops boarding the Blackburn Beverley XB289 prior to its demonstration.

First flown a few weeks before the Show, Hawker Hunter XG131 was fitted experimentally with wing tip tanks.

The Vickers Valiant WB215 gets away smartly with the aid of de Havilland Super Sprite rockets.

1957

THE EIGHTEENTH SHOW
2-9 SEPTEMBER

For the 1957 SBAC Show, apart from drizzle and cloud down on the Hog's Back on Monday morning, there was good weather through the week. Once again there was no increase in prices for admission on the public days. The exhibition area was enlarged to 125,400 square feet (11,165 sq.m) and the trade enclosures – as they were referred to at the time – were now four neat rows of identical chalets on the forward slopes of the hill.

The intrusion upon the scene of the guided missile had made a most unfortunate impact upon the minds of Her Majesty's Ministers – well, one of them at any rate. Under the influence of these new toys Mr Duncan Sandys announced, through the White Paper on Defence, published in April, that no more manned fighters were to be ordered after the Lightning. The asserted dominance of the missile in defence, according to this document, had made fighters obsolete.

The possible effect of this decision upon the future of one of the most successful and flourishing industries in Britain, with exports in 1956 running at over £100 million, may be imagined. The Lightning scraped into existence by the skin of its teeth (it had already had one interesting moment in its career when the restless Mr Petter resigned and went off to fresh woods at Folland). That was back in 1950; Freddy Page took the project triumphantly into reality, a task for which he has never properly been acclaimed. Both the Canberra and the Vulcan were threatened (there were to be no more strategic bombers after the V-bombers) and among many promising projects that went down was the Hawker P.1121 supersonic strike aircraft (to be called the Hurricane), taking with it the de Havilland Gyron engine.

There *was* considerable sense, in a European scenario, in eschewing further expensive squadrons of the increasingly vulnerable high altitude sub-sonic bombers; the French government had made the decision to abandon the bomber as such, but encouraged what was to become a whole family of brilliant strike aircraft from Dassault. In Britain, as a result of Mr Sandys' sweeping decision, there appeared to be no future for the military design teams at all. As one result, it may be noted that there has been no British-designed fighter since the Lightning (the Harrier is really a special case) and in 1988 the United Kingdom was largely defended by the American Phantom. Even the Anglo-French Jaguar is basically a Breguet design.

As late as 1970, the President of the Society, Mr J.H.S.Green, was to refer to the White Paper as "the most calamitous document that was ever published".

On the civil side, the Viscount was selling well, and had got a firm grip on the American market, but the initial ill luck of the Comet had spoiled its chances and there was still a regrettable tendency for the Corporations always to be changing their minds and delaying decisions. The Vickers V.1000, a long range project that could have been competitive in the world market, had Government support withdrawn. Many years later another administration, "warring on another day", tried to keep British Aerospace out of the early Airbus programme. Ah, well, hindsight is a great thing.

During the Show, the announcement of a large Indian order for the Hunter was made.

This was another year when Services participation was to be on the grand scale – indeed, with 93 aircraft it was the largest yet.

Among the new aircraft, the Scimitar and Wessex were destined to see service with the Royal Navy, the latter in some strength. The English Electric P.1B would become the Lightning, and the Gnat, in two-seater from, would serve the Royal Air Force as a trainer and, thanks to the Red Arrows, become one of its best-known aircraft.

The Wessex, flown by "Slim" Sear, was of particular interest in being the first production helicopter in the world powered by a free gas turbine (a Napier Gazelle), on which it went "hissing quietly past....at something like 150 mph" (242 k/h), to quote the Press. The first helicopter for the Fleet Air Arm designed from the start for anti-submarine warfare, it would replace the faithful Whirlwind in three major versions, serving eventually with 18 squadrons. The design was based on the Sikorsky S-58.

The Saunders-Roe SR.53 produced a moment of drama when, shortly after take-off, a light came on in the cockpit to indicate a fire in the engine bay. Morally convinced that it was just a fault in the wiring, John Booth executed a calm but early return to earth.

Miles Aircraft showed their novel jet trainer Student and, in conjunction with the French company Hurel-Dubois, the H.D.M. 105. The company had ceased trading as aircraft constructors in 1947 and the appearance of the Student marked a welcome return of the two gifted brothers. Intended as a better, cheaper and more economical alternative to the Jet Provost, by the time the firm's limited resources at Shoreham allowed completion of a prototype in 1957, the challenge was too late. Duncan McIntosh demonstrated the crisp handling of this delightful aeroplane, flying it for some reason from the right hand seat. It still existed in 1988 and nearly got back into the Farnborough Show.

The H.D.M. 105 was a research aircraft intended to explore the very high-aspect ratio wing as a means of balancing induced drag against structure weight (the very opposite to normal Miles practice). It first flew on 31 March 1957, but had only a brief career, being scrapped after a crash on 28 June the following year. It had a startling performance on its two 155 hp Blackburn Cirrus Majors and Ian Forbes delighted in taking off within the confines of the concrete apron in front of the classic Shoreham control tower. One has a vivid recollection of being shown steep turns into a dead engine at what seemed to be extremely low altitude, the closeness of the grass emphasised by the incredibly long and narrow wing.

The Aviation Traders (Engineering) Ltd Accountant marked that organisation's first and last venture into independent aircraft design, intended to fill a perceived gap in the obviously popular turboprop market. It arrived at Farnborough on its two R.Da.6 Dart 540s with only 15 hours flying since its first flight on 9 July. Apart from being offered as a "DC-3 replacement" (everybody had one in the cupboard in those days), much was hoped for in the American executive market. But nothing came of it and its first appearance was also its last, causing Chris Wren, a little unkindly, perhaps, to suggest that the second prototype should be called the Auditor and the third the Receiver.

With great enthusiasm, "Bea" Beamont, Peter Hillwood and Desmond de Villiers flew both the Sapphire-powered P.1A and Avon-powered P.1B turning in some beautiful flying and pulling 6G on the turns to stay in the arena. The P.1A flew only on Monday, leaving the rest of the week to what was effectively the Lightning prototype. Runs were carefully planned for M:0.98, to avoid the now forbidden sonic boom, but it was difficult to be so precise in practice and many claimed to have heard, if not a bang, at least a premonitory cough.

Besides the 30 Royal Air Force squadrons equipped at the beginning of the year (of which ten fell victim to the run-down of Bomber Command), the Canberra was being delivered to South America, and now India had ordered 80, the largest export order ever received. With the coming into service of the new medium V-bombers, production of basic Canberras for the Royal Air Force had ceased, and the B(I)8 represented the surviving operational role, apart from photo-reconnaissance. Another Canberra at the Show carried the Napier Double-Scorpion. This last, mounted in the capacious bomb-bay, had enabled Michael Randrup and Walter Shirley to regain the Aeroplane Altitude Record for Britain on 29

August at 21,430 metres (70,470.4 ft), beating the two-year old previous Canberra record by 1,347 metres (4,419.29 ft). Ten days previously, in a U.S.Army balloon, Major David G.Simons, USA, had taken the Absolute Height Record to 30,942 metres (101,515.75 ft).

The Hunter team presentation consisted of Duncan Simpson, Hugh Merewether, Frank Bullen and David Lockspeiser. Duncan flew a Mk 4 with Fireflash missiles, the others Mk 6s; the Swiss demonstrator, now with the saw-tooth leading edge and clutching two 100 gallon (454.6 litre) and two 230 gallon (1,045.57 litre) drop tanks; one with Firestreak and nose-mounted AI radar; and one with saw-tooth and 36 25 lb (11.34 kg) rockets in triple tier mountings. Bill Bedford was in the Mk 7 two-seater, complete with saw-tooth, the big Avon 200 and flying tailplane. On Tuesday he had a flying canopy, too, when it came off during his take-off run and he had to transfer to another aircraft.

Rolls-Royce sponsored a Mk 6 with reheat and thrust reversal, and completing the Royal Air Force side of the solo demonstrations was Dick Rumbelow in the Jet Provost T.2, now flying with 50 gallon (227.3 litre) tip tanks and a one-piece canopy, though no ejection seats, as the Mk 3 development aircraft.

Participation by the Service itself in 1957 was spectacular. In addition to the two pairs of Valiant B.1 and Vulcan B.1 representing Bomber Command, there were 27 Javelins from Nos 46, 23 and 141 Squadrons and 27 Hunter 6s from Nos 1, 43 and 34 Squadrons, the latter whistling past at 1,000 ft (304.8 m) and 400 knots (741 k/h). Vapour trails from over fifty exercising Valiants and Canberras at high altitude trellised the sky and, on most days, made an impressive backdrop.

Of the two Valiants, at lead and in the box in the all-white fly-past, one was the 49 Squadron aircraft that had dropped the British hydrogen bomb near Christmas Island. Production of the Valiant had ceased on 27 August and the last aircraft to leave Brooklands was flown out by chief test pilot "Jock" Bryce and his deputy, Brian Trubshaw. Among the crew was Basil Stephenson, the company's chief designer, aircraft. All production Valiants flew out of Brooklands after a sacriligious chunk of the Byfleet banking had been torn from the *voie sacrée* to make room for them.

The Central Flying School contributed its aerobatic team of four Provost T.1s, the "Sparrows", led by F/Lt J.H.Kingsbury; but the high point of the entire Display was provided by the glossy black Hunters of No. 111 Squadron. They had adopted this colour scheme in April that year. Under the inspiration of their leader, S/Ldr Roger Topp and his successor, S/Ldr "Prolific" Pete Latham, the Black Arrows achieved and maintained a standard of excellence that has caused those who came after to labour mightily "to keep the image bright"

1957

Auster Atlantic	G-APHT (3447) fuselage only	
+ Aviation Traders Accountant	G-ATEL (ATL.90)	
Avro Shackleton MR.3	WR977	
+ Avro Vulcan 1	VX770 R-R Conways	
+ Avro Vulcan B.1	XA889	
+ Avro Vulcan B.2	VX777	
Blackburn Beverley C.1	XB262	
Bristol Britannia 101	G-ALBO (12873) Bristol Proteus and Orion test-bed	
+ Bristol Britannia 301	G-ANCA (12907)	
Bristol Britannia 313	4X-AGB (13233)	
Bristol Sycamore 4	G-AMWI (13070)	
Bristol 173	VF785 (12871)	
+ de Havilland Comet 3	G-ANLO (06100)	
de Havilland Dove 6	G-AMZN (04437)	
de Havilland Heron 2D	G-APEV (14125)	
+ de Havilland Sea Vixen FAW.1	XJ475 (10002)	
de Havilland Vampire T.55	L160 (15802) Lebanese AF	
+ English Electric Canberra 1	VN813 R-R Nene, D.H. Gyron Junior in port nacelle	
+ English Electric Canberra B.2	WF909 D.H. Spectre in bomb bay	
+ English Electric Canberra B.2	WH713 Bristol Olympus with silencers	
+ English Electric Canberra B.2	WK163 Napier Scorpion rocket in bomb bay	
+ English Electric Canberra B(I)8	XH234	
+ English Electric P.1A	WG760	
+ English Electric P.1B	XA847 (95004)	
Fairey Firefly U.9	VT413 (F.8313)	
Fairey Gannet AS.4	XG787 (F.9355) RAN	
+ Fairey Gannet T.5	XG889 (F.9418)	
+ Fairey Ultra-light Helicopter	G-AOUJ (F.9424)	
+ Fairey Ultra-light Helicopter	G-AOUK (F.9426)	
+ Fairey F.D.2	WG774 (F.9421)	
+ Folland Gnat F.1	XK740 (FL.4)	
Folland Gnat F.1	GN101 (FL.8) Finnish AF	
Gloster Javelin T.3	WT841	
+ Gloster Javelin FAW.7	XH710	
Gloster Javelin FAW.7	XH714	
+ Handley Page Herald	G-AODF (148)	
+ Handley Page Victor B.1	XA918	
+ Hawker Hunter F.4	XF310	
+ Hawker Hunter F.6	XE587	
+ Hawker Hunter F.6	XF378	
+ Hawker Hunter F.6	XK147	

+ Hawker Hunter F.6	XK148	
+ Hawker Hunter F.6	XF833 R-R Avon with reverse thrust	
+ Hawker Hunter T.7	XJ615	
+ Hawker Hunter T.7	XJ627	
Hunting Percival Jet Provost T.2	G-AOUS (P.84/14)	
Hunting Percival Jet Provost T.2	G-23-1 (P.84/13)	
+ Hunting Percival Pembroke C.1	XL930 (P.66/92)	
Hunting Percival Pembroke C.54	AS-554 (P.66/96) Luftwaffe	
Hunting Percival President	G-AOJG (P.66/79)	
+ Miles Student	G-35-4 (1008)	
+ Miles HDM 105	G-AHDM (105/1009)	
+ Saunders-Roe Skeeter 6	G-AMTZ (SR.907)	
+ Saunders-Roe Skeeter 10P.10	XK773 (SR.904)	
+ Saunders-Roe SR.53	XD145	
Saunders-Roe SR.53	XD151	
Scottish Aviation Pioneer CC.1	XL666 (137)	
+ Scottish Aviation Twin Pioneer	G-AOEO (503)	
Scottish Aviation Twin Pioneer CC.1	XL966 (514)	
+ Sikorsky S-58	XL722 (58-265) for Wessex development	
+ Supermarine Scimitar F.1	XD218	
Vickers Valiant B.1	XD875	
Vickers Viscount 803	PH-VID (175)	
+ Westland Widgeon	G-AKTW (WA/H/001)	
+ Westland Whirlwind 2	G-AOCZ (WA/H/115)	
+ Westland Whirlwind HAS.7	XK941 (WA.168)	

Services participation in flying programme:
Avro Vulcan: two in fly-past.
Fairey Gannet: twelve in fly-past.
Gloster Javelin: 27 in fly-past.
Hawker Sea Hawk: five in RN aerobatic team plus one individual aerobatics.
Hawker Hunter: nine in 111 Squadron "Black Arrows" aerobatic team plus 27 in fly-past.
Hunting Percival Provost: four in CFS aerobatic team.
Vickers Valiant: two in fly-past.
Westland Whirlwind: four in RN demonstration team.

as the Commandant of the CFS once put it.

On this occasion, a "diamond nine" was looped and rolled for the first time, the main team of five subsequently going through seven formation changes in six minutes. Smoke for the final break came, not from exhaust injection, but from underwing tanks.

Not to be outdone, the Royal Navy presented their own show-within-a-show and were, very properly, the first Service item. Five scarlet Sea Hawks of No. 738 Training Squadron, led by a remarkable gentleman called "Spiv" Leahy, and calling themselves the Red Devils, put up a classic display, assisted by a camouflaged solo aircraft.

There was also a formation fly-past by twelve Gannets, in the shape of a naval anchor (not an Admiralty one; the "foul-

ing" was presumably too difficult to do). They were drawn from Nos 737, 796 and 825 Squadrons. No.737 had once rejoiced in the sounding title of Amphibious Bomber Reconnaissance Training Squadron, teaching people to fly Walruses off ships' catapults, but finding there was "not much call for that sort of thing", went on to other pastures. No.796, operating as the Observer and Air Signaller School at Culdrose, also used Sea Balliols, while No. 825 – the oldest of the three, having started in 1934, had spent much of its recent history being disbanded and reformed every two years, which must have been confusing.

The Navy also provided teams of Whirlwinds: two HAS.22s and three HAS.5s. Among naval items in the main, or industrial programme, the de Havilland Sea Vixen and Scimitar

1957

Hunting Percival Jet Provosts G-AOUS and G-23-1 on their way to the Show.

appeared, the former with some spectacular high and low speed runs and flexing its power-folding wings during the taxy. It also deployed a retractable ram air auxiliary turbine, cooked up by Plessey to supply emergency hydraulic power – which was different. The Scimitar carried four under-wing fuel tanks.

On the civil side, de Havilland's John Cunningham and Peter Bugge flew the Comet 3, first seen in 1955, with silenced Avon RA.29s and basically a prototype for the Mk 4, while Bristol deployed the test-bed prototype Britannia again with the Proteus 705 (for the BOAC Mk 102), the Proteus 755 (for the Mk 300/310) and an Orion for good measure. That was on trade days, touring in from its work place at Filton; on public days it was replaced by the stretched and developed Mk 301.

The Aviation Traders Accountant G-41-1 was a bold attempt to enter the DC-3 replacement market but development was abandoned.

The Saunders-Roe SR.53 XD145 was the first of two prototypes of this mixed powerplant (turbojet and rocket) research aircraft.

The Miles HDM.105 G-AHDM was a rebuild of an Aerovan 6 fitted with a high aspect ratio wing designed by French company Hurel-Dubois for research purposes.

Fairey's Ultra-light helicopter G-AOUK lands on the back of a company lorry, apparently stationary here, although this demonstration did take place with a moving lorry.

1958

THE NINETEENTH SHOW
1-7 SEPTEMBER

For the Nineteenth SBAC Exhibition and Flying Display, the Services added considerably to the spectacle of new aircraft presented by the Society, contributing no less than 145 aircraft to a flying total (on the best days, when everything flew) of 202, likely to remain an all-time record for the course.

There were the odd fall-outs, as aircraft suffered minor injury or irritation – or in two cases, total obliteration – and although the weather was generally excellent, Wednesday turned out rotten again, with persistent rain which cleared just in time for Thursday's Show, leaving Friday misty and variable, but perfectly flyable.

The general emphasis of the event was now beginning to change; with the considerable cut-backs in military orders and the fairly drastic pruning of defence spending, visible in the disbanding of many squadrons of the Royal Air Force, and with the continuing success of British turbine airliners, attention was focused largely on the civil scene. Service participation underlined the state of readiness and equipment of both the Royal Air Force and Fleet Air Arm.

In token of all this, the principal speaker at the SBAC eve-of-Show Dorchester Dinner was the Minister of Transport and Civil Aviation, Mr Harold Watkinson (Remember him? Man who closed Croydon Airport) although many of the industry present did not seem to agree completely with his vision of the commercial future. But the long-range Comet 4 and Britannia 312 were now flying and British civil turbine airliners were in service in 33 countries in the hands of 53 operators. The airlines were going through one of their periodic recessions, it was true, and the SBAC President, Mr Aubrey Burke, sounded a note of financial caution and dwelt on the problems of funding development. He also quoted export figures of £116,500,000 for 1957, with a probable 1958 total of £150 million. Since the end of the war, the export earnings of the industry had been £720 million.

The Dinner, normally an all-male occasion, also added to the particularity of 1958; the Guest of Honour, the President of the FAI, was Miss Jacqueline Cochran.

The Show itself differed little in detail from its predecessors; prices to the public remained unchanged. There were 362 stands taken in the big top, still the biggest in the world and now covering 126,000 square feet (11,705 sq. m).

Traffic remained a problem (which was still with us in 1988, 30 years later). Latter-day travellers by road to the Show may or may not agree with the advice given on that earlier occasion:

"To all road-users going to Farnborough, whatever the speed of their vehicle, the motoring organisations offer this simple perennial advice: start early and follow the official routes."

The enclosures and main hall were unchanged, but there was a short row ("E" Row) of guest chalets fronting Lincoln Road, between it and the radar terrace. President's and Press enclosures, separated by a decent interval, were still on the barrier line.

For some reason, official policy dictated that on trade days only the identities of exhibiting aircraft should be given over the Tannoy system, with neither descriptions of the flying nor pilots' names, although the public were treated to a full commentary. Neither the Director, Ted Bowyer, nor Major Oliver Stewart, is now available for questioning, but from the author's recollection of both those strong-minded gentlemen, a clash of titans is not entirely an impossibility. At any rate, the latter described himself pointedly as an "announcer", which is probably as close as he cared to come to open mutiny.

As has been said, a series of incidents contrived to keep the content of the Display changing and the first of these, indeed, occurred before the whole thing had even begun. "Hazel" Hazelden, bringing the new Dart-engined Herald 2 into Farnborough, suffered a fire in the starboard engine not far from the aerodrome and brought the aircraft down to a skilful and successful forced landing without injury to crew or passengers, passing coolly below a line of high tension cables on his final approach.

On Monday, the new Blackburn N.A.39, operating out of Boscombe Down for security reasons (even the model on the stand was placed well out of reach), had to abandon its opening appearance, with an infuriated "Slim" Sear wrestling with a radio button jammed on "transmit", while the Lightning was grounded by a faulty starter switch. The programme commenced with the first circus, containing the now-familiar Scorpion-Canberra (Tom Lampitt), taking-off from Laffan's Plain to centre its near-vertical departure on the chalets, the Canberra T.11, Tyne-Ambassador and Gannet AEW.3.

Trials of the latter began on board HMS *Centaur* shortly after the Farnborough Show; a further 43 were built, equipping only the four dispersed Flights of No. 849 Squadron, and replacing their Skyraiders.

The second circus contained nine helicopters, the four Westland members forming a family circle within it; the

Saunders-Roe P.531 was the prototype of the Navy Wasp and Army Scout, both of which (built by Westland) had distinguished careers. The Bristol 192 was the sole survivor of a number of variants of the 173 proposed to the Royal Navy as the 191, to the Royal Air Force as the 192 and to the Royal Canadian Air Force as the 193. Twenty-six were eventually built, serving with distinction in Africa and the Far East with three squadrons, from 1961 to 1969. It was the first, and until the arrival of the Chinook in 1980, the only Royal Air Force twin-rotor, twin-engined helicopter. As the acquisition of the Chinook had been originally proposed in 1967, but became another defence-cut statistic, the Royal Air Force medium-lift helicopter capacity was pretty emasculated for a decade.

The last of the Westlands, the Westminster, was a most imposing monster, the only one of a series of ambitious Westland projects for very big helicopters to see the light of day. In fact this first (of two) Westminsters let in quite a lot of the light of day through the uncovered, heavy-gauge steel tube structure of what was actually a "proof of concept" test rig. The company sank nearly £1½ million of its own money into the Westminster, but financial and production pressures in other directions killed it off. At the end of their slot, the Westlands gathered themselves into a tidy line and bowed to the President, starting a precedent that has not entirely died out.

This year the Royal Navy were represented by two formation teams, one of seven Sea Hawks from No. 800 Squadron and one of four Scimitars from No. 803 Squadron, in synchronised displays. The Sea Hawks, power-unfolding their wings as they taxied out, took off in formation, the largest such departure at a Show until the Red Arrows, with ten. On the first day, as they rolled out of the top of the opening loop, one aircraft broke from the formation, trailing smoke from an engine fire, and headed for Blackbushe. At 5,000 ft (1,424 m) the pilot, Lt Roger Dimmock, banged out, breaking an ankle in the subsequent landing and being rescued by the duty Whirlwind. This incident did not quench his enthusiasm for flying. At the 1987 DEC Schneider race at Bembridge, Chief Petty Officer "Soapy" Watson, about to take-off as a race competitor, was joined in his naval Chipmunk, slightly to his surprise, by Flag Officer, Naval Air Command, Rear Admiral Roger Dimmock, attired for the occasion in a flying suit (with badges of rank) and a stylish tweed cap.

Other members of the naval teams included Lt David Pentreath of 800 Squadron, who was later appointed to the Distinguished Service Order for his exceptionally spirited handling of 6 Frigate Flotilla in the Falklands, and Lt Ted Anson of 803, who later retired, as Admiral Sir Edward Anson and went to work for British Aerospace in New York. By and large, a vintage year.

Though chronologically true, it would be ridiculous to say that No. 111 Squadron, the Black Arrows, "followed" anybody;

they stole the Show. In three close vics of seven, plus one, 22 Hunter F.6s, nine from "Treble One" and the rest from Nos 1,2,19, 56 and 92 Squadrons, the Hunter OCU (No. 229) and the Central Fighter Establishment, collected and led by Roger Topp, swung magnificently into a loop and followed immediately with a second. On the way down, three wing men a side broke left and right, the 16 left barrelled to port and shed the last seven visitors, leaving Treble One to loop nine smoking, drop four off the top and take the basic five over another loop in fork, change to line abreast, loop and bomb burst. It was a sight no-one present will forget and remains the largest formation ever looped. (The Pakistan Air Force had looped 21 Hunters earlier in the year.)

The Royal Air Force display continued with a fly-past by a No.10 Squadron Victor, with Vulcan (83 Squadron) and Valiant (90 Squadron) accompaniment; a flight-refuelling pass by a Valiant BK.1, feeding a B(PR)K.1, both of No. 214 Squadron; nine Canberras in three vics of three from Nos 9 and 12 Squadrons; six Jet Provosts from the Central Flying School, this time in red, white and blue costume, with smoke from underwing canisters; and a thunderous parade of 45 Hunters under Black leader and 45 Javelins under Pink leader, deftly held in leash by an anonymous whipper-in flying a Meteor.

To follow all *that* with two Austers, a Chipmunk and a Beaver brought everyone down to earth with a bump. The Alpha, kitted out with Britten-Norman Micronair atomisers, sprayed lavender water over the airfield by courtesy of Mr Norman's Crop Culture (Aerial) Ltd, of Bembridge, Isle of Wight. Des Norman, lately Export Officer of the SBAC, carried on a lively agricultural trade from the island, largely with Tiger Moths, flew in displays with the then recently-formed Tiger Club, and hankered after the gentlemanly Meteor 8s so recently and cruelly taken away from him and other Auxiliary pilots. As he was known to be bracing himself to try to get one in and out of Bembridge, at that time just a short, grass slope, perhaps it was just as well.

The single-seat, agricultural Chipmunk of Fison-Airwork (actually everyone called it the Dustmunk) spread phantom dust over phantom furrows, while Ranald avalanched the Aiglet. The Beaver stolidly lifted six hefty soldiers.

There were two Gnats, one armed, one not and a Javelin FAW.8, the first production aircraft, with new AI, 12,300 lb (5,579.2 kg) Sapphire 200s and afterburners. Said *Flight*:

"The difference between the Gnat and the Javelin is that between a pocket cosh and a shillelagh." So now you know.

The Fairey Rotodyne demonstrated the possibilities of a VTOL airliner, rising vertically as a helicopter to 1,000 ft (305 m), translating to forward flight as an autogyro and accelerating in level flight to an impressive 185 mph (297.7 k/h). The complex compound lift and propulsion system, with airscrews and wing to take 50 per cent off the loading of the rotor and

1958

+	Airspeed Ambassador	G-37-3 (62) R-R Tynes
+	Auster Aiglet Trainer J/5L	EP-AIJ (3559)
+	Auster Alpha J/1N	G-APAR (3370) spraying equipment
	Avro Shackleton MR.3	XF701
+	Avro Vulcan B.1	VX770 R-R Conways
+	Avro Vulcan B.1	XA891 Bristol Olympus
	Avro Vulcan B.1	XA903 Blue Steel development aircraft
	Avro Vulcan B.2	VX777 B.2 aerodynamic prototype
+	Avro Vulcan B.2	XH533
+	Blackburn N.A.39 (Buccaneer)	XK486
	Blackburn N.A.39 (Buccaneer)	XK487
	Bristol Britannia 312	G-AOV1 (13418)
	Bristol Sycamore 52	CC-063 (13490) Luftwaffe
+	Bristol 192	XG447 (13342)
+	de Havilland Chipmunk 23	G-APOS (C1/0763) spraying version
+	de Havilland Comet 3B	G-ANLO (06100)
	de Havilland Comet 4	G-APDA (6401)
	de Havilland Dove 6	G-AMZN (04437)
	de Havilland Heron 2D	G-APEV (14125)
	de Havilland Sea Vixen FAW.1	XJ475 (10002)
	de Havilland Vampire T.11	WZ587
+	de Havilland Canada Beaver 2	G-ANAR (80)
+	English Electric Canberra B.2	WK163 Napier Double Scorpion rocket in bomb bay
	English Electric Canberra B(1)8	XM245
	English Electric Canberra U.10	WJ624
+	English Electric Canberra T.11	WJ610
+	English Electric Lightning	XA847
+	English Electric Lightning	XG308
+	Fairey Gannet AEW.3	XJ440 (F.9431)
	Fairey Gannet AS.4	UA-115 (F.9372) German Navy
+	Fairey Rotodyne	XE521 (F.9429)
+	Fairey Ultra-light Helicopter	G-AOUJ (F.9424)
+	Fairey F.D.2	WG774 (F.9421)
+	Folland Gnat F.1	XK741 (FL.5)
+	Folland Gnat F.1	G-39-10 (FL.16)

	Gloster Javelin FAW.7	XH901
+	Gloster Javelin FAW.8	XH966
+	Handley Page Victor B.1	XA930
	Hawker Hunter F.6	XE618
+	Hawker Hunter F.6	XF389
+	Hawker Hunter T.7	XL564
+	Hawker Hunter T.8	WW664
+	Hunting Jet Provost T.2	G-AOUS (P.84/14)
	Hunting Jet Provost T.3	XM348
	Hunting Pembroke C.54	SC-304 (P.54/1014)
+	Hunting President 1	G-AOJG (P.66/79)
	Hunting President 2	G-APMO (PAC/2/1031)
+	Saunders-Roe Skeeter AOP.12	XJ762 (S2/5074)
+	Saunders-Roe Skeeter 51	SC-502 (S2/5070) German Navy
+	Saunders-Roe P.531	G-APNU (S2/5267)
	Saunders-Roe P.531	G-APNV (S2/5268)
+	Scottish Aviation Twin Pioneer	G-APLW (532)
	Scottish Aviation Twin Pioneer CC.1	XM289 (543)
	Short S.C.1	XG900 (SH.1814)
+	Vickers Viscount 812	N248V (360)
+	Westland Wessex HAS.1	XL727 (WA.1)
+	Westland Westminster	G-APLE (WA.1)
+	Westland Whirlwind HAS.7	XL880 (WA/230)
+	Westland Widgeon	G-AKTW (WA/H/001)

Services participation in flying programme:
Avro Vulcan: one from 83 Squadron.
Handley Page Victor: one from 10 Squadron. Formation fly-past.
Vickers Valiant: one from 90 Squadrom.
Vickers Valiant: tanker and receiver fly-past.
Hawker Hunter: 45 in formation fly-past plus 22 from 111 Squadron "Black Arrows" aerobatic team.
English Electric Canberra: nine in formation fly-past
Gloster Javelin: 45 in formation fly-past.
Hunting Jet Provost: four from CFS in fly-past.
Hawker Sea Hawk: seven in fly-past from 800 Squadron. One crashed 1/9.
Supermarine Scimitar: six in fly-past; four in aerobatic team from 803 Squadron.
Avro Vulcan XH481 flew over on return from Canada on 7 September.
Vickers Valiant WP219 flew over on return from Malta on 6 September.

WW664 was converted from a Hawker Hunter F.4 to the prototype T.8 two-seater for the Royal Navy – note arrester hook beneath the rear fuselage.

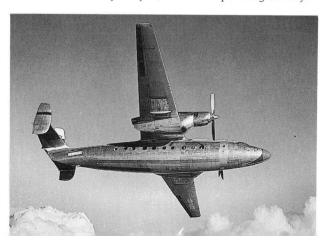

Airspeed Ambassador G-37-4 (ex-G-AKRD), used as a testbed for the Rolls-Royce Tyne, flies on the port engine only.

1958

tip-thrust reducing the stresses further, gave promise of high speeds being attained and in January 1959, in the new FAI record class for convertiplanes (Class E.2) a 100 km (62 mile) closed circuit record of 307 k/h (190.9 mph) was successfully set.

Three white Vulcans took part; a company B.1 with the famous winged triangle badge on the fin, and flown by Jimmy Harrison, demonstrated the Low Altitude Bombing System (LABS), a bombing technique that flung a bomb onto a target from a half-loop and roll-off-the-top. This ensured that you did not have to overfly the target and get hoist by your own petard and was sufficiently startling when performed by V-bombers. XH533, a B.2 with the new wing, set off on Friday to attend a show in Toronto, returning to the Farnborough Display in 5 hours, 47 minutes, or 619 mph (996.18 k/h) over 3,600 miles (5,793.96 km). The third aircraft carried a development round of the Avro stand-off bomb.

From Tuesday, the Show closed with the N.A.39 and Lightning. (The latter name had been announced in August.) Blackburn had successfully tendered to a specification for a low-level, high-subsonic strike aircraft in 1955, the Ministry of Supply ordering 20 pre-production aircraft. The prototype, being shown at Farnborough, was so secret (it was considered to give Britain a three year lead in its field) that it flew in each day from Boscombe Down and the second prototype, on the ground, was only available for inspection by security-cleared visitors.

The English Electric P.1B Lightning did not fly on Monday, as related, nor on Friday but on the other days put up the kind of performance expected by aircraft with "Bea" Beamont in the saddle. On Thursday it was flown by S/Ldr Jimmy Dell, the Royal Air Force Lightning liaison officer, who fell in love with the beast and shortly afterwards joined the firm.

There had been the odd boom, or rumour of boom, during the week and on Sunday, while Jimmy Dell was flying the Lightning, *something* broke some windows in the control tower.

Westland's biggest helicopter to date was the Westminster; G-APLE was the first of two prototypes but development did not take place.

An interesting and unusual shape – and a very noisy one – was the Fairey Rotodyne XE521.

Avro Vulcan XA903 was the development aircraft for the Blue Steel stand-off bomb.

Nine RAF English Electric Canberras, part of the Services participation in the flying programme.

1959

THE TWENTIETH SHOW
7-13 SEPTEMBER

What was new in 1959? There were new and exciting airliners, there was the first (and, one must admit, slightly hilarious) appearance of real VTOL, there was an even grander Royal Air Force appearance, embracing Transport Command for the first time and there were the first semi-official rumblings about SST – the supersonic transport. The Minister of Supply was said to have placed a contract for studies. Exports were up again; during the Show an order for two squadrons' worth of Sea Hawks for the Indian Navy was announced, part of the complement of the new aircraft carrier *Vikrant*. Formerly HMS *Hercules*, the last of the British light fleet carriers, she was currently undergoing modernisation at Harland and Wolff.

The main parameters of the Show were the same: the layout, the timetable, the charges and the traffic. The weather was magnificent; if anything too hot, although it was generally admitted that the recently-installed fans in the main exhibition hall did make their presence felt. The hall was 125,000 square feet (11,612.5 sq.m) this year, with the guided weapons and equipment parks around fifty per cent bigger, making them something over half the size of the main hall.

Emphasising a long period of British ascendancy in international competitive gliding, gliders (or more properly, sailplanes) opened the Show on the three public days.

The Comet 4B opened the programme proper. This was G-APMB, carrying the new scarlet and black BEA livery. It was the second aircraft of the Corporation's order for seven and inaugurated revenue services the following April, to Tel Aviv. G-APMA, the first aircraft, had taken part in the famous "Arch to Arc" London-Paris race, covering the Northolt-le Bourget stage in 27 minutes. It had been chartered by a team of British business men (and one business lady), led by Peter Brookes, complete with briefcases, bowler hats and umbrellas (except the lady). They did the whole trip by "public transport" from Marble Arch ro Paddington (taking a short cut from the start through the gents' loo, including the lady), by chartered London Transport bus, thence by railcar to Northolt and Comet to le Bourget. The final stage, le Bourget to the Arc de Triomphe, was done in *traction avant* Citroën taxis. Those who know that route will appreciate the average time for the stage of thirteen minutes.

Following the Comet, the Royal Air Force presented its own contribution. There were three Victor B.1s (the first Victor formation at Farnborough) from No.15 Squadron, Cottesmore, three Vulcan B.1s from No. 230 OCU, Waddington, representing Bomber Command, then three No. 46 Squadron Javelin FAW.2s and three No. 25 Squadron FAW.7s (with Firestreak), all from the Waterbeach Wing.

After them, Treble One. Nine Hunters looped, seven Hunters rolled in opposition. Following the break away of two from the smaller formation, there was a beautifully-timed display of synchronised formation aerobatics, culminating in the celebrated downward bomb-burst by the nine, followed immediately by the five, who reverse burst upwards through the smoke. The black Hunters cleared to reassemble themselves off-stage and Transport Command took over, headed by a Twin Pioneer flanked by two single dittos, respectively from No. 21 Squadron at Benson and No. 230 at Upavon. They led on a succession of singletons, representing all the main equipment of the Command; Whirlwind HAR.2, from JEHU (Joint Experimental Helicopter Unit), Beverley C.1 (No. 47 Squadron, Abingdon), Hastings C.2 (No. 24 Squadron, Colerne), Comet C.2 (No. 216 Squadron, Lyneham) and Britannia C.1 (No.99 Squadron, Lyneham).

The Jet Provosts from CFS came back for their slot and were followed by the Black Arrows, to loop 16 and break for landing.

The Beaver and Twin Pioneer followed the solo display by the Bristol 192, the latter being the fourth of an order for 20 for the Royal Air Force, eight of which had been delivered and would equip No. 66 Squadron in two year's time. After stopping briefly to disembark a full load of 18 soldiers, the 192 made a neat and rapid hook-up to a 4,000 lb (1,814.2 kg) Bloodhound missile, complete with its travelling carriage, subsequently depositing it equally neatly back on the ground. (It fell over on Thursday.)

The "Twin Pin", a civil demonstrator destined for Rio Tinto, carried two large endplates on its wing, containing some sort of MAD gear for locating minerals.

After the solo Jet Provost, the spectators were treated to the first public appearance of the remarkable Hovercraft, or more properly, the Saunders-Roe SR.N1. The principle and history of the hovercraft are sufficiently well-known today, but in 1959 this swirling, ungainly but obviously effective (and British) invention was a very strange sight indeed. Its presence at Farnborough and B type registration reflected the convoluted and not entirely disinterested decision by various bodies that "hovercraft" were aircraft. Subsequently, air cushion vehicles took on an identity of their own and disappeared from the SBAC Show scene.

It was, however, sufficiently impressive, taking aboard each day a load of 20 Royal Marines and skirling them along the runway at 25 knots (46.23 k/h) on the 435 bhp of a single Alvis Leonides. Among other things, it brought out the worst in Oliver Stewart, who described it on Tuesday as a "seaside bandstand" and on Wednesday as a "director's inkpot". But he still wasn't allowed to mention pilots' names.

The Vickers Vanguard was the launch customer, so to speak, for the powerful Rolls-Royce Tyne Mk 506. The design emerged from requirements by BEA and Trans-Canada for a Viscount follow-on, with greater speed, range and capacity. The "double-bubble" fuselage evolved from BEA's requirement for high freight utilisation. Although, later on, the lure of speed and the magic word "jet" would force airlines to re-equip with turbo-jets, when the Vanguard was designed it was a more efficient vehicle for its purpose than a jet, let alone a swept-wing jet. BEA milked an extra advantage, introducing economy-class seats on short-range sectors. The 1959 Farnborough aircraft was the second for BEA and lived on until 1973, when it was broken up at Heathrow. Although economical and efficient, the jet age eventually overtook the Vanguard and only 43 were built.

The Armstrong Whitworth Argosy 101, G-APVH, was actually the fifth airframe of a batch of ten that the company decided to lay down in order to reduce lead time, and subsequently appeared on the United States register, Riddle Airlines having ordered four to replace their fleet of adapted piston-engined airliners. The first civil aircraft produced by the Hawker Siddeley Group, which included Armstrong Whitworth among its members, it was a bold advance in that market area. Designed as a fast, medium-range freighter of average capacity, it was pressurised and had been very carefully tailored to its task. The floor of the capacious fuselage was at truck-bed height and could be loaded or unloaded from either end (dictating the twin-boom arrangement, which saved weight over a conventional ramp).

The project was set up at the Group's own financial risk and they spent some £10 million on it. For those who did not make it to the Paris Show in June, Farnborough was their first chance to see the aircraft.

Riddle increased their order to seven and used the Argosy on military contracts for the United States Air Force. Eventually, the contract ended and the aircraft came back to Armstrong Whitworth, to be solemnly sold back to the company who had taken up the renewed USAF contract. One pilot attempted unsuccessfully to land one on a highway – excusable conduct, one feels, as he was enjoying an emergency at the time.

British European Airways bought three, having decided to run a specialised freight service instead of filling up half a Vanguard and the Royal Air Force ordered 56 as the Argosy C.1 for Transport Command, equipping six squadrons. The type served in a wide variety of tasks until 1974 and might well, but for continuing defence cuts, have served much longer. Its civil rôle was to disappear before the capacious holds of the big jets.

Service aircraft occupied most of the rest of the 1959 Show, apart from the helicopters. The Gannet AEW.3, seen the previous year, was now the only variety still in production; the Javelin this year was an F(AW).8. With a full complement of Firestreak missiles, it demonstrated its agility with an eight point roll (it now had a power-operated rudder, which may have helped) and confused purists of language by "lowering" the undercarriage in the inverted position.

The Vulcan B.2, flown by Jimmy Harrison, was complete with in-flight refuelling probe (trials with this equipment with a Valiant tanker had just been completed), and took off from the Laffan's Plain end of the runway.

The Blackburn N.A.39 was the first production British aircraft to be area-ruled to reduce drag at very high speeds. It was the only Service aircraft to be powered by the de Havilland Gyron Junior, and aids to its dedicated high speed very-low-level rôle included blown leading edge slots and powerful speed brakes at the back end. The latter were there largely to balance speed requirements against drag, when the engines were spooled-up on the approach to make re-circulation over slots and flaps effective.

This was the "year of the spin" as far as the Hunter was concerned, with the bright orange T.66A hurtling in at high speed and low level (the attention a trifle diverted by the simultaneous inverted passage of the ground-attack FGA.9, the last of the fighting Hunters) before ploughing up to 15,000 ft (4,572 m) and returning in a multi-turn, dizzying, smoking spin. On Monday, there were eight turns, later ten and on the closing Sunday, in deference to the date, thirteen.

It is impossible to convey, after all these years, the sensation of watching this display at the time, but it was well summed-up by Robin d'Erlanger, who had a tendency to stutter when excited: "That's not a s-s-spin; that's t-t-t-torque off the altimeter."

This year's Lightning (most unkindly described by one journalist as an "aerodynamic meat cleaver"), flown by Beamont and therefore frequently seen in a series of tight, high-g turns, was the T.4 two-seat trainer, in parallel production with the F.1. It had been ordered in 1956 and first flew on 6 May 1959. Shortly after the Display, on 1 October, J.W.C.Squier had to eject from this aircraft at M:1.7 and 40,000 ft (12,192 m) in one of the first very-high-speed, very-high-altitude departures. Neither the sophisticated aids employed to try to recover him, nor the intensive air-sea rescue operation, produced the

1959

+	Armstrong Whitworth Argosy	G-APRN (AW.6654)
	Armstrong Whitworth Argosy	G-APVH (AW.6655)
+	Auster Aiglet Trainer J/5L	G-APVG (3306)
	Avro Lincoln B.2	G-APRJ Napier de-icing research
+	Avro Vulcan B.1	XA902 R-R Conways
+	Avro Vulcan B.2	XH536
+	Blackburn N.A.39 (Buc-caneer)	XK490
+	Bristol 192	XG451 (13346)
+	de Havilland Comet 4B	G-APMB (06422)
	de Havilland Dove 6	G-AMZN (04437)
	de Havilland Heron 2D	G-APEV (14125)
+	de Havilland Sea Vixen FAW.1	XJ516 (10025)
	de Havilland Vampire T.11	XD624
+	de Havilland Canada Beaver 2	G-ANAR (80)
	English Electric Canberra PR.9	XH134 (SH.1724)
+	English Electric Lightning F.1	XG331
+	English Electric Lightning T.4	XL628
+	Fairey Gannet AEW.3	XL452 (P.9435)
+	Fairey Rotodyne	XE521 (F.9429)
+	Folland Gnat F.1	XN326 (FL.24)
+	Folland Gnat T.1	XM691 (FL.501)
+	Gloster Javelin FAW.8	XJ125
+	Handley Page Herald	G-AODF (148)
	Hawker Hunter T.7	XJ615
+	Hawker Hunter FGA.9	XG135
+	Hawker Hunter T.66A	G-APUX
+	Hunting Jet Provost T.2	G-AOUS (P.84/14)
	Hunting Jet Provost T.3	XM370
	Hunting Jet Provost T.51	CJ701 Ceylon AF
	Hunting President 2	G-APVJ (P.66/114)
+	Saunders-Roe Skeeter 8	G-APOI (S2/5081)
+	Saunders-Roe Skeeter AOP.12	XL813 (S2/5098)
+	Saunders-Roe P 531-2	G-APVL (S2/5311)
	Saunders-Roe P.531-2	G-APVM (S2/5312)
+	Saunders-Roe SR.N1 Hover-craft	G-12-4 (S2/5081)
+	Scottish Aviation Twin Pioneer	G-AOER (505)
+	Short S.C.1	XG905 (SH.1815)
+	Vickers Vanguard 951	G-APEB (705)
	Vickers Viscount 816	VH-TVR (435)
+	Westland Wessex HAS.1	XM301 (WA.6)
+	Westland Westminster	G-APLE (WA.1)
+	Westland Westminster	G-APTX (WA.2)
+	Westland Whirlwind 2	G-AOCZ (WA.115)
	Westland Whirlwind HAR.5	XJ398 (WA.62)
	Westland Widgeon	G-ANLW (WA/H/133)

Services participation in flying programmes:
Avro Vulcan: three from 230 OCU.
Blackburn Beverley: one from 47 Squadron.
Bristol Britannia: one from 99 Squadron.
Bristol Sycamore: one.
de Havilland Comet: one from 216 Squadron.
Gloster Javelin: three from 25 Squadron, three from 46 Squadron.
Handley Page Hastings: one from 24 Squadron.
Handley Page Victor: three from 15 Squadron.
Hawker Hunter: 16 from 111 Squadron "Black Arrows" aerobatic team.
Hunting Jet Provost: two from CFS, synchronised aerobatics.
Scottish Aviation Pioneer: one from 21 Squadron.
Scottish Aviation Twin Pioneer: two from 230 Squadron.
Supermarine Scimitar: six from 807 Squadron, four in aerobatic team.
Westland Whirlwind: one from JEHU.

Other flying participation:
Elliott Eon Olympia 403 G-APEW; Eon Olympia 419; Slingsby Eagle BGA740; Slingsby Skylark 2 BGA899; Slingsby Skylark 3 BGA 739, tug aircraft de Havilland Chipmunk WB758 and WG466, Miles Messenger G-AILI, Percival Prentice G-APIY and G-APJE.

slightest result and in fact he came ashore on his own after 28 hours in his dinghy and rang in from a farm. So much for technology.

There were two Westminsters this time in the helicopter circus, the second slightly better clad and sporting large external fuel tanks and the first prototype toting a 3,500 lb (1,587.6 kg) bridge span. This was carefully lowered onto prepared ramps and the Wessex, underslinging a Land Rover and some kind of gun, and a Whirlwind, lifting an Austin Mini-moke, deposited their cargoes, which then drove across the bridge so thoughtfully provided. The Widgeon appeared with fat, three-piece inflated pontoons, looking for all the world like cocktail sausages, and with the Skeeter, Saunders-Roe P.531 and a second Whirlwind, made up the eight helicopters that, after their various cavorts, formed up in line abreast to salute the President and his guests.

The finale was provided by No. 807 Squadron of the Fleet Air Arm, from Lossiemouth, whose six Scimitars (four in box and two solos) were led by Lt Cdr Keith Leppard - except

on Monday, when his aircraft went u/s. Several special features were brought to this item: one was a demonstration of LABS bombing techniques, with one of the Scimitars equipped with a lurid red "atom bomb" and producing a convincing ball of fire on the airfield; another was a high-speed target snatch by hook off the runway. Uniquely among Farnborough extravaganzas, as the two singleton Scimitars landed in one direction, folding their wings, they gave just sufficient room to let through another landing in the opposite direction.

As a prelude to Saturday's Show, five British sailplanes were allotted the task of opening the programme. British sailplanes and British pilots were well in front on the competition scene and with preparations for the next World Gliding Championships well under way, it was appropriate to show some of the best of British designs.

From Elliotts of Newbury came the 17-metre Olympia 403 and the 19-metre 419; both had done well in the Nationals. Slingsby Sailplanes showed the Eagle T.42 advanced trainer and the Skylark 2 and 3 single-seaters. Slingsby were as well-

known for training as for competition types and had just become the Shaw Slingsby Trust Ltd, with "Sling" as managing director of Slingsby Sailplanes and Philip Wills chairman of both. The main function of the new Trust was to support British gliding as the Kemsley Flying Trust already did.

This year the Show dinner was held after, not before, the Show. Sir Aubrey Burke, the SBAC President, acknowledging that with British engines flying in more than fifty different foreign aircraft, there was considerable pressure to allow the latter to appear at Farnborough, claimed that lack of space was the main reason for excluding them – but "it is a matter which we have always in our minds."

The 16 Hawker Hunters of No.111 Squadron, the Black Arrows aerobatic team.

On a more personal note, it must have been a great consolation to Tom Brooke-Smith, whose display of the VTOL Short S.C.1 had been cut short by the ingestion of a complete carpet of cut grass into his vertical engine intakes, and who had had a pretty rotten week as far as flying was concerned, to read in *Flight* (the Russians having just launched their Moon-probe) that his Farnborough performance was equally interesting if not quite as spectacular.

The orange and white Hawker Hunter two-seater G-APUX – Bill Bedford's spinning mount.

A neat static park and useful aircraft recognition test! Making their first appearance were the Vickers Vanguard, Armstrong Whitworth Argosy and de Havilland Comet 4B in the left foreground.

An interesting comparison between Folland Gnats – the camouflaged single-seater XN326 and two-seater XM691.

The Saunders-Roe SR.N1 "flies" down the runway with its cargo of soldiery – the lowest fly past at the Show.

1960

THE TWENTY-FIRST SHOW
5-11 SEPTEMBER

There was a Press and technicians' preview day on Monday, followed by the three trade days and three public days. For the more fortunate invited guests, who were not following the recommended road route to the Show (via the A3 from London to Guildford and then suit yourself) RAF Odiham accepted aircraft and the SBAC had organised a coach shuttle on to Farnborough. That the service was popular soon became evident and 1,738 passengers came to the Show in 198 aircraft.

The helicopter park, open on trade days for the even more privileged guests, was located in the clutter of grass and concrete between Southern Squadron and the N/S runway and doubled as a static aircraft area on public days. For more mundane approaches, British Railways offered a train-coach ticket from Waterloo for 10s (50p).

The Exhibition Hall again increased in size and now covering 126,000 square feet (11,705 sq.m.) taken up – apart from the gangways – by 382 exhibitors. Curling round the hill were the four lines of chalets, making up what *Flight* called the "tented jamboree". It cost a member of the public £1 to get in on Friday, plus another £1 to "abide his auto" and five bob (25p) on Saturday and Sunday. On the two latter days 30s (£1.50) brought in a car with six bodies therein, while motorcycles cost 5s and pedal cycles 1s.

The Show was opened each day by a demonstration of the striking power of the Royal Air Force. Four V-bombers "scrambled" from the western end of the airfield to a starter's gun fired from the President's Enclosure, in response to a telephoned order from the Air Officer Commanding, Bomber Command. Three squadrons were involved: on Monday, Thursday and Sunday four Valiants from No. 148 Squadron, based at Marham; on Tuesday and Saturday, four Vulcans of No. 617 Squadron, Scampton; and on Wednesday and Friday, four Victors of No. XV Squadron, Cottesmore.

The Valiant was the first V-bomber to enter service and in 1960 had the additional distinction of being the Royal Air Force's only air-refuelling tanker, operated by No. 214 Squadron. As the only aircraft kitted to indulge in air-to-air refuelling were the rest of the V-force (Victor and Vulcan) and later Marks of Javelin, one squadron was probably enough. The Valiants at Farnborough were all airborne on Monday in one minute 56 seconds and by the end of the week they had cut this to one minute 37 seconds.

This was the last time Farnborough spectators would ever see the Black Arrows, who were shortly to disband prior to reassembling with the Lightning. Led still by the redoubtable S/Ldr Pete Latham (who had adopted a motor scooter as the only way of getting about on the ground) they performed splendidly, with a sequence consisting largely of a variety of loops, one of which was called Farmer Loop – which might have been a tribute to the bucolic appearance of the boss, if it had not been for its resemblance to a well-known MiG fighter. Mikoyan was not at Farnborough to appreciate the compliment, but Oleg Antonov and Aleksandir Yakovlev were there on Wednesday and may have told him.

The importance of the V-force had been underlined by a government announcement in February that it was abandoning the ballistic missile as a nuclear deterrent and would henceforth rely upon the bombers, armed with the American Douglas Skybolt missile. (Co-incidentally, in May, a ceremony marked the completion of the last of the Thor ballistic missile complexes for the Royal Air Force.) As Skybolt was almost immediately cancelled on grounds of expense and complication, the move towards it turned out not to have been one of government's brighter ideas. But neither had the decision to abandon manned bombers, taken earlier. There was also a British air-ground missile, Blue Steel, under development (it was on display at the Show along with a Vulcan) and it was issued to No. 617 Squadron (and later No.27) to be carried briefly by their Vulcans before it was decided that they had become too vulnerable and the whole thing was handed over to the Royal Navy and Polaris.

In the same month as the Skybolt decision was made public, Mr Duncan Sandys, then filling the newly-created post of Minister of Aviation, announced that the government would fund the construction of a supersonic airliner and invited tenders. He also pledged official support for the VC10 and Trident programmes. At the SBAC Dinner, which now took place on the Wednesday of Show week rather than preceding or following it, the new Minister, Mr Peter Thorneycroft, speaking of the supersonic transport, commented that "There is apparently a limited market for supersonic commercial aircraft" and that, "We are very ready to consider how we might collaborate with the Americans, the French, or other overseas friends who are interested."

This was the year in which the complex process of mergers, that had been initiated under a previous administration, finally came about. The process had been protracted and in the end turned out to be less of a political dragooning than many people declared it to be. Economic common sense would certainly have brought about much the same result eventually.

There were now two major airframe groups and one helicopter company and two engine manufacturers. This was very much the structure that had been forecast by the Minister of Supply, Mr Aubrey Jones, in May 1958 when he was surveying the future level of work within the industry.

The Hawker Siddeley Group had been formed round Hawker Siddeley Aviation, which in 1935 had been born of a merger of Hawker Aircraft with Avro (including Avro Canada), Gloster, Armstrong Whitworth and Armstrong Siddeley Motors. Now, during the previous twelve months, it had also absorbed Folland Aircraft, Blackburn Aircraft and Blackburn Engines and the world-wide empire of de Havilland Aircraft, Engines and Propellers, along with their Canadian and Australian subsidiaries.

British Aircraft Corporation might be said to have come into existence on 24 May 1960, when the board of directors was announced. For the time being, the three constituent partners, Bristol Aircraft, English Electric and Vickers-Armstrong (Aircraft), would continue to operate under their own names. Shortly after the reorganisation the three were joined by Hunting Aircraft. With English Electric came D.Napier and Sons, though retaining independence in the engine industry and with the Bristol Aeroplane Company came a 50 per cent holding in Bristol Engines, 15¼ per cent in Short Brothers and Harland and 10 per cent in Westland. The link with Shorts was a very real one; Cyril Uwins, for example, for so many years Bristol's chief test pilot and since the war a director of the company, was also a director of Shorts and had just become chairman and managing director.

Bristol Siddeley Engines was structured with 50 per cent holdings by Bristol Aeroplane Company and the Hawker Siddeley Group. The original merger that was to create the company came about between Armstrong Siddeley and Bristol Aero-Engines in 1958. Rolls-Royce were Rolls-Royce.

Westland, having made their original decision to abandon fixed-wing aircraft for helicopters had been quietly acquiring the helicopter interests of everybody else and now combined under their name Bristol's helicopter division, Saunders-Roe (who had already taken over Cierva) and Fairey Aviation. In gaining Fairey's aviation interests they had also inherited the Gannet production line but in keeping with their earlier decision, were not pursuing that line once the current production orders had been completed.

Chris Wren, that most loved and gentlest of satirists of the aviation scene, evidently suffering from a surfeit of mergers on this occasion, went so far as to describe the Show as "a Hawker Siddeley Air Show with guest artistes".

In the Display itself, one of the more impressive items was the daily departure of a Shackleton from No. 201 Squadron (originally the senior unit of the Royal Naval Air Service) on a 22-hour patrol. The aircraft took-off towards the latter end of the Show and returned to land the following morning. On Monday, a day of impeccable met., L-Lima, numbering the Squadron Commander and the Air Officer Commanding No. 19 Group among the crew, headed out into the Atlantic, via Lisbon, into the appalling mix of driving rain and low cloud that was to come in and make Tuesday miserable. On Tuesday afternoon it landed back, having covered 80,000 square miles (207,199 sq.km) and flown 3,700 nautical miles (6,857 km), and all done below 1,000 ft (305 m).

The weather improved gradually through the week and ended with a week-end of blazing sunshine.

There was one other military event of note in 1960, though it had nothing to do with Farnborough: older readers might recall that 1960 saw the end of National Service.

It was a very successful Show, by and large, with orders announced at the end for £20 million and official trading figures up to the end of July of well over £87 million. Just over half that total (£44.5 million) were sales of engines.

This year, foreign engines were admitted – in British aircraft but definitely not in the flying programme. As a result, both the Austers remained firmly wedged in the static park. All the same, it was an interesting pointer to the future, for with the healthy state of the home aero-engine industry there can have been no general feeling that it was necessary then to admit the opposition.

The fatness of the Westland presentation was due to their having taken over all rotary wing activity under their name. Among the offerings the admirable little P.531 evolved, via a number of prototypes, into the Wasp and Scout, respectively for naval and military use. It also evolved under a confusing variety of names, starting as the Sprite (and Sea Sprite for shipboard use) before becoming the Scout, with a Sea Scout naval version that was later renamed the Wasp. Flying at Farnborough was the pre-production P.531-2 Sprite Mk. 1, with Nimbus A.129 engine. The first production version, the Scout AH.1 flew on 6 March the following year. Also flying in the Show was the P.531.0/N Sprite, the last of a batch of three service evaluation aircraft for the Navy and fitted with a Blackburn Turmo engine on this occasion.

Among the other aircraft flying, the Herald embarked 30 troops and took off in under 600 yards (549 m). The Victor B.2, Conway-powered, anti-radiation white painted and deploying a braking parachute that might have lowered a howitzer in safety, was appearing in public for the first time. The similarly-painted Vulcan B.2 was the first pre-production aircraft. Two of the six Gnats then flying appeared at the Show, the second with full dual control and ejection seats;

Westland Belvedere XG451, with natty spats on its rear wheels, prepares to deposit a Bloodhound on the grass.

By this year, the Westland Westminster G-APLE had been given a protective skin in contrast to its previous skeletal appearance.

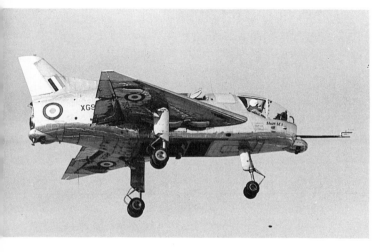

The Short S.C.1 in the hover – an extremely noisy experience for the onlookers.

Edgar Percival's E.P.9 appeared at the Show in a new agricultural guise as the Lancashire Prospector with an Armstrong Siddeley Cheetah engine. The original Lycoming-engined version was shown statically.

Armstrong Whitworth Argosy G-APRN appeared at the 1959 and 1960 Shows.

The de Havilland Canada Beaver 2 G-ANAR was a one-off variant with enlarged fin and rudder and an Alvis Leonides engine; it appeared at a number of Shows, but 1960 was the last.

1960

Armstrong Whitworth Argosy	G-APRN (AW.6654)	
+ Armstrong Whitworth Argosy	G-APRL (AW.6652)	
Auster D.4/108	CS-AMA (3602)	
Auster D.6/180	G-ARDJ (3704)	
Avro Lincoln B.2	G-29-1 Napier icing research	
+ Avro Vulcan B.2	XH534	
+ Avro 748	G-APZV (1534)	
Blackburn Buccaneer	XK488	
+ Blackburn Buccaneer	XK489	
de Havilland Comet 2E	XN453 (06026)	
de Havilland Dove 8	G-ARDH (04519)	
de Havilland Heron 2D	G-APEV (14125)	
de Havilland Sea Vixen FAW.1	XJ578 (10060)	
de Havilland Canada Beaver 2	G-ANAR (80)	
+ English Electric Lightning F.1	XG332	
+ English Electric Lightning T.4	XL629	
+ Folland Gnat T.1	XM691 (FL.501)	
Folland Gnat T.1	XM693 (FL.503)	
+ Gloster Javelin FAW.9	XH844	
+ Handley Page Herald 100	G-APWA (149)	
+ Handley Page Victor B.2	XH669	
+ Hawker Hunter FR.10	XG168	
+ Hawker Hunter T.66A	G-APUX	
Hunting Jet Provost T.3	XN462 (PAC/W/10141)	
+ Hunting Jet Provost T.4	XN468 (PAC/W/10147)	
Lancashire Prospector 1	G-APXW (43)	

+ Lancashire Prospector 2	G-ARDG (47)	
+ Scottish Aviation Twin Pioneer 3	G-APPH (540)	
+ Short S.C.1	XG905 (SH.1815)	
+ Vickers Vanguard 952	CF-TKB (725)	
+ Westland Belvedere HC.1	XG451 (13346)	
Westland Belvedere HC.1	XG452 (13347)	
+ Westland Rotodyne	X E521 (F.9429)	
+ Westland Scout AH.1	XP165 (S2/8437)	
+ Westland Skeeter AOP.12	XM563 (S2/5117) Blackburn Turmo	
Westland Wessex HAS.1	XM839 (WA.20)	
+ Westland Westminster	G-APLE (WA.1)	
+ Westland Whirlwind HAR.3	XJ398 (WA.62) B.S. Gnome	
+ Westland P.531-0	XN334	

Service participation in flying programmes:
Avro Shackleton: XF711 of 201 Squadron took off for 22 hour patrol; XF708 of 201 Squadron landed after 22 hour patrol.
Avro Vulcan: four of 617 Squadron.
English Electric Lightning: four of 74 Squadron aerobatic team.
Hawker Hunter: 18 of 111 Squadron "Black Arrows" aerobatic team.
Handley Page Victor: five of 15 Squadron.
Hunting Jet Provost: four from CFS, aerobatic team.
Vickers Valiant: five of 148 Squadron.

Other flying participation:
Elliott Eon 460 G-APWL; Elliott Eon Olympia; Slingsby Skylark and Swallow; Auster 6A G-ARDX and D.H. Tiger Moth G-AOFR glider tugs.

---

there were two Lightnings, which did not fly on Tuesday because of the water on the runway and two Hunters. The Mk 10 was designed for low-level reconnaissance and featured variable gearing to the ailerons to desensitize them for very fast, very low flying. The red and white two seater was largely occupied in finding out how many spins Bill Bedford could manage (15 was the most). The Jet Provost T.4 was originally privately funded, featured a more powerful Viper that added considerably to its performance and ensured an order from the Ministry of Defence.

Most exciting of all, though, was the Short S.C.1 vertical take-off aircraft. It was flown by "Brookie", whose bow tie was as famous at Farnborough as Mike Hawthorn's had been at Goodwood, and who was making his final appearance as chief test pilot before hanging up his boots, as they say, and going out with a triumphant display that must have made up for the embarrassment of the grass carpet. The S.C.1 was now well into its test programme, with over 100 transitions to its credit and gave a performance whose novelty of sight and sound was not equalled until the arrival of the P.1127. That particular "mystery ship" was not on display, though the

engine was and a sketch showing what the complete aircraft looked like had slipped past the censors onto the stand, before being hastily spirited away . The aircraft itself *was* on view to carefully selected spectators from the United States and NATO, at the Hawker Siddeley airfield at Dunsfold. There was also a rash of VTOL projects on the stands, of a complexity and credibility varying from a proposal for a vertical take-off Argosy to a Rolls-Royce fantasy involving 24 lift and six propulsion engines, to fly at M:2.26 with 72 passengers but no pilots.

The man behind Rolls-Royce's initial concept of a mix of lift and propulsion engines, which culminated in the S.C.1, and who had been prophesying VTOL in 1941, had retired in August after 21 years of service with the company. He was Dr A.A.Griffith, whose connections with Farnborough went back to his early career at RAE, where, in 1926, he made his first proposals for a turbine engine. Unlike Frank Whittle, whose designs were based on a centrifugal compressor, Dr Griffith worked from the start on axial flow and was responsible for the early ideas that led Rolls-Royce to the Avon.

1961

THE TWENTY-SECOND SHOW
4-10 SEPTEMBER

In many ways, the 1961 SBAC Show marked a low point for the British aircraft industry (it had not yet expanded into "aerospace"). The civil market at that time was far from buoyant and the military picture, still suffering from the appalling decisions of the Defence White Paper, had not yet sorted itself out from the effects of a more recent White Paper on the aircraft industry. The series of amalgamations that had resulted had some of the characteristics of the shot-gun marriage, but the necessity for action in this direction was not disputed.

Numbers of aircraft at Farnborough were the lowest ever but the second biggest-ever Service invasion of the Show took place with no less than 139 aircraft and looked like turning the event back into a Hendon Display. Nevertheless, the Show continued to grow.

Three hundred and ninety-seven exhibitors took part (remember that this was still an all-British event) and occupied 130,400 square feet (12,114 sq.m) of exhibition hall space – the largest to date. Among the distinguished guests were Oleg Antonov and Sergei Ilyushin, attending under the baleful eye of the Deputy Chief of the Soviet State Committee for Aircraft Production, Sergei Leschenko.

If there were few new aircraft in the round, the stands gave promise of an exciting crop in 1962. Exports continued to be strong, with 1960 figures standing at £142 million. European co-operation was in the air (we had just made one of our attempts to join the Common Market) and the international spirit was represented by the first Rolls-Royce Continental engines from their Light Aircraft Division. Official interest in the supersonic transport had taken another step forward and, indeed, the evidence that at least low-speed research was under way was present with the Handley Page H.P.115.

Government concern in the civil field was planned to include a risk-sharing scheme of initial support for certain programmes. Mentioned at the time were the Argosy Series 200, Trident, VC10 and Super VC10 and BAC One-Eleven. There were forty British engines on the stands, including the big Rolls-Royce Conway, first of the new high by-pass, low-consumption power plants, already flown in a test-bed and on offer commercially for the first time. Orders announced during the week included five VC10s for the Royal Air Force, bringing the total on the books to 57, a launch order for the D.H.125 (which at this stage of its career was called the Jet Dragon) and new batches of Wessex for the Royal Air Force

and of Wasp for the Royal Navy. Handley Page now had orders for 15 Heralds.

The "no more fighters" threat was receding; now seen to be nonsensical, especially in the light of United States activity and the evidence of formidable Soviet progress given at the Tushino Air Day. The commonsense views of the Royal Air Force on future defence needs were beginning to be heard. Question of the day: was it time for the Show to go biennial, as Paris had done immediately after the Second World War? Many members thought it was. The SBAC President, the Hon. H.G.Nelson, made it clear at the Flying Display Dinner that there would be a Show in 1962. For the rest, questionnaires had been sent out to member companies and the SBAC would wait and see.

The weather, after the preview day, was kind, with a fine Friday, magnificent Saturday, but dull closing Sunday. On Monday, despite the efforts of Air Traffic and radar, few aircraft flew; the Royal Air Force set piece was weather-bound at its various bases (the Navy got through – perhaps HMS Hermes had better weather) and at one stage, the nose of Blue Streak, at an altitude of 65 ft (20 m) QFE in the guided weapon park, was in cloud. Someone worked out that Thursday was the SBAC's 100th flying display day.

The occasion gave birth to a new noun of assembly, with a journalist describing the chalet rows, guarded by "a ribbon of commissionaires".

The year was notable for the number of formation and aerobatic teams that took part, quite apart from anything else. The Royal Air Force aerobatic display team was now the Blue Diamonds, 14 Hunter T.6 and two T.7 of No. 92 Squadron, led by S/Ldr Brian Mercer, whose last posting, by a curious chance, had been deputy leader to Pete Latham in Treble One. No. 74 Squadron, under S/Ldr John Howe, produced their unforgettable "burner take-off", nine flame-tipped Lightnings pitching effortlessly up to the vertical at lift-off, the last few almost invisible in the heat-haze, conveyed the power unleashed by those roaring Avons in the most dramatic way possible. If you happened to watch it from the runway's edge – as one could in those days – you also smelled of kerosene for the rest of the day.

The Fleet Air Arm was represented by six Scimitars of No. 800 Squadron, led by Lt Cdr Danny Norman and by three formations from HMS Hermes, ten Sea Vixens of No. 890 Squadron (diamond nine and solo), six Scimitars of No. 804 Squadron (five and solo) and finally four Gannets from No.849 Squadron. The two solo aircraft gave LABS demonstrations and the naval contribution was completed by a flight refuelling demonstration by two Sea Vixen.

For the first time, the Army Air Corps were represented. Apart from demonstration drills with Thunderbird and Blue Water from No. 37 (GW) Regiment, Royal Artillery in the guided weapons park, eight Skeeters in two four-ship boxes, operating out of Queen's Parade gave a synchronised formation display. The former Army Air Corps, formed in 1942, had been an assault unit, and closed in 1950 with the withdrawal of gliders. The name was revived in September 1957 when the War Office took over Air Observation Post and light liaison aircraft from the Air Ministry.

Attention was being focussed on the possibilities of supersonic civil transports as it had become obvious that militarily, the subject was a dead duck. In fact, the first meeting of the Supersonic Aircraft Transport Committee had taken place at the end of 1956. Handley Page proposed long-range and medium range SSTs, the H.P.109 and 110 and selected cruising speeds of M:1.8 and 1.3, but official preference then went on to M:2.2 (any higher speed took one out of the heat-absorption capabilities of existing alumunium alloys) and A.V.Roe and Bristol, but not Handley Page, were told to go ahead with studies. Bristol took over the modified F.D.2 and turned it into the Bristol 221 for high-speed research (their design eventually became our half of Concorde) and the H.P. contribution was limited to the low-speed end and the 115. Over the next four years the aircraft was to accumulate a great deal of useful data for the Concorde programme.

The overlay of the Beagle label on both Miles Aircraft at Shoreham and Auster aircraft at Rearsby caused the final Auster productions, the D. 4/D. 5/D. 6 and civil Auster 6 conversions to become first Beagle-Austers in 1961 and then Beagles in 1962 and acquire canine labels. Priority in 1961 was being given to a new light twin, originated by Peter Masefield at Bristol and brought with him as a project to Shoreham when he arrived as managing director of Beagle.

This was the 206. In prototype form, the Rolls-Royce label on its Continental engines qualifying it for the flying display, it aroused intense interest. A five-seater, with 260 hp engines it cruised at 228 mph (367 k/h) and proved, like all subsequent Beagle designs, delightful to fly. The Airedale, got up like an airliner, and consequently 350 lb (158.75 kg) heavier than the Husky on the same horsepower, was never terribly popular, the extra weight tending to erode the performance "No little and then somewhat", as Damon Runyon would have said.

The Short S.C.1 flew again, still using its protective platform, displayed by Denis Tayler, now chief test pilot. Compared with the solution of vectored thrust adopted by Bristol for their VTOL designs, the Rolls-Royce battery of five separate engines seemed complicated. One engine provided forward thrust only, the lift engines being pivoted in pairs, providing forward thrust or braking thrust as required in transition. Shorts had also erected in the equipment park, what appeared to be a novel two-storey chalet with double staircase and balcony, but which turned out to be a section of a Belfast fuselage with viewing facilities.

The Comet 4C, final variant of the Mk 4, combined the longer fuselage of the 4B with the Comet 4 wing and fuel tanks, giving better loadcarrying over shorter distances. Five were ordered by the Royal Air Force for Transport Command.

Westland flew virtually their complete range of helicopters. The Belvedere was a production aircraft and the Scout one of the pre-production batch. The Whirlwind was the company demonstrator, converted from Leonides to Gnome turbine power; production airframes were being turned out at Yeovil as the HAR.10 and older airframes converted at Weston. The production naval Wessex HAS.1 carried full autostabilization gear and equipment for its anti-submarine role and distinguished itself by towing up the runway a flat-bed truck on which were a pick-up truck and a Scout helicopter, with a trailer carrying a Saladin armoured personnel carrier, the whole lot weighing 50 tons (50.8 tonnes). On the grounds, presumably, that it was neither flying nor static, the Scout did not appear in contemporary lists of participating aircraft.

On the public days there was a delightful *hors d'oeuvre* consisting of the Tiger Club's nine-ship Turbulent formation and the Shuttleworth S.E.5A (which they were having some difficulty in extracting from the RAE). Nobody, apparently, complained that the Turbulents' Volkswagen engines and the S.E.5A's Hispano-Suiza were not British. The Commanding Officer, Experimental Flying, Pat Hanafin, was flying the S.E.5A. James Baring of the Tiger Club, who tended to live in a world of his own at times and patently had not been listening when introduced, baffled COEF – and everybody else – by addressing him consistently as Group Captain Parafin.

The set piece at the end of the day involved a noisy and spectacular attack on the control tower by aircraft of No.38 Group and others. Hunter FGA.9s from Nos 1 and 54 Squadrons and No.229 OCU provided fire and movement, under cover of which four Beverleys of No. 53 Squadron landed some 200 troops with three Land Rovers, two Ferret scout cars and some 105 mm recoil-less rifles. Parachutists (six instructors from No. 1 Parachute Training Centre) dropped in from 9,000 ft (2,743 m) after a spectacular free fall, No.230 Squadron's single and Twin Pioneers dropped supplies, and more material was ferried in to the troops by six Whirlwind HAR.2 of No. 225 Squadron and Belvederes from the Belvedere Training Unit at Odiham. All very exciting, especially when viewed from the roof of the target.

1961

+ Armstrong Whitworth
  Argosy C.1   XN814 (AW.6743)
  Avro Lincoln B.2   G-29-1. Napier icing research
+ Avro Vulcan B.2   XH557 Bristol Olympus
+ Avro 748   G-ARMV (1536)
+ Beagle Airedale   G-ARKE (B.501)
  Beagle Airedale   G-ARNP (B.503)
  Beagle Airedale   G-ARNS (B.505) fuselage only
+ Beagle Terrier   G-ARRN (B.630)
+ Beagle AOP.11   XP254 (B.701)
+ Beagle B.206X   G-ARRM (B.001)
+ Blackburn Buccaneer S.1   XK534
+ de Havilland Comet 4C   G-AROV (06460) MEA
  de Havilland Dove 8A   G-ARDH (04519)
+ English Electric Lightning T.4 XM974
+ Folland Gnat T.1   XM693 (FL.503)
+ Folland Gnat T.1   XM698 (FL.508)
+ Gloster Javelin FAW.1   XA554 D.H. Gyron Juniors
  Gloster Meteor U.16   WH505
+ Handley Page Herald 200   G-ARTC (148)
+ Handley Page Victor B.2   XL164
+ Handley Page H.P.115   XP841
+ Hawker Hunter T.66A   G-APUX
+ Hunting Jet Provost T.4   XP547 (PAC/W/14130)
  Hunting Jet Provost T.51   G-23-1 (PAC/W/13903) marked
                              124 for Sudan AF

  Scottish Aviation Twin
  Pioneer CC.2   XP294 (572)
+ Short S.C.1   XG900 (SH.1814)
+ Westland Belvedere HC.1   XG459 (13354)
+ Westland Rotodyne   XE521 (F.9429)

+ Westland Scout AH.1   XP165 (S2/8437)
+ Westland Skeeter   XM563 (S2/5117) Blackburn
                              Turmo
+ Westland Wessex HAS.1   XM300 (WA.5)
+ Westland Whirlwind 3   G-APDY (WA.241)

Services participation in flying programmes:
Auster AOP.9: three aircraft for parachutists from AAC Middle Wallop.
Blackburn Beverley: four to land 200 troops plus one for parachutists, 53 and 47 Squadrons.
Bristol Belvedere: two carrying field guns and carriages plus one with troops.
de Havilland Sea Vixen: nine from 890 Squadron, two in refuelling demonstration, one in LABS demonstration.
English Electric Lightning: nine from 74 Squadron, aerobatic team.
Fairey Gannet: four from 849 Squadron.
Hawker Hunter: 16 from 92 Squadron "Blue Diamonds" aerobatic team plus eight of 54 Squadron.
Hunting Jet Provost: four from CFS, aerobatic team.
Scottish Aviation Pioneer: one plus one Twin Pioneer, 230 Squadron.
Supermarine Scimitar: six from 800 Squadron, aerobatic team, six from 804 Squadron fly-past, one from 804 Squadron in LABS demonstration, one photographing show.
Westland Skeeter: two teams of four from AAC Middle Wallop.
Westland Whirlwind: six from 225 Squadron.

Other flying participation:
Druine (Rollason) Turbulent: G-APLZ, 'PNZ, 'PTZ, 'PVZ, 'PZZ, 'RGZ, 'RIZ, 'RJZ, 'RNZ.
RAE S.E.5A D7000.

The photographer in a Westland Widgeon took this corner of the aircraft park on a damp 4 September. Right in the centre is the bronze and white Beagle B-206X G-ARRM.

Gloster Javelin XA552 in an overall dark blue scheme was used as a test-bed for the Gyron Junior engines of the Bristol T.188 research aircraft.

The Skeeter, now under Westland's name, was XM563 fitted experimentally with a Blackburn Turmo engine. It later reverted to standard AOP.12 configuration.

Beagle's AOP.11 XP254 made its Farnborough debut looking more like a two-seat tourer than an Army air observation post.

Beagle were well represented; also making its first appearance was the Airedale of which G-ARNP was the third production aircraft.

The Handley Page H.P.115 XP841 was built as a low speed research aircraft for the delta wing; it provided much useful handling experience for the Concorde.

1962

THE TWENTY-THIRD SHOW
3-9 SEPTEMBER

Any number of reasons might be given for proposing the importance of the 1962 SBAC Show. For one thing, it was finally made public and official by the President of the Society, Sir Roy Dobson, that there would be no Show in 1963. Agreement had been reached among Members on the subject and the next one would be in 1964 and, for good measure, he emphasised that it would still be confined to British products or products made in Britain.

After 1964, he would not commit himself, but it was generally felt that no return to an annual event would be made. The Paris Salon occurring in uneven years, the SBAC Display would alternate neatly with it.

Tented accommodation for 348 exhibitors had gone up to 134,000 square feet (12,449 sq.m). Agreement had been reached between Britain and France over the decision to press on with the supersonic airliner, which would be basically an amalgamation of the (very similar) ideas contained in the Bristol 198 project and the Sud Aviation Super-Caravelle. Signed in London shortly after the Show on 29 November, the agreement provided for equal cost-sharing by both partners, the final bill being then estimated at between £75-85 million – a sum that was to rise a little later to £280 million. It was expected that the prototype would fly in 1967 and production aircraft be in service in 1971.

Among the international *sturm und drang* that accompanied the short-lived NATO proposal for a VTOL supersonic strike fighter, the announcement of the proposed formation of a tripartite evaluation squadron, using the subsonic private venture Hawker P.1127, passed almost un-noticed in 1962 except among those directly involved in the UK, Germany and the USA.

Six new aircraft appeared this year. The three transports, D.H.125, D.H.121 Trident and Vickers VC10, all paid obvious tribute, in their rear-mounted engines, to the current design philosophy of a clean wing, suitable for the installation of a variety of high-lift devices. The P.1127 went on to become the Harrier. The other two newcomers were the diminutive, Bensen-derived Wallis autogyro and the remarkable Bristol 188.

On a more sinister note, the Avro Vulcan B.2 of No. 617 Squadron in the static park was seen to be carrying the British Blue Steel stand-off bomb, with which the squadron was carrying out development trials.

Due note was taken of the fact that 1962 marked the fiftieth anniversary of the founding of the Royal Flying Corps; there was a splendid and nostalgic parade of vintage and veteran aircraft, many of which were still flying more than 25 years later.

Service participation, down a little, inevitably, from the previous year's exuberance, included no less than seven formation teams, a No.114 Squadron Argosy C.1 dropping eight parachutists as weather permitted, a brace of Sea Vixens of No. 899 Squadron demonstrating flight refuelling and a singleton Scimitar, photographing them at it as he shot past and delivering processed prints onto the President's table very shortly afterwards.

For the Royal Navy, Cdr A.J. "Spiv" Leahy was back, leading a piratical team of four Buccaneers from No. 700Z intensive flying unit, the pilots wearing black bonedomes decorated with large skulls and cross bones. There were five Scimitars of No. 736 Squadron, pushing their luck with what the Press, with an eye on the rules and the Navy's reputation, delicately called "audible near-sonic almost-bangs" and repeating the famous "twinkle" roll with a quartet in formation. There was "Fred's Five" of Sea Vixens from No. 766 Squadron and seven more from No. 893.

The Royal Air Force was represented by the Hunters of the Blue Diamonds, by No. 74 "Tiger" Squadron's eight Lightnings, led by S/Ldr Pete Botterill and by the Central Flying School four-ship Jet Provost team. On the final Sunday both fighter teams combined to produce a diamond 25 and F/Lt Doug Bridson, reserve pilot in 92 Squadron, drilled his Hunter up to 21,000 ft in a series of vertical rolls. On the lighter side, the nine Tiger Club Turbulents were back and Andrei Tupolev, having failed to receive an official invitation, paid his £1 happily on Friday like a good proletarian and was rewarded by having lunch with Sir George Edwards.

It was not the best of years for weather. After a dull Monday it rained heavily on Tuesday, but cleared grudgingly in the afternoon. On Wednesday low cloud prevented much in the way of vertical manoeuvre, on Thursday the afternoon was clear after a rainy morning and on the public days the sun shone. One really begins to wonder about that "first week in September is best" stuff from the met. records.

Pioneering work was done by Dowty, who seem to have been the first to introduce the company logo plastic bag and by Elliott's, who went UDI in their own little exhibition marquee. But authority soon put a stop to that sort of thing. At any rate, it does not seem to have happened again. There was no Comet, for the first time in 13 years, but the Dove was still nestling in the static at its 17th Display. There was no Viscount, but BAC had a display on their stand recording the total hours flown (four and a half million-odd by the time the Show started), rather like those clocks in St James's Park Underground station that tell you how often trains go by.

The autogyro in the Show was one of a long line of similar craft built by W/Cdr Ken Wallis in Norfolk and represented a rare attempt at series production. Ken Wallis had taken the basic American Bensen design and shaken it out engineering-wise into quite a different animal. He was continuously refining or altering his basic design for domestic, aerial work or record-breaking purposes and among other achievements in 1988 held every one of the FAI records in the particular weight class for the type.

Although its Farnborough appearances were rare, and two further commercial ventures, through Airmark and Vinten, came to nothing, "Little Nell", one of the series, gained enduring fame as a "goodie" in a James Bond film. Like most of the early versions, the WA.116 was powered by a modified McCulloch flat-four two stroke of some 72 horsepower and at 580 lb (263 kg) total weight, must qualify for being one of the lightest aeroplanes, bar microlights, ever shown at Farnborough. As their creator could never bear to throw one away, there are still 21 on the civil register.

At the other end of the scale was the Bristol T.188, built almost entirely out of steel and looking rather as if it had been oval-turned from the solid. The first and as it happened the last, turbojet built by Bristol Aircraft Ltd, before all turned into BAC, it had but a brief and unglamorous career. It was designed to provide data on kinetic heating effects on aircraft structures in prolonged flight at twice the speed of sound, for the benefit of the Concorde programme.

With this in mind, it was built of stainless steel and raised all sorts of problems in application of this material, notably in fastening or welding it, for the flight conditions it would meet. Virtually the whole fuselage was full of fuel, with a complex refrigerated compartment in front for the pilot and a vast mass of electronic recording and telemetering equipment. This was monitored by a pilot and engineer on the ground, who fed back to the pilot in the aircraft "only information requiring definite action, so saving him from the distraction of indications and warnings about which he could do nothing" – to quote Chris Barnes' *Bristol Aircraft since 1910*. It was an awe-inspiring concept and under the circumstances it was perhaps not surprising that at the Empire Test Pilots School Dinner the company's chief test pilot, Godfrey Auty, was voted the man most likely to eject in 1963. After all the effort, the Gyron Juniors proved so thirsty in this airframe that it never did manage to fly fast enough long enough to get hot enough. Two were built and flown, plus a test airframe,

out of the six originally ordered.

After that tragic but inspiring tale, it is nice to be able to turn to a number of more successful aircraft, the Trident, the 125 and the VC10. This being a period when aircraft constructors were merging with bewildering rapidity, one has to be careful with the nomenclature of the Trident. It was designed as the Airco 121 by a consortium of de Havilland, Fairey and Hunting, calling itself the Aircraft Manufacturing Company, which just happened to be the name under which de Havilland had originally commenced trading. Design responsibility fell on de Havilland when Airco was disbanded and the 121 became the D.H.121. After the formation of the Hawker Siddeley Group it became the H.S.121 and as such, it displayed at the 1962 Farnborough.

The Trident was designed to a close specification from BEA for a short-haul jet capable of working from short runways. Normally a 75 seater, the aircraft was exactly what BEA wanted, with the right characteristics for short sectors and later proved fully compatible with the Autoland fully automatic landing system – incidentally, Smiths' first commercial application of this. Rear mounted engines gave a clean wing and greatly reduced cabin noise. Powered by Rolls-Royce Speys, the third production aircraft had flown for the first time only two weeks before the Show and it was joined at the Show when airborne by the first and second off the line. These were Trident 1s, with an 800 mile (1,287.5 km) range carrying 77 passengers and freight. BEA had ordered a full fleet of 24 off the drawing board. The later Trident 1C carried 1,000 gallons (4,546 litres) more fuel which extended the range to 1,500 miles (2,414 km). A very well-designed aircraft, its prospects were to be considerably hampered by loyal compliance with parameters that were of interest solely to BEA, thus inhibiting orders from other airlines with quite different requirements.

The H.S.125, which had shed the rather cumbersome name of Jet Dragon between last Farnborough's model and reality, was a 6-8 seat, 365 knot (676.5 km/h) twin-Viper business jet with a range of 1,650 miles (2,656 km). The first prototype being shown had only twenty hours' flying behind it, but on Tuesday, the Minister of Aviation, Julian Amery, announced that it would be ordered for the Royal Air Force. It was to become a clear leader in an increasingly important – and competitive – area and like the Viscount, achieve major export sales in North America.

The Vickers VC10, one of the best-looking airliners ever built, with handling characteristics to match its looks, was powered by four Conways and like the Trident, was tailored only to one airline's requirements, in this case BOAC, for its African and Australian routes. This involved catering for a large payload (35,000 lb/15,876 kg) over a range of some 4,000 miles (6,437 km) and involving take-offs at some very

1962

	Armstrong Whitworth Argosy C.1	XN817 (AW.6746)
+	Avro Vulcan B.1	XA894 R-R Olympus beneath fuselage, flying only
	Avro Vulcan B.2	XL361 with Blue Steel
+	Avro 748-2	C-91-2500 (1550) Brazilian AF
	Beagle Airedale	G-ASBY (B.523)
	Beagle Terrier 2	G-ASBU (B.613)
+	Beagle AOP.11	G-ASCC (B.701)
+	Beagle B.206X	G-ARRM (B.001)
+	Beagle B.206Y	G-ARXM (B.002)
+	Beagle B.218	G-ASCK (B.051)
+	Beagle-Wallis WA.116	XR942 (B.202)
	Blackburn Buccaneer S.1	XN929
	Bristol Britannia C.1	XL640 (13449)
+	Bristol T.188	XF923 (13518)
	de Havilland Dove 8	G-AREA (04520)
+	de Havilland Trident 1	G-ARPA (2101) flying only
+	de Havilland Trident 1	G-ARPB (2102) flying only
+	de Havilland Trident 1	G-ARPC (2103)
+	de Havilland D.H.125	G-ARYA (25001)
+	English Electric Lightning F.3	XG310
	English Electric Lightning T.4	XM974
+	English Electric Lightning T.5	XM967
+	Folland Gnat T.1	XM691 (FL.501)
+	Folland Gnat T.1	XM698 (FL.508)
+	Handley Page Herald 200	CF-MCK (161)
+	Handley Page H.P.115	XP841
+	Hawker Hunter T.66A	G-APUX
+	Hawker P.1127	XP831
+	Hawker P.1127	XP972
+	Hunting Jet Provost T.4	XP666
	Hunting Jet Provost T.4	XP667
	Vickers Varsity T.1	G-ARFP (546)
+	Vickers VC10	G-ARTA (803)
+	Westland Scout AH.1	XP848 (F.9474)
+	Westland Scout AH.1	XP849 (F.9475)
	Westland Scout AH.1	XP853 (F.9479)
	Westland Wasp HAS.1	XS463 (F.9541)
+	Westland Wessex HAS.1	XM837 (WA.18)
	Westland Wessex HAS.31	WA202 Royal Australian Navy (WA.202)
+	Westland Whirlwind 2	G-AOCZ (WA/H/115)
+	Westland Whirlwind 3	G-APDY (WA.241)
+	Westland Whirlwind HAR.2	XK991 (WA.147)
	Westland Whirlwind HAR.10	XP301 (WA.341)
+	Westland Whirlwind HAR.10	XP400 (WA.388)

Services participation in flying programmes:
Armstrong Whitworth Argosy: one from 114 Squadron.
Blackburn Buccaneer: four from 700Z Flight and 801 Squadron.
de Havilland Sea Vixen: five from 766 Squadron, "Fred's Five" aerobatic team and seven from 893 Squadron. Two flight refuelling from 899 Squadron.
English Electric Lightning: eight from 74 Squadron.
Hawker Hunter: 16 from 92 Squadron, "Blue Diamonds" aerobatic team.
Hunting Jet Provost: five from CFS, aerobatic team.
Supermarine Scimitar: five from 736 Squadron aerobatic team.

Veteran and vintage aircraft:
Bristol F.2b Fighter D8096.
de Havilland Mosquito T.3 TW117.
Fairey Fulmar N1854.
Fairey Swordfish LS326.
Gloster Gladiator K8032.
Hawker Hart J9933.
Hawker Hurricane PZ865/G-AMAU.
RAE SE.5A D7000.
Supermarine Spitfire AB910.

Civilian aircraft:
Druine (Rollason) Turbulent: G-APNZ, 'PTZ, 'PVZ, 'PYZ, 'RCZ, 'RGZ, 'RJZ, 'RNZ, 'RRZ.

high, hot and short airfields en route. Here the advantages of the clean wing/rear engine combination showed up, offering improved airfield performance and economy and lower approach speeds.

During the design, certain modifications to weight, wing area and fuel capacity gave the VC10 trans-Atlantic capability; there was a gain of 16,000 lb (7,257.5 kg) of fuel and an increase in gross weight of 52,000 lb (23,587 kg). BOAC signed a contract for 35, with 20 more on option, in 1958, thus bringing the order book to break-even point in one fell swoop. However, with the announcement of the Super VC10 in 1961, they cut the original order to 12 and ordered 30 Supers. The prototype VC10 flew for the first time on 29 June and the second was in the factory when the first aircraft appeared, in BOAC livery, at Farnborough – though the first actual service aircraft would not fly until the following month. Eleven had been ordered for the Royal Air Force and more were to follow. The VC10, too, following the rationalisation of the industry, was the last aircraft to appear under its parents' original name.

The most exciting aircraft has been left to the last. This was,

of course, the VTOL Hawker P.1127; two of them, in fact, with the first prototype, flown by Hugh Merewether, being joined, until Thursday, by the third prototype, which then left to return to its test duties at Dunsfold while XP831 displayed solo in the pouring rain.

The principle of vectored thrust had been carefully described well before the First World War and in May 1954

Avro Vulcan XA894 was used as a test-bed for the Bristol Olympus intended for the TSR.2.

Star of the Show was the Hawker P.1127; two were shown and one of these, XP831, is seen here in an early test hover.

Westland Whirlwind HAR.10 XP301; the Hillman Minx was not part of the Show but the Hawker P.1127 was.

Westland flew a Nene-powered Meteor with jet deflection nozzles ranging over 60 degrees. By a happy chance the pilot on that occasion, S/Ldr Leo de Vigne, was to bring a Whirlwind HAR.10 in to Farnborough on the Saturday.

At a time when the 1957 Defence White Paper had virtually wiped clean the drawing boards in the Hawker Design Office, they were approached by Bristol with an initial proposal for vectored thrust. What had started as a French idea to drive compressors with swivelling volutes from a Bristol Orion had evolved, via an intermediate design, into the BE.53 Pegasus, a most elegant and satisfactory powerplant. Around it grew up the P.1127, which first flew on a tether on 21 October 1960, achieving full and free hover on 19 November. Transition was achieved in the first half of 1961 and four more airframes were commenced. Progress was swift, despite the loss of the second aircraft in December 1961 and by July, Duncan Simpson and David Lockspeiser had joined the programme. Further aircraft, which were to become the Kestrel, were ordered to equip the proposed tripartite squadron.

At an early and critical stage the chief test pilot had the misfortune to break his ankle in a car crash, thereby holding up the whole programme. Under considerable pressure from the company to renew his medical, the Ministry of Civil Aviation grudgingly and only partially gave way. One of Bill Bedford's most cherished possessions is a Private Pilot's Licence endorsed "for tethered flight only".

Another de Havilland newcomer was the first D.H.125 G-ARYA which made its maiden flight three weeks before the Show.

The first pre-production Gnat T.1 was accompanied by the eighth, in an unfamiliar bright yellow paint scheme evolved by Folland, who tried to convince the Air Marshals that this tough, epoxy-resin finish gave better protection than the Service silver and dayglo red. This aircraft carried pylons for Sidewinders. One wonders if that yellow Gnat, XM698, finished up at Valley and inspired the Yellowjacks.

G-ARPB was one of three de Havilland Tridents appearing in the flying programme. The first Trident had made its maiden flight only eight months earlier.

1964

THE TWENTY-FOURTH SHOW
7-13 SEPTEMBER

On 26 February 1964, the Society of British Aircraft Constructors, reflecting the large expansion of interests among its members, became the Society of British Aerospace Companies, retaining the famous initials that, at the height of the Sandys White Paper mergers, was cynically supposed to refer to the Society of Both Aircraft Companies.

In 1964, at the first of the biennial Shows, although there were a lot of innovations, two intriguing prototypes did not appear. TSR.2 was running a bit late on its first flight and the curious BAC H.126, which had been flying for about eighteen months, was withdrawn in favour of continuing its research programme at Luton. The TSR.2 never did appear at Farnborough; it was cancelled by Mr Denis Healey, who had very strong views on the subject and was airing them in 1964 in attacks on Mr Julian Amery. The H. (for Hunting) 126 was built purely to engage in jet flap research and presumably had little commercial attraction. All the same it would have been nice to see it fly; it looked a little like a Barracuda that had been badly frightened by a Sabre.

The new two-year cycle would continue, despite the Society's cautious refusal to commit itself at the time. After all, Members might yet change their minds after this first experiment with time. At any rate, it looked as if the longer interval was a factor in increasing the interest taken in the Display.

The weather, apart from dull mornings on the first two days, was impeccable; there were 320 exhibitors and the Great Exhibition Hall again covered 134,000 square feet (12,448.6 sq.m).

Prices had not increased and you could still bring in your bicycle for 1s (5p) or 2s 6d (12½p) on Friday. Ken Pearson, who had been working in the control tower for some years, was the commentator, the suave, charming, irrepressible Major Oliver Stewart, MC, RFC, ex-fighter pilot, author, editor – and *chef manqué* – having retired to the Isle of Wight to indulge his twin passions of sailing and gastronomy and continue his stubborn campaign for the metric system. One may be forgiven for thinking that the SBAC, who never quite knew what Oliver was going to say next, watched his retirement with mixed feelings. Pilots' names were still unmentionable.

This year the now familiar souvenir public programme was introduced for the first time and on public days, vintage and ultralight aircraft displayed during the lunch period – an innovation that did not survive. Sadly, nor did one of the vintage aircraft; the beautifully-restored Bristol Bulldog crashed during its demonstration, never to be rebuilt.

Service participation again was on the grand scale; two Royal Air Force aerobatic teams displayed simultaneously and 58 aircraft took part in a co-ordinated demonstration, producing 109 movements in 11 minutes. Royal Air Force and Army parachute teams jumped on the public days.

From the Fleet Air Arm came eight Scimitar F.1s of No. 803 Squadron (for the record, among the eleven aircraft from which the team was drawn was one from No. 736 Squadron). There were eight Sea Vixen FAW.1s, drawn from Nos 890 and 766 Squadrons and no less than twelve Wessex HC.5s of No. 848 Squadron.

For the Royal Air Force, No.92 Squadron were there again, now re-equipped with the Lightning and showing six F.2 and T.4. The second formation aerobatic team was the familiar Jet Provost one from CFS, now with six T.4s painted blood-red all over and calling themselves the Red Pelicans, a title patently drawn from the unit badge. There was also a new and dashing team of five yellow-painted Gnats from No. 4 FTS at Valley, billed as the Yellowjacks and led by a remarkable young officer called Lee Jones. They put on synchronised displays each day with the Red Pelicans and produced several new manoeuvres, including "leader's benefit" (sound familiar?) and "candy stripe delta". This last has left no impression over the years, but one feels it must have combined the liveries of both teams.

During the course of the Show, several orders for aircraft were announced, including a repeat, said to be for 30-40 units, of Westland Scouts and one announced by the Minister of Aviation, for thirteen H.S.125s. (In fact he got it wrong; he forgot the one ordered for Her Britannic Majesty's Ambassador in Washington.) Handley Page announced the sale of two Heralds.

Farnborough International 1990 (and le Bourget) exhibitors might look a little wistfully at a comment heard in 1964: charges for space at Paris were three times those at Farnborough – sixteen guineas (£16.80) a square metre.

Beagle had one brand-new aircraft flying. The B.242 was a re-think of the B.218, but with metal replacing the many glass fibre elements in the latter, as it turned out that tin was cheaper and lighter. The initial miscalculation cost Beagle dear, for neither got past a solitary prototype.

The BAC One-Eleven was at the start of a most successful career, in the course of which it was to break into the North American market, like the Viscount it was planned to replace and also, unlike the Viscount, to sell behind the Iron Curtain. The original design for a rather smaller aircraft came to BAC from Hunting, but was enlarged to meet market requirements. American orders, several times repeated, were particularly satisfactory, in competition with the native DC-9. At Farnborough time there were 65 orders, 55 from overseas and with the British launch customer, British United Airways, who had ordered ten, due to receive the first for crew training, shortly after the Show. Over 200 were sold in various versions.

Many political and economic factors could distort the pattern of aircraft sales and upset plans. BOAC announced that they were abandoning all services to South America. Their defence was that the route, in the face of local political pressure which would not allow them to introduce the highly-suitable 707, was uneconomical.

Buying more VC10s for such an uneconomic area would be no answer, said the Corporation. This hardly cheered Vickers, faced with the muddle over BOAC's requirements for the VC10 and rejection of the VC11 in favour of the BAC One-Eleven. Nor, in view of the cancellation of the V1000 long range military transport, could they find much comfort in Parliament's criticism of official neglect of this important area of Royal Air Force activity (made in the course of taking a closer economic look at the management of the Service's overseas bases).

At least the Super VC10 was flying at Farnborough. Rolls-Royce had raised the thrust of the Conway to 22,500 lb (10,205.8kg) and careful detail redesigning of wing and nacelle had notably reduced drag and increased range, thus giving BOAC an aircraft suitable for trans-Atlantic routes, where runway lengths equated greater gross weight. Twenty-seven were built of this version.

Godfrey Auty flew the BAC 221 research aircraft, which was in fact one of the two Fairey Delta 2 airframes, lengthened by six feet or so and married to an entirely new wing and set of controls and given rather more fuel. The new wing, a slender, ogival delta matching that proposed for Concorde, was, of course, the reason for the existence of the BAC 221 and was to be tested at various speeds, for comparison with wind-tunnel and theoretical data, up to a planned M:1.6; pretty much the speed reached by the original F.D.2 in its record flight.

With the bigger R.Da.12 Dart of no less than 3,000 shp and Dowty-Rotol airscrews 14 ft 6 in (4.42 m) in diameter the military 748 could operate out of rough airstrips down to 300 yards (274.3 m) in length, using an impressively steep approach, and could take-off in 100 yards (91.45 m) at 33,000 lb (14,968.5 kg). Jimmy Harrison used these advantages to give an impressive flying display in the prototype, which was

the aerodynamic test-bed for the production Andover C.1. This aircraft did not have the hydraulically-operated "kneeling" undercarriage fitted to the C.1 to adjust the floor height for loading different vehicles. On the opening Tuesday (Monday was still rehearsal day) he made a one-engine pass, with doors open, at 90 knots (167 k/h) and by engaging reverse thrust on final approach, achieved a landing run short enough to draw a spontaneous burst of applause from the spectators.

Not to be outdone, the Trident 1C produced an equally impressive short landing, reversing the centre engine's thrust well short of touch-down.

When the Andover C.1 finally disappeared from squadron service on the disbandment of No. 46 Squadron at Thorney Island in August 1975, a victim of one of the numerous Treasury "Defenceless" cuts, an obituary notice appeared in the *Daily Telegraph* "C.C.Andover: quietly at his home at Thorney Island, on 29 August 1975....". It is sad to have to record that authority did not think this tribute amusing – and said so to the officer concerned.

For Short Brothers (and, of course, Harland, who did not disappear from the company name until the 1976 restructuring) the Skyvan marked a most important moment in the 64 years that the Short brothers had been building aircraft, for it represented the return of the firm to the main stream of civil aircraft design, through its recently-formed Light Aircraft Division. At the other end of the scales of size and weight was the Short Belfast, whose empty weight was about the equivalent of ten loaded Skyvans and which could lift nearly seventeen times as much cargo.

Ten Belfasts were ordered for Transport Command, going to No. 53 Squadron at Brize Norton. They performed prodigies of airlift, carrying such loads as a Chieftain tank or three Whirlwinds, sharing with No. 216 Squadron's Comets the almost unique distinction in the Royal Air Force of having names for all the squadron aircraft. (These units chose names from astronomy and the classics; faced with the same problem of naming aircraft, No. 8 Squadron, for their Shackleton AEW.2s, went to *Magic Roundabout).*

Government decisions to pull out of all Far Eastern commitments cut short the career of the Belfast C.1 (and made any further order out of the question) and no response to extensive propaganda in the civil market was made for new airframes. However, several of the C.1s were bought by HeavyLift Cargo Airlines, who were still employing them most effectively in 1990.

One might close by quoting from the SBAC President's speech: "Government policy on ordering military and sponsoring civil projects has been anything but consistent." Many Members would have agreed with him.

1964

	Airspeed Ambassador 2	G-ALZP (5213)
+	BAC Jet Provost T.4	XS230
	BAC Jet Provost T.52	603 Iraqi AF
+	BAC Lightning F.3	XP697
+	BAC One-Eleven 201	G-ASJE (H.009)
+	BAC Super VC10	G-ASGA (851)
	BAC VC10	G-ASIW (819)
+	BAC 221	WG774 (13521) converted from Fairey F.D.2.
	Beagle Airedale	G-ASWF (B.537)
	Beagle Husky	G-ASNC (3678)
+	Beagle B.206S	G-ASMK (B.005)
	Beagle B.206Z (Basset)	XS743 (B.008)
+	Beagle B.242	G-ASTX (B.242/001)
+	Beagle AOP.11	G-ASCC (B.701)
+	Beagle-Wallis WA.116	G-ARRT (B.201)
	Handley Page Herald 200	G-ASVO (185)
+	Handley Page Herald 400	FM-1024 (180) Malaysian AF
	Handley Page Victor B.2	XL233 with Blue Steel
+	Handley Page H.P.115	XP841
+	Hawker Siddeley Buccaneer S.2	XN976
	Hawker Siddeley Dove 8	G-AREA (04520)
+	Hawker Siddley Gnat T.1	XM691 (FL.501)
+	Hawker Siddley Hunter FGA.59	580 no marks, for Iraqi AF
	Hawker Hunter 12 (two-seater)	XE531
	Hawker Siddeley Shackleton MR.3	XF708
+	Hawker Siddeley Trident 1C	G-ARPB (2102)
	Hawker Siddeley Vulcan B.2	XM595 with Blue Steel
+	Hawker Siddeley H.S.125	G-ASEC (25004)
	Hawker Siddeley H.S.748-1	G-ASJT (1559)
+	Hawker Siddeley H.S.748-2	G-ARAY (1535)
+	Hawker Siddeley H.S.748MF	G-ARRV (1548)
+	Hawker Siddeley P.1127	XP984
+	Hawker Siddeley Kestrel FGA.1	XS688
+	Hawker Siddeley Kestrel FGA.1	XS689
	Saunders-Roe Skeeter AOP.12	XL764 (S2/5076)
+	Short Belfast C.1	XR362 (SH.1816) flying only
+	Short Belfast C.1	XR363 (SH.1817) flying only
+	Short Belfast C.1	XR364 (SH.1818)
+	Short Turbo-Skyvan	G-ASCN (SH.1828)
+	Westland Scout AH.1	XP907 (F.9508)
+	Westland Scout AH.1	XP910 (F.9511)
+	Westland Wasp HAS.1	XS572 (F.9583)
	Westland Wasp HAS.1	XT414 (F.9584)
+	Westland Wessex HAS.1	XM837 (WA.18)
+	Westland Wessex HC.2	XR526 (WA.148)
+	Westland Wessex HU.5	XS484 (WA.158)
	Westland Wessex HU.5	XS510 (WA.179)
+	Westland Whirlwind 3	G-APDY (WA.241)
	Westland Whirlwind HAR.10	XJ764 (WA.110)
+	Westland Whirlwind HAR.10	XP299 (WA.342)
+	Westland SR.N5 Hovercraft	(001)

Services participation in flying programmes:
BAC Canberra: four from 14 Squadron.
BAC Jet Provost: six from CFS, "Red Pelicans" aerobatic team.
BAC Lightning: six from 92 Squadron.
de Havilland Canada Beaver: one from 6 Flight, AAC.
Handley Page Victor: one each from 100 and 139 Squadrons.
Hawker Siddeley Gnat: five from 4 FTS, "Yellowjacks" aerobatic team.
Hawker Siddeley Hunter: four each from 1 and 54 Squadrons.
Hawker Siddeley Sea Vixen: eight from 890 and 766 Squadrons.
Hawker Siddeley Vulcan: one from 9 Squadron.
Supermarine Scimitar: eight from 803 Squadron.
Westland Wessex: twelve from 18 and 72 Squadrons; twelve from 848 Squadron.
Whitworth Gloster Argosy: three from 267 Squadron.

Veteran and vintage aircraft:
Blackburn B.2 G-AEBJ.
Bristol Bulldog K2227. Crashed 13/9
Comper Swift G-ABUS.
de Havilland Mosquito T.3 RR299.
Fairey Swordfish LS326.
Gloster Gladiator K8032.
Hawker Hurricane PZ865/G-AMAU.
Hawker Hart J9941.
RAE S.E.5A D7000.
Supermarine Spitfire AB910.

Civilian aircraft:
Druine (Rollason) Turbulent: G-APNZ, 'RNZ, 'RRZ, 'SAM, 'SDB.

A taste of things to come; few who saw the first appearance of the Folland (by now Hawker Siddeley) Gnats of the Yellowjacks – seen here above the red Hunting (by now BAC) Jet Provosts of the Red Pelicans – could have expected the direct progression to the Red Arrows, still the RAF's official aerobatic team 26 years later.

Only the second hovercraft to appear at the Show, the Westland SR.N5 lifts up its skirts prior to a fast sprint down the runway.

Prototype of the Hawker Siddeley H.S.748MF G-ARRV which, in production form became the Andover C.1.

Short Belfast XR364, flew in the Show and was joined by XR362 and '363, but '364 was the only one shown statically.

By 1964, camouflage was being applied to the V bombers and the Hawker Siddeley Shackleton MR.3 XF708 with tricycle undercarriage was shown.

1966

THE TWENTY-FIFTH SHOW
5-11 SEPTEMBER

The whole period of the 1960s was one of change for the aircraft industry and the general reshaping of the companies for future requirements was usually echoed by the SBAC Show. In 1966, for the first time, foreign aircraft, provided that they employed a British engine or used major British components, were permitted in the flying display. They had, however, to be sponsored by their British partners. Apart from that, the Show seemed to have stabilised, there being no change in the number of exhibitors nor in the size of the Hall.

Despite the wave of cancellations that had hit the industry in 1964, killing off the Vickers 1000, the TSR.2 and P.1154 and considerably delaying the eventual introduction of the HS.146, exports for the previous year totalled £217,181,000. The SBAC had organised for the foreign Press a series of visits around its members – who now numbered 520 – to underline the generally healthy state of the industry. It is interesting to note how many important British aircraft at the Show, in a period of governmental control of everything, were private ventures; the Beagle 206, the Islander, the Jetstream, the BAC One-Eleven, the Skyvan and the HS 125.

Among various financial wheelings and dealings, the Government announced on the second trade day that it would provide around £1¼ million support for the Handley Page Jetstream and £¼ million for the Islander. They also confirmed that the cost of Concorde had risen to £400 million, to be equally shared between Britain and France, but failed to sugar this particular pill by pointing out that £182 million had been spent in the United States by the rival SST proposers, without a design having even been agreed for construction.

On the following day, Rolls-Royce announced a £26½ million transfer fee for Bristol Siddeley Engines from Hawker Siddeley to themselves (which was felt to be a good thing). Shortly after the Show, on 15 September, the Government added £100 million to the Concorde bill and on 21 November Fred Mulley, the Minister, told BAC and Hawker Siddeley to consider merging their airframe activities (which did not seem to raise quite the same enthusiasm at the time). Prior to the Show, on 2 August, the Minister had instructed BEA to buy British for its next spread of aircraft. Possibilities here included the VC10 and BAC One-Eleven, Government having already fatally compromised a sale of Super VC10s to Middle East Airlines by refusing financial backing. But they offered

Shorts, in January, £1 million to permit a fresh batch of Skyvans to be started.

This last transaction, in advance of any orders for the aircraft being made stemmed from the British government's majority holding in the company. Shorts were unable to commit capital in this way on their own account.

The Show marked the fiftieth anniversary of the SBAC and during the week, sales were announced to a total value of £62½ million, including 134 aircraft.

Earlier in the year, on 12 March, the death had occurred at the age of 72 of Sir Sidney Camm, director of design at Hawker Siddeley Aviation, chief designer at Hawker Aircraft since 1925 and responsible for a whole series of admirable designs including the Hurricane and the Hunter.

Service participation was not on quite the lavish scale of previous occasions, but included a mass display from the four squadrons of HMS *Hermes*' Air Group and the first appearance of the new Royal Air Force aerobatic display team, the Red Arrows. The mantle of the Firebirds, the Blue Diamonds, the Black Arrows and a long line of fighter squadrons had been placed on the shoulders of the Central Flying School.

A fine collection of veteran and vintage aircraft was assembled to add to the entertainment on the three public days and the Tiger Club were there again, this year with six Turbulents.

BAC were showing two One-Elevens. The demonstrator Series 400 was being employed for trials of the Elliott Automation autoland equipment for initial certification in Cat.2, or 100 ft (30.5 m) decision height and 440 yard (402 m) runway visual range.

Newest, and as it would turn out, most successful of all the new British aircraft present, were the two Britten-Norman Islanders. The prototype had first flown on 13 June 1965, exhibiting later at Paris; it was now at Farnborough, with the first production ten-seater in Loganair colours. As design work had only started just after the previous SBAC Show, this was a remarkable achievement. With 210 hp Rolls-Royce Continentals, weighing 1,000 lb (454 kg) less than the Rapide it was intended to replace and marketing at £17,500, it could hardly fail. In fact, it was to become a resounding success.

Beagle, who had (temporarily, they hoped) shelved the B.242 to concentrate on the forthcoming Pup, focussed their Farnborough effort on the B.206 and supercharged B.206S. Orders were picking up for the light twin, with production running at five a month and demonstrators were active in Europe, Australia, South Africa and North America. All 20 of

1966

Aermacchi MB.326	I-FAZD
+ Aermacchi MB.326	MM54183
+ Agusta-Bell 204B	I-AGUG
+ Airspeed Ambassador 2	G-ALZP (5213)
BAC Canberra TT.18	WJ632
+ BAC Jet Provost T.4	XR669
BAC Lightning F.6	XP697
+ BAC Lightning F.53	XR770
+ BAC One-Eleven 301AG	G-ATPL (W.035)
+ BAC One-Eleven 400	G-ASYD (H.053)
+ BAC 221	WG774 (F.9421)
+ BAC VC10 C.1	XR807 (827)
Beagle Basset C.1	XS777 (B.025)
Beagle Husky	G-ASNC (3678) crop spraying equipment
+ Beagle Husky	G-ATMH (3684)
Beagle AOP.11	G-ASCC (B.701)
+ Beagle B.206	G-ASOF (B.007)
+ Beagle B.206S	G-ATUK (B.032)
+ Beagle B.206S	G-ATVT (B.035)
+ Beagle B.206S	G-ATYD (B.040)
+ Beagle B.206S	G-ATYE (B.041)
+ Breguet Atlantic	(15.)
+ Britten-Norman Islander BN-2	G-ATCT (001)
+ Britten-Norman Islander BN-2	G-ATWU (002)
+ de Havilland Chipmunk	G-ATTS (C1/0765) Rover turbine
+ de Havilland Canada Turbo Beaver	CF-UBN (1622/TB13)
+ de Havilland Canada Twin Otter 100	CF-UXE (9)
+ Fiat G.91T/1	MM6432 (113)
Fiat G.91T/1	MM6433 (114)
+ Fokker F.27-400	PH-FKA (10306) (PK-PFB for Indonesia)
+ Handley Page Herald 204	G-ASBP (163)
Handley Page Victor B(SR)2	XL193
+ Hawker Siddeley Andover C.1	XS595 (1573)
Hawker Siddeley Buccaneer S.2	XV157
Hawker Siddeley Dominie T.1	XS738 (25077)
Hawker Siddeley Gnat T.1	XS101 (FL.595)
Hawker Siddeley Hunter FGA.9	708 Jordanian AF
+ Hawker Siddeley Kestrel FGA.1	XS695
+ Hawker Siddeley P.1127	XV276
Hawker Siddeley Shackleton MR.3	WR973

+ Hawker Siddeley Trident 1E	AP-AUG (2133)
+ Hawker Siddeley Vulcan B.1	XA903 R-R Olympus under fuselage
Hawker Siddeley Vulcan B.2	XL443
+ Hawker Siddeley H.S.125	G-ATSP (25097)
Hawker Siddeley H.S.748-1	G-ASJT (1559)
Hawker Siddeley H.S.748-1	VP-LIO (1535)
+ Hawker Siddeley H.S.748-1	G-ATMJ (1593)
+ Piaggio-Douglas PD.808	MM578 (502)
+ Short Skyvan 2	G-ASCO (SH.1829)
Short Skyvan 2	G-ATPG (SH.1835)
Slingsby Capstan	
+ Slingsby Dart	367
+ Transall C.160	WV (V.1)
+ Wallis WA.116	G-ATHL (401/212)
+ Westland Scout AH.1	XT640 (F.9646)
+ Westland Wasp HAS.1	XT782 (F.9664)
Westland Wasp HAS.1	NZ3902 (F.9679)
+ Westland Wessex HAS.3	XT225 (WA.239)
Westland Wessex HC.2	XR521 (WA.143)
+ Westland Wessex HC.2	XT606 (WA.533)
Westland Wessex HU.5	XT484 (WA.306)
+ Westland Wessex HU.5	XT759 (WA.481)
+ Westland Whirlwind HAR.9	XN386 (WA.316)
+ Westland-Bell Sioux AH.1	XT245 (WA.404)

Services participation in flying programmes:
Fairey Gannet: three from 849 Squadron.
Hawker Siddeley Buccaneer: six from 809 Squadron.
Hawker Siddeley Gnat: nine from CFS, "Red Arrows" aerobatic team.
Hawker Siddley Argosy: one from 114 Squadron with "Falcons" parachutists.
Hawker Siddeley Sea Vixen: ten from 892 Squadron.
Westland Wessex: five from 826 Squadron.

Veteran and vintage aircraft:
Avro Triplane replica.
Bristol Boxkite replica.
de Havilland Mosquito T.3 RR299.
English Electric Wren 4.
Fairey Swordfish LS326.
Hawker Hurricane LF363.
Hawker Hart J9941.
RAE S.E.5A D7000.
Sopwith Pup N5180.
Supermarine Spitfire AB910.
Vickers Gunbus replica 2345.

Civilian aircraft:
Druine (Rollason) Turbulent G-APNZ, 'RLZ, 'RRZ, 'RZM, 'SAM, 'SDB.
de Havilland Dragon Rapide G-AEML.
Stampe S.V.4B G-ASHS.

the military version, the Bassett CC.1, had been delivered to the Royal Air Force. Intended originally for transport of V-bomber crews, it was found unsuitable for that purpose and indeed never achieved a very happy Service life.

The sharp end of the Hawker Siddeley Group's activities was represented by the eighth production Kestrel of the evaluation batch ordered for the Tripartite Training Squadron and the first production standard P.1127 to Royal Air Force requirements.

Westland tried hard for the prize for quantity, with ten helicopters, including the licence-built Bell Sioux for the British army, but came second to Hawker Siddeley, who had 14 of their Group products on display. The Canberra took over from the Dove (not present) as oldest inhabitant, with 15 Shows in 17 years.

Among the Europeans, pride of place had to go to the polished aerobatics of Captain Ricardo Perrachi on the MB.326, resplendent in the orange livery of the Italian Air Force's Experimental Flight Centre. He finished his display on the "Macchino" by landing off a loop, a manoeuvre he embellished by adding gear down, flaps down and a roll on finals. As regular visitors to Farnborough will know, the tradition of this controlled flamboyance by Aermacchi pilots has not been lost.

Macchi built their first aircraft to their own designs in 1914; they built fighters in the Second World War and a number of light aircraft in the 1950s and 1960s, but really re-established themselves in the international market with the MB.326.

Designed in the early 1950s, when the introduction of *ab initio* jet training was beginning to look attractive, the prototype MB.326 flew for the first time on 10 December 1957. It was ordered by the Aeronautica Militare Italiana and entered service in 1962.

With the MB.326, Macchi were among the first to grasp the possibilities of the "two-tier" trainer that doubled in ground-attack/light bombing and weapon training and eventually over 800 were sold in 13 countries, with licence production in Australia, South Africa and Brazil. In 1990 it was still employed by the Royal Australian Air Force, equipping their formation aerobatic team, the Roulettes.

Equally stimulating was the display by the Fiat G.91. The type won the NATO light fighter competition and served with the Italian and German air forces.

Of the two other European aircraft displayed, the Transall 160 was another international programme, the parent company, Transporter Allianz, being formed by Aérospatiale of France, MBB of Germany and VFW-Fokker in 1959 for the production of a new medium transport. The first prototype had flown in 1963, but production did not commence until four years later, when 110 German and 50 French aircraft were built at the three production facilities at Bremen, Hamburg and Bourges. One hundred and eighty-five were eventually built, but apart from this one appearance by the French-roundelled prototype, it did not fly again at Farnborough until a new version was being promoted, in 1976.

The large proportion of collaborative designs among these first foreign entries was a significant pointer to the future trend of European aerospace policies.

The Breguet Atlantic was developed by a five-nation consortium and first flew in 1961. Intended to replace the Lockheed Neptune in NATO air forces, 40 were ordered for the Aéronavale and 20 for the Kreigsmarine. Later the Netherlands government ordered six, largely to fill the gap caused in their naval air cover by the sale of their aircraft carrier HrMs *Karel Doorman*, formerly HMS *Venerable*. (The Dutch sold her to Argentina, where she became the *Veinticinco de Mayo*.). The Dutch order would not itself have re-opened the production line, but an Italian order for 18 made the proposal feasible.

The Fokker F.27, like so many other similar designs, belongs to the "Dakota replacement" family and, as it turned out, was the most successful of them all, not least because of the choice of the reliable Rolls-Royce Dart engines. Thirty years after it first flew in 1955, 759 had been built, with 205 of those produced by Fairchild in the United States.

Smallest aircraft on display was the Wallis WA.116 autogyro G-ATHL.

The European flavour was provided by several aircraft with British engines; this is the French Transall C.160 prototype coded WV powered by Rolls-Royce Tynes.

Another foreign entrant was the Italian Fiat G.91T/1 with the Bristol Siddeley Orpheus engine; this is MM6432 about to begin its display.

Also from Italy was the Piaggio-Douglas PD.808 MM578; Douglas later withdrew from the programme and only 24 were built.

The BAC Lightning was on order for Saudi Arabia and in honour of the occasion XR770 was shown in Saudi colours.

The Royal Navy on the run in for their fly past with Hawker Siddeley Sea Vixens of 892 Squadron and Buccaneers of 809 Squadron.

The first two prototypes of the Britten-Norman Islander were shown; G-ATCT, the first, flies past on one engine. The Islander was a great success and was still in production 25 years later with over 1,100 sold.

1968

THE TWENTY-SIXTH SHOW
16-22 SEPTEMBER

For reasons not entirely clear, it was decided to slip the Show by two weeks and hold it in the third week of the month, presumably as a result of the unpleasant weather in the last few years. It was a most unfortunate decision; torrential rain fell, flooding the airfield and some hurried land reclamation schemes had to be brought into action when the "Laffan's Plain end" disappeared into the Basingstoke Canal and Monday's flying had to be cancelled. The public days were not much better; the Falcons only managed to drop (mostly sideways) at minimum altitude on Sunday; the Arrows that day did their rolling show.

This year, aircraft of any nationality were allowed in, subject once again to their being sponsored by an SBAC member and featuring major items of British equipment. They included for the first time two (Sud helicopters) not powered by British engines.

Service participation in the flying included a No. 55 Squadron Victor refuelling two Lightnings from No. 5 Squadron and for the first time, on the public days, the Royal Air Force Historic Flight was included, with the classic Hurricane – Spitfire – Lancaster formation.

Japan showed their new twin-engined civil transport, the NAMC YS-11A from, would you believe, Nihon Kokuki Seizo Kabushiki Kaisha. One hundred and eighty-two were eventually built and served, in six different versions, from 1965. Apart from domestic airlines, Olympic ordered six and Piedmont Airlines no less than 22, making its final purchase in 1984.

The Fleet Air Arm were represented by two new naval formation teams, Simon's Circus with Sea Vixens from No. 892 Squadron and Phoenix Five with Buccaneers from No. 809; both units had recently deployed to Yeovilton from HMS *Hermes*' Air Group. The Royal Air Force produced 20 Jet Provosts from the RAF College in a "50" formation to commemorate their half century and, for their second time at the Show, the finest sky-diving team in any Service, the Falcons.

Beside the solo Phantom in the display there were four from No. 700P Phantom Trials Unit and, underlining the increasing importance of the helicopter in naval air, no less than eleven Wessex, from Nos 845 and 707 Squadrons. No.845 Squadron received their HU.5s in January 1966 and were based between 6 and 22 September at Farnborough, prior to moves to Culdrose and HMS *Fearless*. The squadron kept

their faithful Wessex for many years, deploying them to the South Atlantic in 1982. No. 707 Squadron led a busy life at Culdrose, carrying out advanced and operational training in the Commando rule and a variety of related and unrelated tasks involving the HU.5.

Then of course, the Red Arrows. So far, in 25 years, there has been no Farnborough Display since the team formed in 1965 that they have not attended and repeated comment on what has become a national institution would be superfluous; so there will not be a lot about the Arrows in these pages. Because of the later dates of the Show, the public day programmes started early, at 14.00 hours and continued for three hours. The Service set piece was confined to these three days. It included a demonstration of tactical assault by the Sea Vixens, Buccaneers, Phantoms and Wessex, with the enthusiastic support of A Company Group, 41 Royal Marine Commando, as well as co-ordinated aerobatics by the two fixed-wing teams.

In view of this situation generally and the steady increase in importance of the equipment and infrastructure sections of the industry it was significant that the principal guest at the SBAC Annual Dinner, the Right Honourable Anthony Crowland, MP, President of the Board of Trade, underlined the need for new air traffic control systems, telecommunications navigation aids and airports.

He also announced that it was already clear that aerospace was a major UK export earner, a fact of which the 250,000 strong industry had been aware for some time. Export figures for 1968 at Farnborough time were £200 millions.

The Director of the SBAC, Vice Admiral Sir Richard Smeeton, at the concluding press conference, with the Society's traditional reluctance to prophesy, said there *might* be a Show in 1970 and it *might* revert to the traditional first week in September.

Fourteen major orders, totalling £32 million, were announced during the week, bringing the total annual order book so far to £780 million for 1968.

For the second time, the commentator was Charles Gardner, a man of infinite dry jest, ex-BBC Air Correspondent, ex-Catalina pilot and well-known man-about-BAC.

There was no charge for bicycles.

Among the new military aircraft pride of place must go to the Harrier. VTOL had already been demonstrated

1968

+	Aermacchi MB.326G	I-BAGJ (6402/171)	
	Aermacchi MB.326G	I-FAZE (6403/172)	
	Agusta-Bell 204B	MM80473 (3208)	
+	Augusta-Bell 205BG	MM80503	
	BAC Canberra TT.18	WJ639	
	BAC Jet Provost T.3	XN607	
	BAC Lightning F.53	G-AWON (95291) Saudi AF 53-686	
+	BAC Lightning F.53	(G-AWOO) (95293) Saudi AF 53-687	
	BAC One-Eleven 501	G-AVMK (H.139) hand over ceremony	
+	BAC One-Eleven 501	G-AVML (H.140)	
+	BAC Strikemaster 80	902 (2) Saudi AF	
	BAC Strikemaster 80	G-AWOS (6) Saudi AF 906	
	BAC VC10 C.1	XV107 (837)	
	Beagle B.206S	G-AVLK (B.059)	
+	Beagle B.206S	G-AVCG (B.051) survey version	
+	Beagle Pup 100	G-AVZM (B.121/005)	
	Beagle Pup 100	G-AVZN (B.121/006)	
+	Beagle Pup 150	G-AVLN (B.121/004)	
	Beagle Pup 150	N557MA (B.121/015) arrived as G-AWKK	
	Beagle Pup 160	G-AVLM (B.121/003)	
+	Breguet Atlantic	– (43) crashed 20/9	
	Britten-Norman Islander BN-2A8	G-AVRA (6)	
+	Britten-Norman Islander BN-2A6	G-AVUB (9)	
+	de Havilland Canada Twin Otter 200	CF-WTE (96)	
+	Fokker F.28-1000	PH-WEV (11002)	
+	Handley Page Herald 201	G-APWG (155)	
+	Handley Page Jetstream	G-ATXH (198)	
	Hawker Siddeley Andover C.1	XS601	
	Hawker Siddeley Buccaneer S.2	XV863	
	Hawker Siddeley Comet 4C	XS235 (06473)	
	Hawker Siddeley Dominie T.1	XS731 (25055)	
+	Hawker Siddeley Harrier GR.1	XV739	
+	Hawker Siddeley Harrier GR.1	XV740	
+	Hawker Siddeley Harrier GR.1	XV742	
+	Hawker Siddeley Harrier GR.1	XV743	
+	Hawker Siddeley Nimrod MR.1	XV226 (8001)	
	Hawker Siddeley Trident 1E-140	G-AVYE (2139)	
+	Hawker Siddeley Trident 2E	G-AVFI (2148)	
+	Hawker Siddeley Vulcan B.1	XA903 R-R Olympus under fuselage	
	Hawker Siddeley H.S.125	G-AVRG (25144)	
+	Hawker Siddeley H.S.125-3B	G-AVXL (25145)	
+	Hawker Siddeley H.S.748-2	G-AVRR (1635)	
	Hawker Siddeley H.S.748-2	ZK-CWJ (1647)	
	Hawker Siddeley H.S.748-2	A10-603 (1603)	
+	McDonnell Douglas Phantom FG.1	XT859	
	McDonnell Douglas Phantom FGR.2	XT891	
+	NAMC YS-11A	JA8714	
+	SAAB Draken J-35F	35346	
+	Short Skyvan 3	G-ASZI (SH.1830)	
+	Short Skyvan 3	G-AWKV (SH.1847)	
+	Short Skyvan 3	N4917 (SH.1850)	
+	Short Skyvan 3	VH-PNI (SH.1840)	
	Short Skyvan 3	VH-PNJ (SH.1841)	
+·	Sikorsky SH-3D	XV370 (61-393) Sea King Development aircraft	
+	Slingsby Nipper 3	G-AVKK (S.104/1588)	
+	Slingsby T.53B	– (1686)	
+	Soko Galeb	23268	
+	Soko Jastreb	24031	
+	Sud SA.330E	XW241 (08)	
+	Sud SA.341	F-ZWRA (02)	
	Westland Scout AH.1	XP908 (F.9509)	
	Westland Scout AH.1	XR637 (F.9537)	
	Westland Scout AH.1	XV126 (F.9701)	
	Westland Scout AH.1	XV131 (F.9706)	
+	Westland Wasp HAS.1	XV629 (F.9724)	
	Westland Wessex HAS.3	XM923 (WA.44)	
+	Westland Wessex 60	G-ASWI (WA.199)	

Services participation in flying programmes:
BAC Jet Provost: 20 from RAF College in "50" formation.
BAC Lightning: two from 5 Squadron.)
Handley Page Victor: one from 55 Squadron.) Refuelling formation.
Hawker Siddeley Argosy: one from Benson with parachutists.
Hawker Siddeley Buccaneer: five from 809 Squadron, "Phoenix Five" team.
Hawker Siddeley Gnat: nine from CFS, "Red Arrows" aerobatic team.
Hawker Siddeley Sea Vixen: six from 892 Squadron, "Simon's Circus" team.
Hiller HT.2: one from 705 Squadron.
McDonnell Douglas Phantom: four from 700P Squadron.
Westland Wessex: 11 from 845 and 707 Squadrons.
Westland-Bell Sioux: four from AAC, "Blue Angels" team.

Veteran and vintage aircraft:
Avro Lancaster PA474
Hawker Hurricane PZ865
Supermarine Spitfire -

experimentally at Farnborough but here was the real production animal, about to be introduced to the Royal Air Force. The first of six prototype P.1127s had flown tethered on 21 December 1960. Nine production Kestrels followed, the first flying on 7 March 1964, for the Tripartite Squadron, composed of pilots from the Royal Air Force, Luftwaffe, United States Navy and United States Army. (Much of the early encouragement and funding for the Kestrel had come from American sources in the Mutual Weapons Defence Team, based in Paris. They had been approached originally by the French aircraft designer Marcel Wibault, one of the progenitors of

practical vectored thrust.)

Duncan Simpson, at that time Chief Production Test Pilot at Dunsfold, flew the first production aircraft on 28 December 1967. Deliveries to No. 1 Squadron would commence at the start of the next financial Ministry year on 1 April 1969. The Harrier was fitted with a comprehensive Smiths head-up display, the first British aircraft for the Royal Air Force to be so equipped.

By contrast, the Hawker Siddeley Nimrod was a sedate, conventional design, owing much of its design, fairly obviously, to the earlier civil Comet. Indeed, the two prototypes were converted from Comet airframes. The Display Nimrod, the first production MR.1, had first flown on 28 June and the type would enter Royal Air Force service with No. 236 OCU from October 1969, the first operational squadron, No. 201, equipping a year later.

Yugoslavia was exhibiting at Farnborough for the first time, sponsored by Rolls-Royce, whose Viper engines sustained their aircraft. The Galeb trainer was currently in service with their air force and with it the inevitable light strike and armed reconnaissance derivation, the Jastreb, with a more potent version of the Viper.

Westland ran their familiar "chorus line". The Sea King, newest product of Yeovil and based on the Sikorsky SH-3, was in this case the prototype and, like the next three airframes, assembled from Sikorsky-built components. Entering service as the HAS.1 it gave the Fleet Air Arm the best hunter-killer system available, with power-folding main rotor, retractable undercarriage, an automatic flight control system from Louis Newmark and an aggressive armament of four Mk 44 torpedoes or four depth charges.

The Sud SA.340, F-ZWRA, was the second prototype of the SA.341 Gazelle, the subject of a fruitful Anglo-French agreement that was to include the Puma and Lynx (Westland assuming design leadership for the last). F-ZWRA was the first of the series to have the fenestron tail that was a prominent design feature of production Gazelles and had been developed by Sud in collaboration with MBB in Germany. Carrying the RAF serial XW241, the SA.330E was the eighth Puma prototype and Royal Air Force trials aircraft for the production transport Puma HC.1 and had first flown on 30 July.

Confined to the trade days, the Handley Page Jetstream prototype had been aimed at the 12/20 seat turboprop market, ignored by other manufacturers. Although it appeared to have a promising future – and indeed began to sell well – the financial and other problems that overset Handley Page caused it to spend several years in the doldrums before re-emerging to a successful career with British Aerospace. It had the sad distinction of being the last aircraft to appear under H.P.'s name.

The Fokker F.28 Fellowship, with two Rolls-Royce Spey Juniors, Short-built wing, Dowty undercarriage and Smiths autopilot, was only just short of being 50 per cent British-made (and so nearly a domestic product).

Breguet were making their final appearance at Farnborough under their own name before becoming part of Avions Marcel Dassault-Breguet Aviation. On Friday, their big, twin-Tyne Atlantic, making its second appearance, running uphill towards the black sheds and turning into a dead engine that the crew were struggling to relight, cartwheeled slowly into the ground, killing all five on board and an unfortunate RAE employee.

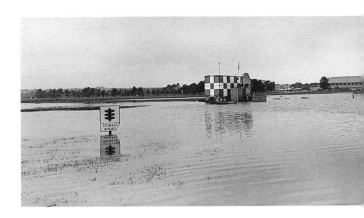

This year was a watershed in the Show's history – looking across the airfield from north to south.

One of five Short Skyvans exhibited, N4917 was destined for Wien Consolidated Airlines.

Farnborough's first Japanese aircraft was the NAMC YS-11A JA8714 powered by Rolls-Royce Darts.

From Yugoslavia came the single-seat Soko Jastreb 24031 and two-seat Galeb 23268 (nearest the camera), both Rolls-Royce Viper powered.

Beagle's newest type was the Pup; G-AVLN was a 150 and G-AVLM a 160.

Hawker Siddeley Vulcan XA903 was flight testing the Bristol Olympus 593 engine for Concorde.

Production models of the Hawker Siddeley Harrier appeared for the first time.

1970

THE TWENTY-SEVENTH SHOW
7-13 SEPTEMBER

During the two-year interval since the 1968 Farnborough Show, a number of events took place which were to have a significant effect on the future of the British aerospace industry. With the first moves into European collaboration already made and gathering momentum, it was becoming clear that it was in this direction that that future largely lay.

Shortly before the start of Farnborough '68, on 8 August, the BAC-Breguet Jaguar prototype, E.01, took to the air for the first time at the *Centre d'Essais en Vol* at Istres, the British prototype following from Warton on 12 October. In common with several other programmes, a new international company was formed to exploit it (in the French sense of that international word). The company was called the *Société Européene de Production de l'Avion d'Entrainement, Combat et Appui Tactique* – or SEPECAT for comparatively short – and is one of the reasons why the aircraft is always just called Jaguar. The title, incidentally, reflects the fact that the aircraft was conceived originally as a trainer with combat potential; in practice, the rôles were reversed.

On 2 March 1969 the French prototype Concorde made its first flight at Toulouse, in the hands of André Turcat and Brian Trubshaw followed with the first British airframe (002) on 9 April.

On a purely national scale, an aircraft that was to become a familiar exhibitor at Farnborough flew at Mach 1 on its first test flight and reached Mach 2.03 on 24 March. The Mirage III, symbol of Dassault's long and successful devotion to the delta wing, was flown by Jean-Marie Saget. This *doyen* of the European test pilots brought to Farnborough techniques in display flying that have seldom been equalled.

On the subject of test pilots, it has always been noticeable that, while the two sides of the various Anglo-French collaborations were occasionally prone to roll their eyes at each other and lay their ears back, no such nationalist tendencies could be laid to the account of the pilots. During conversation with the assembled Breguet-Dassault test pilots at a later Farnborough, it became apparent that they all smoked English briar pipes, bought their caps at Cambrian Flyfishers and drove MGBs. *Quelle délicatesse!*

The Multi-Role Combat Aircraft (MRCA) was formally launched with the announcement on 28 March 1969, of the formation, two days previously, of the BAC, MBB, Aeritalia-sponsored Panavia Aircraft GmbH to design, develop and produce a new multi-national all-weather strike aircraft. An executive agency was set up to control the tri-national contributions, called the NATO MRCA Management Agency (NAMMA) and was itself subordinate to NAMMO (NATO MRCA Management Organisation) run by the three governments concerned. Despite all this, and such off-putting nicknames as Mother Riley's Cardboard Aeroplane and Must Re-invent Canberra Again, the infant survived to become, as the Tornado, one of the world's outstanding military aircraft.

It would be difficult to underestimate the importance of the MRCA programme. That both Britain and West Germany understood that importance fully was shown by their willingness, if necessary, to underwrite the Italian contribution at a time when that country was deeply in political crisis and her industry unlikely even to raise the minimum ten per cent of cost to "buy in". France had her new Mach 2 fighter, the Mirage; Britain had only the memory of TSR.2, over a decade before and West Germany had none.

There was another international programme starting up in 1969, which was to become even more important than Tornado. The French and West German governments signed an agreement (the British government, after a lot of havering, had withdrawn from the programme) to produce an all-European airliner. Showing considerable sense, Hawker Siddeley joined the programme privately some eight weeks later, to act as design consultants and build the wings.

Among engine companies the same strides were being taken and in the same direction, with Rolls-Royce teaming up with Fiat to build the Viper and with Fiat and Motoren Turbinen-Union over the RB199 engines for MRCA. They were already working with Turboméca in France to produce the Adour for the Jaguar and the Turmo, Astazou and Gem for the Anglo-French helicopter programmes.

It was against this background that the 27th SBAC Show took place. It was a period that marked a great turning point in the history of British aerospace achievement and needs to be understood as such.

There were about the same number of exhibitors, with 272 in the hall itself, 22 on the equipment terrace and seven in the space and radar park. Almost a quarter of a million people came to the Show.

Emphasis of the Royal Air Force demonstration was on the power available to Air Support Command, both in the transport role and in its more recently acquired offensive ground support tasks inherited from No. 38 Group. There were 45 minutes of helicopter assault, backed up by the formidable firepower of the Harriers and there was a flight refuelling demonstration. The transport element consisted of a single Belfast (No. 53 Squadron), VC10 (No. 10 Squadron) and Andover (No. 46 Squadron) and four Hercules, which under the central servicing system were not assigned to particular squadrons of the Hercules force. No. 72 Squadron provided eight Wessex HC.2 while the strike element contained four Harrier GR.1s of No. 1 Squadron and six Phantom FGR.2s of No. 6 Squadron.

Strike Command flew samples of its main equipment from No. 57 Squadron (Victor K.1A), No. 43 Squadron (Phantom FG.1), No. 12 Squadron (Buccaneer S.2) and No. 236 OCU (Nimrod MR.1). Solo aerobatics were indulged in by a Lightning; either one of No. 226 OCUs F.3s or No. 23 Squadron's F.6s.

With the triumphant arrival of Concorde 002 for its fly-past just after three o'clock, (flown by Brian Trubshaw and John Cochrane), the civil sector, for once, had the display edge over the military. Concorde has since become a familiar sight in British skies but on that summer afternoon in 1970 it had been seen by very few people, had not yet achieved Mach 2 and had not even achieved the ultimate accolade of being photographed with the Red Arrows by Arthur Gibson. It had cost its parents £500 million so far and in those heady days before universal economic distress tore the pages from the order book, there was talk of 74 options to be taken up and an eventual sale of 250. Which at an "on the road" price of £9 million would have been very nice.

British Aircraft Corporation had the One-Eleven 475 as the core of their display. G-ASYD was the company demonstrator and development aircraft and had previously played the same role for the 500 and 400 series, clocking up its 1,000th flight the previous April and flying for the first time as the 475 on 27 August, twelve days before the Show and a month ahead of schedule. Originating as a sort of 79-seat Viscount replacement but 180 mph (290 k/h) faster (Series 200), it had progressed via the Series 300 with 89 seats and bigger engines and the parallel 400 Series to United States requirements. The 500 Series had a longer fuselage holding up to 107 passengers and bigger Speys yet.

Now, with orders running to 200 at a unit cost around £1½ million and over 130 of them for export to 16 countries, BAC introduced the 475 Series, which in production form would feature a redesigned undercarriage with low-pressure tyres to widen the scope of its employment on gravel or low-strength sealed runways. The engines were now Spey Mk 521, giving 12,550 lb (5,693 kg) of thrust, an increase of 20 per cent.

Test-beds, though no longer in the numbers employed in the early days of the turbine engine, had not entirely died out and the VC10 had its two 21,000 lb (9,525 kg) Conways

on the port side replaced by a single, 40,600 lb (18,416 kg) RB211 – an engine that was expected to be the Derby firm's next great money spinner but very nearly destroyed the company instead before both ultimately recovered. G-AXLR, previously G-36-6, having received civil identity on 30 July 1969 and was actually XV104, the Royal Air Force's ninth VC10 C.1, returning to military duties and identity in May 1973. On the final day of the Show, BOAC were to lose one of their fleet of Super VC10s, G-ASGN, blown up by the Popular Front for the Liberation of Palestine at the so-called "Liberation Airport" in Jordan – which was actually an ex-Royal Air Force landing strip, called Dawson's Field.

The flying opened with the block of foreign aircraft, (Rolls-Royce sponsored, of course) followed by the international jet set (Concorde and Jaguar). The big, swashbuckling Ling-Temco-Vought Corsair II was the 88th of the first production batch of A-7Es for the United States Navy. Apart from the Spey engine, there was another major British contribution to the Corsair, Elliott having announced the sale of Head Up Display equipment for the aircraft in August.

The Aermacchi MB.326GB was the ground attack version of the two-seater and marked the first appearance of their new chief test pilot, Lieut. Col. Franco Bonazzi.

The four Jaguars from SEPECAT were the first, third, fifth and sixth prototypes, respectively the French two seat trainer and single seater for the Armée de l'Air and single seaters for Aéronavale and Royal Air Force, the last (XW560) being the first British-built aircraft.

There was a sudden flurry of small rotary-wing exhibits; the WA.117 from Wing Commander Ken Wallis, now appearing as a commercial offering under the name of Tom Storey's company Airmark, crashed on Friday, destroying its immediate prospects and, sadly, killing "Pee Wee" Judge, one of the best-loved of British test pilots. The Campbell Cricket, built at Membury and flown by Jeremy Metcalfe, was also a gyrocopter, developed out of the Bensen formula. The Cierva Grasshopper, a neat and intelligent twin-engined five-seater with contra-rotating rotors, made but this one appearance before retiring from view.

There was a good deal of speculation at this time about V/STOL airliners, with the capability of vertical as well as very short take-offs, as being the next generation of commercial transports. Rolls-Royce were still pursuing the lift-engine solution (there were some astonishing projects about this time, with lift-engines packed into the wings like snooker balls in their frames) and Dornier even built one, the Do 31. It still exists, on display in the Deutsches Museum in Munich, a monument to one of aviation's more fascinating dead-ends. As it turned out, the future lay immediately with more conventional STOL transports and de Havilland of Canada were at Farnborough with the Series 300 Twin Otter, with the

1970

+	Aermacchi MB.326GB	I-FAZE/MM54290 (6403/172)
	Aermacchi MB.326K	I-AMKK (6477/218)
	Airmark Wallis WA.117	G-AVJV (K/402/X)
+	Airmark Wallis WA.117	G-AXAR (G/403/X) Crashed 11/9
+	BAC Canberra B.62	G-AYHP/B-102 (71234) for Argentine AF
+	BAC Jaguar	XW560 (S.06)
	BAC Jet Provost T.5	XW318
	BAC Lightning F.2A	XN733
+	BAC One-Eleven 475	G-ASYD (H.053)
+	BAC Strikemaster 84	G-AYHS/314 (51) ⎱ Singapore Air
		⎰ Defence
	BAC Strikemaster 84	G-AYHT/315 (52) ⎰ Command
+	BAC VC10 C.1	G-AXLR (829) RB.211 in port pod
+	BAC/Aerospatiale Concorde	G-BSST (002/13520)
+	Britten-Norman Islander BN-2A	G-AXDH (70)
+	Britten-Norman Islander BN-2A	G-AYBI (145)
	Britten-Norman Islander BN-2A-6	G-AYGF (193)
	Britten-Norman Trislander BN-2A Mk.III	G-ATWU (002)
+	Campbell Cricket	G-AXVK (CA.327)
+	Cierva CR.LTH-1 Grasshopper 3	G-AWRP (GB-1)
+	Dassault-Breguet Jaguar	B (E.01)
+	Dassault-Breguet Jaguar	D (A.03)
+	Dassault-Breguet Jaguar	J (M.05)
+	de Havilland Canada Twin Otter 300	CF-YFT (210) water bomber
	Fokker F.27-600	PH-FPN (10438)
+	Fokker F.28-1000	PH-MOL (11003)
+	Grumman Gulfstream II	N804GA (775)
	Hawker Siddeley Buccaneer S.2A	XV350
+	Hawker Siddeley Harrier GR.1	XV742
+	Hawker Siddeley Harrier T.2	XW175

+	Hawker Siddeley Nimrod MR.1	XV241 (8016)
+	Hawker Siddeley Trident 3B	G-AWZB (2303)
+	Hawker Siddeley H.S.125-3B	G-AVRG (25144)
+	Hawker Siddeley H.S.125-400B	G-AXYJ (25217)
	Hawker Siddeley H.S.748-2	G-AVXI (1623)
+	Hawker Siddeley H.S.748-2A	G-AYIR (1681)
+	LTV A-7E Corsair II	156888
	LTV A-7E Corsair II	156889
+	Scottish Aviation Bulldog	G-AXEH (B.125/001)
+	Short Skyvan 3	G-ASZJ (SH.1831)
+	Short Skyvan 3M	G-AXPT (SH.1867)
+	Soko Galeb	23003
	Soko Jastreb	24003
	Victa Airtourer 100	G-ATEX (110)
	Westland Scout AH.1	XR637 (F.9537)
	Westland Sea King HAS.1	XV666 (WA.654)
+	Westland Sea King HAS.1	XV671 (WA.659)
	Westland Wasp HAS.1	XS570 (F.9581)
	Westland Wessex HU.5	XT486 (WA.308)
+	Westland/SNIAS SA.330E Puma	XW241 (08)
+	Westland/SNIAS SA.341 Gazelle	F-ZWRI (02)

Services participation in flying programmes:
BAC Lightning: one from 23 Squadron or 226 OCU.
BAC VC10: one from 10 Squadron.
Handley Page Victor: one from 57 Squadron.
Hawker Siddeley Andover: one from 46 Squadron.
Hawker Siddeley Buccaneer: one from 12 Squadron.
Hawker Siddeley Gnat: nine from CFS, "Red Arrows" aerobatic team.
Hawker Siddeley Harrier: four from 1 Squadron.
Hawker Siddeley Nimrod: one from 236 OCU.
Lockheed Hercules: four.
Short Belfast: one from 53 Squadron.
McDonnell Douglas Phantom: one from 43 Squadron; six from 6 Squadron.
Westland Wessex: eight from 72 Squadron.
Westland-Bell Sioux: five from AAC, "Blue Eagles" team.

The BAC/Aerospatiale Concorde G-BSST makes its Farnborough debut, but in the flying programme only.

lengthened fuselage and higher performance of 200 Series. This particular one was actually fitted up as a water bomber (a type with considerable application in Canada) and on Monday, when the weather was just beginning to be thoroughly beastly, (it brought the flying to a halt by three o'clock on Saturday) it turned in its normal STOL landing despite a 90° cross-wind. Future development of the STOL transport was to ensure the company's place in aviation history and produce some memorable Farnborough flying.

Of light aircraft in the programme the Bulldog, a bulkier and more powerful military trainer version of the Beagle Pup, had been taken over by Scottish Aviation at Prestwick after the demise of Beagle and was being put into production to fill orders from Sweden, Malaysia and Kenya. Later, it would attract favourable attention from the Royal Air Force. Its display, in the experienced hands of John Blair, opened with a lazy multi-turn spin.

Seen once before fading into obscurity was the Cierva Grass-hopper 3 G-AWRP with contra-rotating rotors.

The US Navy provided a pair of LTV A-7E Corsair IIs from the USS Kitty Hawk. Just above the retracted refuelling probe is a rectangle with the pilot's name, Cdr. D.D. Hicks.

Hardly in need of a caption, the legend on VC10 G-AXLR is self-explanatory. It was the only three-engined VC10!

A youthful Prince Charles has the instrument panel of Campbell Cricket G-AXVK explained.

72 Squadron's eight Westland Wessex swing in for their part in the airborne assault.

1972

THE TWENTY-EIGHTH SHOW
4-10 SEPTEMBER

In 1972, after three increasingly "open" Shows, the restrictions upon foreign entries were further relaxed and Farnborough '72 was "Farnborough Europe". In this way, the SBAC and the aerospace industry demonstrated clearly that they had not lost their leading position in the country. The rest of Great Britain did not enter the Common Market until 22 January 1973.

There was some disappointment that initial European participation had not been greater (the French in particular had been expected to turn up in greater strength), but no doubt many potential exhibitors adopted a "wait and see" policy.

Why a European and not an International Farnborough? Basically, because the Society was anxious to establish a solid, working relationship with its European partners before making any widespread attempt to invite collaboration outside - effectively from the United States. It was undoubtedly felt that both government and industry had a lot to absorb about American commercial methods, which several companies had already discovered to be a very different proposition to the more gentle and leisurely world of British government contracts.

There were 225 British companies exhibiting, bringing the total to 250 and causing the main exhibition hall to extend its blue-and-white striped canvas hospitality to 143,000 square feet (13,285 sq.m.). The general layout had not changed, with the President's Enclosure (F Row) up on the hill on ETPS Road, in the position to which it had moved in 1968 and the Press Centre, having come back off the railings in 1970, occupying what had been E Row of chalets on Lincoln Road

Against a background of inflation, wage claims and a floating pound, exports worth over £198.5 million were achieved in the first six months of 1972. Thirty-five orders, worth approximately £122 million were announced during the Show, including those for six more Tridents for the People's Republic of China, and ten Sea Kings Mk 50 for Australia, with the more powerful H.1400-1 engines required by the Royal Australian Navy. This general purpose version, used for Anti-Submarine Warfare, casualty evacuation, Search and Rescue, troop and freight uplifts, was the first to fly, on 30 June 1974, with the uprated Gnome.

Five Concordes for British Overseas Airways were to be built, the contract actually being signed on 28 July. It was swiftly followed by the announcement that Air France had ordered four. China ordered two for CAAC, but nothing came of that one, nor of any of the other optimistic forecasts of sales, which faded away under the cold light of financial realities and a lot of worrying about sonic booms.

The Sea King order confirmed the growing popularity of this excellent anti-submarine helicopter, of which, when the Show opened, 107 had been ordered and all 56 of the Royal Navy's requirement plus six others delivered. The Australian order alone was worth around £10 million.

Another very important announcement made just before the Show concerned the restoration by the Joint Congressional Congress Committee of the follow-up order for 30 Harriers for the United States Marine Corps.

Altogether, the industry, which had suffered some severe shocks over the past year or so, had recovered pretty well; the total workforce, not unnaturally with all the merging going on, was down to 214,000, but European co-operation was now seen to be working and Jaguar production had begun, the first of 200 for the Royal Air Force making its initial flight on 11 October, just after the Show.

Latest excitement on the commercial front was the QTOL (quiet take-off and landing) airliner and both the major British constructors were involved in discussions with European groups; British Aircraft Corporation with Messerschmitt-Bolkow-Blöhm and Saab-Scania in a new company called Europlane Ltd and Hawker Siddeley with Fokker-VFW and Dornier. In Italy, Aeritalia were engaged with Boeing on the same subject. In the event, the successful BAe 146 was the sole outcome of these projects.

One unique item, which is most unlikely to be repeated at future Shows, was the staging of a handicap air race, promoted by the *Daily Express* and organised by the Royal Aero Club of the United Kingdom. The race was a great success (it was held on Saturday, 9 September) and attracted 19 competitors. The course, laid out by the author, as it happens, took pilots down to the west and south and back to Farnborough and was remarkable for lying almost entirely within restricted airspace; most of that part of England consisting of ranges of one sort or another. Fortunately they were all silent on the day and the only race casualty was Peter Bubbear, whose Chipmunk was excluded for an infringement of the rules. The race was won by Roy Paterson (Cessna 310), followed by Alan Dyer (Cherokee Arrow), who was later to become known, as a result of a spectacular forced landing in ripe cereal at Shobdon, as "The Cornflake Kid".

Flying started normally at 14.30 but there were some additional items flying in the public days (Friday 8 September to Sunday 10 September) from 11.30. Prices of admission on Friday were £1.50 for adults, 70p for children under 14 and (additional to occupants) £1.00 for cars or coaches and 30p for motorcycles. Week-end equivalent charges were 70p for adults, 40p for children, £3.00 for a car and four occupants, 50p for a coach and 30p for a motorcycle. (Britain had adopted decimal coinage on 2 February 1971).

"Access by road to the show site" said *Flight International*, "is straightforward." Would that it were still so.

The Red Arrows, in their fourth time of Farnborough displays, opened the flying each day and the Royal Air Force was further represented by the return, on public days, of the Falcons parachute display team and (at 11.30) the Battle of Britain Flight, with the Lancaster, Spitfire and Hurricane.

No. 38 Group, Royal Air Force, mounted a set-piece attack, with a brace of Hercules (No. 30 Squadron), a couple of Andovers (No. 46 Squadron), a Wessex HC.2 (No. 72 Squadron), six Pumas (No. 33 Squadron) backed up by a recce Phantom FGR.2 (No. 41 Squadron) and six FG.1s (No. 6 Squadron), plus six Harrier GR.1 and a T.2A (No. 3 Squadron). The Group also produced a 3 Div. Air Regiment Sioux AH.1 and three Scout AH.1 from No. 665 Squadron. The Army's Blue Eagles were also there.

The Red Arrows were not the only national aerobatic team taking part, for both the French Patrouille de France and the Italian Frecce Tricolori made an appearance.

The successes of the Britten-Norman Islander had been considerable; within some four years of its first flight it was in service in 27 countries and by September 1972, over 360 had been built, at around one a week. Orders for Islanders were being met by construction at Westland's Weston-super-Mare facility and British Hovercraft at East Cowes, with the home port of Bembridge handling final assembly and fitting out the airframes from another production line at Baneasa, in Romania. Also flying at the Show was the Trislander, a new, three-engined 17-seater version which flew into the static park in 1970 on the opening day, which was also the day of its maiden flight. Despite all this success, the company ran into considerable cash-flow problems and called in the receivers in October 1971. A new company, Britten-Norman (Bembridge) Ltd was formed a month later to continue trading while a buyer was being sought. That buyer turned out to be the Fairey Company, who had been out of the aeroplane-building world since 1960 but announced in August that they were acquiring the assets of the Bembridge company.

SAAB brought their new Viggen, successor to the Draken. An immensely complex and sophisticated multi-rôle aircraft, this thunderous and dramatic double-delta monster, which in later versions exceeded Mach 2 and for which the Flygvap-net anticipated a requirement for 350, was to become a long-standing Farnborough favourite and eventually production reached 329 of five main variants, continuing into 1986. SAAB also showed the 105 trainer whose pilot had the misfortune, on Wednesday, to cross that celebrated dividing line between pilots who have landed with the wheels up and those who are going to.

India was represented by the Kiran and the single seater Gnat Mk 1 from Hindustan Aircraft. Conceived in 1958 and first flying in 1964, on 4 September, some 190 of the Kiran basic trainer were built, later production concentrating on a ground attack version. HAL bought manufacturing rights for the single-seat Gnat, its success in this area encouraging the Air Staff in Britain to go ahead with the trainer version. Gnats in Indian service put up an impressive performance in the war with Pakistan (which lasted from 3 to 17 December 1971), managing to keep their engagements at a height band convenient to themselves.

It was, however, the Lockheed TriStar that gained the most attention. Rolls-Royce had been working on an engine for the Airbus, but made the decision to get into a bigger ball game and concentrated all their efforts on the RB211, offering it to Lockheed for their new wide-body. Then everything went wrong. General Electric were already supplying power to the similar DC-10 and now announced an even more powerful version of their engine. Not only did this threaten the success of the RB211 but after a series of technical disasters, the latter was late and distressingly below promised performance. The first engines, with which the prototype TriStar flew on 16 November 1970, delivered 34,000 lb (15,422 kg) thrust instead of the promised 42,000 lb (19,051 kg) and moreover both aircraft and engine were well over weight.

A badly-shaken Lockheed refused to back off the contractual obligations and the delay in deliveries of satisfactory units at a time of peak development expenditure caused a grave cash problem. On 4 February 1971, Rolls-Royce announced that they were going into receivership.

What followed was remarkable. Rolls-Royce were already hard at work to retrieve the engine; Hugh Conway and Stanley Hooker had been drafted in from Bristol Siddeley (which Rolls-Royce had bought): the Conservative Government, which had come to power under Edward Heath in June the previous year, bought Rolls-Royce's aviation assets to protect the company, combining Derby and Bristol aerospace activities as Rolls-Royce (1971) Ltd and after a good hard look at the RB211 decided to buy that too, announcing an injection of £11 million into the programme on 21 January 1972.

In the meantime, Lockheed had been themselves in serious trouble financially and on 2 August 1971, in a move even more unexpected than that by the British government, the Senate voted $250 million in support of the TriStar

1972

+	Aeritalia AM.3C	I-AEAM (6350)	
	Aermacchi MB.326G	I-FAZE/MM54290 (6304/172)	
+	Aermacchi MB.326K	I-AMKK/MM54390 (6477/218)	
+	Aermacchi MB.326K	I-KMAK/MM54391 (6478/219)	
	BAC Jaguar GR.1	XW563 (S.07)	
+	BAC Jaguar T.2	XW566 (B.08)	
	BAC Jet Provost T.5	XW436	
+	BAC One-Eleven 476FM	G-AZUK (H.241)	
+	BAC Strikemaster 88	G-AZXK/NZ6364 (304) for RNZAF	
	BAC Strikemaster 88	G-AZYN/NZ6365 (305) for RNZAF	
+	BAC/Aerospatiale Concorde	G-BSST (002/13520)	
+	Britten-Norman Defender BN-2A	G-AYXE (653)	
	Britten-Norman Islander BN-2A-9R	N20JA (307)	
	Britten-Norman Islander BN-2A-8S	G-BAAE (308)	
+	Britten-Norman Trislander BN-2A Mk.III	G-AZZM (321)	
+	Dassault-Breguet Falcon 20C	F-BTMF (184)	
	Dassault-Breguet Jaguar E	– (E.3)	
+	de Havilland Canada Twin Otter 300	CF-DHA (337)	
+	Dornier Skyservant	D-IMOL (4050)	
	Fokker F.27-400M	PH-FPW (10489)	
+	Fokker F.28-2000	PH-ZAX (11053)	
+	GAF Nomad N22	VH-SUR (02)	
	Hawker Siddeley Buccaneer S.2B	XW525	
	Hawker Siddeley Gnat T.1	XM693 (FL.503)	
+	Hawker Siddeley Harrier GR.1	XV738	
+	Hawker Siddeley Harrier GR.1A	XW770	
+	Hawker Siddeley Harrier 50/AV-8A	158699	
+	Hawker Siddeley Harrier 50/AV-8A	158701	
+	Hawker Siddeley Harrier 50/AV-8A	158709	
+	Hawker Siddeley Harrier T.2A	XW175	
+	Hawker Siddeley Hunter FGA.74	G-BABM	
+	Hawker Siddeley Nimrod MR.1	XV229 (8004)	
+	Hawker Siddeley Trident 3B	G-AWZH (2309)	
+	Hawker Siddeley Trident 3B	G-AWZN (2315)	
+	Hawker Siddeley Trident 3B	G-AWZR (2318)	
+	Hawker Siddeley Trident 3B	G-AWZT (2320)	
+	Hawker Siddeley H.S.125 600B	G-AZHS (25258)	
+	Hawker Siddeley H.S.748-2A	G-AZJH (1698)	
+	Hindustan Gnat I	E1069	
	Hindustan Gnat I	E1070	
+	Hindustan Kiran I.	U-703	
+	Lockheed TriStar	N305EA (1006)	
+	MBB Bo 105D	G-AZOR (S-20)	
+	SAAB Viggen AJ 37	37002	
+	SAAB 105G	SE-XBJ (105-2)	
+	SAAB 105XT	SE-DCX	
+	SAAB-MFI 17	SE-XCF (MFI-15-02)	
+	Scottish Aviation Bulldog 100	G-AXIG (B.125/002)	
+	Scottish Aviation Jetstream 200	G-AXFV (211)	
+	Short Skyliner	G-AZYW (SH.1903)	
	Short Skyliner Executive	G-AZRY (SH.1901)	
+	Short Skyvan 3M	G-AXPT (SH.1867)	
+	SOCATA Rallye Club	G-AZKF (1951)	
+	SOCATA Rallye Minerva 125	F-BTIT (11943)	
+	VFW 614	D-BABB (G-2)	
+	Westland Gazelle HT.2	XW845 (1007)	
	Westland Lynx	XW835 (1/02)	
+	Westland Lynx	XW838 (1/03)	
+	Westland Lynx AH.1	XX153 (2/11)	
+	Westland Lynx HAS.2	XX469 (1/07)	
+	Westland Puma HC.1	XW231 (1195)	
	Westland Scout AH.1	XV126 (F.9701)	
+	Westland Sea King 41	89-50 (WA.744) German Navy	
+	Westland Sea King 43	062 (WA.747) Norwegian AF	

Service participation in flying programmes:
BAC Lightning: one from TTF.
Fouga Magister: eleven from Patrouille de France aerobatic team (France).
Fiat G.91PAN: ten from Frecce Tricolori aerobatic team (Italy).
Hawker Siddeley Gnat: nine from CFS, "Red Arrows" aerobatic team.
Hawker Siddeley Andover: two from 46 Squadron +.
Hawker Siddeley Harrier: seven from 3 Squadron +.
Hawker Siddeley Hunter: one from 4 FTS +.
Lockheed Hercules: two from 30 Squadron +.
McDonnell Douglas Phantom: eight from 6 and 41 Squadrons +.
Westland Puma: six from 33 Squadron +.
Westland Scout: three from AAC, 665 Squadron +.
Westland Sioux: six from AAC, "Blue Eagles" team, plus one from 3 Division Air Regiment +.
Westland Wessex: one from 72 Squadron +.
+ 38 Group joint presentation

Veteran and vintage aircraft:
Avro Lancaster PA474.
Hawker Hurricane PZ865.
Hawker Sea Fury TF956.
Hawker Tomtit K1786.
Miles Magister P6382.
Sopwith Pup N5180.
Supermarine Spitfire P7350.

Civil aircraft participation:
Stampe SV.4: four, Rothmans aerobatic team.
Pitts S-1S G-AZPH.

Daily Express Air Race (9 September only):
In finishing order: Cessna 310 G-ASYV; Cherokee Arrow G-AZOG; Rollason Beta G-AWHX; Falco G-AWSU; Cessna 180 G-ASIT; AA-1 Yankee G-AYLN; Cherokee Arrow G-AZSF; Auster 9 G-AVHT; Mooney Ranger G-AWIH; Airtourer G-AZBE; Condor G-AXGS; Hornet Moth G-ADKM; Condor G-AYFH; Falco G-APXD; Wassmer Pacific G-AZYZ; Jodel DR.1050M1-G-ATLB; Condor G-AWFP; Cherokee 140 G-AVLG.

programme - by a majority of one. Production go-ahead was given on 14 October, the first commercial revenue flight took place on 26 April 1972 with Eastern Airlines and on 7 August British Airways' European Division announced their order for six, with a further six on option. (The two Corporations had merged on 1 April.) In token of that order, the aircraft at Farnborough, the fifth of the Eastern order, bore BEA's insignia and logo on the fin and fuselage.

The wide-body story had begun with the launch of the Boeing 747 on 9 February 1969. The DC-10, tailored to a requirement from American Airlines, and the TriStar were not long in following. The type was new to Farnborough and this 250-400 passenger, 426,000 lb (193,230 kg) aircraft, intended primarily for United States domestic routes, was very impressive.

France's initial contribution to Farnborough was modest, consisting of the Falcon 20 and the Rallye Club and Minerva Club. The first of Avions Marcel Dassault's continuing and successful line of business jets, the first production Falcon had flown on 1 January 1965, under its original name of Mystère XX. It was marketed in the United States of America by Pan American Business Jets, Inc. as the Fan Jet Falcon. Later, all units were officially registered as Falcon 20s, causing the name adopted for the F-16 to be altered to Fighting Falcon to avoid confusion as to what you were actually buying.

The French aircraft industry was at this time going through the same sort of merger traumas that had been facing the British and in 1971 two major companies fused together to become Avions Marcel Dassault-Breguet Aviation (or AMD-BA, unless you were actually practising the language). After a couple of unsuccessful turboprops the company went on to considerable success in the business jet field, building 492 of the 8/10 passenger Falcon 20.

The Rallye series originated with Morane-Saulnier, who came to grips with the requirements of the club and private sector with the MS.880 Rallye Club in 1961, production eventually running to 1,100 units. The example of the standard three-seater with 100 hp Continental O-200A engine flown at Farnborough was the last of a block of six appearing on the British register in December 1971; the Rallye Minerva 125

was a version powered by the 125 hp Franklin 4A-235, later versions being fitted with 220 hp Franklins. The Minerva 125 remained a prototype, but 247 of the more powerful version were sold, being marketed in the United States by Waco Aircraft.

Morane-Saulnier ran into the stock high, demand low cashflow situation and went bankrupt in 1962. Taken over by Etablissments Henri Potez the following year, production of the Rallye continued, the company now being called SEEMS (*Société d'Exploitation des Etablissments Morane-Saulnier*). After three years, Potez handed this mouthful over to Sud-Aviation, who shortened it a bit to GEMS (*Gérance des Etablissments, etc*), absorbed the company into its bosom in 1965 and renamed it again. It was now the *Société de Construction d'Avions de Tourisme et d'Affaires*, or SOCATA, retaining that title (and responsibility for all light aircraft projects) after the 1970 government-inspired merger of Nord and Sud-Aviation into the Société Nationale Aérospatiale, and enabling SOCATA/Aérospatiale to claim that the Rallye was built by "the company that brought you Concorde". Or words to that effect.

There was also the curious over-wing-engined collaborative VFW-Fokker 614 (with bits by Short Brothers) which appeared on Wednesday and subsequently slid quietly into oblivion after 17 had been built for French and Danish operators, no-one apparently being much interested in a 44-seat very-short-range DC-3 replacement. Both collaborators were, if anything, rather relieved by this as it enabled them to get on with the much more successful Fokker F.28 Fellowship.

Dassault's Falcon 20C F-BTMF gets away smartly from the runway to begin its display.

The GAF Nomad VH-SUR can hardly wait to get airborne.

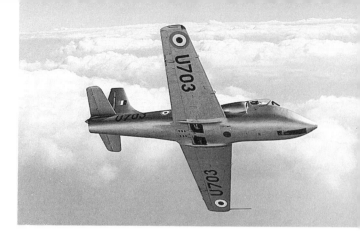

This year marked the first appearance of SAAB's mighty Viggen; 37002 was the second prototype and thereafter the Viggen's display was always watched with keen interest.

Our first Indian visitors were from Hindustan Aircraft, U703 was a Kiran powered by a Viper.

VFW 614 D-BABB shows its strange over wing engine layout.

Dornier Skyservant D-IMOL with German Navy (Kriegsmarine) insignia.

The Hunter, now with the Hawker Siddeley nameplate, was still around in 1972 since there was a market for refurbished examples. G-BABM, formerly an F.6, XF432, became a FGA.74 and was exported to Singapore.

1974

THE TWENTY-NINTH SHOW
1-8 SEPTEMBER

Farnborough, at last, went international. The moves to this momentous decision had been ordered, considered and cumulative and followed the trend towards internationalism within the industry.

The two years between the 1972 and 1974 Farnboroughs had certainly not been conducive to optimism in the industry. As a result of the Yom Kippur War and United States support for Israel, the oil states had increased fuel prices by 70 per cent and cut production severely. The United States was in some political and economic disarray despite the ending of the Vietnam War. In January 1973, Pan Am and TWA cancelled their options on thirteen Concordes.

In Britain the power and fuel industries were still heavily involved in strikes and pay claims, inflation ran at 16 per cent, the three-day week was introduced and in March 1974 the Government fell. Shortly after the Show, in October, Hawker Siddeley announced that as a result of the economic situation they were stopping work on the 146.

Nevertheless, when all the application forms were in on closing day (well, most of them were in) at the end of November, there was no doubt that it was going to be a success. There were no less than 380 exhibitors, 185 from overseas and 77 of those from the United States. To accommodate them, a second exhibition hall was erected to the north of the first, adding 113,000 square feet (10,441 sq.m) to supplement the 133,000 square feet (12,356 sq.m) of the original building, now identified as South Hall.

The weather was not good at the best of times, degenerating frequently into conditions that sometimes prevented aircraft from flying; there were winds gusting 45 knots (83 k/h) and an inch of rain fell during one night. The often dramatic black clouds did, however, provide an ideal backdrop for Concorde's Show-opening runs. There were some anxious moments when South Hall threatened to take off in Force Nine gale conditions and on top of the control tower the commentators were preparing to announce the arrival of the world's largest hang-glider. But the structure held and the organisers (and Black & Edgington, in charge of the canvas) breathed again.

The Show had grown in other dimensions as well. It now ran from Sunday to Sunday. The old preview-rehearsal-technicians'-Press day had gone and there was a dedicated Press day on the opening Sunday, with three trade days and a combined trade and public-premium day on Thursday, followed by the usual three days of public participation.

There were now three different sets of entrance fees for the public, thanks to the new combined day. Adults paid £1.75 (Thursday), £2.00 (Friday) or £1.00 (week-end) and children under 14 £1.75, 70p or 60p – which shows that children were definitely not encouraged on Thursday. Cars cost an additional £1.50 or £1.00 at the week-end, coaches were £2.00 and motorcycles 50p across the board and seats in the grandstand, down where J Row of chalets would later be located, £1.00.

Among the American exhibits the SR-71 Blackbird arrived via the finish gate of a new point-to-point record from New York, announced just after it landed on Press day as 1 hour, 55 minutes, 42 seconds (from *New York*?). Major James V.Sullivan and Major Noel F. Widdifield had crossed the Atlantic at 2,908.026 k/h (1,806.964 mph) in one seventeenth the time it took Charles Lindbergh in 1927. By a rather dismal coincidence, Lindbergh had died six days before this astounding flight.

With the inclusion of American companies came the impressive McDonnell Douglas Eagle, America's answer to the Foxbat – which had been the subject of much international publicity, particularly in the Middle East. The F-15 Eagle was destined to be a consistent and appreciated exhibitor at Farnborough Shows. Not yet in squadron service (18 had been built; this was one of two TF-15 two-seaters) it was put through an eye-opening routine that included high-g tight turns well inside the perimeter and high-drag, high angle of attack approaches. In subsequent years, one would come to expect spectacular displays from the F-15, but this was the first time such behaviour had been seen and fully vindicated the design philosophy of this big, broad-winged fighter.

Orders totalling over £150 million and including sales of nearly two hundred aircraft, were announced at the Show.

Apart from the main display, the first half hour on the public days was devoted to aerobatics, from the four Pitts S-2A Specials of the Rothman's team, led by Iain Watson and the solo Pitts S-1S and Zlin duo, with Z.526 Treners, flown by James Black, Pete Jarvis and Carl Schofield, all of Aerobatics International. After the main display, No. 1 Squadron with seven Harrier GR.3 and one T.4 and No. 6 Squadron (actually using aircraft borrowed from the OCU) with four Jaguar GR.1 or T.2, put on a set piece attack, assisted by a single Harrier GR.3 with cluster bombs, provided by No. 233 OCU. The Red Arrows were led by Squadron Leader Ian Dick.

The Royal Navy's Historic Flight took part this year, with their celebrated Swordfish. This was originally a company "hack", and used to turn up at Royal Aeronautical Garden Parties and suchlike events, usually flown by Peter Twiss, on one occasion with eleven other test pilots in the cavernous rear cockpit. The lugubrious Fairey house colours of dark blue and silver, in which it was then painted, suited it as little as Hawker's blue and gold did the Hurricane and Hart.

Of the international or multi-national programmes represented, only two were Farnborough first-timers, while Concorde was already a familiar sight. The French production prototype had flown on 6 December 1973, followed by the British one in January 1974 and 15 airframes were under construction, enough to cater for British Airways' and Air France's needs, with long lead items for a further half dozen in case the Iranians or Chinese actually put any money down. The British pre-production prototype, G-AXDN, flying at Farnborough, was to end its days in the Imperial War Museum collection at Duxford.

A significant and unusual honour had come the way of the two chief test pilots on the Concorde the previous year when, on 20 August 1973, President Nixon presented the Harmon Trophy for aeronautical achievement to Brian Trubshaw and André Turcat.

The Dassault-Breguet/Dornier Alpha Jet was developed jointly by France and Germany to fill a requirement in the Armée de l'Air for an advanced trainer and in the Luftwaffe for a tactical strike/ground attack aircraft. Unlike its rival Hawker Siddeley Hawk it was twin-engined, "for safety" and, more practically, to add multi-engine training in its rôle. Belgium was interested, ordering 33 on top of the 175 each required by the French and Germans and it was to sell in areas of French influence in Africa and in Egypt.

Two of the four wide-bodied transports appeared at Farnborough; the Lockheed TriStar was there in 1972 and to the extent that it was designed round the Rolls-Royce RB211, had a multi-national flavour; but the Airbus Industrie A300B2 was certainly multi-national and was at the Show for the first time.

The problems that seemed to accompany the TriStar onto the market were not entirely over. The first one to operate in the United Kingdom was Court Line's initial aircraft (the second, incidentally, made the first fully-automatic trans-Atlantic crossing on delivery from Palmdale), and Court Line had gone into voluntary liquidation on 15 August. Under the circumstances, the company may have regretted naming the first one *Halcyon Days*.

Back in July 1972, the EEC Commission had issued a document detailing at some length proposals for a unified aviation industry policy for Europe, which envisaged a common financial support policy and integration of national aerospace industries. After two years' frustrating work, it was admitted that the scheme had foundered. National interests were too powerful, especially in defence; the Italian industry was already heavily involved in American programmes; the British aerospace industry, having survived its earlier rationalisation, was in a strong independent position with national – and international – programmes.

With 200,000 employees (the whole of the rest of Western Europe came to about the same) and over £500 million in export sales in 1973 its major preoccupation was with the proposed nationalisation of the British Aircraft Corporation and Hawker Siddeley Aviation (among others) in a British National Aerospace Corporation. Involved were the Minister of State, Lord Beswick, whose background and interests brought him close to Roger Bacon's definition of a total aviation person and the Secretary for Industry, Mr Wedgewood Benn, whose background did not. A Government White Paper entitled "The Regeneration of British Industry" and good value at 14p, outlined proposals for implementing control of the aerospace industry through a National Enterprise Board and named Rolls-Royce (1971) as a founder member.

The new government was trying to re-negotiate the terms of Britain's entry into the EEC – and the aerospace industry was a powerful bargaining counter. There was still no national involvement in Airbus, a programme that was beginning to look healthy, but on 14 August 1974, Paul Millett, the BAC project test pilot had made the first flight in MRCA at Manching, at the start of what was to become an extremely important international programme.

Anglo-French co-operation had produced the admirable Jaguar, of which the first GR.1 for the Royal Air Force was delivered to Lossiemouth on 30 May 1973 and the first French squadron formed at St Dizier on 19 June and an £80 million overseas order was announced for two overseas customers at the start of the Show. As the French were busy trying to sell their own Mirage F.1, BAC had been perfectly happy to take on sales of Jaguar International. Another project, the Anglo-French Variable Geometry aircraft foundered upon familiar national rocks. This was rather a pity, because French determination to pursue their own ends tended to split them from the rest of Europe and put them into a posture of opposition (which, of course, they may enjoy) that persisted into EFA and Rafale.

By and large, by 1990, the Commission's dream was still a long way off, but in one most important move, in which the SBAC is deeply committed on behalf of its members, the technical infrastructure has been consolidated already in the work of the Association Européenne des Constructeurs de Matériel Aérospatial (AECMA), where common standards, procedures and certifications are agreed.

Passing from the overall European situation at the first International Farnborough, a look at the list of aircraft in the Dis-

1976 The McDonnell Douglas YC-15 01876 impressed with
its STOL performance.

1976 The Polish PZL TS-11 Iskra SP-DOE was making the
type's first appearance in the West.

1980 Colourful de Havilland Canada Twin Otter G-BDHC was used by the Transglobe Expedition.

1980 General view of the static park with, left to right, top: Dassault-Breguet Mirage 4000, McDonnell Douglas TF-18A Hornet and F-15B Strike Eagle. Below: British Aerospace Jaguar, Tornado IDS and Tornado ADV.

1984 Ilyushin Il-86 CCCP-86066 was the latest Soviet airliner this year; unfortunately it did not take part in the flying programme.

1984 It was particularly interesting to see the world's largest helicopter, the Mil Mi-26, CCCP-06141, flying daily.

Airship Industries' Skyship 600 G-SKSC over the site on 5 September.

1984 de Havilland Canada Dash 8 C-GGPJ demonstrates its short landing ability. (Peter Nicholson)

1986 Prototype of the Norman Freelance G-NACI stands next to Norman's Fieldmaster. The Freelance featured folding wings for easy storage.

1986 The intriguing little Chichester-Miles Leopard G-BKRL light business jet had not yet made its first flight.

1986 Boeing E-3A Sentry LX-N90448 flew past on 3 September.

1986 Early morning check on the Dassault-Breguet Mirage 2000N.

1986 The prototype Dassault-Breguet Rafale made its first appearance at Farnborough this year.

1986 Another new shape at Farnborough in 1986 was the British Aerospace EAP, ZF534, seen taxying to the tune of "Chariots of Fire". (Peter Nicholson)

1988 The first EHI EH 101, ZF641, assembled by Westland.

1988 The Mikoyan MiG-29A lands after its stunning display.

1988 British Aerospace Hawk 200 ZH200 is dwarfed by Antonov An-124 CCCP-82007. (Peter Nicholson)

1988 A new sound at Farnborough; McDonnell Douglas MD-81UHB, (Ultra High Bypass) N980DC, was powered in its port nacelle by a General Electric GE36 unducted fan engine. (Peter Nicholson)

play will show to what extent different countries were setting up their national participation.

Dassault, while still not displaying the new autumn line of Mirages, had added to their executive suite the Falcon 10 and 30 business jets, respectively carrying 4/7 and 30 passengers, complementing the 8/14 passenger Falcon 20. Two hundred Falcon 10s were sold, but the 30 did not enter production. From Aérospatiale came the new SA 360 Dauphin, with the fashionable fenestron tail. Intended as a replacement for the Alouette, this was the second prototype, production being about to commence. In the event, despite several speed records set up by the prototype, the Dauphin turned out to be underpowered and only 34 were built, but a later twin-engined development sold in larger numbers. The SN.601 Corvette twin-jet fixed wing transport sold only in small numbers to an over-subscribed market.

Cessna, on the other hand, who entered the same market with the Citation in 1972 – to a lot of head-shaking – sold 51 in the first year and 81 in the second.

Not to be outdone by the heavy brigade, Maurice Serré provided an equally memorable performance in the SOCATA Rallye Minerva, one of the very few light aircraft in the flying display.

On the helicopter side, recent advances in the design and construction of rotor hubs and blades permitted rolling manoeuvres and both the light-weight Lynx and very heavyweight Sikorsky S-65 went through the motions; in the case of the latter, an HH-53C weighing some 36,400 lb (16,511 kg) with a 72 ft 3 in (22.02 m) rotor disc, an awe-inspiring

sight. Tragically, on the opening Sunday, the Sikorsky Black Hawk prototype crashed from a similar manoeuvre, killing one crew member and fatally injuring the other. It hit not far from the control tower, narrowly missing the RAE rescue Wessex and finishing up on a spot vacated minutes before by a Starlifter of 60th Military Airlift Wing.

On the British side, despite the claim by IATA that it had been the worst year ever in commercial operation and military economies all along the line, the position was by no means gloomy. The order books stood at over five hundred for the Islander, 215 for the BAC One-Eleven and over one hundred for the Skyvan. All the Westland-Aérospatiale helicopters were doing well and the Sea King order book stood at 121. Over eighty countries had purchased and were operating British aerospace products.

The Handley Page Jetstream, subject of various rescue packages, had now emerged under the wing of Scottish Aviation (like the Bulldog) and was displaying again, this time as a production Royal Air Force T.1 from the Central Flying School. The new Short SD3.30 airliner, based on the Skyvan experience, was also at the Show and arousing interest, having first flown as recently as 22 August. On the day before that, Duncan Simpson, by then chief test pilot at Dunsfold, had lifted the new Hawk off the ground for the first time and was flying it at the Display. The Royal Air Force had ordered 175 as an advanced trainer to replace the Gnat and the single-seat version, mooted in the company's original Hawk proposals, was now being trawled by the company.

SAAB's MFI-15 Safari LN-BIV was basically a civil version of the MFI-17 Supporter.

Scottish Aviation Jetstream XX480 runs up – note the depressed nose wheel leg.

1974

+	Aermacchi MB.326K	I-AMKK/MM54390 (6477/218)
	Aermacchi MB.326K	I-KMAK/MM54391 (6478/219)
+	Aerospatiale SA.360 Dauphin	F-WSQX (002)
+	Aerospatiale Corvette	F-BUQP (4)
	Agusta A.109	(7101)
+	Airbus A300B-2	F-WUAA (2)
+	BAC Jaguar GR.1	XX108 (S.1)
+	BAC Jaguar T.2	XX136 (B.1)
	BAC Jet Provost T.5A	XW425
	BAC One-Eleven 401 Executive	N111NA
	BAC One-Eleven 475	G-ASYD (053)
+	BAC/Aerospatiale Concorde	G-AXDN (01)
	Beech Baron B55	G-BBSD (TH-429)
	Beech King Air C90	G-BBVK (LJ-631)
+	Beech Super King Air 200	N925B (BB-6)
	Bell 206B JetRanger II	G-BASE (969)
+	Boeing-Vertol CH-47C Chinook	20952
	Britten-Norman Defender BN-2A-21	G-BCEM/303 (402) Sultan of Oman AF
+	Britten-Norman Islander BN-2A-3	G-BAYH (696)
	Britten-Norman Islander BN-2A-3	G-BCJY (392)
	Britten-Norman Trislander BN-2A Mk.III-1	G-BCEG (372)
+	Britten-Norman Trislander BN-2A Mk.III-2	G-BCJX (391)
+	Cessna Citation 1	N142CC (550-142)
	Cessna Citation 1	G-BCII (550-176)
+	Dassault Falcon 10	F-BSQU (1)
+	Dassault Falcon 20F	F-BSTR (246)
+	Dassault Falcon 30	F-WAMD (01)
	Dassault-Breguet/Dornier Alpha Jet	D-9594 (02)
+	Dassault-Breguet/Dornier Alpha Jet	F-ZWRV (03)
	Dornier Skyservant	58-20 (4095)
+	Dornier Skyservant	D-IKAS (4030)
+	Enstrom F-28A	G-BBBZ (138)
	Enstrom F-28A	G-BBVI (182)
	Fokker F.27-400M	PH-EXI (10502) Imperial Iranian AF
+	Fokker F.27-600	I-ATIC (10349)
+	Fokker F.28-6000	PH-JHG (11001)
	Gates Learjet 25B	G-BBEE (25B-135)
	Gates Learjet 36	N362GL (36-002)
+	Hawker Siddeley Harrier 52	G-VTOL (B3/41H/735795)
+	Hawker Siddeley Hawk T.1	XX154
+	Hawker Siddeley Nimrod MR.1	XV229 (8004)
+	Hawker Siddeley H.S.125-600B	G-BBAS (256017)
+	Hawker Siddeley H.S.748-2	G-AVXJ (1624)
	ICA-Brasov IAR-823	YR-MEA (02)
	ICA-Brasov IS-28B2	YR-1009 (03)
+	ICA-Brasov IS-29D	729 (17)
+	Lockheed TriStar	N10114 (1079)
	Lockheed C-5A Galaxy	00454
	Lockheed P-3C Orion	159327
	Lockheed S-3A Viking	158873
	Lockheed SR-71A Blackbird	17972

+	McDonnell Douglas TF-15A Eagle	10291
+	MBB Bo 105C	D-HDBY (S-74)
	MBB Bo 105D	D-HDCH (S-83)
+	Partenavia P.68B	G-BCFM (19)
	Piper Cheyenne	N331PT (31T-740004)
	Piper Navajo Chieftain	G-BCJI (31-7405242)
	Piper Pressurised Navajo	G-BCBO (31P-7400196)
	Piper Seneca 200	G-BCDB (34-7450110)
	PZL SZD-30 Pirat	
+	PZL SZD-36 Cobra 15	
	PZL SZD-37 Jantar 19	
	PZL Wilga 35	G-BCIC (74210)
	Rockwell Commander 112A	D-EHXM (191)
	Rockwell Commander 685	G-BCAY (12053)
	Rockwell Shrike Commander 500S	G-BSLK (3180)
	Rockwell Turbo Commander 690A	N57108 (11108)
+	SAAB Viggen AJ 37	37052
	SAAB Viggen AJ 37	37053
+	SAAB Viggen AJ 37	37055
	SAAB Viggen SK 37	37808
+	SAAB 105G	SE-XBZ (105-2)
+	SAAB MFI-15 Safari	LN-BIV (MFI-15-006)
	SAAB MFI-17 Supporter	SE-XCF (MFI-15-02)
+	Scottish Aviation Bulldog	G-AXEH (B.125/001)
	Scottish Aviation Bulldog T.1	G-BBPF (BH.120/282) for Nigerian AF
+	Scottish Aviation Jetstream T.1	XX480 (262)
	Short Skyliner 3	G-BCFI (SH.1930)
+	Short Skyvan 3M-400	G-BCFJ (SH.1931)
+	Short SD3-30	G-BSBH (SH.3000)
+	Sikorsky HH-53C	31647
+	Sikorsky S-67 Blackhawk	N671SA (67001) Crashed 1/9
	SOCATA Rallye Sport	G-BBLM (2392)
	SOCATA Rallye Club	G-BAOG (2249)
	SOCATA Rallye Commodore	G-BBHX (12211)
+	SOCATA Rallye Minerva	F-BPDG (12200)
+	VFW 614	D-BABC (G-3)
+	Westland Gazelle HT.2	XW864 (1116)
+	Westland Lynx	XW839 (2/09)
+	Westland Lynx HAS.2	XX910 (WA.3/16)
+	Westland Sea King 50	N16-098/G-17-1 (WA.787) RAN

Service participation in the flying programmes:
Hawker Siddeley Gnat: nine from CFS, "Red Arrows" aerobatic team.
Hawker Siddeley Harrier: eight from 1 Squadron, one from 233 OCU.
BAC Jaguar: four from 6 Squadron.

Veteran and vintage aircraft:
Avro Lancaster PA474.
Fairey Swordfish LS326.
Hawker Hurricane LF363.
Supermarine Spitfire AB910.

Civil aircraft participation:
Pitts S-1S G-AZPH aerobatics.
Pitts S-2A: four, Rothmans Aerobatic Team.
Zlin Z.526 Trener: G-AWPG, G-AWSH aerobatics.

*BAC Strikemaster 80 G-BECI for the Royal Saudi Air Force
surrounded by a mass of weaponry.*

*Lockheed's SR-71 Blackbird 17972 set a Transatlantic record
on its way to the Show.*

*Aermacchi MB.326Ks 1-AMKK and 1-KMAK on their way to
the Show.*

1976

THE THIRTIETH SHOW
5-12 SEPTEMBER

Farnborough 1976 posed one important question for the organisers. The country had sweltered and gasped and sun-bathed its way through one of the hottest and most perfect summers in recent history; would the weather hold until the final Sunday of the Show? After that, *Aprés moi le deluge* as far as the SBAC was concerned.

It very nearly did hold. The first four days were a continu-ation of the summer, but on Thursday the customary proces-sion of fronts resumed their sway and produced squalls, rain and a vicious, gusting cross-wind that taxed many pilots and defeated one or two. (The Bullfinch, still in the very early stages of its flight test programme, did not risk it, for one.) On Friday, it just drizzled, but that did not prevent the public from attending the Show. Nor did the quite considerable increases in prices of admission.

The SBAC is not permitted to make a profit out of the run-ning of the Farnborough Display under its terms of reference, but "times was hard" in the seventies, with inflation in Europe well into double figures, the aftermath of large pay awards and industrial unrest to pay for and the dollar at 1.6-odd to the pound. In retrospect, it is surprising for how long the Show ran without any increase in entrance charges.

This year, the three-tier system for admittance on Thurs-day, Friday and the week-end continued. The new prices were, respectively (1974 in brackets): Adults £2.50(£1.75), £3.50(£2.00), £2.50(£1.00): Children under 14 £2.50(£1.75), £1.50(70p), £1.00(50p): cars additional to occupants £2.00(£1.50), £1.50(£1.50), £2.00(£1.00). Coaches went up from £2.00 to £5.00, motorcycles from 50p to £1.00. The increase looks large, but actually did no more than reflect the general rise in costs.

Taking heed of the lessons learned in 1974, arrangements for traffic control were improved and included the realign-ment of entry gates into the present pattern. The extension of motorways was also beginning to make itself felt.

There was now a continuous row of chalets along Lincoln Road (E and H Rows) and an extra 4,000 square feet (372 sq.m) of covered stand space to accommodate the require-ments of the 376 exhibitors (146 of them from overseas).

There was a curious and short-lived attempt made this year to solve the problem of putting a programme together by sending off aircraft in alphabetical order by manufacturer, switching the two halves of the show at mid-week in order

to appease the exhibitors like Westland who lived far down the alphabet. It was not, by and large, a success.

Multi-national programmes included the Transall 160, which was appearing rather in the capacity of a *ballon d'essai*, no decision to re-open the production line having yet been taken; someone was busily spreading the rumour that France's Armée de l'Air was looking at the Fiat G.222 as an alterna-tive – which was authoritatively denied. While this was the first public appearance of the Tornado, the Jaguar programme was well under way, the 100th aircraft for the Armée de l'Air having been delivered on 19 May.

The go-ahead for initial production of 40 Tornados had been given on 29 July. These would probably be built equally in Britain and Germany, with Italian production participation not yet being clear. The clearance to production was wel-comed, enabling the speeding-up of equipment orders so that these and other matters hitherto subject to tri-national agree-ment, could now be settled more swiftly at purely national level.

The aircraft at Farnborough were the third Warton proto-type, engaged in stores release and gun firing trials, which was in the flying display and the fourth and last Warton pro-totype – the third Tornado fitted with radar and the second two-seater, both in the static.

Service participation was confined to the Red Arrows, led by Dickie Duckett, the Vintage Pair Meteor T.7 and Vampire T.11, who had appeared in 1974 and were to remain a popu-lar display item round the country for a decade to come, the Lancaster, Spitfire and Hurricane and the Fleet Air Arm's Sea Fury – the latter in the capable hands of the piratical Lieu-tenant Commander Pete (the Bad) Sheppard.

These items flew on the public days only, the Battle of Bri-tain Flight arriving after flying had ceased on Friday even-ing and providing an unforgettable sight as they passed the chalets in the general direction of Laffan's Plain and the set-ting sun.

No entries had been received from the Soviet Union (who appeared at Paris, which had been international all its days) but they advertised in *Flight International*, which was gener-ally conceded to be a good sign.

The F-14 Tomcat, a "swing-wing" aircraft, like the Tornado, had been designed, in competition with a McDonnell Douglas project, for the Navy's VFX contest following the cancella-tion of the naval version of the F-111, the F-111B, in 1968 and not un-naturally followed the basic lay-out of that aircraft. Grumman had, in fact, built the first US combat aircraft with vg, the extraordinary XF10F-1 Jaguar, around the time of the Korean War. It looked like an aerodynamic joke in dubious taste and only two were built; one was expended testing a crash barrier and the other became a tank target at Aberdeen Proving Ground.

Tornado, of course, was one of the aircraft that everyone had come to Farnborough to see. Just too late to get into the previous Show, it represented a most ambitious programme; the nine prototypes were being built and tested simultaneously among the three design partners in Britain, Germany and Italy. The tri-national RB199 had taken rather longer to come on line in quantity than planned, but there were now enough engines to go round and eleven pilots had been cleared on the aircraft.

Wing sweep was manual, though auto-sweep had been proposed and would be implemented on the F.3 version. The skills required to achieve optimum change of sweep – for instance, in minimum drag or turn radius - did not turn out to be difficult to learn. Curiously, an early request for practice time on F-111s was turned down by the United States Department of Defense, but the requirement turned out to be unnecessary anyway.

The TF-15A Eagle was the second two-seater and twelfth aircraft built. Considering its maximum gross weight of 66,000 lb (29,937 kg) and the rejection of the advantages of variable geometry (on grounds of complexity and weight) the Eagle showed remarkable agility. Shortly after the previous Farnborough, in an operation named Streak Eagle, it had broken all eight of the world time-to-height records, culminating in a streak to 30,000 metres (98,425 ft) in three minutes, 27.8 seconds. That is a vertical speed of 144.37 m/s (473.65 ft/sec) or, if you prefer it, 520 k/h (323 mph). Confronted with such ballistic virtuosity, the FAI countered with a new record category for Altitude in Horizontal Flight.

The other contribution from McDonnell Douglas was the YC-15. This was one of two designs submitted to the USAF AMST (Advanced Medium STOL Transport) proposal, the other being the Boeing YC-14. To meet the requirements, the company used a supercritical wing with double-slotted flaps covering three-quarters of the span. The latter, when fully deployed on the approach, were startling to look upon, the general effect from the vantage-point of the control tower roof being, as someone said, that of a wide-body triplane. The YC-15 was a year ahead of its rival, and McDonnell Douglas embarked on a programme of development, but someone changed their minds, or there was not enough cash and the AMST went into suspended animation. Where, at the time of writing, it remains; nevertheless, the programme provided valuable data for the C-17.

There were many memorable moments at Farnborough '76; not least being Tom Appleton's display of virtuoso

STOL on the Buffalo. The DHC-5 Buffalo was a 41-seat turboprop military transport developed out of the DHC-4 Caribou (and indeed initially named Caribou II). Taking-off in just about its own length, it proceeded to give a demonstration of steep turns and low-speed handling, culminating in a vertiginously steep final approach and possibly the STOLest landing ever seen at the Show. With its later stablemates the Dash 7 and Dash 8 it continued to amaze for ten years, going out finally in 1986 in a blaze of glory, landing on, rather than in, its own length.

As a result of some reshuffling in the Italian aerospace industry and the SBAC's novel method of deciding who flew when, Aermacchi opened the Show. The MB.326K had been joined by the new MB.339 (a kind of Lamborgini-Hawk) and for the first time we were treated to a synchronised display of great complexity and perfect precision by Franco Bonnazi and Ricardo Durione – test pilots to Aermacchi and known to everyone in the pilots' tent as "The Macchi Twins". Universally liked and universally respected, they are the only pilots at the Farnborough Show ever to have received a standing ovation at the morning briefing for their display.

Fairchild and their remarkable A-10 were newcomers to the Show. This "simple, effective and survivable twin-engine jet aircraft", to quote the USAF press kit, was designed as a dedicated tank-killer, armoured up to the eyebrows. Redundant wherever you looked and capable of carrying 16,000 lb (7,258 kg) of appropriate ordnance, as well as its main offensive weapon, the seven-barrel, 30 mm, GAU/8A Gatling gun. A big aircraft for battlefield work, spanning 57 ft 6 in (17.5 m) it could provide 1.8 hours loiter time 250 miles (402 km) from base, remaining on call to a theatre commander, able to operate in far worse weather conditions than more sophisticated attack aircraft and built to refute the old tag that the second pass is the one where they get you. Later named Thunderbolt II for sentimental reasons, it also answered to the less resounding title of Warthog.

On 1 May 1975, the government introduced its Nationalisation Bill for the aircraft industry, and 1976 was to be the last Farnborough at which the British Aircraft Corporation and Hawker Siddeley names would appear. In fact, British Aircraft Corporation involvement in the flying was confined to the Jaguar and Concorde with a One-Eleven (220 of which had been sold) and export Strikemaster (700 Jet Provost/Strikemaster sold) in the static, as well as a Concorde.

Concordes overflew the Show on Monday and Thursday, in the course of scheduled runs to Bahrain and there was one on the ground for the first time, that the public could walk through. Which they did; 28,000 of them. When the queue reached something like 6,000 on the final Sunday the police called a halt and it was announced that no-one joining after that would reach the aircraft before closing time. The tail of the queue promptly and predictably doubled.

On 1 August 1975, the fourth production Concorde made the first double-double Atlantic crossing in one day; out-and-back twice in twenty-four hours. British Airways and Air France began the first supersonic passenger service to Rio de Janeiro on 1 January 1976, following with the first trans-Atlantic regular services on 24 May.

TriStar was also on the ground and open for the first time and 115,000 went through its wide body.

Main delight of the Hawker Siddeley presentation was the elegant and workmanlike Hawk. Duncan Simpson in the third production Royal Air Force aircraft and Andy Jones in the company demonstrator, G-HAWK (in sand-and-dust camouflage and therefore the "Desert Hawk") were joined by the sixth RAF aircraft, and on Wednesday by six more for an impressive formation Hawk display that upstaged the Arrows by four years.

On the civil side the last of the Viper-powered H.S 125s, the Series 600, with more power and more room, was accompanied by the prototype Series 700, which featured Garrett AiResearch fan jets. Over 150 125s had been sold and it was doing very well in the United States.

Dassault-Breguet flew the Falcon 10 and 20; the 30 had been dropped in favour of the later, three-engined Falcon 50. Aérospatiale fielded three helicopters; their rotary wing activities were to develop very powerfully in the next few years, but they were to drop the Corvette, which had cost them a great deal of money but failed to attract many orders.

The World Aerospace Conference organised in London by the *Financial Times* just prior to Farnborough reinforced the evident European realization that "co-operate or die" was a good working principle, but national projects, though becoming fewer, still proliferated; the French industry, for instance, launching a national airliner, Airbus or no Airbus. This was to be the CFM56-engined Mercure 200. The Mercure 100 had been a financial disaster, but there was talk of McDonnell Douglas coming in on the 200 – except at McDonnell Douglas – and in the end nothing came of it.

Other newcomers that were to gain a place in world markets in subsequent years included the Spanish C.212 Aviocar, still being flown by Guillermo Delgardo six Farnboroughs later, and the Pilatus Turbo-Porter and PC-7. One must not forget Airbus test pilot Pierre Baud, who flew the largest and heaviest jet aircraft in the Display – the A300 – and the smallest and lightest – the Bede BD-5J. The latter, available in kit form in a rather haphazard way, fell victim to Jim Bede's marketing methods, which tended to represent the triumph of optimism over common sense, but one reappeared later, minus its stubby wings, as a racing car. Not many aircraft have done this.

A rare but welcome appearance by the Australian aircraft industry was made with the Nomad N22. It was an aircraft arising originally from the Australian government's determination to maintain their aerospace industry's building capability. It sold steadily over the next seven years to a total of 172 when the shut-down of production was announced at the end of 1984, the last 20 being completed that year. Eight of those were 24As, for civil commuter work, joining 20 already engaged in that activity.

Service participation in flying programmes:
Hawker Siddeley Gnat: nine from CFS, "Red Arrows" aerobatic team.

Veteran and vintage aircraft:
Avro Lancaster PA474.
de Havilland Vampire, T.11 XH304 } Vintage Pair team
Gloster Meteor T.7 WF791 }
Hawker Hurricane LF363.
Hawker Sea Fury TF956.
Supermarine Spitfire P7350 and PM631.

Civil aircraft participation:
BAC/Aerospatiale Concorde G-BOAA on 8/9; G-BOAC on 6/9.
Mudry CAP.10 G-BECZ aerobatics.
Pitts S-2A: four, Rothmans aerobatic team.
Supermarine S.5 Replica G-BDFF.

The McDonnell Douglas YC-15 STOL transport gave a most impressive display; note the large flaps and rather odd nose wheel door configuration. C

1976

+	Aermacchi MB.326K	I-IVAO/MM54390 (6477/218)
	Aermacchi MB.326K	I-IVAP/MM54391 (6478/219)
+	Aermacchi MB.339	I-NOVE/MM568 (6573/001)
+	Aerospatiale SA.360 Dauphin	F-WVKJ (1001)
+	Aerospatiale SA.365 Dauphin	F-WVKE (004)
	Aerospatiale SA.342 Gazelle	F-WTNA (1185)
+	Aerospatiale Corvette	F-BVPI (24)
+	Agusta A.109A	I-DCVM (7109)
	Agusta A.109A	I-CDMV (7113)
+	Agusta-Bell AB.212ASW	MM80936
+	Airbus A300B-2	F-WUAD (3)
+	BAC Jaguar GR.1	XZ358 (S.125)
	BAC Jaguar International	XZ362 (S.129)
	BAC One-Eleven 401 Executive	N111NA (055)
	BAC Strikemaster 80	G-BECI/1124 (355) R. Saudi AF
+	BAC Tornado IDS	XX948 (P.06)
	BAC Tornado IDS	XX950 (P.08)
	BAC/Aerospatiale Concorde	G-BBDG (002/13523)
	Bede BD-5J	F-WZAV (50005)
	Beech King Air 100	G-BBVM (B-201)
+	Bell 206L LongRanger	N9954K
	Boeing 707-3J9C	5-249 (21123) Imperial Iranian AF
	BHC SR.N6 Hovercraft	GH-9003
+	CASA Aviocar	EC-CRV (09)
	CASA Aviocar	EC-CRX (10)
	Cessna FR.172E	SE-FBT (0034)
+	Dassault Falcon 10	F-BVPR (5)
	Dassault Falcon 20E	G-BCYF (304)
+	Dassault-Breguet/Dornier Alpha Jet	F-ZWRU (02)
	de Havilland Chipmunk	G-ARWB (C1/0621) Bonner Super Sapphire engine
+	de Havilland Canada Buffalo	C-GBUF (60)
+	Enstrom 280 Shark	G-BDIB (1017)
	Enstrom 280C Shark	(G-BEEL) (1038) no markings
+	Fairchild A-10A	75-264
	Fairey Britten-Norman Defender BN-2A-21	G-BDLN (492)
	Fairey Britten-Norman Islander BN-2A-21	G-BCZD (759)
	Fairey Britten-Norman Islander BN-2A-26	G-BDHU (767) Firefighter
	Fairey Britten-Norman Islander BN-2A-26	G-BDMT (772) Agricultural
	Fairey Britten Norman Trislander BN-2A-III-2	G-BDTR (1029)
+	Fairey Britten-Norman Trislander BN-2A-III-2	G-BDTS (1030)
+	FFA Bravo 18A	HB-HEY (015)
	FFA Bravo 18A	HB-HFD (023)
+	Fokker F.27 Maritime	PH-FCX (10183)
+	Fokker F.28-1000	PH-ZBM (11048)
+	GAF Nomad N22B	VH-AUN (26)
	Gates Learjet 24	SE-DCW (24-109)
	Grumman Gulfstream II	G-BDMF (103)
	Grumman E-2C Hawkeye	160010
+	Grumman F-14A Tomcat	158955
	Grumman American AA-1B Tr.2	G-BDLS (0564)
	Grumman American AA-5A Cheetah	G-BEBE (0154)
	Grumman American AA-5B Tiger	G-BDLR (0128)
+	Hawker Siddeley Harrier 52A	G-VTOL (B3/41H/735795)
+	Hawker Siddeley AV-8A Harrier	159374
+	Hawker Siddeley Hawk T.1	G-HAWK (41H/4020010)
+	Hawker Siddeley Hawk T.1	XX156
+	Hawker Siddeley Hawk T.1	XX158
+	Hawker Siddeley Hawk T.1	XX159
+	Hawker Siddeley Hawk T.1	XX160
+	Hawker Siddeley Hawk T.1	XX161 } included in total of
+	Hawker Siddeley Hawk T.1	XX162 } nine aircraft formation
+	Hawker Siddeley Hawk T.1	XX163 } on one day, flying only
+	Hawker Siddeley Hawk T.1	XX164
+	Hawker Siddeley Nimrod MR.1A	XZ282 (8044)
+	Hawker Siddeley H.S.125-700	G-BFAN (25258)
+	Hawker Siddeley H.S.125-600B	G-BDJE (256052)
+	Hawker Siddeley H.S.748-2A	CS-03 (1743) Belgian AF
+	ICA-Brasov IS-28BM2	YR-1013 (01)
	Lockheed TriStar 100	A40-TY (1138)
+	Lockspeiser LDA-01	G-AVOR (PFA/1346)
+	MBB Bo 105C	D-HDDV (S-128)
	MBB Bo 105C	D-HDER (S-150)
+	McDonnell Douglas TF-15A Eagle	71-291
+	McDonnell Douglas YC-15	72-1876
+	Northrop F-5E Tiger II	74-1543
+	Northrop YF-17 Cobra	72-1570
+	Partenavia P.68B	G-BCDK (32)
	Partenavia P.68 Observer	D-GERD (15)
+	Piaggio P.166-DL3	I-PJAG (416)
+	Pilatus PC-6B2/H2 Turbo-Porter	HB-FFW (735)
+	Pilatus PC-7 Turbo-Trainer	HB-HOZ (509)
	Pilatus PC-11 B-4	HB-1253 (175)
	PZL SZD-41A Jantar	SP-3060 (B-719)
	PZL SZD-45A Ogar	G-BEBG (B-655)
	PZL TS-11 Iskra	SP-DOE (3H 1606)
	PZL Kruk	SP-WUF (26006)
+	PZL Wilga 35	SP-WRE (86225)
	Rockwell Sabreliner 75A	N64 (380-35)
+	SAAB 105G	SE-XBZ (105-2)
+	SAAB Safari	SE-XCF (MFI-15-02)
	SAAB Supporter	T-405 (15-205)
+	SAAB Viggen AJ 37	37091
	SAAB Viggen SF 37	37907
	SOCATA Rallye 100ST	G-BDED (2553)
	SOCATA Rallye 100ST	G-BDWA (2695)
+	SOCATA Rallye 235E	F-BXDT (12193)
	SOCATA Rallye 235GT	G-BEEA (12770)
+	Scottish Aviation Bulldog 120	G-ASAL (239)
+	Scottish Aviation Bullfinch	G-BDOG (381)
	Scottish Aviation Jetstream	G-AWVK (208)
+	Short Skyvan 3M	G-BDVO/YV-O-MC-9 (SH.1949)
	Short SD3-30	G-BDMA (SH.3002)
+	Short SD3-30	G-BEEO (SH.3006)
+	SIAI-Marchetti SF.260W	I-ARGI (20-01)
+	Transall C.160	61-MZ (54)
+	VFW 614	D-BABI (G.9)
+	Westland Lynx	G-BEAD (WA.001) P&W PT-6A engines
+	Westland Lynx AH.1	XX907 (WA.1/8)
+	Westland Lynx HAS.2	XX910 (WA.3/16)
+	Westland Lynx HAS.2	XZ166

The nine British Aerospace Hawk formation on its way to Farnborough.

David Lockspeiser's LDA-01 (Land Development Aircraft) G-AVOR was a scale model of a proposed transport aircraft with a detachable pod in the centre fuselage. There was no further development and it was destroyed in the fire at Brooklands' Old Sarum factory several years ago.

The first Westland Lynx airframe, XW835, was re-engined with two Pratt & Whitney Canada PT6B-34 engines and flew in July 1976 under civil marks G-BEAD.

Latest variant of the Piaggio family was the P.166-DL3 1-PJAG.

1978

THE THIRTY-FIRST SHOW
3-10 SEPTEMBER

Space available to exhibitors in 1978 totalled 138,791 square feet (12,894 sq.m). There was now a new row of 16 chalets, J row, down by the woods where the old grandstand had formerly been, raising the total number available to 208.

For the public period, which had now reverted to the traditional "long week-end" of three days, there were in addition to the Red Arrows, the Royal Air Force and Royal Navy historic presentations, Concorde and a full house from Leisure Sport, who fielded all the available items from their reconstructions of World War One scouts. Of these the D.H.2 suffered some indignity in its motor and did not fly. One Camel sported a genuine rotary, the rest conceding modern radial or flat-four engines under the bonnet. Entry charges remained the same as for 1976.

A late arrival for the full display was the remarkable Tri-Turbo 3 from Specialised Aircraft, a DC-3 powered by three PT-6s. The latest brain-child of Jack Conroy of Guppy fame, it was intended to compete in the search and surveillance market, but despite eloquent pleading by its proud parent, was not permitted to fly. In any case, McDonnell Douglas, with one eye on the original stress calculations for the DC-3 and another on the product liability laws, were by no means keen on the idea.

Dassault-Breguet had at last brought their "first eleven", the big fighters; de Havilland of Canada had added the Dash 7 to their STOL fleet; the Macchi Brothers now had an MB.339A apiece and could really let themselves go, and Philip Meeson spent a happy week demonstrating the aerobatic capabilities of the Cranfield A1. Intended to be the great white hope of the British World Aerobatics team, circumstances, including the death of Neil Williams, its original, if not "onlie begetter", slowed down its development and although it was still appearing handsomely in competition ten years later, it never did fulfil its original destiny.

Events played firmly into the hands of the French as far as the flying was concerned. SAAB of Sweden had brought no Viggen (though it was to return in 1980) and after the startling decision by the President of the United States that it was immoral to demonstrate fighting aeroplanes at international exhibitions (or words to that effect), American military front-line aircraft were conspicuously absent. There was a Chinook in the air and an A-10 in the park and that was it; the presence of the Chinook was of particular interest

because of the order for 30 for the Royal Air Force placed by the Ministry of Defence on 31 January. A curious situation indeed. Only the Tornado was there to challenge this temporary French air superiority.

In one area, however, Britain (in the person of British Aerospace) still remained unquestionably supreme. The ski-jump take-off ramp for heavily-loaded Harriers was demonstrated twice daily, once by a Sea Harrier, once by a very comprehensively stocked GR.3. The Royal Air Force Harriers had now all been delivered, as had those for the United States Marine Corps – indeed the RAF had recently ordered 24 more GR.3s – and Nos 1, 3 and 4 Squadrons had all been equipped. The Sea Harrier FRS.1 had made its first flight at Dunsfold on 21 August in the hands of John Farley, now chief test pilot, Duncan Simpson having joined SBAC and the Display Flying Control Committee. The aircraft involved, demonstrating at Farnborough, was to go on to trials in HMS *Hermes* from 14 November.

The withdrawal of military aircraft by the United States government, leaving only a few business aircraft, helicopters and British-sponsored club singles (mostly on static display), gave the British exhibitors a dominating position in the flying programme with twenty aircraft, half of them appearing for the first time under the new name of British Aerospace. The formation of a national company had been under discussion for some time and was formally announced in Parliament on 29 April 1977. It became reality for most people on 1 January 1978, when the names of its constituent members, British Aircraft Corporation, Hawker Siddeley Aviation (and Hawker Siddeley Dynamics) and Scottish Aviation were finally dropped.

For a great variety of reasons, of which perhaps the single most compelling one was the steadily increasing complexity of modern civil and military aircraft operations at every level, it had now become evident that the "balance of power" at the Exhibition had changed. The importance of the exhibitor in the main halls who was marketing systems, equipment, electronics and materials was now being demonstrated. They represented a growing percentage of the trade generated by the Show. New materials were now as important as new aircraft; British Aerospace was investigating carbon-fibre reinforced plastics for the Tornado and Dunlop were becoming leaders in carbon-fibre brakes.

On 31 August, the British government finally announced its intention to back British Aerospace's desire to continue in the Airbus programme and take up a 20 per cent stake. This programme, the most exciting European one to date, was now well under way, with orders and options at the end of 1977 standing at 56. Production was running at 22 units a year and the aircraft at Farnborough in 1978 was a production B2, with a passenger capacity of between 220 and 345 over ranges from 2,500 miles (4,023 km) to 4,000 miles (6,437 km). The first of the new A300B4, with greater weights and more fuel, had flown on 26 December 1974. Freddie Laker, currently the *enfant terrible* of the airline world with his Skytrain, had ordered six of them with an option on four more and the short-span, 250-seat A310, with redesigned wing, was beginning to attract orders.

The curious thing about the decision to go for a stake in Airbus was the fact that no-one seemed to have noticed. There was still a lot of muttering at Farnborough about Britain making up its mind before it was too late (some people said it was too late) and whose side were we on anyway? There were tales of British Aerospace having talks with McDonnell Douglas and the rumour that British Airways were going to buy Boeing 757s raised a few French eyebrows. They did, too; signed a contract for 19 on 2 March 1979.

Nobody seemed to be worried by the British government's heavy backing of the RB211-535, but Fokker-VFW, backed by *their* government, raised a stink with the European Commission over a similar sum (£250 million) allocated for development of the revived BAe 146. This protest over an alleged contravention of EC rules was regarded as being not entirely disinterested, as the 146 might conceivably be seen to compete with the F.28 Fellowship. In any case, the complaint came to nothing.

Back on the national front, the SBAC had announced half-yearly export figures for the aerospace industry in 1978 as £550 million in round figures, with a 50 per cent increase in instrument sales and over 100 per cent increase in those for simulators and trainers.

The Italians were showing the new Aermacchi MB.339A trainer. It was based on the strengthened single seater MB.336K and retained that version's capability for carrying armament. the Aeronautica Militare were expected to order about 100 and they would replace the Fiat G.91PAN in the national aerobatic team, the Frecce Tricolori.

Designed originally by Fiat, who became part of the nationalised Aeritalia group in the mid-seventies, the G.222 was making its first Farnborough appearance. It was of particular interest because production aircraft were to receive the Rolls-Royce Tyne 20, causing the production line for that useful engine to be re-opened. Apart from an order for 44 from the Aeronautica Militare useful enquiries were coming in from other parts of the world.

The Italian aircraft industry was in a curious position, with strong order books balanced against serious economic and political problems. Despite the nationalisation of much of the industry (Agusta was 51 per cent owned by the government financing organisation EFIM) it was a continual complaint that, unlike other European countries, the Italian government gave no support whatsoever to its aerospace industry.

Agusta were showing their A.109 Hirundo (the name was soon dropped) and the licence-built Agusta-Bell AB.212ASW. The 109 was a native product; a military and naval helicopter of which 100 out of a current order for 250 had been built. The 212 was one of a number of types built under the long-standing Bell licence (early Sioux for the British Army were Agusta-built).

Rinaldo Piaggio was principally involved in contract work for the G.222, Tornado and Viper engine, but was assiduously marketing the new version of the unpressurised P.166 with Lycoming turboprop engines. Ten had been laid down in anticipation of repeating at least some of the numerous sales of earlier versions.

Partenavia were only exhibiting statically, but SIAI-Marchetti (part of the Agusta group) flew the SF.260W Warrior version of Dott Ing Stelio Frati's highly-successful design of which some 700 had been sold. It had begun as a three-seat light aircraft, but all his designs were potential fighters. The SM.1019, which the company were hoping to export, completed a powerful Italian presence.

Against slightly disturbing economic conditions, the French aircraft industry at this time was in a very powerful position, possessed of aggressive marketing techniques and strongly government-backed. Moreover, French participation in a number of multi-national programmes put her in a commanding position. Of the aircraft at Farnborough the twin-jet Falcon 20 was No. 375 of 435 ordered. The SOCATA Rallye had the inimitable Maurice Serré demonstrating its remarkable aerodynamic capability and the Dauphin 2 was now twin-engined to improve its performance – which also greatly increased its sales. On 2 July 1980, Aérospatiale would announce a contract for the assembly of 50 in the People's Republic of China.

Orders for the Atar-powered Mirage F.1 swept-wing single-seat fighter totalled 554 for nine countries; versions in the flying display were the F.1B and F.1E, respectively the two-seat all-weather interceptor and multi-role export single seater, the Mirage 2000, the "ten-tonne fighter" with SNECMA M53 turbofan, selected as the next generation air superiority and interceptor fighter for the Armée de l'Air, was spendidly displayed by Guy Maurouard, a first-class display pilot, but one whose name was a permanent challenge to a British commentator. Fully fly-by-wire, with full span leading edge slats almost permanently deployed, the big delta's display was outstanding and included a fly-past at around 100 knots (185 k/h) at nearly 25 degrees angle of attack. Although plans for acquisition of 20 production aircraft in the first year had been cut to four, development of the 2000 had a high priority, absorbing the lion's share of the French defence budget. There was a planned initial requirement for 127 units.

Among British Aerospace aircraft in the flying display, the One-Eleven was the company demonstrator, G-ASYD, configured to the 670 Series short-field version. Of the 220 One-Elevens sold, 43 were executive versions and 46 per cent of the total sales were European, with 31 per cent to the United States. Apart from that, a contract was signed with the Romanian government on 15 May for the building and marketing of up to 80 One-Elevens at Bucharest.

From Woodford was the latest version of the 748, the Coastguarder, with an eye on the increasing market for affordable and economic off-shore patrol, surveillance and ASW aircraft. Basically, it was a version of the Series 2A, which had more powerful engines; well over three hundred civil and military 748s had been sold and it was in production in India.

The first of the Sea Harriers, complete with ski-jump, was on display, with the Mk 3 Harrier, which featured the more powerful Pegasus 103. Lt Cdr D.R.Taylor RN, had invented the ski-jump in 1977. A curved launching ramp, fitted to the navy's three new carriers, at seven degrees in HMS *Invincible* and *Illustrious* and twelve degrees in the later HMS *Ark Royal*, it enabled a Harrier to lift an extra 2,500 lb (1,100 kg) and take-off in a shorter distance. The ramp at Farnborough was erected by the Royal Engineers from parts of a Fairey Engineering Medium Girder Bridge – a fine example of the capacity for improvisation that characterises that most ingenious regiment. Anchored at the base and supported only at the lip, the curve of the ramp, following a quartic equation, gave a surprisingly bland take-off (when tried out one evening in G-VTOL).

The two Hawks presented were both company aircraft, the T.1 being the third production trainer, retained for attack configuration trials and the 50 being G-HAWK, the "desert" version. Deliveries to the Royal Air Force were progressing nicely, the static aircraft at the Show being number 52. At this time, the negotiations to provide, through Valmet, 50 Hawks for the Finnish government were in their final stages.

Britten-Norman (Bembridge), with sales of the Islander now at around 900, plus 30 Defender military versions and some 50 Trislanders, and production continuing in Romania and the Philippines, found itself, thanks to the dissolution of the Fairey Group, back in the market-place. Their time in the wilderness was short, on this occasion however, as it was announced a month before Farnborough that an offer had been made by Pilatus for the whole operation.

This Swiss company was part of the large Oerlikon-Bührle group, producing the successful Porter and Turbo-Porter and the PC-7 trainer and saw the Islander/Trislander as a useful extension of their operation. Their main factory at Stans had achieved undying fame as the site of Auric Enterprises in the film *Goldfinger*.

Shorts, who were demonstrating the 3-30 and Skyvan 3, the former with the popular Pratt and Whitney of Canada PT-6A, the latter with the Garrett TPE-331, were also heavily involved with subcontracting work to Boeing, Lockheed and McDonnell Douglas, as well as running a full guided weapon programme and delivering 140 wing sets for the Fokker F.28. The company would shortly be provided with a £60 million government investment for a new capital re-equipment plan, and at the time of Farnborough, when they were expecting to be able to announce fresh orders, those for the 3-30 stood at 24, while virtually all of the 123 Skyvans ordered had been delivered.

Westland's contribution to the flying this year consisted of a Sea King and two Lynx. The Sea King was the first production HAR.3 for the Royal Air Force; 19 having been ordered to replace the ageing Whirlwind HAR.10 with No. 202 Squadron, who began to receive them in July and were fully equipped just before Farnborough. This was the biggest helicopter the Royal Air Force had ever had and a special training unit was set up at Culdrose to take advantage of Royal Navy experience on the type. A total of 166 Sea Kings had been sold, together with some 50 of the Commando version, including 15 for the Royal Marines and 28 for Egypt.

The Lynx was the 20th production airframe for the Royal Navy; the HAS.2 for the Small Ship's Flights would replace the Wasp and could carry either anti-submarine torpedoes or the new Sea Skua air-surface missile. The first ones delivered went to No. 700L Squadron in 1976, which also trained Lynx crews for the Netherlands Marineluchtvaartdienst, who received the first of their MK 27s in September 1979, and the first ship-borne Lynx joined the Leander class frigate HMS *Sirius* on 3 January, 1978 when the Ship's Flight reformed. Headquarters squadron at that time was No. 702. There were already orders for 285 Lynx and the type was to become the standard NATO naval helicopter.

The SIAI-Marchetti SM.1019 I-AFRI shows clearly in this view how it was developed from the Cessna L-19 Bird dog.

1978

+	Aeritalia G.222	MM62112 (4018)
	Aeritalia G.222	MM62114 (4019)
	Aermacchi MB.326K	MM54391 (6478/219)
	Aermacchi MB.339A	I-NEUF/MM54401 (6597/004)
+	Aermacchi MB.339A	I-NINE/MM589 (6574/002)
	Aerospatiale AS.350B Ecureuil	F-GBBQ (1003)
+	Aerospatiale SA.365C Dauphin II	F-WXFG (5011)
	Aerospatiale Fouga 90	F-WZJB
	Agusta A.109A	I-CVMD (7107)
+	Agusta A.109A	MM81014 (7118)
+	Agusta-Bell AB.212ASW	MM80954
+	Airbus A300B-2	F-WUAD (3)
	Bede BD-5	N502BD (50003)
+	Boeing-Vertol CH-47C Chinook	77-22684
+	British Aerospace Bulldog 124	G-ASAL (239)
+	British Aerospace Comet 4C	XW626 (06419) Nimrod fin and AEW nose
+	British Aerospace Harrier GR.3A	XV789
+	British Aerospace Harrier 52	G-VTOL/ZA250 (B3/41H/735795)
	British Aerospace Hawk T.1	XX156
	British Aerospace Hawk T.1	XX205
+	British Aerospace Hawk 50	G-HAWK/ZA101 (41H/4020010)
+	British Aerospace Jaguar GR.1	G-27-313/XX108 (S.1)
	British Aerospace Jaguar GR.1	XX766 (S.74)
	British Aerospace Jet Provost T.5A	XW322
+	British Aerospace Sea Harrier FRS.1	XZ450
+	British Aerospace Tornado IDS	XX947 (P.03)
+	British Aerospace Tornado IDS	XX950 (P.08)
+	British Aerospace H.S.125-700B	G-BEFZ (257001)
	British Aerospace H.S.125-2A	G-BDVH (1746)
+	British Aerospace H.S.748 Coastguarder	G-BCDZ (1662)
+	British Aerospace One-Eleven 670	G-ASYD (053)
+	Britten-Norman Islander BN-2A-27	G-BEGL (812)
	Britten-Norman Islander BN-2B-26	G-BESG (846)
+	Britten-Norman Islander BN-2A-3	G-FANS (251) Dowty ducted propulsors
	Britten-Norman Maritime Defender BN-2A-21	G-BCMY (419)
+	Britten-Norman Trislander BN-2A-III-2	G-BEDR (1040)
	CASA Aviocar	EC-T-104 (139)
+	CASA Aviocar 200	EC-T-103 (138)
+	CASA Aviojet	EC-ZDF (XE25-01)
	CASA Aviojet	EC-ZDI (XE25-04)
+	Cranfield A1	G-BCIT (001)
+	Dassault-Breguet Falcon 20	F-GBMD (375)
+	Dassault-Breguet Mirage F1B(F-ZJTJ)	
+	Dassault-Breguet Mirage F1EF-ZJTK)	
+	Dassault-Breguet Mirage 2000	(F-ZWRS) (01)
	Dassault-Breguet/Dornier Alpha Jet	98-33 (0001)
+	Dassault-Breguet/Dornier Alpha Jet	118-BQ (E2)
+	de Havilland Canada Buffalo	C-GQUT
+	de Havilland Canada Dash 7	C-GNBX (1)
+	de Havilland Canada Twin Otter 300	C-GDHA (428)

	Dornier Skyservant	58-37 (4112)
+	Dornier TurboSky	D-IBUF (4302)
+	Embraer Bandeirante	G-BWTV (110153)
+	Embraer EMB-111	FAB-7052
	Embraer Xingu	PP-ZCT (121001)
+	Enstrom 280C Shark	G-BENO (1060)
	Fairchild A-10A	77-0192
	FFA Bravo 18A	HB-HFD (023)
+	FFA Bravo 26A	HB-HEY (015)
+	FMA IA-58 Pucara	A-19
	GAF Nomad N22B	VH-BFH (35)
	GAF Nomad N22B Searchmaster	VH-AUH (4)
+	GAF Nomad N24A	VH-BLY (46)
	Gates Learjet 35A	D-CCCA (35A-160)
	Grumman American AA-5A Cheetah	G-BFRC (0631)
	Grumman American AA-5B Tiger	G-BFVS (0784)
	Grumman American GA-7 Cougar	N29699 (0033)
+	Hughes 500D	G-BFAY (67-0148D)
+	Hughes 500MD	N58235 (78-0323D)
	ICA-Brasov IS.28M2	G-7-100 (09)
+	MBB Bo 105CB	D-HDGV (S-311)
+	MBB Bo 105CBS	D-HDFQ (S-179)
	Mooney 201	OO-JPG (M20J-24-0534)
+	NDN Firecracker	G-NDNI (001)
	Partenavia P.68R	I-VICR (40)
	Piaggio P.166-DL3	I-PIAC (465)
+	Piaggio P.166-DL3	I-PJAG (416)
+	Pilatus PC-6 Turbo-Porter	HB-FFW (735)
	Pilatus PC-6 Turbo-Porter	HB-FHA (794)
	Pilatus PC-7 Turbo-Trainer	HB-HAO (101)
+	Pilatus PC-7 Turbo-Trainer	HB-HOZ (509)
	Pilatus PC-11 B4	HB-1253 (175)
	Piper Turbo Lance II	G-BFYD (32R-7887057)
+	Piper Tomahawk	G-OATS (38-78)
+	PZL-110	SP-WGC (2855)
+	PZL TS-11 Iskra	SP-DOF
+	PZL Wilga 35	SP-WHN (96332)
	Rockwell Commander 114	N5808N (14375)
	Rockwell Sabreliner 60	N9NR (306-135)
	Rockwell Sabreliner 75A	JY-AFL (380-56)
	Rockwell Turbo Commander 690B	N81767 (11465)
+	Short Skyvan 3	G-BFUJ (SH.1960)
	Short 330	G-BDBS (SH.3001)
+	SIAI-Marchetti SF.260W	I-FOUR (305-28-002)
	SIAI-Marchetti SF.260W	I-SEAW (304-28-001)
+	SIAI-Marchetti SM.1019E	I-AFRI (065-02-002)
	SOCATA Rallye 180GT	F-GBCP (13109)
+	SOCATA Rallye 180T	F-GBCS (3205)
	SOCATA Rallye 235CA	F-GBKH (13073) tailwheel, spray gear
	SOCATA Rallye 235G	(F-GAFE/F-ZWRT) (12105)
	Specialized Aircraft Tri-Turbo 3	N23SA (4903)
+	Transall C.160	G1-MQ (F.45)
+	Westland Lynx AH.1	XZ179 (WA.047)
+	Westland Lynx HAS.2	XZ248 (WA.080)
+	Westland Sea King HAR.3	XZ586 (WA.852)

Service participation in the flying programmes:
British Aerospace Hawk: one from CFS.
Hawker Siddeley Gnat: nine from CFS, "Red Arrows" aerobatic team.
Hawker Hurricane LF363.
Hawker Sea Fury TF956.
Supermarine Spitfire P7350.

Civil aircraft participation:
BAC/Aerospatiale Concorde G-BOAE.
Leisure Sport replicas: de Havilland D.H.2, Fokker Dr. 1, Fokker D.VII, Albatros D.VA, Sopwith Camel (2), Spad XIII.

Some of the smaller types in the aircraft park.

Britten-Norman Islander G-FANS with its Lycoming engines driving Dowty ducted propulsors – "the power to kill noise" as Dowty put it.

The Pilatus Turbo-Porter HB-FFW makes its usual steep take-off.

Management Aviation's Aerospatiale Dauphin II F-WXFG operating from a North Sea platform.

1980

THE THIRTY-SECOND SHOW
31 AUGUST-7 SEPTEMBER

The principal changes to the site for 1980 reflected the growing demand for space from the exhibitors. The main chalet rows (A to D) had been extended a considerable distance to the south-west, involving the removal of a large chunk of hill and the resiting of all the roads in the area. At the same time, South Hall was extended to the south, necessitating the re-alignment of ETPS Road and raising the total exhibition area to 176,142 square feet (16,364 sq. m).

Ticket prices on the public days were now £4 (adults), £2 (children), £4 (cars) and £10 (coaches) on Friday, and, respectively, £3, £1, £3 and £10 at the week-end.

The Government, in pursuance of its announced purpose to return British Aerospace, British Airways and Rolls-Royce to private ownership, proposed to release half of its holding in British Aerospace as an initial move.

Changes were becoming evident during the early eighties which were affecting the content of the flying display. Economic and political forces in Europe had already shaped the path for military aircraft; very few fresh projects were launched without the requirement for a risk-sharing partner, even among helicopters and trainers and the highly-successful British Aerospace Hawk might well be almost the last truly national military programme in Europe – and even this had an international engine.

Commercial transport programmes had been influenced by growing concern over economic and environmental considerations; superior aerodynamics and fuel efficient engines with low noise levels were beginning to mould the new airliners' characteristics, while the rising tempo of tourist travel and the limitations of existing airports has tended to make for more capacious aircraft. Development, and not invention, had been for some time the name of the game.

The trainer war was hotting up with more and more different designs appearing at each Show and progress in equipment, systems and materials, propelled by fast-growing new technology, could be seen in the increasingly important displays in the exhibition halls. Significant development was evident, for example, in flight simulation, some revolutionary new concepts in cockpit design and the use of new composites.

Japanese aircraft were back, for the first time since 1968, the appearance of the twin-turboprop Mitsubishi Marquise and Solitaire coinciding with the appointment of a new distributor in Britain.

The flying demonstrations were outstanding, with the three new American fighters and the Mirage 2000 and 4000 as well as Viggen and Tornado. The quality of the whole exhibition was reflected in the number of foreign missions and high-ranking defence officials doing the rounds of the stands, both independently and on conducted tours. The Soviet Union was there, though not officially represented.

There was one political move in 1979 which turned out to have a considerable bearing upon the aerospace scene; when the regime of the Shah was toppled on 16 January by followers of the exiled Ayatollah Khomeni, virtually the whole of the massive defence contracts that had so incensed the opponents to the Shah's policies were cancelled. In the United States these amounted to about £3,500 million and in the UK for almost the first time in its life the British army found itself knee-deep in tanks.

Looking forward beyond the Mirages and the Tornados, British Aerospace, MBB and Dassault-Breguet were completing their first drafts for the ECA, or European Combat Aircraft. The Inspector General of the Luftwaffe said it would never work and the French view of the desired product differed considerably from everyone else's.

One programme already well under way was Jaguar International, an export version of the aircraft with uprated Rolls-Royce Turboméca Adours. A dozen each had already been delivered to Ecuador and Oman and not long after the previous Show, on 30 October 1978 the Indian government announced that it was procuring a substantial number. Following purchase of an initial batch of 40, up to 150 would be built in India. The first two aircraft were handed over on 19 July 1979.

On 5 June 1979, the first production Tornado was rolled out at Warton. Production at the three Panavia companies was running at between eight and nine a month and was working up to the planned twelve aircraft a month. There were orders for 805 and Tornado would take over from the elderly Vulcan and other strike aircraft. If you wanted to buy one it would cost you, in 1980, £8.64 million. The two flying at Farnborough were the GR.1 (IDS) and F.2 (ADF), the two basic variants for the Royal Air Force.

Most of Europe's next generation of front-line aircraft was on view at Farnborough. In Sweden, the JA 37 Viggen, of which 149 had been ordered, was starting to re-equip the eight Draken Wings (280 aircraft) and the ones at Farnborough bore the markings of F13 Wing from Norrköping. In France, the Mirage 2000 would succeed the Mirage F1C.

Among the new United States aircraft in the flying display (the business of the morality of airshows having been sorted out since 1978) was the General Dynamics F-16A, officially named Fighting Falcon on 21 July 1980. Like the Sentry, it had only recently entered service – on 6 January 1979, with the 388th Tactical Fighter Wing.

Another aircraft making its first appearance at Farnborough which had first flown soon after the 1978 event was the McDonnell Douglas F-18 Hornet. The designation covered a joint programme between McDonnell Douglas and Northrop and was based on the latter company's YF-17 Cobra entry for the United States Air Force's LWF programme. The one at Farnborough was one of the two-seat TF-18As.

The third of the United States combat aircraft present at Farnborough had recently become the first to see combat, when five Syrian MiG-21s were shot down, on 27 June 1979 by F-15s of the Israeli Air Force.

One sign of the changing circumstances surrounding future military procurement was the growing concern in the (supposedly) endlessly wealthy United States over inflationally-spiralling costs for F-16 and F-18 and other programmes, some of which suffered procurement cuts in consequence.

Dassault-Breguet were formidably present. The first Dassault fighter, the Ouragan, flew in February 1949, developing into the swept-wing Mystère as the company gained experience of high-speed design. The Mystère family ended in French service in 1977 with the Super-Mystère, having been replaced by the new Mirage series. Although early Mirages were deltas, taking advantage of the benefits of that configuration, the ultimate service Mirage, the F1 (displaying at Farnborough) was a swept-wing design, Dassault's capabilities now enabling them to revert to a layout giving better performance in the current state of the art. The advent of fly-by-wire techniques enabled them to combine the best of both worlds in the very sophisticated Mirage 2000. In 1978 the intervening fighter design, the Mirage G8/F8 was cancelled, on grounds of expense, enabling the Mirage 2000 to be selected as the F1 replacement.

The delta provides low drag, low radar signature, considerable fuel storage, fewer controls and excellent manoeuvrability. The relaxed stability of fly-by-wire, aided by a number of high-lift devices, gives the big delta the advantages of conventional aircraft that it had hitherto lacked, including shorter take-off and landing runs and less speed loss in violent manoeuvres. The extrapolation of the design into the "20-tonne" thrust, twin-engined Mirage 4000 anticipated an extension of the graph that did not appear, various circumstances making it clear that the current generation of fighters would continue to serve, with mid-life updates, until the arrival of a completely new breed.

On top of the 50 Hawks for Finland, orders were announced from Indonesia for eight and the Kenya order for twelve was partially complete. Just in time to work up for the coming season, the last of the Red Arrows' Hawks was delivered on 15 November 1979.

The Aermacchi MB.339K or Veltro 2, new to Farnborough, was a single-seat attack version of the trainer. Other newcomers included an intriguing new British trainer from Desmond Norman's company, now called NDN. The Firecracker had been designed with a number of ingenious features intended to provide maximum efficient utilisation out of a small and simple airframe and was aerodynamically aimed at reproducing some of the more thought-provoking characteristics of the next generation of combat aircraft.

In a class new to Farnborough were the miniature Microjet 200, with two 200 lb (91 kg) thrust jets and the "powered glider" Caproni Vizzola C22J.

Two impressive military aircraft represented contenders for the next generation of AWACS (Airborne Warning and Control System). The Boeing E-3A Sentry was another touring item, that flew in over the Black Sheds during the week. The majestic approach of this impressive aircraft was hardly helped on its first appearance by the commentator, who – stumbling over its "giant rotating radar dish", announced to a startled world that it was "topped by a giant rotating radish". It was already in service in the Continental United States with the 552nd Airborne Warning and Control Wing and in March 1979, extended its duties to include monitoring the war in the Yemen. It was the successful contender for the NATO Early Warning role, with 18 aircraft ordered and training for the crews beginning in the United States. The British Aerospace Nimrod AEW.3, whose remarkable nose and tail radomes had already been seen in 1978 attached to a rather embarrassed-looking Comet 4C, was also appearing for the first time, being put forward as a national alternative for the Royal Air Force in the AWACS role.

The Airbus story continued to unfold with new orders being recorded with gratifying frequency. The A300B4 at the Show bore French prototype registration, but was in the livery of Singapore Airlines, to whom it would shortly be delivered. Eastern Airlines had introduced leased A300B4s on 13 December 1977 and subsequently ordered 23 on 6 May 1978, while Swissair placed an order for ten A310s and options on ten more in March 1979. Air France had started a Paris-Moscow Airbus service on 4 May 1978.

The last production Concorde, number 16, made its maiden flight on 20 April 1979. Being no longer a prototype, in production or about to enter production, it was no longer eligible to fly in the main Farnborough Display, but continued to appear at each Show, on the public days.

One display aircraft at least was working harder than most for its living; the curious-looking Edgley Optica, whose first flight was made on 14 December 1979, was being used by the Hampshire Constabulary to monitor the arrangements to expedite traffic into and out of the Show. The process was enlivened by the (private) comments of the police inspector on board – who was familiar with the duty roster – on the efforts of individual officers on the ground.

Helicopters were plentiful; Agusta were again showing their fast, medium-size A.109A, which was designed to fill the gap between the Bell 206 and 212, also built by Augusta. Available in civil or military form, some ninety had been delivered at Show time.

Bell's offering, the YAH-1 Model 249, was an interesting one, being an experimental version of the Huey Cobra with four rotor blades, which had first flown the preceding December. The Huey Cobra, with 959 ordered for the United States' services in various forms, was the first of the new battlefield helicopters seen at Farnborough, not counting the unfortunate S-67 Blackhawk.

MBB, who had shown the model 105 in previous Shows, now displayed with it the MBB/Kawasaki Bk 117, a risk-sharing joint venture that replaced independent projects by each company. Very largely a developed, larger version of the 105, with 50 per cent more power, it entered production in late 1979 and 120 had been sold by September 1980.

At the end of May, Westland had announced orders for 14 more Lynx for Aéronavale, ten for the Royal Navy and eight for other customers. No less than 151 British warships, including Royal Fleet Auxiliaries and merchant ships conscripted in 1982 for the Falklands campaign, were to be fitted to accept helicopters – mostly the Lynx – as were 26 with Commonwealth navies and with the Netherlands Marineluchtvaartdienst.

The Pilatus PC-6 and PC-7 were this time teamed with the newly-acquired Britten-Norman Islander, Turbine-Islander, and Trislander. Just before the Show, in what was said to be their largest single order to date, 15 Islanders were ordered for Mexico, with an option on 21 more.

This year saw yet another episode in the chequered history of the Jetstream with the statement by Mr Geoffrey Pattie, the Royal Air Force Under Secretary of State, that no decision could be taken to confirm the order for 14 Jetstream 31s that Mrs Thatcher's government had insisted should be ordered, rather than the Beech Super King Air, (which some of the Service apparently were secretly hoping to find in their stocking).

Shortly before Farnborough the Ministry of Defence imposed a three month moratorium on defence spending and announced that the life of the current Devons and Pembrokes, which the Jetstream was intended to replace, would continue for some considerable time. In the meantime, British Aerospace Scottish Division (Scottish Aviation that was) continued

with the Jetstream programme and wondered what would transpire when the three months was up.

From Canadair came the Challenger. Although it had been around for two years, its first flight, on 8 November 1978, was too late to let it be seen at Farnborough that year. It was present in 1980, however, operating out of Blackbushe each day to open the flying programme.

The aircraft was basically a new version of the LearStar 600, but Canadair had been investing money in an improvement programme and were planning an increase of 2,000 lb (907 kg) in gross weight, with a consequent bigger fuel uplift and increased range, up to 3,350 nautical miles (6,023 km).

Aérospatiale's Tampico, was the first of a new generation of club and touring single engined types, owing nothing to the familiar style of the older Rallye. Successful though the latter had been, it was getting a bit long in the tooth as a design. Maurice Serré, incidentally, whose demonstrations of the low-speed handling of his beslotted and beflapped mount enriched any flying display, having discovered the ski-jump, had put in a request to take-off and land on it. The request had been turned down apparently on the grounds that there was no time to rehearse. No-one on the Committee, it seems, had doubted for a moment that he could do it. Sadly for all concerned, there never was a second chance.

One aircraft present at the Show, though not in the flying programme, deserves mention. In the static park was an Evans VP-2, powered by a Volkswagen engine and sponsored by BP, which bore on its fin the arms of Truro School where it had been built by more than 80 of the pupils over a period of 18 months. An event of considerable rarity in the history of English schools, it was certainly unique at Farnborough.

Two interesting flying exhibits in the light aircraft category were the Chipmunk 200, powered by Bill Bonner's beautifully-built Super Sapphire water-cooled V-6 of 230 horsepower and Tom Storey's Airmark Cassutt IIIM Formula One single-seat racer, now offered as a production aircraft.

Services participation in flying programmes:
British Aerospace Hawk: nine from CFS, "Red Arrows" aerobatic team.
British Aerospace Sea Harrier: three from 800 Squadron.

Veteran and vintage aircraft
Avro Lancaster PA474.
de Havilland Dragon Rapide G-AIYR.
Douglas A-26C Invader N3710G/43-22612.
Fairey Firefly WB271.
Fairey Swordfish LS326.
Hawker Hurricane PZ865.
Hawker Sea Fury TF956 and WG665.
Supermarine Spitfire P7350 and PS853.

Civil aircraft participation:
BAC/Aerospatiale Concorde G-BOAA.
Pitts S-2A; four, Rothmans aerobatic team.
Volmer VJ-23 powered hang-glider.

1980

	Aircraft	Registration
+	Aermacchi MB.339A	I-NEUN/MM54443 (6602/009)
	Aermacchi MB.339A	MM54444 (6603/010)
+	Aermacchi MB.339K	I-BITE (6662/001)
+	Aerospatiale AS.355E Twin Star	F-WZJI (002)
	Aerospatiale SA.341G Gazelle	F-WXFI (1515)
+	Agusta A.109A	I-DCVM (7109)
	Agusta A.109A	I-DMCV (7110)
+	Agusta A.109A	I-DVCM (7156)
+	Airbus A300B4-203	F-WZER (117) to be 9V-STA
	British Aerospace Bulldog 124	G-ASAL (239)
+	British Aerospace Harrier 52	G-VTOL/ZA250 (B3/41H/735795)
	British Aerospace Hawk T.1	XX278
+	British Aerospace Hawk 50	G-HAWK/ZA101 (41H/4020010)
	British Aerospace Jaguar GR.1	XX979 (S.101)
	British Aerospace Jaguar GR.1	XZ104 (S.105)
	British Aerospace Jetstream 31	G-JSSD (227)
+	British Aerospace Nimrod AEW.3	XZ286 (8048) flying only
	British Aerospace One-Eleven 201AC	XX105 (008)
+	British Aerospace Sea Harrier FRS.1	XZ457
	British Aerospace Strikemaster 80A	G-16-27
+	British Aerospace Tornado IDS	XX947 (P.03)
+	British Aerospace Tornado ADV	ZA254 (A.01)
+	British Aerospace H.S.125-700B	G-OBAE (257094)
	British Aerospace H.S.748-2A	G-BDVH (1746)
+	British Aerospace H.S.748-2B	G-BGJV (1768)
+	Canadair Challenger CL-600	C-GBKC (1007) to be HZ-TAG
+	Caproni Vizzola C22J	I-CAVJ (001)
+	CASA Aviocar 200	EC-DHO (139)
	CASA Aviocar 200	N37838 (169)
+	CASA Aviojet	EC-ZDZ (XE25-01)
+	Cassutt IIIM	G-AXDZ (PFA/1341)
+	Dassault-Breguet Falcon 50	F-BNDB (1)
+	Dassault-Breguet Mirage FIC	5-NE (241)
+	Dassault-Breguet Mirage 2000	(02)
+	Dassault-Breguet Mirage 2000	(04)
+	Dassault-Breguet Mirage 4000	(01)
+	Dassault-Breguet/Dornier Alpha Jet	F-ZJTI
+	Dassault-Breguet/Dornier Alpha Jet	40-67 (0067)
+	de Havilland Chipmunk	G-ARWB (C1/0621) Bonner Super Sapphire engine
+	de Havilland Canada Buffalo	C-GCTC (103)
+	de Havilland Canada Dash 7	132002 (12) CAF
	de Havilland Canada Twin Otter 310	G-BDHC (414)
	Dornier Do 128-2	D-IDWM (4331)
+	Dornier Do 128-6X	D-IBUF (4302)
+	Dornier TNT	D-IFNT (4330)
+	Edgley Optica	G-BGMW (EA7/001)
+	Eiri PIK-20E	G-BGZL (20218)
	Embraer Bandeirante	PT-SBW (110287)
+	Embraer Bandeirante	G-BHYT (110277)
+	Embraer EMB-111	PP-ZDT (110159)
+	Embraer Xingu	G-BGIE (121014)
+	Embraer Xingu	G-XING (121030)
	Enstrom 280C Shark	G-BIBJ (1187)
	Evans VP-2	G-BTSC (PFA/63-10343)
	Fairchild A-10A	79-0126
	FFA Bravo 18A	HB-HEX (026)
+	FFA Bravo 26A	HB-HEY (015)
	Fokker F.27M Maritime	PH-FTU (10595) for Angolan AF
	Fokker F.28-4000	PH-ZBW (11157) to be PK-GKC
+	Gates Learjet 35A Maritime	N80SM (35-205)
+	General Dynamics F-16B	78-089
	General Dynamics F-111F	70-412
+	Hughes 300CQ	G-HUSH (890826)
+	Hughes 500D	G-HOOK (700708D)
+	Hughes 500MD	N8337F (1060070D)
+	Hughes 500MD	N1109D (800686D)
+	Lockheed TriStar 500	G-BFCA (1157) flying only
+	Lockheed TriStar 500	G-BFCD (1165) flying only
+	Lockheed TriStar 500	G-BFCF (1174) flying only
+	Marmande Microjet 200B	F-WZJF (01)
+	MBB Bo 105CB	D-HDML (S-438)
+	MBB Bo 105CBS	D-HDNI (S-455)
	MBB Bo 105DBS	D-HDLR (S-382)
+	MBB Bk 117	D-HBKA (P.2)
+	McDonnell Douglas F-15B Strike Eagle	71-291
+	McDonnell Douglas TF-18A Hornet	160784
+	Mitsubishi Mu-2 Marquise	N266MA (779)
+	Mitsubishi Mu-2 Solitaire	F-GCJS (406)
	Nash Petrel	G-AXSF (P.003)
+	NDN Firecracker	G-NDNI (001)
	Piaggio P.166-DL3	I-PIAE (466)
+	Pilatus PC-6B2 Turbo-Porter	HB-FHO (809)
+	Pilatus PC-7 Turbo-Trainer	HB-HAO (101)
	Pilatus Britten-Norman Islander BN-2B-21	G-BFNW (879)
+	Pilatus Britten-Norman Turbine Islander BN-2T	G-BPEN (419)
+	Pilatus Britten-Norman Trislander BN-2A-III-2	G-BEGX (1043)
	Piper Cheyenne I	G-BHTP (31T-8004022)
	Piper Cheyenne III	N442PC (42-8001001)
	PZL Wilga 35	G-BHUN (140548)
	PZL Wilga 35	SP-WDC (140542)
	PZL Mewa	SO-PKD (1AHP01-04)
	SAAB Viggen JA 37	37304
+	SAAB Viggen JA 37	37305
+	Short Skyvan 3M	G-BHVK (SH.1973)
+	Short 330	G-BHYL (SH.3054) to be YV-374C
	SIAI-Marchetti SF.260	I-LELF (568/41-004)
+	SOCATA Rallye Gabier	F-GBKL (13020)
	SOCATA Rallye Gaucho	F-GBXF (13078)
+	SOCATA Tampico	G-BIAA (141)
	SOCATA Tobago	G-BIAM (144)
	Swearingen Merlin IIIB	G-IIIA (T-342)
	Swearingen Metro II	N116BS (TC-331)
	Valmet L-70 Miltrainer	VN-2
+	Westland Lynx AH.1	G-LYNX/ZB500 (WA.102)
+	Westland Lynx HAS.2	XZ727 (WA.199)
+	Westland Sea King HAR.3	XZ587 (WA.852)
+	Westland Sea King HC.4	ZA296 (WA.910)
+	Westland Sea King HC.4	ZA297 (WA.911)
+	Westland 30	G-BGHF (WA.001P)

The British Aerospace Nimrod AEW.3 XZ286 flew in daily from Woodford for its slot in the programme.

British Aerospace Tornado IDS XX947 with every stores position occupied still manages a short take off.

Fitting Pratt & Whitney PT6A turboprops into the basic Dornier Skyservant airframe resulted in the Do 128-6 Turbo Skyservant D-IBUF.

de Havilland Canada's improved 5D model Buffalo C-GBUF first appeared at Farnborough in 1976 during a world demonstration tour; it was back again in 1980.

Edgley's Optica prototype G-BGMW appeared for the first time at the 1980 Show.

The sole Dassault-Breguet Mirage 4000 with air brakes extended.

1982

THE THIRTY-THIRD SHOW
5-12 SEPTEMBER

To meet the requirements of what was patently going to be a greatly expanded attendance, the SBAC had managed to squeeze in quite a lot of extra accommodation. A New North Hall was created on the site of the radar terrace, the latter being pushed forward into the space behind H Row of chalets and the exhibition hall total area now came to 311,349 square feet (28,925 sq.m). The charges to the public for adults, children and cars were £5, £3 and £5 on Friday with a quid off all round at the week-end. Coaches £10.

As usual, during the week preceding the actual Show, rehearsal flying was taking place continuously as pilots went through their routines before the Flying Control Committee. It was mandatory; not even the Red Arrows were exempt and at the end everyone's display conformed to the stringent safety regulations, though sometimes a little judicious re-arranging of a sequence was required to achieve this. This supervision continued throughout the week, during the display and it was not unknown for a pilot to be excused flying for repeated violations. One year a particularly volatile gentleman was actually taken off on Press Day and spent the rest of the week quite happily serving behind the bar in his company's chalet.

It was now 50 years since the first SBAC Flying Display and Exhibition and a far cry even from the relaxed, all-British family atmosphere of 25 years ago. The press of aircraft and the relentless pace of technology had turned the picnic on the grass into something more resembling a working breakfast at a take-over bid.

Discounting the boot *fêtes champêtres* of the PR car lines in the early days, there really was a picnic one year, when visiting royalty turned up complete with a large family party who had been promised tea on the lawn – and got it, following some rapid re-alignment of security measures.

The 1982 Farnborough Show could lay some claim to being the biggest and best so far in a long and generally escalating series. There were 480 exhibitors. Among the exhibiting aircraft there was, uncharacteristically, a fair number of microlights. ICA-Brasov brought three gliders and a powered glider and for the first time ever, there was an airship.

Fifteen countries were represented by aircraft, but the majority were from Great Britain. The spread of different types was interesting, and no doubt symptomatic of the state of the market, for while there were six airliners, four of them new to Farnborough, there were no less than 20 in the category generally referred to as feeder, commuter, third-level or what-have-you. On the military side, market trends were certainly evident, with 16 different kinds of trainer, forming half the total fixed-wing presentation, and 21 helicopters.

Stars of the Show were two aircraft that were not in the flying display at all; the Rockwell B-1 bomber and the Lockheed TR-1 development of the much-publicised U-2. The first of the single-seat TR-1As was rolled out at Palmdale on 15 July 1981 and made its first flight on 1 August. There were 35 on order for the United States Air Force, of which 18 would be based at Alconbury in England. The implication of the presence at Farnborough of these two aircraft, apart from being a useful training exercise for the B-1, (and Lockheed's pious hope that they might sell up to 15 TR-1s to the Royal Air Force) was a reaffirmation of the support of NATO by the United States. The U-2 carried on in service until finally retired in 1989, their 1960's technology and tired airframes finally giving way to satellite reconnaissance.

The presence of the B-1 in particular underlined the changes in policy that followed the induction of Ronald Reagan as the new President in November 1981, for the 241 ordered had been cancelled by President Carter in 1977, when they were regarded as too vulnerable to Soviet defences. The programme was reinstated to the extent of 100 B-1Bs, to take over from the B-52 force until the Advanced Technology Bomber from Northrop was ready. The latter became better known in the media as the "stealth bomber", a description, incidentally, which has given the French yet another opportunity to demonstrate the charm of their native tongue; the French for stealth bomber is *avion furtif*. The B-1 at Farnborough was actually the fourth prototype, taken out of mothballs for the purpose.

There were, however, other stars at the Show, from rather nearer home, for the Falklands campaign, conducted briskly and skilfully between April and June 1982, had focussed attention sharply upon the triumphant Sea Harriers and Harriers that had so distinguished themselves in the South Atlantic.

Two well-known Farnborough performers were in the news shortly after the end of the previous Show; on 1 November, British Airways closed down its Bahrain-Singapore Concorde service and on the 14th the last revenue flight of a Comet 4C took place. Appropriately enough, the final flight by a civil Comet 4C in Britain was to a museum, eleven months later.

At least the start of the 1982 Show was relaxed, for it was opened by the majestic Skyship 500, its silver skin gleaming in the bright sunlight and its swivelling, ducted propulsors working competently, with the powerful elevators, to maintain an even progress in a strong and turbulent cross-wind. The envelope was built by Zodiac, a French company who had built their first airship in 1909 and their last, for the French navy, in that same year of 1932 that saw the first SBAC Display. The engines were Porsche six cylinder car units and drove the five-bladed reverse-pitch propulsors through gear boxes originally designed to drive the tail rotor of the Lynx helicopter, but now much-modified. Interest in the airship was reviving quite rapidly; there were numerous projects under way, and a few aerostats flying, in different countries. In the Soviet Union there was a remote-control airship whose designer, Comrade Bauman, was optimistic enough to christen it *Boomerang*. (Actually, of course, he called it byMepaHr, but no matter).

The aerospace world is subject to market pressures less easy to predict accurately, especially in the time dimension, than most other major industries. There seems never to have been a time when predictions came true – or if they did, then not at the time and place expected. In this, it somewhat resembles the art of meteorology. It was still a time of heavy recession in 1982; airlines were going out of business and trade in single engined light aircraft had almost come to a standstill, with major American constructors laying off staff and closing lines. The fuel crisis was still not over and its effect at the fuel pumps on America's roads had been a major cause of the previous President's lack of popularity. All of which helps to explain the explosion of interest in the cheap, simple and supremely economical microlight and their sudden – and as it would turn out, brief – appearance in quantity at Farnborough.

There were probably several reasons for their subsequently vanishing from the Farnborough scene. As the market found its level, sales proceeded adequately without such upmarket exposure, for one thing; their parameters, financial, marketing and operational, could not be made to fit readily into the British or French exhibitions, for another. The reverse was also true, apparently, when established organisations looked at microlights; one of the more interesting newcomers at the SBAC Show was the Dragon, sponsored by British Air Ferries and marketed by the sales organisation of CSE at Oxford. Even with such influential parents, the Dragon did not survive and by 1988 there were only 15 on the British register.

In spite of the prevailing gloom in the airline marketplace, there were four entirely new aircraft displaying at Farnborough. All were significant of the forthcoming upturn in both prospects and competition for sales among engine and airframe manufacturers.

Boeing were showing both their new twin-engined designs, the 757 and 767 and attempted to take a neat advantage over their rivals by turning their arrival into an extra display period. Although this did not succeed, they were permitted to combine customer demonstration with their display slot as a consolation. The 757 was Boeing's current standard-body, (it first flew on 19 February 1982), carrying between 178 and 233 passengers – the latter configuration being referred to as "high-density", which sufficiently describes it. It came in short or medium range versions. The 767-200 represented a slightly earlier wide-body, first taking the air on 26 September 1981 and carried 211-255 passengers over rather longer distances than the lighter 757.

Both Boeings were significant advances on previous models. Both featured two-man cockpits, though with cautious provision for a third member. By no means everyone had yet come to terms with the two-crew concept.

They were the first big Boeing twins and the 757 had the added distinction in being the first Boeing airliner offered with a foreign engine – the Rolls-Royce 535C. This was basically a scaled-down RB211, de-rated to 37,300 lb thrust (16,920 kgp) and running that easy, was to become one of the most reliable of the big turbofans.

Airbus Industrie had been regular exhibitors at Farnborough since 1974 and were to continue to be prime supporters. This year they were showing the new A310, a short fuselage version of the basic A300. The first A300 flew on 28 October 1972; the production B2 version, seating 281-345 passengers, going into service with Air France on 23 May 1974. It was followed by the A300B4 long-range version, with added fuel in the centre-section and higher gross weight by some 61,000 lb (27,000 kg) and engines with 1,000 lb (454 kg) more poke. Aimed directly at breaking the Boeing near-monopoly and at creating a powerful European airliner industry, Airbus Industrie was a consortium consisting initially of Aérospatiale in France, MBB and VFW-Fokker in Germany (later combined to become Deutsche Airbus), CASA in Spain and Hawker Siddeley Aviation in Britain. There was also Fokker-VFW in the Netherlands. This combination of VFW-Fokker (or Fokker-VFW, depending where you were standing) was very confusing and it was a great relief to all when they finally merged with MBB in December, 1980 – not least to Airbus, as the merger released some £65 million in funds from the West German government for their research programme.

The A310 had covered most of its test programme in July 1982, running at that time four weeks ahead of schedule and returning performances handsomely ahead of expectation. The advanced wing of the A310 was the responsibility of British Aerospace (who had, of course, absorbed Hawker Siddeley) and contributed to much of the aircraft's good performance. It was completely free of vortex generators and fences and suchlike aids and entered service in that same clean configuration, the first airliner wing so to do. It was very largely responsible for the fact that the A310 was able to erode the advantages at height and over long distances of the bigger-winged rival 767 and it was on 4 July (three months exactly after the first A310 flight) that an A310 drew attention to this with a non-stop flight from Kuwait to Singapore against a 45 knot (83 km/h) headwind, covering 4,216 miles (6,785 km) with the equivalent of 210 passengers and baggage in 8 hours 40 minutes.

At the start of 1982 (at the end of January, to be precise), there were 160 A300s in service with 28 airlines, against 173 767s and total sales of all Airbuses had reached 346, with 159 options, for 43 customers.

Fifteen years after its first Farnborough appearance, the design having been in the hands of several owners in the interval, a completely new version of the Jetstream 31 was about to start a new and successful career with British Aerospace. In its new form it first flew on 28 March 1980, having being converted from one of the old Series 1 aircraft. It was now powered by two Garrett AiResearch TPE 331 and the first production delivery took place in the December after the Show.

Among the military, apart from the B-1 and TR-1 there was not a lot of completely new material. With the absence of McDonnell Douglas, only the General Dynamics F-16A (a single-seater this time) represented the American scene. With production lines running in the United States, Belgium and The Netherlands, the F-16 programme was gaining momentum and at the start of 1982, 560 had been delivered. In the shape of the F-16E the Fighting Falcon was due to shoot it out with the F-15E for a mid-life improvement programme, the winner to equip the United States Air Force until the new radical fighters came along – if they ever did. The Air Force said never mind the shoot-out; they'd like to have both, but while the USAF was funding a development F-16XL and MDD had gone ahead with their own Strike Eagle update of the F-15, the whole project was put into limbo as part of a general cut back in government spending (and partly, too, from the lack of a clear requirement from the Air Staff).

Tornado progress was marked by the display of four of No. 9 Squadron's GR.1s (in service since June) and the prototype F.2. Both the Trinational Tornado Training Establishment and Weapons Conversion Unit were up and running, with 79 aircraft between them. Two of a required 30 stretched Hercules C.3 for the Royal Air Force were on display, one flying, one static. The adding of 40 per cent volume to the fuselage was being done by Marshall's of Cambridge, who had handed over the first conversion on 11 December 1979.

The Dassault-Breguet Atlantic NG (Nouvelle Génération) that took part in the flying was the subject of an Aéronavale order for 42, made its first flight on 8 May the previous year, and gave a welcome top-up to the production of the Rolls-Royce Tyne.

One new item in the air was the first of the converted VC10 K.2 tankers for the Royal Air Force, making an interesting comparison with another airliner-turned-bowser, the KC-10 Extender that accompanied the B-1.

Trainers there were galore, a trend that was still continuing in a healthy fashion in 1988. The most conventional were the TB 30 Epsilon and Piper/FAC Pillan, both tandem-seat and piston-engined and both basic/primary in scope. The Epsilon was destined for pupils coming off the CAP 10 in the Armée de l'Air, the Pillan (using a variety of Piper parts) for the Chilean Air Force.

Slingsby's T.67 was new to Farnborough. It came in two varieties with different engine sizes and John Taylor and Brendan O'Brien, who did the same sort of thing at other shows with two Fournier RF-4s, gave a neat and polished synchronised aerobatic demonstration. By coincidence, the T.67 was basically a Fournier design. The MBB (ex-Rhein Flugzeugbau) Fantrainer, in prototype form and like the Slingsby new to Farnborough, drew attention to itself by having the engine and propeller in mid-fuselage behind the crew. The little Caproni Vizzola C 22J, with side by side seats and two diminutive 200 lb (92 kg) thrust Microturbo jets, was aimed at primary and continuation training and "light reconnaissance". A nice thought, the latter; for hussars rather than dragoons?

Microturbo were themselves once more presenting the Microjet 200, with twin jets, a butterfly tail for lightness and staggered seats to claim the benefits of tandem seating (pupil gets an operational view) and side-by-side (Sir can see what pupil is thinking and where his eyes are resting). With full side-by-side seating, however, the pupil's view to one side was always blocked by the instructor.

Pilatus' successful PC-7 turboprop was already in service to the tune of 300 with ten air forces and Embraer had the brand-new Tucano to the same formula. The Alpha Jet had been hustling around the United States to try to beat the Hawk to the United States Navy VTX-TS competition for its new trainer, but the Hawk was announced the winner on 19 November 1981. Alpha Jet was also being extended experimentally with a supercritical wing fitted by Dornier. The Aermacchi MB.339A and K were there, of course, solely for the aerobatic convenience of the pilots – still our old friends Bonazzi and Durione, though Franco Bonazzi was about to hang up his boots as chief test pilot. The two-seater had been selected in January to equip the national aerobatic team, the Frecce Tricolori.

Aircraft	Registration
Aeritalia AP.68TP	I-RAIK
Aeritalia (Partenavia) P.68 Observer	D-GEMG (246-04- OBS)
+ Aermacchi MB.339A	I-TOCA/MM54443 (6602/009)
Aermacchi MB.339A	MM54487 (6684/)
Aermacchi MB.339K	I-BITE (6662/001)
+ Aerospatiale AS.332B Super Puma	F-WZLB (2005)
+ Aerospatiale AS.355F	F-GBON (5044)
Aerospatiale SA.342M Gazelle	F-WXFI (1515)
+ Aerospatiale SA.365N Dauphin	F-WZJS (6004)
+ Aerospatiale Epsilon	VO (01)
Aerospatiale Epsilon	VJ (02)
Agusta A.109A	I-DACC (7274)
Agusta A.109A Mk.II	I-DVCM (7156)
Agusta AB.212ASW	MM81098
Agusta AB.412	I-DACB (25507)
Agusta AB.412	I-MDCV (33003)
+ Airbus A310-221	F-WZLI (172)
Airmass Sunburst	
Airmass Sunlight	
Airmass Sunset	
+ Airship Industries Skyship 500	G-BIHN (1214/2) flying only
+ Beech Super King Air 200	G-BIZX (BB-963)
Bell 206B JetRanger III	VH-DIK (3653)
Bell 214ST	G-BKFN (28109)
+ Boeing 727-100	N199AM (19262)
+ Boeing 757-225	N505EA (22195)
+ Boeing 767-232	N102DA (22214)
+ British Aerospace Hawk 50	G-HAWK/ZA101 (41H/4020010)
British Aerospace Hawk T.60	G-9-490/604 for Zimbabwe AF
British Aerospace Jaguar International	G-27-367 for Indian AF
British Aerospace Jetstream 31	G-JBAE (602)
+ British Aerospace Jetstream 31	G-TALL (601)
+ British Aerospace Nimrod AEW.3	XZ286 (8048) flying only
+ British Aerospace Nimrod AEW.3	XZ287 (8049) flying only
British Aerospace One-Eleven 201AC	XX105 (008)
+ British Aerospace Sea Harrier FRS.51	G-9-478/IN601 for Indian Navy
British Aerospace Tornado GR.1	ZA368
+ British Aerospace Tornado F.2	ZA254 (A.01)
British Aerospace H.S.125-400B	3D-AVL (25254)
+ British Aerospace H.S.125-700B	G-OBAE (257094)
+ British Aerospace BAe 146-100	G-SSCH (E.1003)
British Aerospace BAe 146-100	G-OBAF (E.1004)
+ British Aerospace BAe 146-200	G-WISC (E.2008)
+ British Aerospace H.S.748-2B	G-11-22 (1787)
+ British Aerospace H.S.748 Coastguarder	G-BDVH (1746)
+ British Aerospace VC10 K.2	ZA141 (809) flying only
+ Canadair Challenger CL-600	N637ML (1024)
+ Caproni Vizzola C22J	I-CAVJ (001)
Caproni Vizzola C22J	I-GIAC (002)
CASA Aviocar 200	EC-DHO (139)
+ CASA Aviojet	EC-ZZZ (XE25-01)
+ Dassault-Breguet Atlantic NG ATL2	(01)
+ Dassault-Breguet Falcon 50	F-BINR (2)
+ Dassault-Breguet Mirage FIC	5-NH (275)
+ Dassault-Breguet Mirage 2000	(04)
+ Dassault-Breguet Mirage 2000B	(01)
+ Dassault-Breguet Mirage 4000	(01)
Dassault-Breguet Super Etendard	(31)
+ Dassault-Breguet/Dornier Alpha Jet	F-ZJTJ
+ de Havilland Canada Buffalo	C-GCTC (103)
+ de Havilland Canada Dash 7	132002 (12) CAF
+ de Havilland Canada Twin Otter 300M	C-GFJQ (774)
Dornier Do 128-6	D-IBUF (4302)
+ Dornier Do 228-100	D-ICOG (7001) to be LN-HPG
+ Dornier Do 228-200	D-ICDO (4359)
Dragon Light Aircraft Dragon	G-MMAC (003)
+ Edgley Optica	G-BGMW (EA7/001)
Eipper-Formance Quicksilver Aerobat	
Eipper-Formance Quicksilver MX1	
Eipper-Formance Quicksilver MX2	
Embraer Bandeirante	PT-SFA (110383)
Embraer Xingu II	G-XTWO (121030)
+ Embraer Tucano	PP-ZDK (312005)
+ ENAER Pillan T-35	CC-EFP (001)
Enstrom 280C Shark	G-BKCO (1226)
Enstrom 280C Shark	G-OFED (1195)
Eurowing Goldwing	G-MBZH (EW-50)
Fairchild A-10A	81-009
Fairchild-Swearingen Merlin IVC	N3010Q (AT-452)
Fairchild-Swearingen Metro III Sentry	N3108X (AC-517)
Fokker F.27-500	PH-FSK (10608)
Fokker F.28-4000	PH-ZCD (11177)
Gates Learjet 55	N3797C (55-044)
+ General Dynamics F-16	661 for Norwegian AF
Grob G.109	G-BJVK (6074)
Gulfstream American Gulfstream III	F-313 (313) Danish AF
Gulfstream American Jetprop Commander 1000	OY-BPA (96003)
Hughes 300C	G-BNBH (1078)
Hughes 500D	G-SOOD (1142D)
+ Hughes 500MD	N8337F (106-0010D)
+ Hughes YAH-64 Apache	73-22248
ICA-Brasov IS-28MA	YR-1026 (01)
ICA-Brasov IS-29D2	YR-1028 (93)
ICA-Brasov IS-30	(104)
ICA-Brasov IS-32	YR-1027 (03)
ICA IAR 825TP	YR-IGB (01)
ICA IAR 827A	YR-MGF
Lockheed 10 Electra	NC5171N (1037)
Lockheed Hercules C.3	XV212 (382-4238)
+ Lockheed Hercules C.3	XV294 (382-4259)
Lockheed P-3C Orion II	160761
Lockheed TR-1	80-1068
+ Marmande Microjet 200B	F-WZJF (01)
+ MBB Bo 105CB	D-HDER (S-150)
+ MBB Bo 105LS	D-HDMU (S-422)
+ MBB Bk 117	D-HBKC (7001)
McDonnell Douglas F-15C Eagle	79-036
McDonnell Douglas KC-10A Extender	79-0433
Mitsubishi Diamond I	N300DM (A.003-SA)
Nash Petrel	G-AXSF (P.003)
+ NDN Fieldmaster	G-NRDC (004)
NDN Firecracker	G-NDNI (001)
Piaggio P.166-DL3	I-PIAQ (471)

Pilatus PC-6B2-H2 Turbo-Porter	HB-FHM (816)	
+ Pilatus PC-7 Turbo-Trainer	HB-HAO (101)	
Pilatus PC-7 Turbo-Trainer	HB-HOO (394)	
Pilatus Britten-Norman Maritime Defender BN-2T	G-HOPL (2112)	
+ Pilatus Britten-Norman Turbine Islander BN-2T	G-MAFF (2119)	
Piper Cheyenne III	G-BJIZ (42-8001055)	
+ RFB Fantrainer	D-EATJ (D1)	
Rockwell B-1A	76-0174	
+ SAAB Viggen JA 37	37319	
SAAB Viggen JA 37	37322	
+ Short Skyvan 3M	G-BJDC (SH.1978)	
+ Short 330-200	G-BKDO (SH.3091)	
+ Short 360	G-WIDE (SH.3601)	
+ SIAI-Marchetti S.211	I-SIJF (C1/002)	
+ SIAI-Marchetti SF.260TP	I-TPTP (60-001)	
SIAI-Marchetti SF.600TP	I-CANG (001)	
SIAI-Marchetti SM.1019	I-AFRI (065/02-002)	
Sikorsky S-76	N5415X (76-0199)	
Sikorsky UH-60A Black Hawk	81-23548 (70-269)	

+ Slingsby T.67A	G-BJCY (1990)	
+ Slingsby T.67A	G-BJIG (1992)	
+ Slingsby T.67B	G-BJNG (1993)	
Slingsby T.67M	G-BKAM (1999)	
SOCATA Rallye Guerrier	F-ZWRT/F-GAFE (12105)	
SOCATA Tampico	G-BKEM (316)	
SOCATA Tobago	G-BKEN (315)	
SOCATA Trinidad	G-TBXX (276)	
+ Valmet L-70 Miltrainer	OH-VAA (31)	
+ Valmet PIK-23 Towmaster	OH-TOW (001)	
Vinten Wallis WA-116	G-SCAN (001)	
Vinten Wallis WA-116	G-VIEW (002)	
+ Westland Sea King HAS.5	XZ916 (WA.876)	
+ Westland Lynx HAS.2	ZD253 (WA.257)	
+ Westland Lynx Utility	G-LYNX (WA.102)	
+ Westland 30	G-BIWY (901)	

Services participation in flying programmes:
British Aerospace Hawk: nine from CFS, "Red Arrows" aerobatic team.
British Aerospace Sea Harrier: six from 800 and 899 Squadrons.
British Aerospace Tornado: four from 9 Squadron.

The Rockwell B-1A made its first appearance in Europe when 76-0174 arrived at Farnborough.

Embraer Bandeirante PT-SFA in the static line up; on its right is Brazilian stablemate Xingu G-XTWO.

From Finland came the Valmet PIK-23 Towmaster appropriately registered OH-TOW.

◄ *Pilatus PC-7 Turbo-Trainer HB-HOO was delivered to Swissair after being statically exhibited at the Show.*

A newcomer from Chile was the ENAER T-35 Pillan CC-EFP; the design was based on the Piper PA-28R using these wings and tail unit but a redesigned tandem-seat fuselage.

Romania was represented by four powered aircraft and two sailplanes. Their largest exhibit was the ICA IAR-827A YR-MGF crop sprayer – note spray bars still to be attached to the wing.

1984

THE THIRTY-FOURTH SHOW
2-9 SEPTEMBER

Out of the 79 displaying aircraft in 1984, no less than 23 were new to Farnborough and a further 14 newcomers in the static display ensured a vintage year. Service participation had been virtually eliminated following the cutbacks in defence expenditure in the late fifties and was once more confined to the Red Arrows. Although it would be invidious to say that they were the best aerobatic team in the world, let us say it, nevertheless. After all, we believe it, along with a very large number of people who come to shows to watch them.

The general arrangements in this year were broadly unchanged from the previous Show. There were three Exhibition Halls, with ETPS Road rerouted to give a bigger South Hall and a covered area total of 415,081 square feet (38,562 sq.m) and 269 chalets in the various rows. Rehearsal flying took place as usual during the week before the Show, with the Flying Control Committee pinning everyone down firmly. Not everybody got it right first time (and sometimes more than one pilot had to qualify) and repeated practices by one of the more Wagnerian military types on continuous afterburner could play hob with telephone conversations in the SBAC Site Office.

It cost a member of the public £6 to get in to see the Show (£2 if he or she was under 14) and another two quid to take his car in as well. You could, of course, leave your car in a Farnborough side street beyond the police no-stop area, and walk in – and out; the latter being the main advantage, as it was acknowledged that it did take quite a lot of time to empty very large car parks back into the local traffic system in one fell swoop. Nevertheless, the SBAC felt that it was tactless, to say the least, for the police and the Royal Automobile Club to advertise their belief that it would take at least two hours to get into the Show. Whose side were they on?

Perhaps it was as a result of this that Cabair, an enterprising helicopter operator, were offering charters into Farnborough on public days. The cost, from their helipad at Fleet, where there was free car parking, was £35, including an entrance ticket, but not including VAT. For a further £13 you got a return ticket from Waterloo and transport between railway and helipad thrown in. Enterprising.

For the first time the Soviet Union was taking part with hardware as well as official or not-so-official missions. In the past,

when pressed, they had always said "We'd love to come; why don't you send us the Forms?" We *had* sent the Forms; several usually. But it seemed they never arrived, like that famous cheque. In any case, we were delighted to see them.

They had brought an Antonov An-72, in Aeroflot colours, which had its two Lotarev D-36 turbofans exhausting over the wing, effectively "blowing" its upper surface and multiple flaps for VSTOL performance. There were powerful thrust reversers in the upper part of the tail pipes and in general layout it much resembled the American Boeing YC-14. Also flying was the awe-inspiring Mil Mi-26, the heaviest production helicopter in the world. The four-engined, twin rotor Mi-12 had been heavier but had flown, some seven years earlier, only as a prototype. The 105 ft (32 m) span rotor had eight blades (it was the only eight-bladed helicopter in the world) and that great, many-felloed wheel, absorbing 22,800 shaft horsepower at 132 rpm and converting it into lift for the 54.5-ton (49.5 tonne) monster, was a memorable sight in action.

There was also the appearance for the first – and quite possibly the last time – of two airships together. The Airship Industries Skyship 500 was joined this year by its larger relation the Skyship 600, enclosing 53,423 cu ft (1,513 cu m) more helium and hefting 1,631 lb (740 kg) more payload.

The prototype 500 lifted off for the first time at Cardington, home of much previous British airship activity, on 28 September 1981 and three more had been built by its 1984 Show appearance. Two had been assembled in Canada and one in Japan, the latter, used for advertising purposes, the first Skyship sold outright rather than leased. The second Canadian one, carrying the name *Olympia*, sustained watch and ward over the 1984 Olympic Games in Los Angeles just before the Farnborough Show.

Airship Industries Ltd, like so many other enterprises, had begun to encounter cash-flow problems by 1984 and in October, as a solution to this situation, became a subsidiary of the Australian Bond Corporation. The latter injected further large sums of money within the next 12 months, raising its stake in the company from 31 to 81.5 per cent. Since then, a fifth 500 has been built, which in 1988 was advertising for Fuji in the United States of America. (This was G-SKSH, c/n 500-06; there was no -01, the prototype being 500-02, just to confuse things). In 1987, the second Canadian-assembled ship, G-SKSB, was converted into a heavy-lift version for hot-and-high operation, becoming the 500-04HL.

The first Skyship 600, with more powerful, supercharged, Porsche engines, first flew on 6 March 1984 and could carry up to 20 passengers. Since then, a further seven have been delivered and an eighth was under construction in Tokyo early in 1989. The prototype, after a variety of advertising contracts, returned to Britain at the end of 1988 for pilot training at Cardington. The second, registered in Australia as VH-HAA, went to work for another Bond subsidiary, Swan Breweries, and other companies. The third advertised a Canadian brewery and later trained Tokyo police officers in the USA. Japan continued to be a major client for the company, with two more ships being used for advertising in Japan and the ninth ship being built for the Tokyo Metropolitan Police. Number five went to the United States for advertising purposes and number eight to the Korean government where, after some confusion caused by a rival organisation producing a similar, but apparently bogus, contract for the job, it covered the Seoul Olympics.

Skyship 600-04 later became the demonstrator for the world's first optical fibre, "fly-by-light" primary control system. As a matter of historical interest, when the full Public Transport Category Certificate of Airworthiness was issued to the 500 series two months after the Show, it was the first since the rather dubious one hastily written out to cover the R.101's ill-fated start for India in 1930.

By 1984 the effects of the intense recession that had been gripping the aerospace activities of the world, was showing signs of lifting and this seemed to be reflected in the quality of aircraft at Farnborough. Military orders were beginning to pick up again for the better-established production aircraft and the business and regional/commuter market was healthy. Although many old-established major airlines in the United States had gone under or were qualifying as a theatened species from the results of uninhibited deregulation, world demand for new airliners showed no signs of slackening. Traffic figures for major European airlines in June, for example, had risen 13 per cent on Atlantic routes over 1983 and comparable air freight figures by 14.6 per cent.

British Aerospace deployed the BAe 146-200 in their corporate presentation. A strong contender in the 100-110 seat bracket, over short and medium ranges, its delayed launch came at a time when turbine – as opposed to propeller turbine – power in this end of the market was becoming extremely attractive, by reason of new-found economy and lack of noise. The 146 was not only about the quietest in the business; it added the emotional appeal of four engines to that of jet power.

Among regional airliners, a proliferating breed, the SAAB-Fairchild 340, Embraer Brasilia and de Havilland of Canada DHC-8 were new, as was the latest British Aerospace 125, the 800 series, using the Garrett TFE engines introduced in the 700 series (and displayed at the previous Show) but with an improved performance resulting from 450 lb (204 kg) of

extra thrust, a new and longer-span wing and increased fuel in a ventral tank, as well as a redesigned flight deck.

SAAB had the first and third prototypes of the 340 flying in the Display, but were plagued by a continuance of engine problems that had given Crossair, the Swiss regional launch customer, three shut-downs on their first two aircraft. Stricken by the same *malaise*, the Farnborough demonstrators suffered some interruption to their flight demonstrations and gave their United Kingdom publicity manager Mike Savage a strong temptation to live up to his name. The problem was odd; the engines, 1,700 shp GE CT7s, were derived from the very successful CT700 helicopter engine, which had by then logged 314 million hours of operation with 99.7 per cent despatch reliability. Anyway, eventually the problem went away.

The Embraer Brasilia was attacking the same 30-seat market as the 340. It was set for a European tour immediately after Farnborough and Embraer were much encouraged, in the wake of over 400 sales of the smaller Bandeirante, by over 100 options on the Brasilia. It featured a very sophisticated flight deck with EFIS/TV, which had been seen at a previous Show in mock-up form on the company stand.

The de Havilland Canada DHC-8, or Dash 8, looked set to continue the success of the four-engined Dash 7, of which nearly 100 had been sold and which had had, until the arrival of the BAe 146, the distinction of being the only four-engined commuter in the business – bar the now rather aged Heron. Several new sales for the STOL Dash 8 were announced during the Show, including the first order from the Canadian Armed Forces/Forces Canadiennes Armées for six. Four would be used in Canada, based at Winnipeg, for navigation training and the other two would go to join the two Dash 7s on transport and communication duties at CFB Lahr, in Germany. Other orders included the first from an African customer, for oilfield duty and two for the Flight Services Directorate of Transport in Canada for flight inspection and calibration work.

Accompanying the STOL transports in their interlocking demonstration of very short landing and take-off, the Buffalo, on 4 September, inadvertently provided a rather more startling arrival than had been intended, trapped between an approach that had suddenly gone sour and the imminent arrival of the other two aircraft. The programme called for their landing successively over the top of the Buffalo, and they were rather too adjacent to allow it an overshoot, had one been possible. In the event it was they who had to overshoot and they trundled off to Boscombe Down, one of the designated diversion airfields, instead of landing at Farnborough. The Buffalo disassembled itself neatly without hurting anyone or, as it turned out, closing the runway for the rest of the week, but the rest of that afternoon's display was a bit truncated. Fortunately the next item, the Firecracker, was already airborne and was called in ahead of time. The pilot, W/Cdr Doug. Barden, was Chief Flying Instructor of Specialist Flying Services, who employed two Firecrackers at Carlisle. Before the Show he had unsuccessfully protested against having his normal polished and practised eight-minute sequence cut to half its length in the display. Having at last given way and redesigned it, he was now understandably a touch frustrated to be told he had all the time he liked and would he stretch it out a bit? Like twelve minutes?

The Hughes 530 followed him into the air and the Russians gallantly, and with commendable speed, some time before their slot was due, wound up the big Mil and motored it around the arena. After that the Committee ran out of helicopters and that was that.

Some little time after all this, a large Coles crane came rubbering up to remove the portions of Buffalo garnishing the runway. The driver's mate dragged the hook and chain over to the carcase and before hooking on was heard to shout back at the driver:

"Do you want a wing or a leg?"

On the military side, interest was being stimulated by two Air Staff Targets. The Royal Air Force had stated requirements to AST 404 for between 75 and 125 replacements for the Wessex/Puma transport fleet. Westland were naturally interested and could offer the WG30 with Rolls-Royce RTM322 engines, while Aérospatiale countered with the Super Puma. Just before the Show, Shorts declared an interest by announcing a Memorandum of Understanding with Sikorsky to produce the S-70A Black Hawk tailored to AST 404. In the event, it was Westland who teamed up with Sikorsky and anyway, AST 404 rather hung fire.

Of more immediate interest was the contest for the new Royal Air Force trainer to replace the Jet Provost. AST 412 set out a very demanding specification. Of the four aircraft that were to be offered, three originated outside the United Kingdom and therefore teamed up with British aerospace companies in order to have friends at court and to meet the obvious requirement that the successful aircraft must be built in Britain.

When the battle lines were finally drawn, Pilatus were allied to British Aerospace (who had an interest in selling the Hawk to Switzerland); Shorts announced an agreement with Embraer around the Tucano and began to study the changes required to meet the AST; Westland teamed up with the Australian Aircraft Consortium, whose contender, the Wamira, had actually not yet been built, let alone flown; and Firecracker, offering the only wholly native product and campaigning heavily to promote a "Buy British" solution. They had found financial and industrial backing from Hunting to tackle the project, confident that their aircraft would meet all the requirements. PC-9, basic (Brazilian) Tucano and Turbo-Firecracker were all flying at Farnborough, the PC-9 prototype having exchanged its sober black civilian coat, in a mood of optimism, for the red and white Royal Air Force training colours. (Somebody once asked the late Sir James Martin why a certain aeroplane was painted black and he replied, "To emphasise my lovely red and white triangles, of course.") Pilatus had always been convinced of the propriety of the geared turboprop trainer and with 1,000 shp available and CRT displays and HUD standard equipment, aiming at the very top of the market, already exceeded the AST requirements in some areas.

Dassault-Breguet presented the greatest number of new aircraft of any one company in the display. The Mirage 2000C1 was claimed to be the first operational combat aircraft with multichromatic head down data displays, in which coloured graphic or alphanumeric navigation, attack or computer data was superimposed on a radar or sensor generated video image. It had entered service on 2 July with 1/2 Cigognes and would next equip 3/2 Alsace and 2/2 Côte d'Or at Dijon/Longvic as well as the Ecole de Combat Tactique. The 2000N would re-equip five Jaguar and Mirage IIIE squadrons in the deep penetration rôle as the powerful French nuclear strike force.

This was to be the last appearance of the elegant and beautifully-displayed Northrop F-20 Tigershark. It had been conceived as a larger, more powerful single-engined successor to the twin-engined F-5, with a single, 18,000 lb (8,165 kg) thrust GE F404, (two of which powered the F/A-18 Hornet), replacing the two 5,000 lb (2,268 kg) GE J85s in the F-5E. Unfortunately, it was butting its head against the phenomenal track record of the F-16 and when a large potential sale to Taiwan was politically blocked that was the last straw.

Lack of interest from the United States Air Force did not help sales prospects, but then they had also rejected the F-5, despite which it went on to equip 31 air forces. Later, they did order Tiger IIs as an economical advanced trainer and employed 66 as aggressors at Nellis AFB and RAF Alconbury, while the United States Navy used them for Top Gun training at Miramar. Altogether Northrop spent $1 billion of their own money on the F-20, which certainly deserved better treatment from fate than it received.

Rhein Flugzeugbau, a subsidiary of MBB, were showing the Fantrainer 600, with a more powerful engine and containing a large amount of composite material in its highly modular construction. RFB already had experience of a similar pusher design with an earlier and not very successful civil two seater, but it was difficult to see any large advantage in this type of layout over more conventional trainers in a rapidly overflowing market.

Hindustan Aeronautics flew the HTT-34 and HJT-16 Kiran II, the former a two-seat, side-by-side basic trainer and light ground attack aircraft, the latter a two-seat turbo-prop light trainer with, uniquely, a fixed undercarriage. Both aircraft were updates of previous designs. Sixty-six Kiran IIs had been ordered for the Indian armed forces.

One-off, experimental aircraft modified as test-beds had become rare at Farnborough displays, as were items from the RAE itself, but in 1984 they flew the Jaguar ACT, resplendent in the Establishment's British Airways-style red, white and blue livery (sometimes referred to by the vulgar as "raspberry ripple"). Intended for exploratory work on fly-by-

wire, it featured prominent extensions between the inboard leading edge of the wing and the intake cowling, while the desired instability was effectively introduced by inserting 500 lb (227 kg) of lead into the back end.

Let us wind up this remarkable year of 1984, not in the flying display, but in the CT5A simulator on the Rediffusion stand. Designed for the latest F-15 training programme, it featured secondary scenarios for those more elderly visitors who might not feel up to the Eagle and you could take on the Red Baron from the cockpit of a No.65 Squadron Camel or mix it in your Spitfire I with the *Geschwaderkommodore* of JG 26 – who was, at that time, Adolf Galland.

1984

Aeritalia P.68 Observer	I-OBSV (316-12-OB)	+ British Aerospace Tornado F.2	ZD901
+ Aeritalia AP.68-300 Sparta-cus	I-RAIZ	+ British Aerospace BAe 125-800	N800BA (258001)
+ Aermacchi MB.339A	I-RAIA	British Aerospace BAe 146-100	G-OPSA (E.1002)
Aermacchi MB.339B	I-GROW/MM54502 (6711/106)	+ British Aerospace BAe 146-200	G-WAUS (E.2008)
+ Aermacchi MB.339K	I-BITE (6662/001)	British Aerospace BAe 748-2B	G-BLGJ (1800)
Aerospatiale AS.332L Super Puma	F-WZJN (2004)	+ Canadair Challenger CL-601	N601CL (3001) until 5/9
Aerospatiale AS.355M Ecureuil	F-WYMC	Canadair Challenger CL-601	N778XX (3017)
Aerospatiale SA.365N Dau-phin	F-WZJV (6005)	Canadair Challenger CL-601	N778YY (3023)
Aerospatiale Epsilon	(F-ZKFZ) (3)	+ Canadair Challenger CL-601	N779XX (3018) from 6/9
Agusta A.109A	G-GBCA (7272)	Caproni Vizzola C22J	I-GIAC (002)
+ Agusta A.109A Mk.II	I-DACI (7257)	+ CASA Aviocar 200	EC-DHO (139)
Agusta A.129	MM590 (001)	CASA Aviocar 300	ECT-131 (323)
Agusta AB.412 Griffon	I-DACB (25507)	+ CASA-Nurtanio CN-235	ECT-100 (001)
+ Airbus A300-600	F-WZLR (252)	+ CASA Aviojet	EC-DUJ (98)
+ Airbus A310-203	G-BKWU (306) 5/9	Cessna 206 (Soloy conver-sion)	HB-CHK (05567)
+ Airship Industries Skyship 500	G-BIHN (1214/2) flying only 2/9, 3/9, 6/9, 8/9	Cessna Conquest I	N1222K (425-0197)
		Cessna Conquest II	N441AG (441-0327)
+ Airship Industries Skyship 600	G-SKSC (1215/01) flying only 2/9, 7/9, 8/9	Cessna Citation II	N141AB (550-0483)
		CFM-Metalfax Shadow	– (007)
+ Antonov An-72	CCCP-72000	CNIAR One-Eleven 560	YR-BRC (VH403)
Beech King Air E90	N940SR (LW-158)	+ Dassault-Breguet Atlantic NG ATL2	(F-ZWRW) (02)
+ Bell 206L Long-Ranger	G-LONG (45227)	+ Dassault-Breguet Falcon 50	HB-IEP (67)
+ Bell 222B	N2226W (47131)	+ Dassault-Breguet Falcon 200	N200FJ (507)
Bell 222UT	N3179U	+ Dassault-Breguet Mirage IIING	(F-ZWVA) (01)
Bell 406CS Combat Scout	N2500B (2500)	+ Dassault-Breguet FICR	(F-ZJTI) (602)
Boeing 707-320C	N792TW (18757)	+ Dassault-Breguet Mirage 2000C	(F-ZJTO)/2-EP (1)
+ Boeing 737-300	N352AU (22952)	+ Dassault-Breguet Mirage 2000N	(F-ZWVG) (01)
+ British Aerospace Hawk 50	G-HAWK (41H/4020010)	+ Dassault-Breguet/Dornier Alpha Jet	F-ZJTD
British Aerospace Hawk 60	G-9-518 for UAE	+ Datwyler MD-3-160	HB-HOH (001)
+ British Aerospace Jaguar ACT	XX765 (S.62)	de Havilland D.H.88 Comet	G-ACSS (1996)
British Aerospace Jaguar International	G-27-397/NAF710 for Nigerian AF	+ de Havilland Canada Buffalo	C-GCTC (103) crashed 4/9
		+ de Havilland Canada Dash 7	C-GNBX (1)
+ British Aerospace Jetstream 31	N331BA (613)	+ de Havilland Canada Dash 8	C-GGPJ (4)
British Aerospace Jetstream 31	G-31-629 (629) to be VH- OSW	de Havilland Canada Twin Otter 300	LN-BNS (536)
+ British Aerospace Nimrod AEW.3	XV263 (8038) flying only 4/9, 5/9, 7/9	de Havilland Canada Twin Otter 300	VP-FAZ
		+ Dornier Do 228-100	D-IBLO (7036)
British Aerospace Tornado GR.1	ZD744	+ Dornier Do 228-200	D-IASX (8035)

The Trago Mills SAH-1 G-SAHI made the first of its three Show appearances so far in 1984. After strenuous efforts it now seems that it will go into production and by the 1988 Show it was being promoted under the Trago/Orca title.

	Aircraft	Registration
	Edgley Optica	G-BGMW (EA7/001)
+	Edgley Optica	G-BLFC (EA7/003)
+	Embraer Brasilia	PT-ZBB (120003)
+	Embraer Tucano	PP-ZTC (312007)
+	Embraer Tucano	PP-ZTT (312053)
+	ENAER Pillan T-35	CC-EFS
	Fairchild Metro IIIA	N3113H (PC-562)
+	FFA Bravo 26A	HB-HEY (015)
	Firecracker NDN-1T Turbo Firecracker	G-SFTR (005)
+	Firecracker NDN-1T Turbo Firecracker	G-SFTS (006)
	Fokker F.27 Enforcer	PH-FSY (10670)
	Fokker F.27 Sentinel	PH-FSR (10655)
	Gates Learjet 35A	G-LEAR (35A-265)
	Gates Learjet 35A	N59DM (35A-205)
	Gates Learjet 35A	N3798P (35A-408)
	General Dynamics F-16A	80-602
	General Dynamics F-16A	81-737
+	General Dynamics F-16A	80-612
	General Dynamics EF-111A	67-041
	Grob G.109B	G-BLGY (6269)
	Grob G.109B	D-KEOL (6204)
	Gulfstream Aerospace Commander Jetprop 1000	N96GA (96088)
	Gulfstream Aerospace Gulfstream III	F-249 (249) Danish AF
	Gulfstream Aerospace SRA-1	N47449 (420)
+	Hindustan HJT-16 Kiran II	U-2462
+	Hindustan HTT-34	X-2335
+	Hughes 530MG	N530MG (106001OD)
	Ilyushin Il-86	CCCP-86066
	Marmande Microjet 200B	F-WDMT (3)
+	MBB Bo 105CBS	D-HDQE (S-582)
	MBB Bo 105LS	D-HDTV (S-652)
+	MBB Bo 105LS	D-HDTY (S-655)
	MBB Bk 117	D-HBKR (7016)
+	MBB Bk 117	D-HBKS (7017)
	McDonnell Douglas F-15C Eagle	79-036
+	McDonnell Douglas F-15C Eagle	79-038
+	McDonnell Douglas F-15C Eagle	79-050
+	Mil Mi-26	CCCP-06141
+	NDN Fieldmaster	G-NBDC (004)
	NDN Freelance	G-NACI (NAC.001)
	Northrop F-20 Tigershark	N3986B (GI1001)
+	Northrop F-20 Tigershark	N4416T (GG1001)
	Pilatus PC-6B2 Turbo-Porter	HB-FHZ (840)
+	Pilatus PC-7 Turbo-Trainer	HB-HAO (101)
	Pilatus PC-7 Turbo Trainer	HB-HOO (394)
+	Pilatus PC-9	HB-HPA (001)
	Pilatus PC-9	HB-HPB (002)
	Pilatus Britten-Norman AEW Defender BN-2T	G-TEMI (2143)
+	Pilatus Britten-Norman Turbine Islander BN-2T	G-DLRA (2140)
	Pilatus Britten-Norman Turbine Islander BN-2T	G-OPBN (2034)
	Piper Cheyenne IIIA	N4117V (5501018)
+	RFB Fantrainer 600	D-EATR (001)
	Robin R.3120	F-WDYQ (105)
	Robinson R.22	– no marks
	SAAB-Fairchild SF.340	SE-E04/N340CA (04)
+	SAAB-Fairchild SF.340	SE-ISB (003) to 4/9
+	SAAB-Fairchild SF.340	SE-ISF (001) from 5/9
	Shorts Skyvan 3	G-BLLI/8P-SKY (SH.1980)
	Shorts 330 UTT	G-BLJB (SH.3099) for Thai Police
+	Shorts C-23A Sherpa	(G-BLLK)/83-0513 (SH.3101)
+	Shorts 360	G-BLIL/OY-MMB (SH.3648)
	Shorts 360	G-BLJR (SH.3651)
+	Shorts 360	G-BLJS (SH.3652)
	Sikorsky AUH-76	N5415X (76-0199)
	Sikorsky S-76A	N4937M (76-0032)
	Sikorsky UH-60A Black Hawk	81-23585
+	SIAI-Marchetti S.211	I-SIJF (01/002)
+	SIAI-Marchetti SF.260TP	I-SMAZ (677/60-005)
	SIAI-Marchetti SF.600TP Canguru	I-KANG (003)
	Slingsby T.67B	G-BIUZ (2005)
+	Slingsby T.67M Firefly	G-BKAM (1999)
+	Slingsby T.67M Firefly	G-BKTZ (2004)
+	Slingsby T.67M Firefly	G-FFLY (2007)
+	SOCATA Guerrier 235	F-GAFE (12105)
	SOCATA Tobago	G-BKTY (363)
+	SOCATA Trinidad	G-TBZO (444)
+	Soko Super Galeb	23005
+	Trago Mills SAH-1	G-SAHI (01)
+	Valmet L-70 Miltrainer	OH-VAA (31)
	Wallis WA.116	G-ATHL (401/212)
+	Westland Lynx 3	ZE477 (WA.001P)
+	Westland Sea King ABW.2	XV704 (WA.675)
+	Westland Sea King HAS.5	ZD630 (WA.939)
+	Westland 30	G-EFIS (014)
	Zenith Barodeur	

Service participation in the flying programmes:
British Aerospace Hawk: one from 4 FTS; nine from CFS, "Red Arrows" aerobatic team.
British Aerospace Sea Harrier: one from 899 Squadron.
British Aerospace Tornado: one from 27 Squadron.
Lockheed Hercules: one.

Veteran and vintage aircraft:
Avro Lancaster PA474.
Fairey Swordfish LS326.
Hawker Hurricane LF363.
Hawker Sea Fury WG655.
Supermarine Spitfire P7350.

Antonov AN-72 CCCP-72000 gave an impressive demonstration; its bank over the vertical on Press Day brought a knuckle wrapping from the Flying Control committee!

British Aerospace's Tornado F.2 ZD901 and ACT Jaguar XX765 on their way home from the Show.

1986

THE THIRTY-FIFTH SHOW
31 AUGUST-7 SEPTEMBER

As the popularity of the Farnborough Show grew, year by year, so did the problem of fitting everybody in on a site that was capable of accepting only a limited amount of stretching. While the requirements for more space in the exhibition halls and the static park increased every two years, the acreage (*metrage carré*) on the ground did not, and with the best will in the world, the Royal Aircraft Establishment could do little to enlarge the total space available to the SBAC.

The immediate answer lay in making more effective use of the space that was available and in 1986 the first major moves in this direction were made. Two new chalet rows were inserted, one (K Row) to the west of the main rows on the hill and another, short one (L Row) squeezed into the space between the pedestrian entrance at Dairy Gate and the grounds of No.1 Officers' Mess. Behind K Row was created a kind of Press village and into this area was moved the Press Centre from its previous location alongside the SBAC Site Office at the west end of North Hall. To that site went the President's Chalet and where the latter and its car park had stood was erected a fourth Exhibition Hall.

The Exhibition now boasted not only a North Hall and South Hall, but a New North Hall and New South Hall as well and covered (literally) 459,644 square feet (42,702 sq.m). There were 291 chalets.

These arrangements just about contained the upturn in demand for exhibition space, though the SBAC's Flying Liaison Officer, Ted Derbyshire, derived little consolation from that in his attempts to fit some 140-odd aircraft into the static park – from which those for the flying display had to be extracted every day and towed over to the north side (and returned afterwards, ready for the next day's intake of visitors to inspect).

In addition, several of the exhibiting aircraft were "touring" items. The Super Guppy, Concorde, Nimrod and Sentry, among the latter, only appeared on certain days, the SR-71 only once. The Harrier GR.5 and the three ARV Super2s flew every day, but came in respectively from Dunsfold and Blackbushe, returning afterwards – except one Super2, which landed at Farnborough, to complicate the life of the recorders of these things. Further to confuse the issue, the same Sentry did not turn up each time.

Among the brand new aircraft in the flying display, the most interesting were undoubtedly the British Aerospace EAP and

the Dassault-Breguet Rafale, which, owing to the general inability of the British to appreciate the finer points of French pronunciation, was universally referred to as the "Raphael". Except by the commentator, of course, who knew better. Others included the Sikorsky S-70C, presented by Rolls-Royce and bearing their new engine and two Brobdignagian visitors in the curious shapes of the AWACS Sentry and the Super Guppy.

Dominating the static park, though unfortunately not flying in the display, was the 392 ton (405 tonne) bulk of the Antonov An-124 Ruslan, the heaviest aircraft in the world.

The British aerospace industry had a very successful year in 1986, with SBAC figures showing total sales of more than £5 billion – an astonishing rise over the £2.4 billion of 1985 – of which aircraft and simulators accounted for over £5 million. Moreover, those figures did not include the Saudi order of about the same value again. During this Farnborough year 231 aircraft were delivered, the majority from British Aerospace, and included 27 BAe 125-800, 25 BAe 146, 46 Jetstream 31s and 29 Tornados. Among deliveries by other companies were twelve Westland Sea Kings, 15 PB-N Islanders and 24 Shorts 360s.

Among the aircraft in the British Aerospace combine, the two Tornados were Royal Air Force aircraft; one, an F.2, from the Operational Conversion Unit, flew on the public days only. The other, a GR.1 from the Tornado Weapon Conversion Unit (which led an alternative life as No. 45 Squadron), took part on the trade days.

A word on the parentage of the Tornado. The parent company, Panavia, was set up to design and produce the aircraft and each of the three partners (Britain and West Germany, 42.5 per cent each, Italy with the rest) builds part of the aircraft. Britain makes the front and rear fuselage; Germany the centre fuselage; Italy, the wings and each partner assembles its own aircraft. Moreover, the ADV Tornado, with its longer fuselage, extended range and Sky Flash missiles, and the F.3 are purely British variants. British-built aircraft appearing at Farnborough are regarded here as British Aerospace aircraft.

The two at Farnborough were part of a spectacular and very carefully-orchestrated presentation; the military formation starting from the Laffan's Plain end and led by the EAP in its smart two-tone blue livery, taxied up to the Black Sheds end, where they were joined by the civil aircraft from the cross runway and the whole lot took off to return (joined by the Nimrod). The entire operation took place to the theme music from *Chariots of Fire*, which British Aerospace had previously adopted as the background to their mainstand display in the exhibition hall.

On the first afternoon, it did not quite work out like that, as the EAP fell victim to some small hydraulic malaise at the western holding point and the formation set off without it. The EAP subsequently appeared as a solo item to close the display in great style, leaving one exhibitor muttering darkly about the whole thing being a cunning wheeze to get extra exposure on Press Day.

Apart from the EAP, which was the ultimate version of a series of British Aerospace studies which would be available for EFA, (the new European fighter), the new civil airliner from Woodford, the ATP, was appearing for the first time and so was the latest Harrier, the GR.5 for the Royal Air Force, corresponding to the McDonnell Douglas AV-8B. The Harrier 5 featured major aerodynamic changes, including a new super-critical wing, redesigned intakes, and generous use of composites to reduce weight. Fuel capacity was also increased. The heart of the improvement programme, however, was the Rolls-Royce Pegasus 11, delivering 21,000 lb (9,525 kg) of thrust. Two very important developments were to be initiated with the Pegasus about this time. Rolls-Royce, in the course of a renewed series of plenum chamber burning tests, fitted the Pegasus for the first time with variable area front nozzles: and about the time of the 1986 Show, service aircraft were fitted with the Harrier Information Management System (HIMS), which monitored engine health (particularly important in a single-engined aircraft). This was integrated with the Royal Air Force Station Engineering Management Aid computers, allowing Harrier engines to be operated more efficiently.

There had been several proposals for improving Harrier performance and the eventual AV-8B/GR.5 was largely McDonnell Douglas-inspired. The American order for 340 aircraft to replace the AV-8As and five squadrons of A-4s in Marine Corps service had a stormy financial passage through both the Pentagon and the Senate in the wake of various defence budget cuts, but production began in 1983 and was planned to continue well into the 1990s. With the Royal Air Force, the Harrier GR.5 would enter service in 1988, initially with the Harrier Conversion Unit at the Operational Conversion Unit, converting pilots from the GR.3, and then beginning to re-equip the three squadrons, one in the UK and two in West Germany. The initial order for the RAF was 62, with a further twelve for the Spanish Navy, who embarked the AV-8 Matador and not a Sea Harrier variant on their solitary aircraft carrier, Principe de Asturias.

Apart from the bits of ATR 42 put in by Aérospatiale, the French presence in the flying display came entirely from Dassault-Breguet (with the assistance of the Dornier bits in the Alpha Jet). It was to be one of the most impressive com-

bines that the company had assembled in the course of several years of very intensive sales presentations, with two of the NGEA Alpha Jets, two Mirage 2000s and the 4000, back again after missing 1984, and the New Generation Atlantic, which had first flown on 8 May 1981.

The most important of all their aircraft though, was Rafale. Back in the opening months of 1984 there had been a series of meetings to determine the parameters of a next-generation European Fighter Aircraft (EFA). Held between Britain, France, Germany, Italy and Spain, there was sufficient agreement at these meetings to set out the operational requirements for an aircraft primarily dedicated to air-to-air combat, with secondary air defence and ground attack functions. The expected market domestically was about 800, with hoped-for foreign sales (mostly to the Middle East) of some 300 more.

Unfortunately, at this stage, national differences began to emerge; both of requirements and of outlook. British Aerospace and Rolls-Royce, along with other SBAC member companies such as Dowty, Lucas, Smiths Industries and Ferranti, were far along the road to a solution based on Royal Air Force Air Staff Target requirements and offering plenty of employment to British industry. The result of this Experimental Aircraft Programme, the EAP, was flying at Farnborough International 86.

The French, too, had their own solution, the Avion de Combat Tactique (ACT) based on the requirement of the Armée de l'Air for a much lighter, ground attack aircraft than the proposed 9.75 ton (10 tonne) EFA and one powered by the French SNECMA 88 of around 16,500 lb (7,484 kg) thrust. EFA, at least initially, was designed round two Turbo-Union RB199s, of considerably greater power. France, moreover, rejecting the solution of buying McDonnell Douglas F/A-18 Hornets to replace the elderly F-8 Crusaders in their aircraft carriers Foch and Clemenceau, contemplated an Avion de Combat Marine version (ACM) of the ACT.

Eventually, British Aerospace became a major partner in EFA with Germany and Italy, on a 33/33/21 per cent basis, with the remaining 13 per cent being taken up shortly afterwards by Spain. France pursued her own solution to her own problems and went ahead developing Rafale to production standards as the ACT and ACM.

The success of international collaboration ventures had already been shown by such programmes as Jaguar and Concorde, now complete, and current collaborative aircraft were flying at Farnborough. Of these, some, like Tornado, were already successful; others, like the Aérospatiale/Aeritalia ATR 42, were just beginning their profitable careers. By the time Farnborough came round again, sales of the ATR would have risen to around 160. The ATR 42 teams had 50/50 design and manufacturing responsibility for the 42-50 seater, which first flew just before Farnborough International 84, on 16 August. It did not appear that year, as the makers wished to consolidate the test programme, but it was said that at that time orders already totalled 60.

Presented with the French company's combine in the flying display was the Dassault-Breguet/Dornier Alpha Jet NGEA, offered as an "across-the-board" training and combat aircraft with greatly increased capacity over the earlier version, including uprated engines and much of the cockpit technology of the Mirage 2000, as well as greatly increased weapon capability. The brochure listed 21 combinations of nine standard weapons, plus a centre-line 25 mm cannon, as examples. NGEA (*Nouvelle Génération Ecole-Appui*) first flew in April 1982, and 60 were ordered by Egypt, with co-production in that country running at two a month in 1986.

Dornier themselves, at this time, were the subject of a take-over bid by Daimler-Benz, who were later to try to extend their aerospace horizons with a similar bid for MBB. They were already the owners of Motoren-und Turbinen-Union, the German partner in Turbo-Union, who built Tornado's RB199 engines.

Helicopter international programmes were proliferating as well, quite apart from the many that were licence-built by Agusta and others. The Franco-German PAH-2/HAP Eurocopter seemed to be in a permanent state of "now you see it, now you don't", but the collaboration between Westlands and Agusta over the EH 101 was progressing. MBB had a working partnership with Kawasaki in Japan over the Bk 117, which was available to customers in 1983 but selling only slowly, in contrast to the purely German MBB Bo105, of which 1,100 had been delivered by Farnborough time. This included some 450 for the German Army as well as being licence-built in Indonesia, the Philippines and Spain. Both helicopters were present at the Show, though statically displayed only – which was a pity, because the demonstrations given on other occasions by the company's chief test pilot, were among the most awe-inspiring rotary displays ever seen.

Rolls-Royce were presenting their new helicopter engine, the RTM 322, in a Sikorsky S-70C, in place of its more usual General Electric CT7s, the first non-US engines so to be installed. Derived from the military UH-60 Black Hawk, of which 750 of an ordered 1,100 for the United States Army had been delivered, the S-70 at this time had only attracted an order from the People's Republic of China for 24.

The Agusta A.129 Mangusta was the first European dedicated attack and anti-armour helicopter, powered again by Rolls-Royce, this time with two of the popular Gem turboshafts. Flying for the first time on 15 September 1983, initial deliveries of 66 for the Italian Army, to whose requirement it had been designed, were about to begin. It contained considerable areas of composites in its construction and featured a

sophisticated mechanical/electronic flight management, weapons aiming and firing and monitoring system.

The Italians' presence at Farnborough was impressive, with no less than 17 aircraft in which they were directly or indirectly involved. The industry had been undergoing a steady process of amalgamation across the board and was now about equally grouped around Aeritalia, Aermacchi (in whom Aeritalia had a 25 per cent stake) and Agusta, the latter being part of the public holding company EFIM. Of the other well-known Italian aircraft companies, Fiat had been a founding constituent of Aeritalia in 1969, SIAI-Marchetti was the aircraft division of Agusta, (who also aquired Caproni, the oldest Italian aircraft company, in 1983) and the youngest, ten-year old Partenavia, was still independent.

The Aeritalia G.222 demonstrated a novel form of crop-dusting with the spraybars fixed to the tailplane and the Aermacchi MB.339B and K were once more in the Terpsichorean hands of the Macchi Twins. The SF.600TP (for Turbine Power) had first flown as long ago as 8 April 1981, but had not yet entered production, though a batch of nine would be laid down in 1987. It followed the familiar pattern of multi-rôle light utility transports.

Another newcomer that was to attract considerable commercial attention was the Fokker 50. Fokker had made their re-entry into the post-war airliner market place with the very successful Rolls-Royce Dart-powered F.27. The 50-60 seater Fokker 50 was based on the 500 series F.27, which superficially it much resembled, but with new engines (the new-technology Pratt & Whitney of Canada PW 124s), a longer fuselage and considerable use of composites.

Several aircraft made brief rushes onto the stage from airborne starts in the course of the week. A NATO Boeing E-3A Sentry made an impressive entry from over the black shed on three of the trade days; LX-N90451 on Press Day, '449 on Wednesday and '454 on Thursday. On the latter day it was confronted (almost) by the British Aerospace Nimrod AEW.3, sweeping in from the Laffan's Plain towards the end of the day's flying and not in the company combine. The battle for the Royal Air Force early warning aircraft order had by no means been settled at this time, but it was a little unkind of someone to suggest they be sent on simultaneously and allowed to fight it out. In the event, of course, the order went to the Sentry; perhaps the only truly memorable aspect of an otherwise messy affair was that the delays imposed on the introduction of the new aircraft would probably give the Shackleton an unassailable record of longevity in front-line service.

On one occasion only, at mid-week, on a dull day with a pounding cross-wind from the south, we were treated to the unforgettable sight of the Aero Spacelines Super Guppy of Airbus Industrie, taking in the Show on its run south to

Toulouse from Ringway. The original Guppies (the brainchild of Jack Conroy) were conversions by Aero Spacelines of Boeing 377 Stratocruisers in 1962 and were designated B-377PG (Pregnant Guppy) and B-377SG (Super Guppy), the latter with T34 turboprop engines. They were used to transport space rockets for NASA and were followed by the piston-engined B-377MG (Mini-Guppy), Allison 501 turboprop powered B-377SGT and B-377MG-101 – a Mini-Guppy with turboprops. The one at Farnborough was a B-377SGT-201

in the red and yellow livery of Airbus; fully loaded, it would weigh as much as 170,000 lb (77,110 kg) and stood 45 ft 10 in (13.97 m) tall on the ground. From the roof of the control tower, its unmistakable and unlikely silhouette could be picked out far to the west. It swept majestically up the runway, like some vast aluminium galleon from the Spanish Armada, the pilot angling its unwieldy bulk into the cross-wind. One of the most imposing sights since the Princess.

Quite the most exciting thing to happen however at the

1986

Aircraft	Registration
+ Aeritalia G.222	I-CERX (4043)
+ Aeritalia/Aermacchi/Embraer AMX	X595 (A.02)
Aeritalia/Aermacchi/Embraer AMX	X599 (A.05)
+ Aermacchi MB.339B	I-GROW/MM54502 (6711/106)
Aermacchi MB.339C	I-AMDA (6775/147)
+ Aermacchi MB.339K	I-BITE (6662/001)
Aerospatiale AS.332M1 Super Puma	F-WZJN (2004)
Aerospatiale AS.350L1 Ecureuil	– (1945)
Aerospatiale SA.365M Panther	F-ZVLO (6005)
Aerospatiale Epsilon	(F-ZKFZ) (3)
+ Aerospatiale/Aeritalia ATR 42	F-WWEC/OY-CIC (024)
Agusta A.109A Mk.II Widebody	I-AGSC (7352)
Agusta A.109A Mk.II Widebody	I-AGSE (7354)
Agusta A.109GDF	– (7338)
Agusta A.109K	I-DACE (7340)
+ Agusta A.129	MM592 (29002)
Agusta A.129	MM598 (29005)
Agusta AB.412	I-DACB (25507)
Agusta AB.412 Griffon	– (039)
+ Airbus A300B-2	F-WUAD (3)
+ Airbus Super Guppy	F-BPPA (002) flying only
Antonov An-124	CCCP-82005
+ ARV Super 2	G-BMSJ (010) one a/c landed 31st,
+ ARV Super 2	G-DEXP (003) otherwise all to
+ ARV Super 2	G-OARV (001) Blackbushe.
ARV Super 2	G-STWO (002)
Bell 206L Long-Ranger	N3902X (45615)
Bell 406CS Combat Scout	N2500B (2500)
Bell 412AH	N412AH (33119)
Bell OH-58D	85-24693 (41556)
+ Boeing E-3A Sentry	LX-90451 on 31/8, '48 on 3/9, '54 on 4/9
British Aerospace Andover E.3	XS610
+ British Aerospace Harrier GR.5	ZD320 flying only ex-Dunsfold
British Aerospace Jetstream 200	G-AWVK (208)
+ British Aerospace Jetstream 31	G-BLKP (634)
British Aerospace Jetstream 31	G-31-705/VH-TQK (705)
British Aerospace Jetstream T.3	G-31-667/ZE441 (667)
+ British Aerospace Nimrod AEW.3	XZ287 (8049) flying only
British Aerospace Tornado GR.1	(ZD714) painted in Saudi AF colours
British Aerospace Tornado F.3	ZE164
+ British Aerospace ATP	G-MATP (2000)
British Aerospace BAe 125-1B	G-DJMJ (25106)
+ British Aerospace BAe 125-800	G-UWWB (258001)
+ British Aerospace BAe 146-100	G-XIAN/B-2701 (E.1019)
+ British Aerospace BAe 146-200	G-BMYE (E.2008)
+ British Aerospace BAe 146-200	G-OHAP/N403XV (E.2061)
British Aerospace BAe 146-200	G-ECAL/N148AC (E.2058)
+ British Aerospace BAe 146-200QT	N146QT (E.2056) 31st only
+ British Aerospace EAP	ZF534
Canadair Challenger CL-601	N226G (3012)
Caproni Vizzola C22J	I-CAVT (003)
CASA Aviocar 200	ECT-134 (321)
+ CASA Aviocar 300	ECT-131 (323)
+ CASA Aviojet	EC-DUJ (98)
+ CASA/IPTN CN-235	ECT-100 (001)
CASA/IPTN CN-235	ECT-135 (P.1)
Cessna T.210M Centurion	G-BMSW (62326)
Cessna Caravan II	F-GEUP (406-0003)
Cessna Citation II	N586CC (550-0086)
Cessna Citation III	N142AB (650-0042)
Cessna Citation III	N65OM (650-0044)
Cessna Conquest II	G-BMTZ (441-0207)
CFM Shadow	G-MJVF (002)
CFM Shadow B	G-MNIS (014)
Chichester-Miles Leopard	G-BKRL (001)
+ Dassault-Breguet Atlantic ATL2	(F-ZWRI) (01)
Dassault-Breguet Falcon 20 (EW)	N909FR (209)
+ Dassault-Breguet Falcon 900	F-GFJC (2)
+ Dassault-Breguet Mirage F1CR	(F-ZJSC) 33-NN (655)
+ Dassault-Breguet Mirage 2000C	(F-ZJRB)/2-LM (27)
+ Dassault-Breguet Mirage 2000N	(F-ZWVH) (02)
+ Dassault-Breguet Mirage 4000	(F-ZWRM) (01)
+ Dassault-Breguet Rafale	(F-ZJRE) (01)
Dassault-Breguet Super Etendard	(F-ZJRD) (5)

	Dassault-Breguet/Dornier Alpha Jet	41-08 (0108)
+	Dassault-Breguet/Dornier Alpha Jet NGEA	F-ZJRO
+	Dassault-Breguet/Dornier Alpha Jet NGEA	F-ZJTJ
	de Havilland Chipmunk	G-AKDN (11)
+	de Havilland Canada Dash 7	C-GNBX (1)
+	de Havilland Canada Dash 8	C-GAAC (47)
	de Havilland Canada Twin Otter 310	VP-FBB (783)
+	Dornier Do 228-100	D-ICOG (7001)
	Dornier Do 228-200	G-MAFS (8084)
	Dornier Do 228-201	98-78 (8068)
	Embraer Brasilia	PT-SIT (120024) to be LN-KOC
	Embraer Tucano	PP-ZTK (313249)
	Everett Autogyro	G-OFRB (006)
	Fairchild Metro III	N2687U (AC-651)
+	FFA Bravo 18A	HB-HFY (135)
+	Fokker 50	PH-OSI (10688) flying only from Cranfield
	Gates Learjet 35A	N3815G (35A-614)
	Gates Learjet 35A	G-LEAR (35A-265)
	Gates Learjet 55	N7260J (55-126)
	Grob G.109B	G-BLGY (6269)
	Grob G.109B	G-BMCG (6362)
	Gulfstream Aerospace Gulfstream III	N800CC (472)
	Gulfstream Aerospace SRA-I	F-313 (313) Danish AF
	Lockheed SR-71A Blackbird	64-17980
+	Marmande Microjet 200B	F-WDMX (02)
	MBB Bo 105CBS	D-HDQE (S-582)
	MBB Bk 117A	D-HBKS (7017)
	MBB Bk 117A-3M	(D-HBKA) (P.2)
+	Norman Fieldmaster	G-NRDC (004)
+	Norman Freelance	G-NACI (001)
+	Norman Turbo Firecracker	G-SFTR (005)
	Norman Turbo Firecracker	G-SFTA (006)
+	Optica Industries Optica	G-BLYZ (EA7-005)
	Optica Industries Optica	G-BMPE (EA7-009)
	Partenavia P.68TC	I-VIPY (351/36TC)
	Partenavia P.68-OBS	G-OBSV (329/20 OBS)
+	Partenavia AP.68TP-600 Viator	I-RAIL (9001)
	Pilatus PC-6B2 Turbo-Porter	HB-FHZ (840)
+	Pilatus PC-7 Turbo-Trainer	HB-HOO (394)
	Pilatus PC-7 Turbo-Trainer	HB-HMP (480)
+	Pilatus PC-9	HB-HPA (001)
	Pilatus PC-9	HB-HPF (107)

+	Pilatus Britten-Norman AEW Defender BN-2T	G-TEMI (2143)
+	Pilatus Britten-Norman Islander BN-2B-26	G-TWOB (2159)
+	Pilatus Britten-Normal Turbine Islander BN-2T	G-DEMO (2146)
	Piper Cheyenne IIIA	G-BLSA (42-5501029)
	Piper Cheyenne 400LS	N44OWH (42-5527009)
	Promavia Jet Squalus	OO-SQA (1)
	RFB Fantrainer 400	D-EATP (011)
+	RFB Fantrainer 600	D-EATR (001)
	Robin R. 3000-120	G-BMTI (120)
	Robinson R.22 Beta	G-HUMF (0534)
+	SAAB SF.340A	SE-ISV (045)
	SAAB SF.340A	SE-E63 (063) for Business Express
+	Shorts 330 Sherpa	G-BKMW (SH.3094)
+	Shorts 360	G-BMXP (SH.3700)
	SIAI-Marchetti S.211	I-SRSV (015)
+	SIAI-Marchetti S.211	I-SMJT (030)
	SIAI-Marchetti SF.260TP	I-SFTP (661-601004S)
	SIAI-Marchetti SF.600TP Kanguru	I-KANG (003)
+	Sikorsky S-70C	G-RRTM (70-583)
+	Slingsby T.67M-200 Firefly	G-BLUX (2027)
	SOCATA Guerrier 235	F-GAPE (12105)
	SOCATA Trinidad TC	G-GENV (617)
	Southdown Pipistrelle 2C	G-MJTM (DA1/8869/83)
+	Trago Mills SAH-1	G-SAHI (001)
+	Valmet L-90TP Redigo	OH-VTP (001)
	Westland Lynx	G-LYNX (WA.102)
+	Westland Lynx 3	ZE477 (WA.310)
+	Westland Super Lynx	ZD267 (WA.307)
+	Westland 30-160	G-BLKR (WA.017)
	Westland 30-160	VT-EKG/G-17-9 (WA.019)
+	Westland 30-TT300	G-HAUL (WA.020)

Service participation in the flying programmes:
British Aerospace Hawk: one from CFS; nine from CPS, "Red Arrows" aerobatic team; 3-5th.
British Aerospace Sea Harrier: one from 899 Squadron.
Panavia Tornado: one from TWCU/45 Squadron; one from 229 OCU.

Veteran and vintage aircraft:
Supermarine Spitfire P7350 and RM689 (G-ALGT).

Civil aircraft participation:
BAC/Aerospatiale Concorde G-BOAD on 6/9.

British Aerospace BAe 146 G-XIAN was handed over to CAAC during the Show and departed mid-week.

British Aerospace's BAe 125-800 demonstrator had the odd registration G-UWWB until the realisation dawned that the company's advertising motto was "Up Where We Belong".

Dassault-Breguet's Rafale gave the polished performance one has come to expect from this company's demonstration pilots.

The British Aerospace EAP ZF534 lifts off with reheat shimmering.

1986 Show has yet to be recorded. This was the first public appearance of the world's first fly-by-wire airliner. It was, in fact, an Airbus A300B2, the test and demonstration vehicle for the later models that would incorporate fly-by-wire as their normal system of control. Spectators, particularly on the trade days, were already familiar with the visual effects (one will not say tricks) that could be arranged thus with military aeroplanes, notably in terms of high alpha passes at very low speeds. They were certainly not prepared for the sight of the massive Airbus pursuing its stately way about the sky at very low speeds and power settings, and responding with instant amiability, to the most outrageous demands made upon its attitudes and trajectory by Airbus's chief engineering test pilot, Gordon Corps. It was, in its way, a far more impressive demonstration of the system than anything done by the big fighters, from whom, after all, one expected that sort of behaviour.

New from Finland was the Valmet L-90TP Redigo OH-VTP, another entrant in the turboprop trainer field.

Pilatus Britten-Norman's AEW Defender G-TEMI, grossly disfigured by the radome enclosing Thorn EMI's Skymaster radar.

1988

THE THIRTY-SIXTH SHOW
4-11 SEPTEMBER

The shape of the exhibition changed again in 1988. A new hall was fitted in, to the north of New North Hall, absorbing the area that had up to then been the radar and equipment terrace, and swallowing up E and H rows of chalets. In order to avoid the problems of referring to a New New North Hall, tradition was abandoned and the halls numbered 1 to 5. The radar terrace was transferred to the 1986 Press area and the Press Tent itself installed on the grass in front of Hall 1, by the static Park. To cope with demand, a number of chalets were converted into two-storey structures.

As a result of the late withdrawal of all Italian participation, following a confrontation over their government's policy towards the industry, quite large adjustments had to be made and in the end, Hall 5 was not built, the final extent of the exhibition buildings being 618,758 square feet (57,484 sq. m).

At the mid-week SBAC Flying Display Dinner, the President, Mr Ivan Yates of British Aerospace, referred to the steady increase in overall and export trade figures, comparing the £9 billion turnover for the industry in 1987, to £2.5 billion in 1978 and touched upon the great changes the industry had seen over the period of the Farnborough Shows.

"Twenty years ago, as we watched the first flight of the Jaguar together, my French opposite number, George Ricard, who was 64, told me he had worked on 24 projects. By contrast, by the time I reach that age, I might have worked on five. This is a five to one reduction in 25 years in new types of aircraft . . . In the UK, in 1948 we had 23 airframe companies. Now we have only one major airframe company, with two smaller ones, including helicopters, and one major engine company where we had five."

He also referred to the greatly extended gestation period of new projects; in the case of EFA, twelve years from the first discussions on performance to the signing of the Memorandum of Understanding to proceed.

It had always been a strict rule that if an aircraft was entered for the flying display, then it flew, subject to acceptable force majeure, every day of the show. There had always been problems enforcing this; test programmes beckoned, as did the hope of sneaking home for the week-end in the case of one or two exhibitors (not British ones, of course) and occcasionally the Flying Control Committee had to get tough. This time, however, underlining the individuality of the 1988 display, there were quite a number of exceptions to that admirable rule.

Misfortune overtook the great Antonov An-124 – the "big Ant" – flying at Farnborough for the first time, on Press Day. As the pilot opened up for take-off, there was a spectacular fireball from the port inner engine when the air bleed unit failed and he had to abort with a damaged engine. With impressive speed (marred slightly by documentation problems at the German border), a fresh engine was flown in by an An-22 and fitted with Ruslan taking its place in the show, flying on Thursday.

The MiG-29 also missed out on one day's flying on Friday; the story that everyone had gone off shopping in Harrods was generally believed to be untrue.

Several exhibiting aircraft "doubled up" in the flying display, with British Aerospace fielding one ATP on Press Day and a different one for the rest of the week, and swapping about the two Tornado F.3s borrowed from No. 229 OCU for the occasion. Westland did the same with two Army Air Corps Lynx. Airbus, having just fitted the prototype A320 with the International Aero Engines V2500, were able to fly it up from Toulouse on Tuesday, display it for two days and return it to its test programme. Aircraft number six and seven were scheduled to be the first production A320s with the engine. IAE were new to the aero-engine scene, made up of a combine of Rolls-Royce, Pratt & Whitney, MTU, Fiat and the Japanese Aero-engine Consortium. After suffering some initial delays in development the engine, delivering 25,000 lb (11,340 kg) of thrust, was beginning to make headway against its principal rival, the GE/SNECMA CFM56, which had up to then had that slice of the market pretty well sewn up.

The de Havilland D.H.88 Comet, beautifully restored to near original condition, flew on Press Day and on the Friday in the competent hands of George Ellis, remaining for the rest of the week parked alongside the MiG-29. It was a splendid sight to see in the circuit, against the bright, piled-up, wind-blown cumulus, for all the world like the Norman Wilkinson painting commissioned by de Havilland in 1934.

The Red Arrows, this year, had been reduced by a series of mishaps to seven aircraft. Indeed, earlier in the season, when five of the team had been stricken with illness after an event, only the synchro pair arrived at the next venue, reducing the team manager to threats of resignation. Nevertheless, the three of them carried it off.

One other exhibitor, his pilot having collected a "full house" of yellow cards (warnings from the Flying Control Committee) by Friday and been excused flying, was left sadly contemplating his aeroplane in the Static Park over the week-end.

Even after forty years of British weather, conditions were quite remarkable in 1988. Right up to the Saturday before the Show Farnborough suffered a succession of lows and troughs, with crowded isobars, high winds and torrential rain. Assembly of the exhibition halls and stand construction became a misery and at one point the BDLI stand designers rang the site office to complain that they had not ordered a swimming pool. But on Sunday, the wind dropped and the sun came out and for the whole Show week conditions were near perfect. Mind you, there was a fairly powerful crosswind at times, which did not help the An-22 on Wednesday evening when it came in with the spare engine for the "big Ant", but added considerably to the entertainment value of its arrival.

Without going into detail, it turned out to be a marvellous demonstration of the rough field capability of the aircraft, even if it put the pilot's workload well on the wrong side of the curve. All the same, when it departed at lunch time on Friday, the pilot's offer to Air Traffic to do a little display on leaving was politely declined. The navigator of the An-22 returned to England the following April for the purpose of flying to the Soviet Union and back in the front seat of one of three Tiger Moths undertaking a 5,000 mile (8,047 km) tour.

On the Monday after the Show, with commendable promptness but too late to spoil the fun, the lows and troughs resumed their sway.

British Aerospace's Hawk 200 was making its debut at Farnborough, with a launch order from Saudi under its belt. Following the Show, in company with a Series 100 two-seater, it would embark on a 30,000 mile (48,280 km) tour round the world, taking in the Australian Bi-Centenary and astonishing the Australians by completing an eight-day, seven nation demonstration out to Richmond with not only no problems but no back-up party.

The Hawk trainer order book was running over 650, including the 302 Goshawks for the United States Navy. Replacing the Rockwell T-2C Buckeye and McDonnell Douglas Skyhawk, the Goshawk was expected to halve training costs while adding many new capabilities. McDonnell Douglas, already heavily involved with British Aerospace over the AV-8 Harrier, were the partners in this programme. Shortly after the Show, the 1989 United States Defense Authorisation Bill approved the purchase of a further 72 Harriers, to provide 288 of the US Marines' target of 328 aircraft. Funding, for the first time in American history, would be spread over several fiscal years.

The Tornado F.3, latest version of the ADV to enter service with the Royal Air Force, was borrowed for the occasion by British Aerospace from No. 229 OCU, aka No. 65 Squadron. Deliveries during the year totalled 44, enough to equip not only the OCU but Nos 5 and 29 Squadrons at Coningsby and No. 11 Squadron at Leeming. Two of the No.5 Squadron aircraft escorted the MiG-29s to Farnborough. (Not to be outdone, the Royal Navy provided a Sea Harrier on each side of the departing Russians for their final flypast after the Show.)

Leeming had previously been in Training Command and at Show time was absorbing another F.3 unit, No. 23 Squadron. Nos 5 and 11 had been the last two Lightning squadrons; the others had flown Phantoms and No. 23, reformed from a flight of No. 29, had been serving at Mount Pleasant in the Falklands.

In March 1987, a Tornado F.3 had become the first British aircraft to fly with the Joint Tactical Information Distribution System (JTIDS), designed to an Air Defence requirement for a jam-resistant ECM communications system. The first of 35 of another Tornado variant, the IDS-based Electronic Combat and Reconnaissance (ECR) version for the German Air Force, began testing during Farnborough week.

"*Glasnost* on the Wing" said a *Flight International* leader, and that was a pretty good description of the effect of the MiG-29 on the assembled (and fascinated) experts of the West. The aircraft first flew in 1977-78 and entered service in 1983-84, with some 400 estimated to be in squadron service by Farnborough time. Its appearance, the first at a western show, was part of the current hard drive for export sales by the Soviet Union and deliveries had already been made to Syria, Iraq, North Korea and Yugoslavia. Just before the Show, it was announced that the Luftstreitkrafte of the German Democratic Republic were receiving the MiG-29 – the first non-Soviet Warsaw Pact Air Force to do so. Aircraft sold outside the Pact were without certain sophisticated or restricted equipment. Recently – at the expense of the Mirage 2000, also on offer, 86 had been sent to India, with an option to licence-build around 100 more. A similar sales drive on behalf of the An-124 had so far produced no results.

It was a remarkable mixture of high technology and – to the West – outdated practices, with very old-fashioned instrumentation and flight control systems, equally highly-advanced fire control, laser ranger, look-down, shoot-down capability, a "thinking hat" for the pilot that impressed the Americans no end, and an ingenious double intake system with shutters to prevent FOD ingestion during take-off. Take-off was at a very flat angle of attack, to keep the big tail pipes clear of the ground and for the same reason the final approach, aided by a tail parachute, was markedly fast and flat.

Construction, where it mattered, was meticulous and

sophisticated. Where it didn't, it wasn't. Its performance was stunning, equalling the best the western fighters were doing and without the benefit of fly-by-wire, with an eye-catching tail-slide the talk of the week. Interestingly, stencilled instructions and instrument information were in English. The aircraft was demonstrated by the Mikoyan Design Bureau's chief test pilot, Anatoly Kvotchur – fellow test pilot Roman Taskaev brought the two-seater.

Dassault-Breguet, this year, had a very much smaller team. Military sales had been very slow in 1987, but Jordan bought 20 Mirage 2000s in April 1988 and there looked like being a healthy trade in refurbishing many of the different versions of the Mirages – foreign sales of all versions, including the 2000, totalled 2,510.

Rafale was, effectively, a proof of concept for the *Avion de Combat Futur* (ACF), currently running slightly ahead of the pack of initials representing 21st century combat thinking. EFA we have met; from the United States come the Advanced Tactical Fighter, the Advanced Tactical Aircraft and the Navy's A-12; from Spain the AX; from India the Light Combat Aircraft and from Taiwan the Indigenous Combat Aircraft. There was also the Yugoslavian Novi project, Brazil's MFT/LF fighter-trainer project to replace the F-5, Mirage and EMB-326 and – the only one among them in the flesh, the Swedish SAAB JAS-39 Gripen. In mid-1989 the future for Gripen looked bleak, as the inevitable problems arose and how many of the rest would see the light of day remained to be discovered.

In the meantime, other aircraft than the Mirage were in line for mid-life upgrading to fill the gap. It was perhaps significant that Belgium decided to refurbish its Mirages rather than join the Rafale programme. The Netherlands was also planning to upgrade its F-16s into the 21st century.

Two of the American fighters whose lives looked like being indefinitely extended in this way were flying at Farnborough. The CF-18 was provided by Canadian Forces in Europe; one of the 138 ordered to replace their CF-104s in NORAD and NATO. Since its previous appearance at Farnborough in 1980, the F/A-18 had been ordered also by Australia, where the cost of acquiring and servicing the initial order of 75 was to raise several political storms and strain an already taut budget. Spain had ordered 72 and it was about half way through its introduction into the attack aircraft carriers of the United States Navy, replacing the A-4, F-4 and F-8, with some 600 delivered of an USN/USMC order for 1,150 aircraft. In October it was announced that Switzerland were to buy 34 as their next generation fighter, the order being won against the Mirage 2000 and JAS-39 Gripen.

The F-16C was the upgraded version of this popular aircraft and the presence of a Turkish example underlined that country's recent membership of the world's largest combat aircraft club. By September 1988, 16 countries were involved

in a total of 4,207 planned orders – nearly 3,000 of which were required for the United States alone. Twelve countries were involved in the production of components, equipment or airframes under the Multi-national Co-production Programme.

There were no fewer than 13 different military trainers on display and there seemed to be little sign of interest waning in this rather over-crowded segment of the market. British Aerospace's trainer Hawk was represented by a Service T.1 from 4 FTS – flown by Flight Lieutenant Andy Wyatt, the current Wright Jubilee Trophy winner. CASA of Spain again flew their C-101, 88 of which had been ordered by the Ejercitu del Aire as the Mirlo. In July, they had sold licence production rights for the armed version, the C-101BB, to Chile, who called it the T-36 Halcón, and brought ENAER Pillans in exchange. The latter was also flying; ENAER were conducting a serious international sales promotion and had recently taken the Pillan round the Middle East. It was unusual among other current trainers in being piston-engined. The company were hopeful, though they had so far received no encouragement, that it might one day form a suitable Bulldog replacement for the Royal Air Force.

This year Shorts appeared with their upgraded Tucano, which had turned out to be the successful contender to AST 412 and featured a more powerful, 1,100 shp Garrett turboprop to give the required performance and strengthened spar to put up the fatigue life by 50 per cent. It also featured the Tucano Information Management System (TIMS), similar to the Harrier's HIMS but also monitoring the airframe. Implementation of the quite considerable changes needed to meet Air Staff requirements resulted in slower initial deliveries than forecast.

Among the regional airliners on display, the ever-increasing public demand for air transport had promoted sales comfortably, for both the Fokker 100 and the ATR 42. By February 1989, the Fokker 100, which had first flown in November 1986, would have 118 orders on the books (and there were orders and options for nearly 100 of the turboprop Fokker 50) and in March Fokker were contemplating an American order expected to bring orders for the jet to 212 with 178 options. The one flying at Farnborough was the prototype, now with more powerful Rolls-Royce Tay 650s and came touring in from Amsterdam each day. The F50 had similarly operated out of Cranfield in 1986.

Airbus 320 sales had reached 370 before the Show, with a further 218 options and the British Aerospace 146 order book had reached 139, including the first sales announced of the -300, which received its CAA airworthiness certificate during the Show. By March 1989, total sales were 154.

In the category of flying test-bed, now rare at Farnborough, McDonnell Douglas flew their UHB (Ultra-High-Bypass)

1988

Aircraft	Registration
+ Aeritalia/Aermacchi/Embraer AMX	MM X599 (A.02)
Aeritalia/Aermacchi/Embraer AMX	MM X599 (A.05)
Aerospatiale AS.332M1 Super Puma	F-WZJN (2004)
Aerospatiale AS.350L1	– no marks
Aerospatiale AS.355F2	G-BOOV (5374)
Aerospatiale SA.365K Panther	– (6011) no marks
Aerospatiale SA.365N1 Dauphin	G-PDES (6096)
Aerospatiale Epsilon	(F-ZKFZ) (3)
Aerospatiale/Aeritalia ATR 42	F-WWEW (070) to be I-NOWI
+ Airbus A320-110	F-WWDC (4)
+ Airbus A320-130	F-WWAI (01)
+ Antonov An-124	CCCP-82007
Beech Beechjet	G-RSRS (RJ-36)
Beech Super King Air 300LW	F-GGFB (FA-118)
Bell 406CS Combat Scout	N2500B (2500)
Bell 412	N32072 (33172)
Bell OH-58D	87-0729 (41606)
+ Boeing 707-351B	N351SR (18586)
+ British Aerospace Hawk 200	ZH200
+ British Aerospace Hawk T.1	XX165 from 5/9 to 10/9
+ British Aerospace Hawk T.1	XX310 on 4/9 and 11/9
British Aerospace Jetstream Super 31	(N370MT)/G-31-800 (800)
+ British Aerospace Tornado F.3	ZE251 on 5/9, 10/9, 11/9
+ British Aerospace Tornado F.3	ZE295 on 4/9 and from 6/9 to 9/9
+ British Aerospace ATP	G-BZWW (2005)
+ British Aerospace ATP	G-BTPA (2007)
British Aerospace BAe 125-1B	G-BOCB (25106)
British Aerospace BAe 125-800B	G-BNEH (258078)
British Aerospace BAe 146-100STA	G-BSTA (E.1002)
British Aerospace BAe 146-300	G-BOWW (E.3120) to be N611AW
+ British Aerospace BAe 146-300	G-LUXE (E.3001)
+ Brooklands/ASTA Scoutmaster	G-BMPF (010)
Canadair Challenger CL-601-3A	N49UR (5016)
CASA Aviocar 200	SE-IVE (343)
+ CASA Aviocar 200M	ECT-130 (369)
CASA Aviocar 300	ECT-131 (323)
CASA/IPTN CN-235	EC-011 (011)
+ CASA/IPTN CN-235	ECT-135 (P.3)
+ CASA Aviojet	EC-DUJ (98)
Cessna 208 (U-27A)	N9698F (208-0129)
Cessna 208B Caravan I Super Cargomaster	N9709F (208- 0138)
Cessna F-406 Caravan II	F-Geul (406-0025)
Cessna Citation III	N657CC (650-0157)
CFM-Metalfax Shadow	G-MJVF (002)
Dassault-Breguet Falcon 900	F-GIDE (1)
+ Dassault-Breguet Mirage 2000B	(F-ZWRE)/BX1
+ Dassault-Breguet Rafale	(F-ZJRD) (01)
+ de Havilland D.H.88 Comet	G-ACSS (1996)
de Havilland Canada Dash 8	C-FCTD (113) for Hamburg Airlines
Dornier Do 228-100	D-CIMA (7116)
+ Dornier Do 228-100	D-ICOG (7001)
Dornier Do 228-200	G-CAYN (8108)
+ EH Industries EH101	ZF641 (PP.1/50001)
Embraer Brasilia	N24706 (120093)
+ Embraer Brasilia	PT-SKY (120081)
+ Embraer Tucano	PT-ZTK (312149)
+ ENAER Pillon T-35	CC-PZF (166)
Enstrom 280FX Shark	N86259 (2024)
Fairchild Merlin IVA	F-GMTO (AT-031)
Fairchild Metro III	G-BOJN (AC-629B)
+ Fairchild Metro III	88003 (AT-421B) Swedish AF, roof radar
FFV Aerotech BA-14 Starling	SE-KFV (1)
+ Fokker 100	PH-MKH (11242) flying only
Gates Learjet 35	N53FN (35-053)
Gates Learjet 35A	G-LEAR (35A-265)
Gates Learjet 55C	N1055C (55C-135)
General Dynamics F-16A	78-0198 Danish AF
+ General Dynamics F-16C	87-0009 Turkish AF
+ General Dynamics F-16C	87-0239
Grob G.115	G-BOCD (8024)
Gulfstream Aerospace Gulfstream SRA-4	N413GA (1034)
Highland Aero Dynamics Sparrow Hawk	N8728A (87005-26)
+ Island Aviation Super2	G-DEXP (003)
+ Island Aviation Super2	G-STWO (002)
Island Aviation Super2	G-BNHD (028)
Israel Aircraft Industries Astra	N30AJ (019)
LET L-41OUPVE-9	OK-TZA (2039) for Liz-Air
+ Marmande Microjet 200B	F-WDMT (03)
MBB Bo 105CB-3	09212 (S-1762) Swedish Army
MBB Bo 105CBS	LN-OSE (S-634)
MBB Bk 117A-4	D-HNBE (7057)
+ McDonnell Douglas AH-64A Apache	86-8981 (PV351)
McDonnell Douglas AH-64A Apache	86-8983 (PV353)
McDonnell Douglas CF-18A Hornet	188745
+ McDonnell Douglas CF-18A Hornet	188745
+ McDonnell Douglas MD-81UHB	N980DC (48000)
McDonnell Douglas MD.500E	G-TMJH (0033E)
+ McDonnell Douglas TAV-8B Harrier II	162747
+ Mikoyan MiG-29A	10 (2960522971)
Mikoyan MiG-29UB	53 (50903008134)
Pilatus PC-6B2-H2 Turbo-Porter	HB-FKG (858)
Pilatus PC-7 Turbo Trainer	HB-HMP (480)
Pilatus PC-7 Turbo-Trainer	HB-HOQ (549) for Swissair
+ Pilatus PC-9	HB-HPE (176)
Pilatus PC-9	HB-HPF (107)
Pilatus PC-9	HB-HPG/C-401 (119) target tug for Swiss AF
Pilatus Britten-Norman AEW Defender BN-2T	G-TEMI (2143)
+ Pilatus Britten-Norman Islander BN-2B-26	G-TWOB (2159)
Pilatus Britten-Norman Turbine Islander BN-2T	G-DEMO (2146)
+ Piper Aztec E	G-HFTG (27-7405378)
+ Powerchute Raider	G-MTVZ (80104) plus four in Hall

+	Promavia Jet Squalus	I-SQAL (001)
	PZL Dromader	SP-DBR (IZ019-08)
	PZL Mewa	SP-DMA (1AHPO1-01)
	RFB Fantrainer 400	D-EATP (011)
+	RFB Fantrainer 600	D-EIWZ (005)
	Robin ATL	F-GFSZ (111)
	Robin DR.400/180	G-BOGI (1821)
	Robin R.3000/160	F-GGJZ (132)
	Robinson R.22 Beta	G-RENT (0758)
	SAAB 340	N125CH (125)
+	Shorts Tucano	G-BTUC (312007)
	Shorts Tucano T.1	ZF142 (11)
+	Shorts 360-300	G-BOEJ (SH.3736)
	Shorts 360-300	G-OLGW (SH.3741)
+	Sikorsky S-70C	G-RRTM (70-583)
+	Slingsby T.67M-200 Firefly	G-BLUX (2027)
	SOCATA Tobago	F-BOIT (810)
	SOCATA Trinidad	F-GFQN (747)
+	Trago/Orca SAH-1	G-SAHI (001)
+	Valmet L-90TP Redigo	OH-VTP (002)
	Westland Lynx	G-LYNX (WA.102)
+	Westland Lynx AH.1	XZ175 (WA.030)
+	Westland Lynx AH.1	XZ649 (WA.188)
+	Westland Super Lynx	ZD249 (WA.243)

Service participation in the flying programmes:

British Aerospace Hawk: nine from CFS; "Red Arrows" aerobatic team.
Westland Lynx: two from 829 Squadron.
Westland Gazelle: four from "Sharks" team.
Westland Sea King: one each from 706, 707, 771 and 849 Squadrons.

Veteran and vintage aircraft:
Avro Lancaster PA474.
Auster AOP.9 XR244.
Hawker Hurricane LF363.
Saro Skeeter XL814.
Supermarine Spitfire PS915.
Westland-Bell Sioux XT131.
Westland Gazelle XZ333.
Westland Scout XT644.

Civil aircraft participation:
BAC Aerospatiale Concorde G-BOAB on 10/9 only.
Pitts S-1T G-WILD.
Lo 100 D-0959 and D-5793, synchronised aerobatics.
SOCATA Rallye G-BTUG glider tug.
Vickers Viscount G-AOYR on 4/9 only.

demonstrator, prototype development aircraft for the MD-90 family and consisting of an MD-80 airframe with the port JT8D replaced by the GE unducted fan (UDF), driving ungeared 12 ft (3.7 m) contra-rotating eight-blade rotors. With a bypass ratio of 36 compared to one of two for the JT8D and producing 25,000 lb (11,340 kg) of thrust, it was a most unusual sight – and sound – in the Farnborough sky. Public reaction to a quite new style of vibration and noise remained to be assessed.

Apart from the Apache, all the helicopters in the flying display were grouped in the Westland combine, which included the Rolls-Royce S-70C and the naval version of the big, three-engined EH101, seen for the first time and flown by Westland chief test pilot Colin Hague. On 9 September Rolls-Royce announced that their RTM322 had won the order for British production versions of the aircraft, which would replace the Royal Air Forces's Pumas and Chinooks and, as the Merlin, equip the Navy's latest Type 22 frigates. In the interval, these ships would work up with Sea King HAS.5s.

Jointly produced by Westland and Agusta the EH101 provided a long range high capacity military, naval and civil helicopter – the first time, said the designers, that this had ever been done as an integrated programme.

The Army Lynx added to the impact of its display by arriving backwards at 60 mph (97 k/h) from the Laffan's Plain end and gave a sprightly aerobatic display with a reasonably full military load. The Army were already taking delivery of the new Lynx Mk 7 and had ordered the Mk 9, which featured advanced composite blades and improved engineering. Those new blades had helped give Lynx the World Helicopter

Speed Record at 400 k/h (249.1 mph).

The Black Hawk demonstrated was the first Westland-assembled airframe under the manufacturing and marketing licence from Sikorsky, who had recently become rather more intimately involved with Westland than before.

It was the solo Apache, however, that caught the immediate attention of the audience, and not just because it was the first item each day. Billed as the world's most powerful attack helicopter – and with 16 Hellfires, 76 70mm rockets and a 30mm cannon, that could well be right – this 17,400 lb (7,892 kg), 48 ft (15 m) rotor aircraft was demonstrated by company test pilots in a sequence of aerobatic manoeuvres that was definitely, as they pointed out "Above and beyond the call of duty" for a military pilot, but which convincingly displayed the aerobatic capability of the twin-engined, anti-armour helicopter, destined for 14 Attack Squadrons in US Forces in Europe.

Several light aircraft, struggling out of economic problems, were shown at Farnborough under new names and with renewed promise; the Trago Mills SAH-1 – whose designer, Sid Holloway, had received the Royal Aeronautical Society's Bronze Medal for his work – had been acquired by Orca, and the Edgley Optica by Brooklands Aerospace, who demonstrated a new loudspeaker-equipped version in conjunction with Aerospace Technologies of Australia, and from which Neville Duke harangued the crowd. ARV, after running into financial and technical problems that stopped deliveries in November 1987, were back under the new name of Island Aircraft. There were 21 of this new British light aircraft, priced at £26,000, on the register. It was powered by the unusual three cylinder two-stroke Hewland engine.

Desmond Norman, whose designs had appeared successively as Britten-Norman, Fairey-Britten-Norman, Pilatus-Britten-Norman, NDN, Firecracker, Hunting-Firecracker and Norman Aircraft, sadly had to retire from the Show, the company having failed to survive – by no means the first victim in post-war British light aviation.

One item, long absent, whose return helped to mark this as a memorable year, was the Service "set piece", in this case an impressive display of co-ordinated formation flying by the Royal Navy and featuring six Sea Harriers, four Gazelles (the Sharks Display Team), four Sea Kings of different Marks and two Lynx. This was one of those items that was immeasurably enhanced by being viewed from a privileged position on the roof of the control tower. The Red Arrows is another.

Other items enriched the occasion including the remarkable PowerChute Raider powered parachute, probably the only aircraft at any Show that you could carry in the boot of your car and demonstrating, in the fresh winds of that week, that it was to be taken seriously. (The winds were too strong for it only once, wrapping it up in a ball and leaving the pilot looking rather like A.A.Milne's Piglet when Wol's house blew down.)

On the Press Day, celebrating its own fortieth anniversary

(the prototype flew at the first Farnborough Show), there appeared a Viscount. It was an 806 of British Air Ferries and added a nice touch of nostalgia. Number two commentator, who had been a Viscount captain with BAF and had 'OYR in his log book, became quite maudlin.

No-one who saw them will forget the two pilots who closed the Show on the Public Days. Ludwig Fuss and Benno Weiss were Bavarian glider pilots, both members of their national championship team. They called themselves the Synchron Pair and they flew 36 year old gliders in an aerobatic routine with smoke and to music (which everyone remembered but no-one could put a name to – actually it was from the sound track of Bilitis). The gliders were Lo 100 Little Bitterns; built by Wolf Hirth in the 1950s and designed by Albert Vogt, they had a ten metre span of vintage Clark Y section and no speed brakes, flaps or spoilers. The two pilots flew them in a taut, carefully-co-ordinated routine that included a very close mirror pass and individual landings that finished within a few metres of each other. To achieve this without go-slow devices of any kind involved them in spectacular, steep approaches, with a yaw of almost 90 degrees.

It was their first British appearance and they were sponsored for the occasion by GEC Marconi and they made a magnificent and unique closer for Farnborough International 88. And for that matter, for this story.

Undoubtedly the stars were a single and two-seat Mikoyan MiG-29 – this is No. 10, the former.

About to be delivered was the first British Aerospace ATP for British Airways, G-BTPA.

Part of the Royal Navy presentation – here are three Sea Harriers, four Sea Kings and two Lynx.

One of the most popular items was the synchronised and silent display by two German Lo 100 gliders, D-0959 and D5793 sponsored by GEC Marconi.

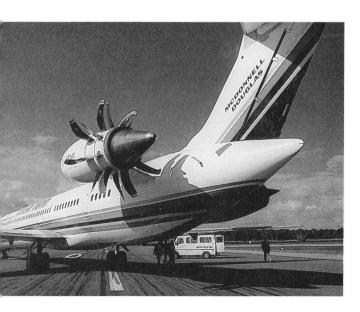

One of the oddest sounds was the McDonnell Douglas MD-81UHB demonstrator N980DC with its normal Pratt & Whitney JT8D on the right side and a General Electric inducted fan on the left.

The tri-company Aeritalia/Aermacchi/Embraer AMX MM X595 was one of two shown – the other was static.

SPEAKER ONE

There appears to be no record of the identity of any of the pre-war commentators at SBAC Displays. The first reference in print is to Captain Rex Stocken, a World War One pilot and, from his position as a director of de Havillands, commanding a wide acquaintance in the aviation fraternity, who spoke for the Radlett Shows. Suave, charming and bi-lingual, he had time, in those days of leisurely presentation, to make his comments in French as well as English. Try that now and you would not get past *Bonjour*! (G'day!).

His successor was the formidable Major Oliver Stewart, MC; author, bon viveur, yachtsman and formerly a very successful World War One fighter pilot. Between the wars he edited a readable magazine called *Popular Flying*, after the Second World War he turned it into an unreadable one called *Aeronautics*. Oliver's commentaries were highly individual, inspired by the briefing in the Pilots' Tent, an intimate knowledge of aerobatics and a tendency to lyrical prose. Working with Oliver from 1961 as a specialist commentator, and later with *his* successor, Wing Commander Charles Gardner, (who flew Catalinas in the Second World War and became a director of British Aerospace) and from whom I took over, has provided an unique view of the SBAC Display scene over thirty years, during which it has changed almost out of recognition.

In many ways, matters have improved considerably; from the comparatively cloistered calm of the two-man greenhouse on the control tower roof, where only Air Traffic, the Flying Control Committee (in the adjacent greenhouse) and the Red Arrows commentator can get at us, it is a far cry to the hectic Air Fair atmosphere of the mid-fifties. To quote Oliver himself, writing in *Aeronautics* of October, 1953:

"The official SBAC Commentator for the Farnborough Display spends a small part of his time on the air, and all the rest of the time on the carpet. He discovers almost directly he has spoken that he has left unsaid those things which he ought to have said, and has said those things which he ought not to have said . . . He is told that all the matters which he believes to be of interest are unworthy of remark and that all the matters which he believes to be devoid of interest should receive special mention. He is handed "scripts" which would take three hours to read at 200 words a minute . . . As he mounts to the tower before the opening of the day's programme his head whirls with the changes and last-minute alterations in pilots and aircraft. He telephones to Control to check something. Control does not know. He telephones to the Pilots' Tent. Those there do not know. He tries to obtain connection with the firm concerned but finds himself talking to one of the two hundred thousand people who want messages put on the air about Little Willie, who has lost his parents, or about Mr Blenkinsop, who wishes to meet Mrs Blenkinsop at the flower bed near the President's Tent . . . A message arrives from the Farnborough Road Safety Com-

mittee requesting that motorists be asked not to have collisions with one another . . . a hand-rolled linen handkerchief, a genuine half-hunter gold watch valued at 27s 6d and a fully fitted luncheon set with ham and tongue sandwiches and a flask of coffee have been lost. Would the commentator immediately put out urgent requests that they be conveyed by their finders to the main SBAC office close to the loudspeaker tower? Is it an official message? Yes, of course. Has it the approval of the SBAC? Yes, of course. Then please send a note signed either by the Director of the SBAC or by the Commanding Officer of the station authorising diffusion. There is a sudden reduction in the number of lost Little Willies who want messages put out on the public address system . . . a merciful lull occurs as the watch-hand ticks towards zero hour. It reaches zero minus one and the control telephone rings . . . A voice requests that we make an excuse for the non-appearance of an aircraft. We glance at our programme. The aircraft is not on the programme at all . . . "

One does still receive weird messages; on the presentation of one twin-engined prototype military aircraft, which was still wearing a development engine on one side that was noticeably not pollution-free, a note appeared asking that we explain that "one engine is *not* making more smoke than the other; one engine is making *less*." but by and large, we are a more sober-minded lot than in the fifties. Commercial pressures, international rivalries and the sheer rapidity of the presentations, ensure that.

Many of the old problems have disappeared. The "Farnborough ghost", an insidious bleep over the speakers caused by one of the ground radars, has almost been exorcised, and no longer is one distracted by the endless whispered repetition of one's last words brought back across the airfield by the line of speakers. On the other hand, fly-by-wire or relaxed stability confers on very noisy aeroplanes the ability to remain throughout their four-minute slot over the centre of the airfield and effectively drown any attempt at commentary. However, the manufacturers do not seem to mind; such presentations get all the attention they need without any help from us.

The use of the plural, by the way, is deliberate, for we are a team of two. Apart from the fact that being a Chief Commentator is no fun if there are no Indians, the preparation and delivery of the "commercials" does need a second body, a function fulfilled by Stratton Richey who splits the work of collecting and checking information and undertakes the essential task of cueing me into the next aircraft – the gaps between the landing of one item (which one is still covering) and the arrival of the next from some quite different angle (like overhead and into sun, out of the hold), being often derisory. He also answers our three telephones, runs the air conditioner and pours out the lemonade. Useful chap.

Index of Aircraft Exhibited at SBAC Shows 1932-1988

Almost 650 basic types of aircraft have appeared at the SBAC Displays since 1932, excluding variants. This listing directs readers to the year in which a particular type appeared and includes a brief mention of the powerplant – to distinguish between various marks of engine and list them separately would have been a gigantic task. Engines, like aircraft, went through various changes in manufacturers' names – for instance the Viper started as Armstrong Siddeley, became Bristol Siddeley and now Rolls-Royce; Lycoming became Avco Lycoming then Textron Lycoming. Specific differentiations for engines has not been attempted as it is not an engine listing. For example the Hunting Jet Provost's Viper engine is shown as Rolls-Royce throughout.

To avoid splitting up long runs of dates where, for instance, the D.H. 125 became the H.S.125 and then BAe 125, these have been cross-referred. In cases where an aircraft has a name it is used in preference to the company designation – Short Belfast instead of Short S.C.5, but basic designations and names are given for US military types. It was considered however, that it was necessary to be more specific in the case of the various Auster sub-types.

Where a type first appeared under a maker's designation and was subsequently named it appears thus: P.1067/Hunter or 541/Swift. Gliders are identified, not surprisingly, by (-) indicating no engine.

Tornados and Jaguars are shown under British Aerospace instead of Panavia and Sepecat respectively. Saro seems to have been the pre-war preferred name for Saunders-Roe.

Aeritalia
  AM-3C (1 x Lycoming 480) 1977
  G.222 (2 x General Electric T64) 1978, 86
Aeritalia/Partenavia
  P.68 (2 x Lycoming 360) 1974, 76, 78, 82, 84, 86
  AP.68 (2 x Allison 250) 1982, 84, 86
Aeritalia/Aermacchi/Embraer
  AMX (1 x Rolls-Royce Spey) 1986, 88
Aermacchi
  MB.326 (1 x Rolls-Royce Viper) 1966, 68, 70, 72, 74, 76, 78
  MB.339 (1 x Rolls-Royce Viper) 1976, 78, 80, 82, 84, 86, 88
Aeromere
  Falco (1 x Lycoming 320) 1972
Aeronca
  100/300 (1 x Aeronca Jap) 1937
Aerospatiale
  Corvette (2 x Pratt & Whitney JT18D) 1974, 76
  Dauphin (1 x Turbomeca Astazou) 1974, 76
  Dauphin (2 x Turbomeca Arriel) 1976, 78, 80, 82, 84, 88
  Ecureuil (1 x Turbomeca Arriel) 1978, 86, 88
  Epsilon (1 x Avco-Lycoming 540) 1982, 84, 86, 88
  Fouga 90 (2 x Turbomeca Astafan) 1978
  Gazelle (1 x Turbomeca Astazou) 1968, 76, 80, 82, 88
  Panther (2 x Turbomeca TM333) 1986, 88
  Puma (2 x Turbomeca Turmo) 1968
  Super Puma (2 x Turbomeca Makila) 1982, 84, 86, 88
  TwinStar (2 x Allison 250) 1980, 82, 84, 88
Aerospatiale/Aeritalia
  ATR 42 (2 x Pratt & Whitney PW120) 1986, 88
Agusta
  A.109 (2 x Allison 250) 1974, 76, 78, 80, 82, 84, 86
  A.109 (2 x Turbomeca Arriel) 1986
  A.129 (2 x Avco-Lycoming LTS 101) 1984
  A.129 (2 x Rolls-Royce Gem) 1986
Agusta-Bell
  AB.204B (1 x Rolls-Royce Gnome) 1966, 68
  AB.205BG (2 x Rolls-Royce Gnome) 1968
  AB.212ASW (1 x Pratt & Whitney PT6T Twin Pac) 1974, 78, 82
  AB.412/Griffon (1 x Pratt & Whitney PT6T Twin Pac) 1982, 84, 86
Airbus
  A300 (2 x General Electric CF6) 1974, 76, 78, 80, 86
  A300 (2 x Pratt & Whitney JT9D) 1984
  A310 (2 x Pratt & Whitney JT9D) 1982
  A310 (2 x General Electric CF6) 1984
  A320 (2 x General Electric/SNECMA CFM56) 1988
  A320 (2 x International Aero Engines V2500) 1988
  Super Guppy (4 x Allison 501) 1986
Airmark-Wallis
  WA.117 (1 x Rolls-Royce Continental 200) 1970
  (see also Beagle-Wallis, Vinten-Wallis and Wallis)
Airmass
  Sunburst/Sunlight/Sunset (1 x Cuyana 430R) 1982
Airship Industries
  Skyship (2 x Porsche) 1982, 84
Airspeed
  Ambassador (2 x Bristol Centaurus) 1947, 48, 49, 50, 51, 64, 66
  Ambassador (2 x Bristol Proteus) 1954
  Ambassador (2 x Napier Eland) 1955

Ambassador (2 x Rolls-Royce Tyne) 1958
  Consul (2 x Armstrong Siddeley Cheetah) 1946, 47, 48
  Courier (1 x Armstrong Siddeley Cheetah) 1934
  Courier (1 x Napier Rapier) 1934
  Courier (1 x Armstrong Siddeley Lynx) 1935
  Envoy (2 x Wolseley A.R.9) 1934
  Envoy (2 x Armstrong Siddeley Lynx) 1935, 36
  Envoy (2 x Armstrong Siddeley Cheetah) 1937
  Horsa (–) 1946
  Oxford (2 x Armstrong Siddeley Cheetah) 1937
Albatross
  D.VA replica (1 x Ranger 6-444) 1978
Antonov
  An-72 (2 x Lotarev D-36) 1984
  An-124 (4 x Lotarev D-18)1986, 88
Armstrong Whitworth
  A.W.16 (1 x Armstrong Siddeley Panther) 1932, 33
  A.W.19 (1 x Armstrong Siddeley Tiger) 1933, 34, 35
  A.W.23 (2 x Armstrong Siddeley Tiger) 1935
  A.W.52 (2 x Rolls-Royce Derwent) 1948
  A.W.52 (2 x Rolls-Royce Nene) 1948
  A.W.52G (–) 1946
  Apollo (4 x Armstrong Siddeley Mamba) 1949, 50
  Argosy (4 x Rolls-Royce Dart) 1959, 60, 61, 62, 64, 66, 68
  Atalanta (3 x Armstrong Siddeley Serval) 1932, 33
  Atlas (1 x Armstrong Siddeley Panther) 1932
  Meteor (2 x Rolls-Royce Derwent) 1950, 51, 52, 54
  Scimitar (1 x Armstrong Whitworth Panther) 1933, 34, 35
  Whitley (2 x Armstrong Siddeley Tiger) 1936, 37
  Whitley (2 x Rolls-Royce Merlin) 1946
ARV
  Super2 (1 x Hewland AE75) 1986, 88
Auster
  AOP.6/6A (1 x de Havilland Gipsy Major) 1946, 47, 60
  AOP.9 (1 x Blackburn Cirrus Bombardier) 1954, 55, 56, 61, 72, 88
  A.2/45 (1 de Havilland Gipsy Queen) 1948
  B.4 (1 x Blackburn Cirrus Bombardier) 1951, 52
  B.8 Agricola (1 x Continental 470) 1956
  C.6 Atlantic (1 x Continental 185) 1957
  D.4/108 (1 x Lycoming 235) 1960
  D.6/180 (1 x Lycoming 360) 1960
  J/1 Autocrat (1 x Blackburn Cirrus Minor) 1946, 47, 48, 49
  J/1B Aiglet (1 x de Havilland Gipsy Major) 1950
  J/1N Alpha (1 x de Havilland Gipsy Major) 1958
  J/2 Arrow (1 x Continental 75) 1946
  J/5A (1 x de Havilland Gipsy Major) 1950
  J/5B Autocar (1 x de Havilland Gipsy Major) 1949, 50
  J/5F Aiglet Trainer (1 x de Havilland Gipsy Major) 1951
  J/5G Autocar (1 x Blackburn Cirrus Major) 1952
  J/5L Aiglet Trainer (1 x de Havilland Gipsy Major) 1952, 53, 55, 58, 59
  J/5R Alpine (1 x de Havilland Gipsy Major) 1956
  J/8L Aiglet (1 x de Havilland Gipsy Major) 1954
  P Avis (1 de Havilland Gipsy Major) 1947, 48, 49
  S (1 x Blackburn Cirrus Bombardier) 1951
  T.7 (1 x de Havilland Gipsy Major) 1948, 49
Aviation Traders
  Accountant (2 x Rolls-Royce Dart) 1957

Avro
626 (1 x Armstrong Siddeley Cheetah) 1932, 33
642 (2 x Armstrong Siddeley Jaguar) 1933
652/Anson (2 x Armstrong Siddeley Cheetah) 1935, 36, 37, 46, 49
707 (1 x Rolls-Royce Derwent) 1949, 50, 51, 52, 53
748/Andover (2 x Rolls-Royce Dart) 1960, 61, 62, 64, 66, 68, 70, 72, 74, 76, 78, 80, 82, 84, 86
Ashton (4 x Rolls-Royce Nene) 1950
Ashton (4 x Rolls-Royce Nene & 1 x Rolls-Royce Conway) 1951
Athena (1 x Armstrong Siddeley Mamba) 1948
Athena (1 x Rolls-Royce Merlin) 1948, 49, 50
Athena (1 x Rolls-Royce Dart) 1949
Cadet (1 x Armstrong Siddeley Genet Major) 1932, 33, 35, 36
Cadet Three-Seater (1 x Armstrong Siddeley Genet Major or Cirrus Hermes) 1933
Club Cadet (1 x de Havilland Gipsy Major or Armstrong Siddeley Genet Major or Cirrus Hermes) 1933
Commodore (1 x Armstrong Siddeley Lynx) 1933
Lancaster (4 x Rolls-Royce Merlin) 1946, 68, 72, 74, 76, 80, 84, 88
Lancaster (2 x Rolls-Royce Merlin & 2 x Armstrong Siddeley Python) 1949
Lancastrian (4 x Rolls-Royce Merlin) 1946
Lancastrian (2 x Rolls-Royce Merlin & 2 x Rolls-Royce Nene) 1946
Lancastrian (2 x Rolls-Royce Merlin & 2 x Rolls-Royce Avon) 1947
Lancastrian (2 x Rolls-Royce Merlin & 2 x de Havilland Ghost) 1947
Lincoln (4 x Rolls-Royce Merlin) 1946, 47, 48, 50, 59, 60, 61
Lincoln (4 x Rolls-Royce Merlin & 1 x Rolls-Royce Tyne) 1956
Lincoln (4 x Rolls-Royce Merlin & 1 x Napier Naiad) 1948
Lincoln (4 x Rolls-Royce Merlin & 1 x Napier Nomad) 1951
Lincoln (2 x Rolls-Royce Merlin & 2 x Bristol Theseus) 1947, 48
Lincoln (2 x Rolls-Royce Merlin & 2 x Bristol Proteus) 1950, 51
Mailplane (1 x Armstrong Siddeley Panther) 1932, 33
Tudor (4 x Rolls-Royce Merlin) 1946
Tudor (4 x Bristol Hercules) 1947
Tudor (4 x Rolls-Royce Nene) 1948
Tutor (1 x Armstrong Siddeley Lynx) 1932, 33
York (4 x Rolls-Royce Merlin) 1946
Shackleton (4 x Rolls-Royce Griffon) 1949, 50, 51, 52, 53, 54, 55, 57, 58, 60, 64
Shackleton (4 x Rolls-Royce Griffon & 2 x Rolls-Royce RB162) 1970, 72
Vulcan (4 x Rolls-Royce Avon) 1952
Vulcan (4 x Rolls-Royce Conway) 1957, 58, 59
Vulcan (4 x Armstrong Siddeley Sapphire) 1953, 54
Vulcan (4 x Bristol Olympus) 1953, 55, 56, 57, 58, 59, 60, 61, 64
Vulcan (5 x Bristol Olympus) 1962, 66
Avro Canada
CF-100 (2 x Avro Orenda) 1955
B.A.
Double Eagle (2 x de Havilland Gipsy Major) 1936
Eagle (1 x de Havilland Gipsy Major) 1935, 36
Swallow (1 x Pobjoy Cataract) 1935, 36
BAC
221 (1 x Rolls-Royce Avon) 1964, 66
Canberra – see English Electric
Jaguar (2 x Turbomeca Adour) 1970, 72, 74, 76, 78, 80, 82, 84
Jet Provost – see Hunting Percival
Lighting – see English Electric
One-Eleven (2 Rolls-Royce Spey) 1964, 66, 68, 70, 72, 74, 76, 78, 80, 82
Strikemaster (1 x Rolls-Royce Viper) 1968, 70, 72, 76, 80
Tornado – see British Aerospace
VC10 – see Vickers
BAC/Aerospatiale
Concorde (4 x Rolls-Royce/SNECMA Olympus) 1970, 72, 74, 76, 78, 80, 86, 88
Beagle
AOP.11 (1 x Rolls-Royce Continental 470) 1961, 62, 64, 66
B.206/Basset (2 x Rolls-Royce Continental 470) 1961, 61, 64, 66
Royce Continental 470) 1961, 61, 64, 66
B.206S (2 x Rolls-Royce Continental 520) 1964, 66, 68
B.218X (2 x Rolls-Royce Continental 300) 1962
B.242X (2 x Rolls-Royce Continental 360) 1964
Airedale (1 x Lycoming 360) 1961, 62, 64
Airedale (1 x Rolls-Royce Continental 300) 1961
Husky (1 x Lycoming 360) 1964, 66
Pup (1 x Rolls-Royce Continental 200) 1968
Pup (1 x Lycoming 320) 1968
Pup (1 x Lycoming 360) 1968
Terrier (1 x de Havilland Gipsy Major) 1961, 62
Beagle-Wallis
WA.116 (1 x McCulloch) 1962, 64
(see also Wallis, Airmark-Wallis Vinten-Wallis)
Bede
BD-5 (1 x Komatsu Xenoah) 1978
BD-5J (1 Microturbo TRS18) 1974
Beech
Baron (2 x Continental 470) 1974, 80
Beechjet (2 x Pratt & Whitney JT15D) 1988
Duchess (2 x Avro Lycoming 360) 1980
King Air (2 x Pratt & Whitney PT6A) 1974, 76, 80, 82, 88
Skipper (1 x Avco Lycoming 235) 1980
Bell
47G (Soloy) (1 x Allison 250) 1980
214ST (2 x General Electric CT7) 1982
222B & UT (2 x Avco Lycoming LTS101) 1984
249/YAH-1S (1 x Avco Lycoming T53) 1980
406S Combat Scout (1 x Allison 250) 1984, 86, 88
412 (1 x Pratt & Whitney PT6T Turbo Twin Pac) 1986, 88
JetRanger/OH-58 (1 x Allison 250) 1974, 82, 86, 88

LongRanger (1 x Allison 250) 1984
Blackburn
B-2 (1 x Blackburn Cirrus Hermes) 1934
B-2 (1 x de Havilland Gipsy III) 1932, 34
B-2 (1 x de Havilland Gipsy Major) 1934, 64
B-3 (M.1/30A) (1 x Rolls-Royce Buzzard) 1933
B-6/Shark (1 x Bristol Pegasus) 1934, 35, 36, 37
C.A.15C Biplane (2 x Armstrong Siddeley Jaguar) 1932
C.A.15C Monoplane (2 x Armstrong Siddeley Jaguar) 1933
N.A.39/Buccaneer (2 x de Havilland Gyron Junior) 1958, 59, 60, 61, 62
N.A.39 Buccaneer (2 x Rolls-Royce Spey) 1964, 66, 68, 70, 72
S.28/43 (1 x Bristol Centaurus) 1947, 48
Y.B.1 (1 x Armstrong Siddeley Double Mamba) 1950
Beverley (4 x Bristol Centaurus) 1955, 56, 57, 59, 61
Firebrand (1 x Bristol Centaurus) 1946, 47, 48
Ripon (1 x Bristol Pegasus) 1933
Segrave (2 x de Havilland Gipsy Queen) 1932
Blackburn & GAL
Universal Freighter (4 x Bristol Hercules) 1950, 51, 52
Universal Freighter (4 x Bristol Centaurus) 1953, 54
Boeing
707 (4 x Pratt & Whitney JT3D) 1976, 84
707 (4 x Pratt & Whitney TF33) 1988
727 (3 x Pratt & Whitney JT8D) 1982
737 (2 x General Electric CFM56) 1984
757 (2 x Rolls-Royce RB211-535) 1982
767 (2 x General Electric CF6) 1982
E-3A Sentry (4 x Pratt & Whitney TF33) 1980, 86
Boeing-Vertol
Chinook (2 x Lycoming T55) 1974, 78
Boulton Paul
P.108 (1 x Bristol Mercury) 1947
P.111 (1 x Rolls-Royce Nene) 1951, 53
Balliol (1 x Armstrong Siddeley Mamba) 1948
Balliol (1 x Rolls-Royce Merlin) 1948, 49, 50, 53, 54
Breguet
Atlantic (2 x Rolls-Royce Tyne) 1966, 68, (see also Dassault Breguet)
Bristol
120 (1 x Bristol Pegasus) 1933
142 (2 x Bristol Mercury) 1936
143 (2 x Bristol Aquila) 1936
171/Sycamore (1 x Alvis Leonides) 1948, 51, 52, 53, 54, 55, 56, 58, 59
173 (2 x Alvis Leonides Major) 1952, 53, 54, 55, 56, 57
188 (2 x de Havilland Gyron Junior) 1962
192/Belvedere (2 x Napier Gazelle) 1958, 59, 61
F.2b Fighter (1 x Rolls-Royce Falcon) 1962
Blenheim (1 x Bristol Mercury) 1937
Bombay (2 x Bristol Pegasus) 1935, 36
Boxkite replica (1 x Rolls-Royce Continental) 1966
Brabazon (8 x Bristol Centaurus) 1949, 50, 51
Brigand (2 x Bristol Centaurus) 1946, 47, 48
Britannia (4 x Bristol Proteus) 1952, 53, 54, 55, 56, 57, 58, 59
Britannia (3 x Bristol Proteus & 1 x Bristol Orion) 1956, 57
Buckmaster (2 x Bristol Centaurus) 1946, 47
Bulldog (1 x Bristol Mercury) 1932, 33, 64
Bulldog (1 x Bristol Jupiter) 1932, 33
Bulldog (1 x Bristol Perseus) 1934, 35
Bullpup (1 x Bristol Aquila) 1935
Freighter (4 x Bristol Hercules) 1946, 47, 48, 49, 50, 51, 52, 53, 54
British Aerospace
ATP (2 x Pratt & Whitney PW124) 1986, 88
EAP (2 x Turbo Union RB199) 1986
VC10 – see Vickers
BAe 125/Dominie (2 x Rolls-Royce Viper) 1962, 64, 64, 66, 68, 70, 72, 74, 76
BAe 125 (2 x Garrett TFE731) 1976, 78, 80, 82, 84, 86, 88
BAe 146 (4 x Avco Lycoming ALF502) 1982, 84, 86, 88
Bae 748 – see Avro
Andover – see Avro
Bulldog – see Scottish Aviation
Comet – see de Havilland
Harrier – see Hawker Siddeley
Hawk (1 x Rolls-Royce Turbomeca Adour) 1974, 76, 78, 80, 82, 84, 86, 88
Jaguar – see BAC
Jetstream (2 x Garrett TPE331) 1980, 82, 84, 86, 88 (see also Scottish Aviation)
Jet Provost – see Hunting Percival
Nimrod – see Hawker Siddeley
One-Eleven – (see BAC and CNIAR)
Sea Harrier (1 x Rolls-Royce Pegasus) 1978, 80, 82, 84, 86, 88
Strikemaster – see BAC
Tornado (2 x Turbo Union RB199) 1976, 78, 80, 82, 84, 86, 88
British Hovercraft Corp.
SR.N6 (1 x Rolls-Royce Gnome) 1976
Britten-Norman
Islander/Defender (2 x Lycoming 540) 1966, 68, 70, 72, 74, 76, 78, 80, 86, 88
Turbine Islander/Defender (2 x Allison 250) 1980, 82, 84, 86, 88
Islander (2 x Rolls-Royce Continental 520) 1968, 70
Trislander (3 x Lycoming 540) 1970, 72, 74, 76, 78, 80
Brooklands/Asta
Scoutmaster (1 x Avco Lycoming 540) 1986, 88 (see also Edgley)
Campbell
Cricket (1 x Volkswagen 1600) 1970
Canadair
Challenger (2 x Avco Lycoming ALF502) 1980, 82
Challenger (2 x General Electric CF34) 1984, 86, 88

Caproni Vizzola
  C22J (2 x Microturbo TRS18) 1980, 82, 84, 86
CASA
  Aviocar (2 x Garrett TPE331) 1976, 78, 80, 82, 84, 86, 88
  Aviojet (1 x Garrett TFE731) 1978, 80, 82, 84, 86, 88
CASA-Nurtanio & IPTN
  CN-235 (2 x General Electric CT7) 1984, 86, 88
Cassutt (1 x Rolls-Royce Continental 200) 1980
Cessna
  FR.172 (1 x Rolls-Royce Continental 360) 1976
  180 (1 x Continental 470) 1972
  206 (Soloy) (1 x Allison 250) 1984
  210 (1 x Continental 520) 1986
  310 (2 x Continental 470) 1972
  Caravan I (1 x Pratt & Whitney PT6A) 1988
  Caravan II (2 x Pratt & Whitney PT6A) 1986, 88
  Conquest (2 x Pratt & Whitney PT6A) 1984
  Conquest (2 x Garrett TPE331) 1984, 86
  Citation (2 x Pratt & Whitney JT15D) 1974, 84, 86
  Citation (2 x Garrett TFE731) 1986, 88
CFM-Metalfax
  Shadow (1 x Rotax 447) 1984, 86, 88
Chichester-Miles
  Leopard (2 x Noel Penny NPT301) 1986
Chrislea
  Super Ace (1 x de Havilland Gipsy Major) 1948, 49
Cierva
  C.30 (1 x Armstrong Siddeley Genet Major) 1934, 35
  W.9 (1 de Havilland Gipsy Six) 1946, 47
  Air Horse (1 x Rolls-Royce Merlin) 1948, 49
  Skeeter (1 x Jameson FF-1) 1948, 49
  Skeeter (1 x de Havilland Gipsy Major) 1949
  CR.LTH-1 Grasshopper (2 x Rolls-Royce Continental 300) 1970
CNIAR
  One-Eleven (2 x Rolls-Royce Spey) 1984 (see also BAC)
Comper
  Swift (1 x Pobjoy R) 1964
Cranfield
  A1 (1 x Lycoming 540) 1978
Cunliffe Owen
  Concordia (2 x Alvis Leonides) 1947
C.W.
  Cygnet Minor (1 x Blackburn Cirrus Minor) 1937
Dassault-Breguet
  Atlantic (see Breguet)
  Atlantic ATL2/NG (2 x Rolls-Royce Tyne) 1982, 84, 86
  Falcon 10 (2 x Garrett TFE731) 1974, 76
  Falcon 20 (2 x General Electric CF700) 1972, 74, 76, 78, 86
  Falcon 30 (2 x Lycoming ALF502) 1974
  Falcon 50 (3 x Garrett TFE731) 1980, 82, 84
  Falcon 200 (2 x Garrett ATF3) 1984
  Falcon 900 (3 x Garrett TFE731) 1986, 88
  Jaguar (2 x Turbomeca Adour) 1970, 72
  Mirage IIING (1 x SNECMA Atar) 1984
  Mirage F1 (1 x SNECMA Atar) 1978, 80, 82, 84, 86
  Mirage 2000 (1 x SNECMA M53) 1978, 80, 82, 84, 86, 88
  Mirage 4000 (2 x SNECMA M53) 1980, 82, 86
  Rafale (2 x General Electric F404) 1986, 88
  Super Etendard (1 x SNECMA Atar) 1982, 86
Dassault-Breguet-Dornier
  Alpha Jet (2 x Turbomeca Larzac) 1974, 76, 78, 80, 82, 84, 86
Datwyler
  MD-3-160 (1 x Lycoming 320) 1984
de Havilland
  D.H.2 replica (1 x Pobjoy Niagara) 1978
  D.H.86 (4 x de Havilland Gipsy Six) 1934, 36, 37
  D.H.108 (1 x de Havilland Goblin) 1946, 47, 48
  D.H.110/Sea Vixen (2 x Rolls-Royce Avon) 1952, 53, 54, 55, 56, 57, 58, 59, 60, 61, 62, 64, 66, 68
  D.H.125 – see British Aerospace
  Albatross (4 x de Havilland Gipsy Twelve) 1937
  Comet (2 x de Havilland Gipsy Six) 1935, 84, 88
  Comet (4 x de Havilland Ghost) 1949, 50, 51, 52
  Comet (4 x Rolls-Royce Avon) 1954, 55, 56, 57, 58, 59, 60, 61, 68, 78
  Don (1 x de Havilland Gipsy King) 1937
  Dove (2 x de Havilland Gipsy Queen) 1946, 47, 48, 49, 50, 51, 52, 53, 54, 55, 56, 57, 58, 59, 60, 61, 62, 64
  Dragon (2 x de Havilland Gipsy Major) 1933, 34
  Dragon Rapide (2 x de Havilland Gipsy Six) 1935, 36, 37, 66, 80
  Dragonfly (2 x de Havilland Gipsy Major) 1936
  Fox Moth (1 x de Havilland Gipsy III) 1932, 33
  Heron (4 x de Havilland Gipsy Queen) 1950, 51, 52, 53, 54, 55, 56, 57, 58, 59, 60
  Hornet/Sea Hornet (2 x Rolls-Royce Merlin) 1946, 47, 48, 49
  Hornet Moth (1 x de Havilland Gipsy Major) 1935, 36, 72
  Leopard Moth (1 x de Havilland Gipsy Major) 1933, 34, 35, 46, 47
  Mosquito (2 x Rolls-Royce Merlin) 1946, 47, 48, 62, 64, 66
  Puss Moth (1 x de Havilland Gipsy III) 1932
  Tiger Moth (1 x de Havilland Gipsy Major) 1932, 33, 34, 35, 36, 47, 60
  Trident (3 x Rolls-Royce Spey) 1964, 66, 68
  Trident (3 x Rolls-Royce Spey & 1 x Rolls-Royce RB162) 1970, 72
  Vampire/Sea Vampire (1 x de Havilland Goblin) 1946, 47, 48, 49, 50, 51, 52, 54, 55, 56, 57, 58, 59, 76
  Vampire (1 x de Havilland Ghost) 1948

  Venom/Sea Venom (1 x de Havilland Ghost) 1949, 50, 51, 52, 53, 54, 55, 56
Canada
de Havilland
  Beaver (1 x Alvis Leonides) 1953, 54, 55, 58, 59, 60
  Beaver (1 x Pratt & Whitney Wasp Junior) 1964
  Buffalo (2 x General Electric CT64) 1976, 78, 80, 82, 84
  Chipmunk (1 x de Havilland Gipsy Major) 1947, 48, 49, 50, 51, 52, 53, 54, 55, 58, 59, 86
  Chipmunk (1 x Rover TP90) 1966
  Chipmunk (1 x Bonner Super Sapphire) 1976, 80
  Dash 7 (4 x Pratt & Whitney PT6A) 1978, 80, 82, 84, 86
  Dash 8 (2 x Pratt & Whitney PW120) 1984, 86, 88
  Turbo Beaver (1 x Pratt & Whitney PT6A) 1966
  Twin Otter (2 x Pratt & Whitney PT6A) 1966, 68, 70, 72, 78, 80, 82, 84, 86
de Havilland Technical School
  T.K.2 (1 x de Havilland Gipsy Major) 1946
  T.K.4 (1 x de Havilland Gipsy Major) 1937
Dornier
  Do 128-2 (2 x Avco Lycoming 540) 1980
  Do 228 (2 x Garrett TPE331) 1982, 84, 86, 88
  Skyservant (2 x Lycoming 540) 1972, 74, 78
  TNT (2 x Garrett TPE331) 1980
  Turbosky (2 x Avco Lycoming LTP101) 1978
  Turbo Skyservant (2 x Pratt & Whitney PT6A) 1980, 82
Douglas
  Invader (2 x Pratt & Whitney R-2800) 1980
Dragon Light Aircraft
  Dragon (1 x Fuji-Robin) 1982
Druine (Rollason)
  Condor (1 x Continental 200) 1972
  Turbulent (1 x Ardem) 1961, 62, 64, 66
Edgley
  Optica (1 x Lycoming 260) 1980, 82, 84 (see also Brooklands/Asta)
EH Industries
  EH101 (3 x General Electric CT7) 1988
Eipper-Formance
  Quicksilver (1 x Rotax) 1982
Eiri
  PIK-20E (1 x Rotax) 1980
Elliott
  Baby EoN (–) 1947
  Intermediate EoN (–) 1948
  Primary EoN (–) 1947, 48
  EoN 460 & Olympia (–) 1947, 48, 59, 60
  Newbury EoN (1 x Blackburn Cirrus Minor) 1947
  Newbury EoN (1 x de Havilland Gipsy Major) 1948
Embraer
  Bandeirante (2 x Pratt & Whitney PT6A) 1978, 80, 82
  Brasilia (2 x Pratt & Whitney PW118) 1984, 86, 88
  Tucano (1 x Pratt & Whitney PT6A) 1982, 84, 86, 88
  Xingu (2 x Pratt & Whitney PT6A) 1978, 80, 82
ENAER
  Pillan (1 x Avco Lycoming 540) 1982, 84, 88
English Electric
  Canberra (2 x Rolls-Royce Avon) 1949, 50, 51, 52, 53, 54, 55, 56, 57, 58, 59, 64, 66, 68, 70
  Canberra (2 x Armstrong Siddeley Sapphire) 1951, 52, 54
  Canberra (2 x Bristol Olympus) 1952, 53, 54, 55, 57
  Canberra (2 x Rolls-Royce Nene & 1 x de Havilland Spectre) 1957
  Canberra (2 x Rolls-Royce Avon & 1 x Napier Scorpion) 1956, 57
  Canberra (2 x Rolls-Royce Avon & 1 x Napier Double Scorpion) 1958
  Canberra (1 x Rolls-Royce Avon & 1 x de Havilland Gyron Junior) 1957
  P.1 (2 x Armstrong Siddeley Sapphire) 1955, 57
  Lightning (2 x Rolls-Royce Avon) 1957, 58, 59, 60, 61, 62, 64, 66, 68, 70, 72
  Wren (1 x ABC) 1966
Enstrom
  F28 & Shark (1 x Lycoming 360) 1974, 76, 78, 80, 82, 88
Eurowing
  Goldwing (1 x Fuji-Robin) 1982
Evans
  VP-2 (1 x Volkswagen) 1980
Everett
  Autogyro (1 x Volkswagen) 1986
Fairchild
  A-10 (2 x General Electric TF34) 1976, 78, 80, 82
  Metro & Merlin (2 x Garrett TPE331) 1980, 82, 86, 88
  Metro (2 x Pratt & Whitney PT6A) 1980, 82, 84
Fairey
  IIIF (various engines) 1932
  G.4/31 (1 x Armstrong Siddeley Tiger) 1934
  P.4/34 (1 x Rolls-Royce Merlin) 1937
  F.D.1 (1 x Rolls-Royce Derwent) 1954
  F.D.2 (1 x Rolls-Royce Avon) 1955, 56, 57, 58
  G.R. 17/Gannet (1 x Armstrong Siddeley Double Mamba) 1950, 51, 57, 58, 59, 61, 66
  Battle (1 x Rolls-Royce Merlin) 1936
  Fantome (1 x Hispano Suiza 12Y) 1935
  Firefly (1 x Rolls-Royce Kestrel) 1932, 33
  Firefly (1 x Rolls-Royce Griffon) 1946, 47, 48, 49, 50, 51, 52, 53, 54, 55, 57, 80
  Fox (1 x Rolls-Royce Kestrel) 1933
  Fulmar (1 x Rolls-Royce Merlin) 1962
  Gordon (1 x Armstrong Siddeley Panther) 1932
  Gyrodyne (1 x Alvis Leonides) 1947, 48
  Jet Gyrodyne (1 x Alvis Leonides & 2 Rolls-Royce Merlin compressors) 1955
  Hendon (2 x Rolls-Royce Kestrel) 1932, 34, 35

Long Range Monoplane (1 x Napier Lion) 1933
Primer (1 x de Havilland Gipsy Major) 1948
Rotodyne (2 x Napier Eland) 1958, 59
Seal (1 x Armstrong Siddeley Panther) 1933, 34
Spearfish (1 x Bristol Centaurus) 1946
Swordfish (1 x Bristol Pegasus) 1936, 37, 62, 64, 66, 74, 80, 84,
Ultra-light helicopter (1 x Turbomeca Palouste) 1955, 56, 57, 58
Fairey Britten-Norman
  Islander & Trislander – see Britten-Norman
FFA
  Bravo (1 x Lycoming 360) 1976, 78, 80, 86
  Bravo (1 x Lycoming 540) 1978, 80, 84
FFV Aerotech
  Starling (1 x Lycoming 235) 1988
Fiat
  G.91 (1 x Bristol Siddeley Orpheus) 1966, 72
Firecracker Aircraft
  Firecracker – see NDN
FMA
  Pucara (2 x Turbomeca Astazou) 1978
Fokker
  Dr.1 replica (1 x Warner Super Scarab) 1978
  D.VII replica (1 x Ranger 6-440) 1978
  F.27 (2 x Rolls-Royce Dart) 1966, 70, 72, 74, 76, 80, 82, 84
  F.28 (2 x Rolls-Royce Spey) 1968, 70, 72, 74, 76, 80, 82
  50 (2 x Pratt & Whitney PW124) 1986
  100 (2 x Rolls-Royce Tay) 1988
Folland
  Gnat (1 x Bristol Siddeley Orpheus) 1955, 56, 57, 58, 59, 60, 61, 62, 64, 66, 68, 70, 72, 74, 76, 78
  Midge (1 x Bristol Siddeley Viper) 1954
Fouga
  Magister (2 x Turbomeca Marbore) 1972
General Aircraft
  GAL.56 (–) 1947
  GAL.61 (–) 1948
  Hamilcar X (2 x Bristol Mercury) 1946
  Monospar (2 x Pobjoy R) 1933, 34
  Monospar (2 x Pobjoy Niagara) 1934, 35, 36
Gates
  Learjet (2 x General Electric CJ610) 1974, 76
  Learjet (2 x Garrett TFE731) 1978, 80, 82, 84, 86, 88
General Dynamics
  F-16 (1 x Pratt & Whitney F100) 1980, 82, 84, 88
  F-111 (2 x Pratt & Whitney TF30) 1980, 84
Gloster
  F.5/34 (1 x Bristol Mercury) 1937
  SS.19B/Gauntlet (1 x Bristol Mercury) 1933, 34
  SS.37 /Gladiator (1 x Bristol Mercury) 1935, 36, 37, 62, 64
  TC.33 (4 x Rolls-Royce Kestrel) 1932
  Javelin (2 x Armstrong Siddeley Sapphire) 1952, 53, 54, 55, 56, 57, 58, 59, 60
  Javelin (2 x de Havilland Gyron Junior) 1961
  Meteor (2 x Rolls-Royce Derwent) 1946, 47, 48, 49, 50, 51, 52, 53, 54, 61, 76
  Meteor (2 x Metrovick Beryl) 1948
  Meteor (2 x Rolls-Royce Avon) 1949, 50
  Meteor (2 x Armstrong Siddeley Sapphire) 1950, 51
  Meteor (2 x Rolls-Royce Derwent & 2 x Rolls-Royce Soar) 1954 (see also Armstrong Whitworth)
Government Aircraft Factory
  Nomad (2 x Allison 250) 1972, 76, 78
Grob
  G.109 (1 x Limbach 1200) 1982, 84, 86
  G.115 (1 x Lycoming) 235) 1988
Grumman
  Cheetah (1 x Lycoming 320) 1976, 78
  Cougar (2 x Lycoming 320) 1978
  Gulfstream II (2 x Rolls-Royce Spey) 1970, 76 (see also Gulfstream American)
  E-2 Hawkeye (2 x Allison T56) 1976
  Tiger (1 x Lycoming 360) 1976, 78
  F-14 Tomcat (2 x Pratt & Whitney TF30) 1976
  Trainer (1 x Lycoming 235) 1972, 76
Hafner
  Gyroplane (1 x Pobjoy Niagara) 1937
Handley Page
  H.P.42 (4 x Bristol Jupiter) 1932
  H.P.47 (1 x Bristol Pegasus) 1935
  H.P.115 (1 x Bristol Siddeley Viper) 1961, 62, 64
  H.P.R.2 (1 x Alvis Leonides) 1950
  Gugnunc (1 x Armstrong Siddeley Mongoose) 1932, 33
  Halifax/Halton (4 x Bristol Hercules) 1946, 47
  Hampden (2 x Bristol Pegasus) 1936, 37
  Harrow (2 x Bristol Pegasus) 1937
  Hastings (4 x Bristol Hercules) 1946, 47, 48, 59
  Herald (4 x Alvis Leonides Major) 1955, 56, 57
  Herald (2 x Rolls-Royce Dart) 1959, 60, 61, 62, 64, 66, 68
  Hermes (4 x Bristol Hercules) 1947, 48, 49
  Hermes (4 x Bristol Theseus) 1949, 50, 51
  Heyford (2 x Rolls-Royce Kestrel) 1932, 34
  Jetstream – see Scottish Aviation
  Victor (4 x Armstrong-Siddeley Sapphire) 1953, 54, 55, 56, 57, 58, 59, 60
  Victor (4 x Rolls-Royce Conway) 1960, 61, 64, 66, 68, 70
Handley Page (Reading)
  Marathon (4 x de Havilland Gipsy Queen) 1948, 49, 51, 52
  Marathon (2 x Armstrong Siddeley Mamba) 1949, 50, 51

Hawker
  P.1040 (1 x Rolls-Royce Nene) 1948
  P.1052 (1 x Rolls-Royce Nene) 1949, 51
  P.1067/Hunter (1 x Rolls-Royce Avon) 1951, 52, 53, 54, 55, 56, 57, 58, 59, 60, 61, 62, 64, 74
  P.1067/Hunter (1 x Armstrong Siddeley Sapphire) 1953, 54
  P.1072 (1 x Rolls-Royce Nene & 1 Armstrong Siddeley Snarler) 1951
  P.1081 (1 x Rolls-Royce Nene) 1950
  P.V.3 (1 x Rolls-Royce Goshawk) 1935
  P.V.4 (1 x Bristol Perseus) 1935, 37
  N.7/46/Seahawk (1 x Rolls-Royce Nene) 1948, 49, 50, 52, 53, 54, 55, 56, 57, 58
  Fury (1 x Rolls-Royce Kestrel) 1932, 34
  Fury (1 x Napier Sabre) 1946, 47
  Hart (1 x Rolls-Royce Kestrel) 1932, 33, 34, 62, 64, 66
  Hart (1 x Bristol Jupiter) 1932
  Hart (1 x Bristol Mercury) 1937
  Hart (1 x Napier Dagger) 1934
  Hart (1 x Bristol Pegasus) 1934
  Henley (1 x Rolls-Royce Merlin) 1937
  High Speed Fury (1 x Rolls-Royce Kestrel) 1933
  High Speed Fury (1 x Rolls-Royce Goshawk) 1935
  Horsley (1 x Bristol Jupiter) 1932
  Horsley (1 x Armstrong Siddeley Leopard) 1932
  Horsley (1 x Rolls-Royce Condor) 1933
  Hurricane (1 x Rolls-Royce Merlin) 1936, 37, 62, 64, 66, 68, 72, 74, 76, 78, 80, 84, 88
  Nimrod (1 x Rolls-Royce Kestrel) 1933
  Sea Fury (1 x Bristol Centaurus) 1946, 47, 49, 50, 72, 76, 78, 80, 84
  Tempest (1 x Napier Sabre) 1946
  Tomtit (1 x Armstrong Siddeley Mongoose) 1972
Hawker Siddeley
  Andover – see Avro
  Buccaneer – see Blackburn
  Comet – see de Havilland
  Dominie – see British Aerospace
  Dove – see de Havilland
  Gnat – see Folland
  Harrier (1 x Rolls-Royce Pegasus) 1968, 70, 72, 74, 76, 78, 80, 86, 88
  Hawk – see British Aerospace
  Nimrod (4 x Rolls-Royce Spey) 1968, 70, 72, 74, 76, 80, 82, 84, 86
  Shackleton – see Avro
  Trident – see de Havilland
  Vulcan – see Avro
  H.S.125 – see de Havilland and British Aerospace
  748 – see Avro
Heston
  A.2/45 (1 x de Havilland Gipsy Queen) 1947
  Phoenix (1 x de Havilland Gipsy Six) 1936, 37
Highland Aero Dynamics
  Sparrowhawk (1 x Rotax) 1988
Hiller
  HT.2 (1 x Franklin) 1968
Hindustan
  HTT-34 (1 x Allison 250) 1984
  Gnat (1 x Bristol Siddeley Orpheus) 1972
  Kiran (1 x Bristol Siddeley Viper) 1972
  Kiran (1 x Bristol Siddeley Orpheus) 1984
Hirth
  LO 100 Bittern (–) 1988
Hughes
  300 (1 x Lycoming 360) 1980, 82
  500 (1 x Allison 250) 1978, 80, 82, 84, 88
  AH-64 Apache (2 x General Electric T700) 1982, 88
Hunting-Percival
  Pembroke/President – see Percival
  Jet Provost (1 x Rolls-Royce Viper) 1954, 55, 56, 57, 58, 59, 60, 61, 62, 64, 66, 68, 70, 72, 74, 78
  Provost – see Percival
ICA-Brasov
  IAR-823 (1 x Lycoming 540) 1974
  IAR-825TP (1 Pratt & Whitney PT6A) 1982
  IAR-827A (1 x PZL-3S) 1982
  IS-28B2 (–) 1974
  IS-28BM2 (1 x Limbach 1700) 1976, 78, 82
  IS-29, 30 & 32 (–) 1974, 1982
Ilyushin
  Il-86 (4 x Kuznetsov NK-86) 1984
Island Aircraft
  Super2 – see ARV
Israel Aircraft Industries
  Astra (2 x Garrett TFE731) 1988
Jodel
  DR.1050 (1 x Continental 200) 1972
Kirkby
  Gull, Kite, Tutor – see Slingsby
Lancashire
  Prospector (1 x Lycoming 480) 1960
  Prospector (1 x Armstrong Siddeley Cheetah) 1960
LET
  L-410 (2 x Walter M601E) 1988
Ling-Temco-Vought
  A-7 Corsair (1 x Allison TF41) 1970
Lockheed
  10 Electra (2 x Pratt & Whitney Wasp Junior) 1982
  C-130 Hercules (4 x Allison T56) 1970, 72, 82, 84